www.wadsworth.com

wadsworth.com is the World Wide Web site for Wadsworth and is your direct source to dozens of online resources.

At *wadsworth.com* you can find out about supplements, demonstration software, and student resources. You can also send e-mail to many of our authors and preview new publications and exciting new technologies.

wadsworth.com
Changing the way the world learns®

FROM THE WADSWORTH SERIES IN SPEECH COMMUNICATION

Adler/Towne *Looking Out/Looking In*, Tenth Edition
Adams/Clark *The Internet: Effective Online Communication*
Albrecht/Bach *Communication in Complex Organizations: A Relational Perspective*
Babbie *The Basics of Social Research*, Second Edition
Babbie *The Practice of Social Research*, Ninth Edition
Benjamin *Principles, Elements and Types of Persuasion*
Berko/Samovar/Rosenfeld *Connecting: A Culture-Sensitive Approach to Interpersonal Communication Competency*, Second Edition
Bettinghaus/Cody *Persuasive Communication*, Fifth Edition
Braithwaite/Wood *Case Studies in Interpersonal Communication*
Brummett *Reading Rhetorical Theory*
Campbell *The Rhetorical Act*, Second Edition
Campbell/Burkholder *Critiques of Contemporary Rhetoric*, Second Edition
Conrad/Poole *Strategic Organizational Communication*, Fifth Edition
Cragan/Wright *Communication in Small Groups: Theory, Process, Skills*, Fifth Edition
Crannell *Voice and Articulation*, Third Edition
Dwyer *Conquer Your Speechfright: Learn How to Overcome the Nervousness of Public Speaking*
Freeley/Steinberg *Argumentation and Debate: Critical Thinking for Reasoned Decision Making*, Tenth Edition
Goodall/Goodall *Communicating in Professional Contexts: Skills, Ethics, and Technologies*
Govier *A Practical Study of Argument*, Fourth Edition
Hall *Among Cultures: The Challenge of Communication*
Hamilton *Essentials of Public Speaking*
Hamilton/Parker *Communicating for Results: A Guide for Business and the Professions*, Sixth Edition
Hoover *Effective Small Group and Team Communication*
Jaffe *Public Speaking: Concepts and Skills for a Diverse Society*, Third Edition
Kahane/Cavender *Logic and Contemporary Rhetoric: The Use of Reason in Everyday Life*, Eighth Edition
Knapp/Hall *Nonverbal Communication in Human Interaction*, Fifth Edition
Larson *Persuasion: Reception and Responsibility*, Ninth Edition
Liska/Cronkhite *An Ecological Perspective on Human Communication Theory*
Littlejohn *Theories of Human Communication*, Seventh Edition
Lumsden/Lumsden *Communicating with Credibility and Confidence*
Lumsden/Lumsden *Communicating in Groups and Teams: Sharing Leadership*, Third Edition
Metcalfe *Building a Speech*, Fourth Edition
Miller *Organizational Communication: Approaches and Processes*, Second Edition
Morreale/Bovee *Excellence in Public Speaking*
Morreale/Spitzberg/Barge *Human Communication: Motivation, Knowledge, and Skills*
Orbe/Harris *Interracial Communication: Theory Into Practice*
Peterson/Stephan/White *The Complete Speaker: An Introduction to Public Speaking*, Third Edition
Rodman/Adler *The New Public Speaker*
Rothwell *In Mixed Company*, Fourth Edition
Rubin/Rubin/Piele *Communication Research: Strategies and Sources*, Fifth Edition
Rybacki/Rybacki *Communication Criticism: Approaches and Genres*
Samovar/Porter *Communication Between Cultures*, Fourth Edition
Samovar/Porter *Intercultural Communication: A Reader*, Ninth Edition
Sellnow *Public Speaking: A Process Approach*
Sprague/Stuart *The Speaker's Handbook*. Fifth Edition
Thomas *Public Speaking Anxiety: Conquering the Fear of Public Speaking*
Ulloth/Alderfer *Public Speaking: An Experiential Approach*
Verderber *The Challenge of Effective Speaking*, Eleventh Edition
Verderber/Verderber *Communicate!*, Tenth Edition
Wood *Communication in Our Lives*, Second Edition
Wood *Communication Mosaics: An Introduction to the Field of Communication*, Second Edition
Wood *Communication Theories in Action: An Introduction*, Second Edition
Wood *Gendered Lives: Communication, Gender, and Culture*, Fourth Edition
Wood *Interpersonal Communication: Everyday Encounters*, Third Edition
Wood *Relational Communication: Continuity and Change in Personal Relationships*, Second Edition

Communicating in Professional Contexts

Skills, Ethics, and Technologies

H. L. Goodall, Jr.
Sandra Goodall

WADSWORTH
THOMSON LEARNING

WADSWORTH

THOMSON LEARNING

Executive Editor: DEIRDRE CAVANAUGH ANDERSON
Publisher: HOLLY J. ALLEN
Editor in Chief: MARCUS BOGGS
Assistant Editor: CYDNEY ERICKSON-FEINSTEIN
Editorial Assistant: MELE ALUSA
Technology Project Manager: JEANETTE WISEMAN
Marketing Manager: KIM RUSSELL
Marketing Assistant: NEENA CHANDRA
Production Project Manager: CATHY LINBERG
Print/Media Buyer: KAREN HUNT
Permissions Editor: ROBERT KAUSER
Production Service: ELECTRONIC PUBLISHING SERVICES INC., NYC

Text Designer: JOHN WALKER
Photo Researcher: ELECTRONIC PUBLISHING SERVICES INC., NYC
Copyeditor: ELECTRONIC PUBLISHING SERVICES INC., NYC
Illustrator: ELECTRONIC PUBLISHING SERVICES INC., NYC
Cover Designer: JOAN GREENFIELD
Cover Images: (from top to bottom) CORBIS/STOCK MARKET, EYEWIRE, AND DIGITAL VISION
Cover Printer: PHOENIX COLOR CORPORATION
Compositor: ELECTRONIC PUBLISHING SERVICES INC., NYC
Printer: R. R. DONNELLEY AND SONS, CRAWFORDSVILLE

COPYRIGHT © 2002 Wadsworth, a division of Thomson Learning, Inc. Thomson Learning™ is a trademark used herein under license.

ALL RIGHTS RESERVED. No part of this work covered by the copyright hereon may be reproduced or used in any form or by any means—graphic, electronic, or mechanical, including photocopying, recording, taping, Web distribution, or information storage and retrieval systems—without the written permission of the publisher.

Printed in the United States of America
3 4 5 6 7 05 04

For permission to use material from this text, contact us:
Web: http://www.thomsonrights.com **Fax:** 1-800-730-2215
Phone: 1-800-730-2214

ExamView® and *ExamView Pro®* are trademarks of FSCreations, Inc. Windows is a registered trademark of the Microsoft Corporation used herein under license. Macintosh and Power Macintosh are registered trademarks of Apple Computer, Inc. Used herein under license.

COPYRIGHT © 2002 Thomson Learning, Inc. All Rights Reserved. Thomson Learning *Web Tutor*™ is a trademark of Thomson Learning, Inc.

Library of Congress Cataloging-in-Publication Data
Goodall, H. Lloyd
  Communicating in professional contexts: skills, ethics, and technologies/H.L. Goodall, Sandra Goodall.
    p. cm.--(Wadsworth series in speech communication)
  Includes bibliographical references and index.
  ISBN 0-534-56331-7
  1. Business communication. I. Goodall, Sandra. II. Title III. Series.
HF5718.G66 2001
658.4'5--dc21

2001046549

Wadsworth/Thomson Learning
10 Davis Drive
Belmont, CA 94002-3098
USA

For information about our products, contact us:
Thomson Learning Academic Resource Center
1-800-423-0563
http://www.wadsworth.com

International Headquarters
Thomson Learning
International Division
290 Harbor Drive, 2nd Floor
Stamford, CT 06902-7477
USA

UK/Europe/Middle East/South Africa
Thomson Learning
Berkshire House
168-173 High Holborn
London WC1V 7AA
United Kingdom

Asia
Thomson Learning
60 Albert Street, #15-01
Albert Complex
Singapore 189969

Canada
Nelson Thomson Learning
1120 Birchmount Road
Toronto, Ontario M1K 5G4
Canada

Contents in Brief

CONTENTS vii
PREFACE xix

Chapter 1   BREAKTHROUGH SKILLS FOR THE GLOBAL WORKPLACE 1

Chapter 2   THE EVOLUTION OF COMMUNICATION IN THE WORKPLACE 31

Chapter 3   PREPARING FOR CONSCIOUS COMMUNICATION IN THE WORKPLACE 60

Chapter 4   LISTENING IN THE WORKPLACE 93

Chapter 5   THE POWER OF VERBAL AND NONVERBAL COMMUNICATION IN THE WORKPLACE 114

Chapter 6   INFORMATION TECHNOLOGY AND CONSCIOUS COMMUNICATION 146

Chapter 7   EXPLORING INTERPERSONAL COMMUNICATION 166

Chapter 8   INTERVIEWING AND CONSCIOUS COMMUNICATION 192

Chapter 9   THE JOB SEARCH AND CONSCIOUS COMMUNICATION 213

Chapter 10   COMMUNICATING IN GROUPS AND TEAMS 243

Chapter 11   INFORMATIVE PRESENTATIONS IN THE WORKPLACE 271

Chapter 12   MAKING THE PERSUASIVE CASE AT WORK 300

APPENDIX 333
GLOSSARY 347
REFERENCES 351
INDEX 361

Contents

Preface xix

Chapter 1
Breakthrough Skills for the Global Workplace 1
Components of Business and Professional Communication 3
- Sender 4
- Receiver 5
- Messages 5
- Noise 5
- Feedback 6
- Channels 7
- Context 7

The Functions of Business and Professional Communication 11
- Organizing Tasks and People 12
- Creating Identities 13
- Sense-Making and Interpretation 13

Conscious Communication in the Workplace 15
- Step 1: Choosing a Communication Goal 16
- Step 2: Creating the Message 16
- Step 3: Coordinating with Others 17
- Step 4: Delivering the Message 18

Principles of Conscious Communication 18

Summary 19

Communicating in Professional Contexts Online 19
- What You Should Have Learned 20
- Activities 20
- Surfing the Net 21
- Key Terms 21
- Breakthrough Skill Development: Building a Communication Profile 22

Chapter 2

THE EVOLUTION OF COMMUNICATION IN THE WORKPLACE 31

Classical Management and Information Transfer 32
- *Scientific Management* 33
- *Bureaucracy* 35
- Communication as Information Transfer 36

Human Relations/Resources and Transaction Process 36
- *Hawthorne Studies* 37
- *Maslow's Hierarchy of Needs* 37
- Communication as a Transactional Process 39

Systems Thinking and Communication Networks 40
- The Links Between Systems Theory and Business and Professional Communication 41
- Tips for Using Formal and Informal Networks Effectively 42

Organizational Cultures, Communication, and Power 43
- *The Influence of the Cultural Approach to Power* 44
- *Organizational Narratives and Dialogue* 47
- *Mindless Communication* 49
- *Mindful Communication* 50

The Next Step: Learning Organizations 52
- *The Five Disciplines* 52
- *Dialogue and Learning Organizations* 53

Why We Learn About Theories of Communication 55

Summary 55

Communicating in Professional Contexts Online 56
- *What You Should Have Learned* 57
- *Activities* 57
- *Surfing the Net* 58
- *Key Terms* 58
- *Breakthrough Skill Development: Moving from Mindless to Mindful Communication* 59

Chapter 3

PREPARING FOR CONSCIOUS COMMUNICATION IN THE WORKPLACE 60

Organizing a Communication Event 63

Step 1: Choosing a Goal for Your Message 64

Assessing Audience Needs and Expectations 64
Determining the Possible Communication Outcomes 66
Establishing Criteria to Measure Success 68
Step 2: Creating a Strategic and Ethical Message 69
Creating a Thesis Statement 70
Determining the Main Points of the Message 72
Developing Supporting Materials 75
Making Transitions 80
Developing an Effective Introduction and Conclusion 80
Step 3: Coordinating with Others 85
Step 4: Delivering the Message 86
Practice, Practice, Practice 87
Fluency 88
Naturalness 88
Vivacity 88
Nonverbal Competence 89
How Beth Fared 89
Summary 89
Communicating in Professional Contexts Online 90
What You Should Have Learned 90
Activities 91
Surfing the Net 91
Key Terms 91
Breakthrough Skill Development: Completing the CCCD Worksheets 92

Chapter 4

LISTENING IN THE WORKPLACE 93
Becoming a Conscious Listener 94
Hearing 94
Tips for Overcoming Blocks to Hearing 96
Informational Listening 96
Tips for Working with Non-Native Speakers 98
Tips for Removing Cultural Barriers to Listening 98
Tips for Overcoming Gender-Related Listening Differences 100
Tips for Surmounting Language Barriers 101
Tips for Dealing with Communication History Barriers 102

Critical Listening 102

Self-Reflexive Listening 104

Conscious Listening 105

Tips for Listening Consciously 105

The Importance of Listening in Business and Professional Contexts 106

Listening in Meetings 107

Tips for Listening in Meetings 107

Listening in Conflict Situations 107

Tips for Listening in Conflict Situations 108

Listening to Complaints 108

Tips for Dealing with Chronic Complainers 109

Listening When Asked for Help 109

Summary 110

Communicating in Professional Contexts Online 111

What You Should Have Learned 111

Activities 111

Surfing the Net 112

Key Terms 112

Breakthrough Skill Development: Moving from Mindless to Mindful Communication 112

Chapter 5

THE POWER OF VERBAL AND NONVERBAL COMMUNICATION IN THE WORKPLACE 114

Communication of Self in the Workplace 117

Developing Awareness in the Workplace 117

Monitoring Our Assumptions About Communication 118

The Principle of Workplace Equity 119

Making Conscious Choices About Verbal Communication 120

Clarity and Ambiguity 120

Tips for Communicating Clearly 121

Upward and Downward Communication 122

Inclusive and Exclusive Messages 123

Confirming and Disconfirming Messages 124

Supportive Versus Nonsupportive Messages 125

Enhancing Personal and Professional Credibility 126

Verbal Communication and Perceptions of Power 127
   Gendered Talk 127
   Verbal Lie Detectors 128
Nonverbal Communication and Perceptions of Meaning 128
   Your Workspace 129
   Tips for Creating the Optimal Workspace 129
   Clothing and Personal Appearance 130
   Tips for Dressing Successfully in the Workplace 131
   Voice 132
   Body Movement, Facial Expressions, and Eye Contact 133
   Benefits of Making Eye Contact 134
   Nonverbal Lie Detectors 136
   Personal Space 136
   Touching 138
Harassment and Communication in the Workplace 139
   What Is Sexual Harassment? 140
   How Can Harassment Be Avoided? 140
What Should You Do If You Are a Victim of Harassment? 141
Summary 142
Communicating in Professional Contexts Online 142
   What You Should Have Learned 143
   Activities 143
   Surfing the Net 144
   Key Terms 144
   Breakthrough Skill: Dealing Ethically with Verbal and Nonverbal Communication Diversity 145

Chapter 6

INFORMATION TECHNOLOGY AND CONSCIOUS COMMUNICATION 146

Information Technology and Communication 148
   The Downside to Information Technology 149
   Revising Our Approach to Information Technology 149
   Information Technology and Gender Differences 150
   Information Technology and Conscious Communication 151
Types of Information Technologies 153
   Computer-Assisted Communication Technologies 153

Electronic and Voice Mail Systems 154
Tips for Using Voice Mail and Email 154
Computer Networks 156
Email and Chatroom Shorthand 157
Video Conferencing 157
Tips for Video Conferencing 158
News You Can Use: Doing Web-Based Research 159
Surfing the Net for Information: A Practical Guide 160
How Much Technology Do I Need? 161
Summary 162
Communicating in Professional Contexts Online 162
What You Should Have Learned 163
Activities 163
Surfing the Net 164
Key Terms 164
Breakthrough Skill: Recognizing the Importance of Technology in the Workplace 164

Chapter 7

EXPLORING INTERPERSONAL COMMUNICATION 166
Choosing: Strategies and Ethics for Relational Development at Work 167
First Impressions 167
Establishing Expectations and Boundaries 170
Behaving Ethically 172
NCA Credo for Ethical Communication 174
Creating: Messages That Reflect Self, Other, and Context 175
Equity: Principles of Everyday Exchange 176
Self-Disclosure and Risk-Taking 177
Tips for Monitoring Disclosures 179
Asking For and Giving Feedback 179
Dialectics and Dialogue 181
Working Through Relational Conflict 182
Coordinating: Making Relational Communities Work 184
Negotiation of Cultural Differences 184
Negotiation of Gender Differences 185
Delivering: Improving Relationships at Work 187
Summary 188

Contents

Communicating in Professional Contexts Online 189
   What You Should Have Learned 189
   Activities 190
   Surfing the Net 191
   Key Terms 191
   Breakthrough Skill: Providing Valuable Feedback 191

Chapter 8

INTERVIEWING AND CONSCIOUS COMMUNICATION 192

Conducting Conscious Interviews 193
   Interrogation 194
   Persuasive or Sales Interviews 194
   Performance Reviews 194
   Tips for Performance Reviews 196
   Information Interviews or Focus Groups 197
   Tips for Information Interviews 198
   Employment Interviews 199
Choosing: Setting the Parameters for the Interview 199
   Setting the Goals for the Interview 200
   Developing a Job Description 201
Creating: Scripting the Interview 204
   Ethical Interviewing 206
Coordinating: Setting Up the Interview 206
Delivering: Ready, Set, Interview 208
   Conducting Phone (Screening) Interviews 208
   Tips for Phone Interviews 209
Summary 209
Communicating in Professional Contexts Online 210
   What You Should Have Learned 210
   Activities 211
   Surfing the Net 211
   Key Terms 211
   Breakthrough Skill: Handling Team Interviews 211

Chapter 9

THE JOB SEARCH AND CONSCIOUS COMMUNICATION 213

Conducting a Conscious Job Search 214

Choosing: Setting Your Job Goals 215
   Job Research 215
Creating: Putting Together a Winning Resume 219
   Selecting the Format 220
   Two Worlds Never to Use on a Resume 224
   Writing a Compelling Cover Letter 225
   Tips for Submitting Resumes and Cover Letters 226
Coordinating: Preparing for the Interview 226
   Participating in a Phone Interview 227
   Arranging the In-Person Interview 228
   Tips for Arranging Interviews 229
   Dressing for Success in the Internet Age 230
Delivering: Practicing and Being Interviewed 230
   Interview Styles 231
   Practicing the Interview 232
   Being Interviewed 235
Summary 238
Communicating in Professional Contexts Online 239
   What You Should Have Learned 239
   Activities 240
   Surfing the Net 240
   Key Terms 240
   Breakthrough Skill: Developing a Smooth Interview Style 241
   Communicating in Professional Contexts in Action! 242

Chapter 10

COMMUNICATING IN GROUPS AND TEAMS 243

Conscious Communication in Groups and Teams 244
Choosing: Strategies for Organizing Teams 245
   Developing Effective Leadership Strategies 246
   Phrases Leaders Shouldn't Use 248
   Participation 248
   Selection of Team Members 249
   Adaptive Skills 250
Creating: Defining the Goals and Strategies for a Team 251
   Agendas 251

Creating a Shared Vision 252

The D&T Vision 253

Coordinating: Establishing a Creative Environment for Team Problem Solving 255

Coordinating with Other Teams 256

Coordinating the Problem-Solving Process 257

Tips for Brainstorming 260

Delivering as a Team 263

Memos and Reports 264

Staff Briefings and Weekly Sessions 265

Planning and Problem-Solving Meetings 266

Virtual Meetings 266

Conferences, Workshops, and Seminars 267

Summary 267

Communicating in Professional Contexts Online 267

What You Should Have Learned 268

Activities 268

Surfing the Net 269

Key Terms 269

Breakthrough Skill: Handling Team Interviews 269

Communicating in Professional Contexts in Action! 270

Chapter 11

INFORMATIVE PRESENTATIONS IN THE WORKPLACE 271

Revisiting the CCCD Process for Organizing a Presentation 272

Choosing a Goal for Your Presentation 273

Informative vs. Persuasive Presentations 273

Developing an Audience Profile 274

Establishing Credibility 274

Establishing Informative Outcomes 276

Developing Criteria to Measure Success 276

Creating an Informative Presentation 277

Conducting Research 279

Tips for Conducting Research 280

Effective PowerPoint Presentations 283

Tips for Using PowerPoint 283

Verbal and Visual Support 287

Effective Transitions 290

Developing an Effective Introduction and Conclusion 292

Coordinating an Informative Presentation 293

Delivering an Informative Presentation 295

Summary 296

Communicating in Professional Contexts Online 296

What You Should Have Learned 296

Activities 297

Surfing the Net 297

Key Terms 298

Breakthrough Skill Development: Developing an Informative Presentation Using the CCCD Worksheets 298

Communicating in Professional Contexts in Action! 298

Chapter 12

MAKING THE PERSUASIVE CASE AT WORK 300

Concierge Persuasion 301

Logos, Pathos, and Ethos 303

Conscious Persuasion in the Workplace 303

Choosing a Persuasive Strategy 303

Creating the Message 305

Coordinating the Message 305

Delivering the Message 306

Tips for Using a Brutal Strategy 307

Persuading Through Reason 308

Choosing the Rational Persuasive Strategy 308

Creating the Rational Persuasive Message 310

Coordinating the Rational Persuasive Message 310

Delivering the Rational Persuasive Message 312

Tips for Using a Rational Strategy 312

Persuading Through Emotion 313

Choosing the Rational/Emotional Persuasive Strategy 313

Creating the Rational/Emotional Message 315

Needs Assessment vs. Audience Analysis 315

Monroe's Motivated Sequence 318

    Steps in Monroe's Motivated Sequence 320
    Coordinating the Rational/Emotional Message 320
    Delivering the Rational/Emotional Message 320
    Tips for Using a Rational/Emotional Strategy 322

Persuading Through Mindful Communication 323
    Creating a Mindful Persuasive Message 324
    Coordinating the Mindful Persuasive Message 326
    Delivering the Mindful Persuasive Message 327
    Tips for Using Mindful Persuasive Strategy 328

Summary 328

Communicating in Professional Contexts Online 329
    What You Should Have Learned 329
    Activities 330
    Surfing the Net 330
    Key Terms 330
    Breakthrough Skill Development: Show What You've Learned 331
    Communicating in Professional Contexts in Action! 331

APPENDIX 333
GLOSSARY 347
REFERENCES 351
INDEX 361

Preface

Business and professional communication textbooks are interesting cultural reflections of their historical eras. Born from an alliance between academic instructors of speech and industry personnel during and after World War II, early examples of textbooks for this market focused almost exclusively on practical tips for making business presentations. Then, as the field began to mature during the latter half of the twentieth century, and as business schools increasingly required communication competencies among their graduates, our texts adopted more theoretical perspectives on communication in organizations that included materials on leadership, teamwork, and interpersonal effectiveness.

Today, as we begin our journey through the 21st century, there is again a need for a new vision for business and professional communication. This vision must be capable of responding to the rapid changes in communication understandings and skills created by a global economy, advances in information technologies, and an increasingly diverse workforce. *Communicating in Business and Professional Contexts* provides this new vision.

Our goal throughout this project has been to incorporate state-of-the-art academic approaches with the most up-to-date skill set on the market. For this reason, readers will find that our text builds, in an evolutionary sense, on time-tested practices common to the best books our field has yet produced. There is, after all, still a strong demand for basic instruction in researching, organizing, and delivering informative and persuasive presentations in business contexts. Likewise, there is still a need to provide materials on effective interpersonal communication at work, employment interviewing, and small group and team work. Of course, no book in this field would be complete without comprehensive discussions of the components of a communication process, listening, and verbal and nonverbal communication.

What makes our approach to these timeless topics unique is:

+ A consistent theoretical orientation to guide each chapter, derived from current research on *mindful* and *ethical* communication practices.
+ A consistent model for building competencies in each chapter, based on the same communication process—in our case, the CCCD system: *Choose* (a communication goal and strategy), *Create* (the message), *Coordinate* (with other people), and *Deliver* (the message).

- A consistent use of *information technologies* to underscore the ways in which exchanges of email, cross-company networking, using the Internet to find information and conduct research, using PowerPoint to develop presentations, and using the telephone to conduct initial employment interviews intersect with everyday interpersonal, group, team, and presentational business contexts.
- Integrated materials and examples of *cultural diversity* and *gender differences* in most chapters.
- A consistent application of *breakthrough skills* in each chapter, designed to build competencies through examples and exercises.
- A *narrative approach,* telling the story of communication in a business context in each chapter as understandings and skills are systematically developed.

The world of business is a messy place. It is rare when communication situations in the workplace conform to scripts learned in a college classroom. In the world of work, valid notions of fairness, political correctness, and gender and racial sensitivity are often at odds with generational, regional, and cultural understandings. The way we *should* treat one another may not be the way we *do* treat one another in the workplace. The narratives in this book are derived from the authors' actual consulting experiences. They were included not as examples of exemplary workplace communication, but as examples of how people actually communicate in the workplace. They are offered as rhetorical openings for classroom conversations and exercises.

In Chapter 1, Breakthrough Skills for the Global Workplace, we introduce our definition and model of the communication process while describing the functions of communication in business and professional contexts: organizing tasks and people; creating identities; sensemaking and interpretation. We also lay out the CCCD system and explain how it can be used to develop understandings and skills. We conclude this chapter with a self-test of communication strategies applied to a variety of business and professional communication contexts.

Chapter 2, The Evolution of Communication in the Workplace, is dedicated to explaining how organizational and communication theories have coalesced over the years into a distinct set of practical understandings and skills. We incorporate the best ideas from the classical, transactional, systems, and cultures approaches, while including new work on organizational narratives, dialogue, and learning organizations.

Chapter 3, Preparing for Conscious Communication in the Workplace, develops our CCCD system within an organizational application. This approach is useful for teachers who assign a presentational speech early in the term. Of particular interest will be the presentational worksheets used to guide the development of a presentation, as well as the step-by-step guide to researching, organizing, practicing, and delivering the speech.

In Chapter 4, Listening in the Workplace, we discuss the types of listening as well as how to become a more conscious listener. We also include new materials on how to listen for cultural and gender differences, self-reflexive listening, and ways in which listening strategies differ in meetings, conflict situations, or when asking a colleague for help.

In Chapter 5, The Power of Verbal and Nonverbal Communication in the Workplace, we discuss the importance of understanding verbal communication in relation to workplace equity as well as individual differences. We discuss various message strategies, including inclusive and exclusive messages, ambiguity, and supportive and nonsupportive messages. In the nonverbal segments, we provide a comprehensive treatment of topics that also includes new materials on the layout of personal workspace, choosing clothing, personal appearance, and voice. A major feature of this chapter is our section on recognizing and dealing with sexual harassment.

Chapter 6, Information Technology and Conscious Communication, discusses communication strategies for using voice and email, networking, video conferencing, and doing Web-based research. We also provide a section on "How much technology do I need?" as a guide to thinking about the relationships between information technology and human communication in the workplace.

Chapter 7, Exploring Interpersonal Communication, begins with a unique format for delivering information on this vital subject by organizing the chapter around a Human Resources Seminar format. In it, new employees are guided through theories and practices associated with scripts; expectations and boundaries; ethical behavior; equity; self-disclosure and risk-taking; asking for feedback; dialectics and dialogue; relational conflict; creating communities at work; and negotiating cultural and gender differences.

Chapters 8 and 9 are dedicated to interviewing. In Chapter 8, Interviewing and Conscious Communication, we explore the organization's perspective on interviews; in Chapter 9, The Job Search and Conscious Communication, we develop the potential employee's perspective on interviewing. Both chapters offer sound information on conducting a job search, writing resumes and cover letters, and developing scripts to guide choices of communication in interviews. We also include information on electronic formats and electronic submission of employment materials, as well as a section on how to make arrangements for an interview.

Chapter 10, Communicating in Groups and Teams, begins by distinguishing between group and team communication. We then focus on the uses of communication to develop teamwork, leadership, and team-based presentations. Throughout the chapter, we highlight the ethical and mindful choices teams must make.

Chapter 11, Informative Presentations in the Workplace, builds on material presented in Chapter 3, and reinforced in every other chapter, on the importance of using the CCCD system to guide communication. The chapter offers a way of thinking about informative presentations in relation to speaker credibility. We also include comprehensive materials on using PowerPoint or other presentation software to develop supporting materials for an informative presentation.

In Chapter 12, Making the Persuasive Case at Work, we develop our conscious communication model to include four types of persuasion in business and professional contexts. We then use the CCCD system to develop appropriate strategies for each type. Unlike other texts, we show how persuasion is used in interpersonal, group, and presentational contexts, and how differences in each context should inform and guide our choice of communication goals and strategies.

Throughout the book we make use of proven instructional aids. Each chapter includes a comprehensive introduction, summary, and Communicating in Professional Contexts Online. Communicating in Professional Contexts Online appears at the end of each chapter and includes a list of key terms (which are defined in the text and in the book's Glossary), and practical student activities, many of which make use of Infotrac College Edition and the Internet. In addition, a "What You Should Have Learned" section provides a review of the chapter material, and the "Breakthrough Skill" section enables students to apply a skill pertinent to the chapter. Select chapters feature a prompt for students to use their Goodall Connection CD-ROM to link to the book's website and to watch, listen to, and analyze model presentations and the interview featured in Chapter 9. Further, we provide a unique way to help students develop communication competencies with charts and worksheets throughout the text.

Overall, we believe we have created a very useful text for anyone interested in providing students with current information and skill development for business and professional contexts in the 21st century.

H. L. Goodall, Jr.
Sandra Goodall

Communicating in Professional Contexts

Chapter One

Breakthrough Skills for the Global Workplace

It takes a smart company to build a tough hog. *Behind all the chrome and leather, behind the brawny bikers and burly bikes, is a company that competes on...brains. Harley [Davidson] is one smart operation—and its top managers see to it that learning is the engine that continues to drive the business.*

In addition to providing workers with 80 hours of training each year...the Harley Leadership Institute focuses on three competencies the company believes all employees should have including communication, conflict resolution, and team skills.

—Gina Imperato, *Harley Shifts Gears*

As you read the excerpt about Harley-Davidson, three things should stand out. First, Harley Davidson is a company committed to the idea of continuous learning. Second, what they are committed to learning about, and to continuously improving, are their employees' communication skills. Third, developing effective communication skills is essential to success in a business or profession.

We begin this chapter with this example because it underscores the fact that the standards have been raised for business and professional communication competence in the workplace. Communication knowledge and skills are viewed by many as *breakthrough skills* for the 21st century (Arygris, 1999).

What is a "breakthrough skill?" It is a communication skill, or skill set, that allows people to act purposefully and competently on what they know. For example, in the field of accounting, it used to be enough to simply be a technically proficient accountant, but not anymore. In a recent article, a senior manager of Allen Gibbs & Houlik L.C. said, "Professional accountants need more than technical knowledge. They need communication and organizational skills. They need to be well-rounded" (Dove, 1998, p. 16). More and more traditional professions—law, accounting, architecture, design, engineering, education, and business—are seeking graduates with *communication* as well as technical skills.

Which is why we have teamed together to write this book. As organizational communication professionals, we recognize that our students spend most of their lives communicating in business and professional contexts. We know that students who study business and professional communication significantly improve their ability to use communication to obtain their personal and career goals. These students use the communication skills they learn in business and professional communication classes to "break through" the human and technological barriers to business effectiveness and professional success. And so can you.

What are those barriers? Consider the following examples:

+ You receive an email message from a colleague in another department about an upcoming meeting. From the tone of his message, you sense that something is wrong. The email was posted last night. You think it is very important to check out your impressions with him prior to that meeting. How do you address your concerns to your colleague?

+ You feel that a supervisor at work is staring at you in a suggestive manner. Is there a way to resolve this form of harassment without totally alienating the supervisor?

+ You have to make a business presentation and want to use colorful graphics and animation to illustrate your main points. What is the best way to ensure that the presentation benefits from the inclusion of these forms of support?

- You are assigned to lead a team work effort. The members of the team come from different departments and none of them know you very well. What is the best way to organize a meeting?
- You are talking to a business counterpart from Brazil. She speaks Portuguese and Spanish with a little English, but you only speak English and freshman-level Spanish. How do you conduct business with someone who doesn't share your native language?
- You and a co-worker are constantly struggling over the best way to complete a project. How would you use communication to effectively manage your differences?

Business and professional communication skills go beyond the ability to engage in casual talk with friends and family or the chitchat we use to pass the time in social settings. Trying to resolve any of the above scenarios with the communication values you learned at home, or skills you routinely use with your friends, may backfire. It is important at the outset that you understand that business settings require *specific communication skills and knowledge.*

Business and professional **communication** is a shorthand term used to refer to *all forms of speaking, listening, relating, writing, and responding in the workplace,* both human and electronically mediated. Human communication includes informal conversations, interviews, group and team meetings, informative briefings and speeches, sales pitches, and persuasive presentations. **Electronically mediated communication** includes telephone conversations and vocal messages on answering machines, satellite conferences, email, and Internet communication, including images and sounds represented on personal and company Web pages, and the use of the Internet for business communication and ecommerce. As you will learn, business and professional contexts require communication skills that are both *appropriate to,* and *effective in,* the workplace.

This course and this textbook are designed to provide you with the breakthrough skills, knowledge, and experiences required for successful business and professional communication. Our goals are to help you understand the new professional standards for communication competency and help you develop the skills and confidence to move ahead in whatever business or profession you choose.

Components of Business and Professional Communication

Early models of business communication posited the idea that communication was simply the instructions (messages) given by a boss or manager (sender) to employees (receivers). (See Figure 1.1.) What this model assumed was that most business communication was *top down.*

Figure 1.1
Top-Down Model of Business Communication

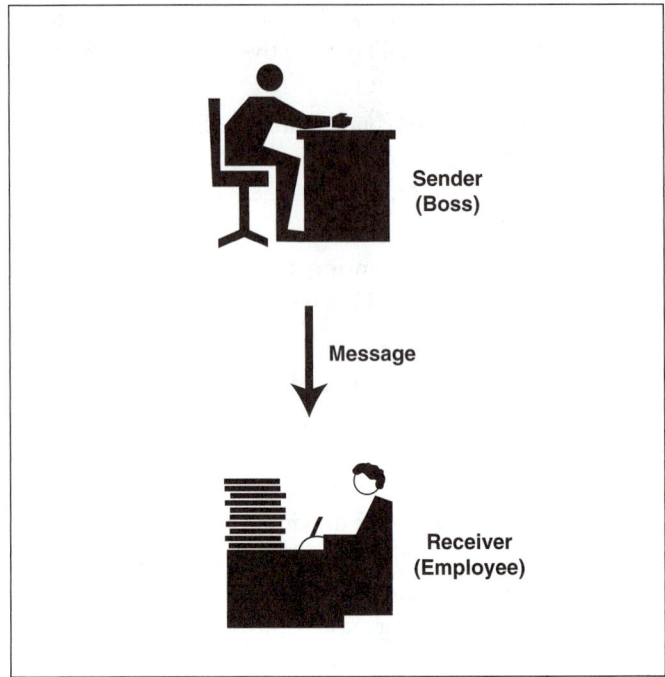

As our understanding of business communication improved, new models included the *responses* (feedback) employees give to bosses and to each other. (See Figure 1.2.) These newer models also included the possibility for misunderstandings caused by disruptions (noise) in, or misinterpretations of, a message. They also introduced the idea that messages are conveyed in different ways (channels), such as airwaves (sound) or lightwaves (sight). This idea of "channel" was expanded to include electronically mediated methods of message delivery, such as radio, television, computers, and satellites, as well as the full range of print media, such as office memos and letters, as well as newspapers, magazines, advertising flyers and brochures, and books.

Later, communication theorists added the *physical, historical, and cultural environments* (context) that inform a communication situation or episode. Today, when we speak of the "components of a communication model," we include all of the terms: sender, receiver, message, channel, noise, feedback, and context. (See Figure 1.3.) Let's take a look at these components in more detail.

Sender

The **sender** is the *originator or source of a message*. In the earliest organizational models, the sender was a boss. What we realize now is that messages originate from a variety of sources, at all levels, inside and outside an organ-

Figure 1.2
Updated Model of Business Communication

ization. For example, a customer entering a department store to make a complaint would be considered the originator of a message to the customer service representative.

Receiver

The **receiver** is *the person to whom a message is initially directed.* In early organizational models, this person was an employee. What we realize today is that anyone can receive messages in an organization. For example, the customer service representative is the receiver of the customer's complaint. However, the customer service representative may report the complaint to any number of people in the organization—the manager of the customer service department, the manager of the department where the product was sold to the customer, co-workers in other departments, even friends and family members. Whoever receives the account is a receiver of the communication.

Messages

The **message** is *what is said and done during an interaction.* Messages are both verbal and nonverbal. Together, these message sources help us arrive at the meaning of a message. In our example, the customer's tone of voice, choice of words, general attitude, facial expression, gestures, and body posture all contribute to the customer service representative's interpretation of the message.

Noise

Noise includes the *physical, semantic, and hierarchical influences that either disrupt or shape the interpretation of messages.* Physical noise may emanate from

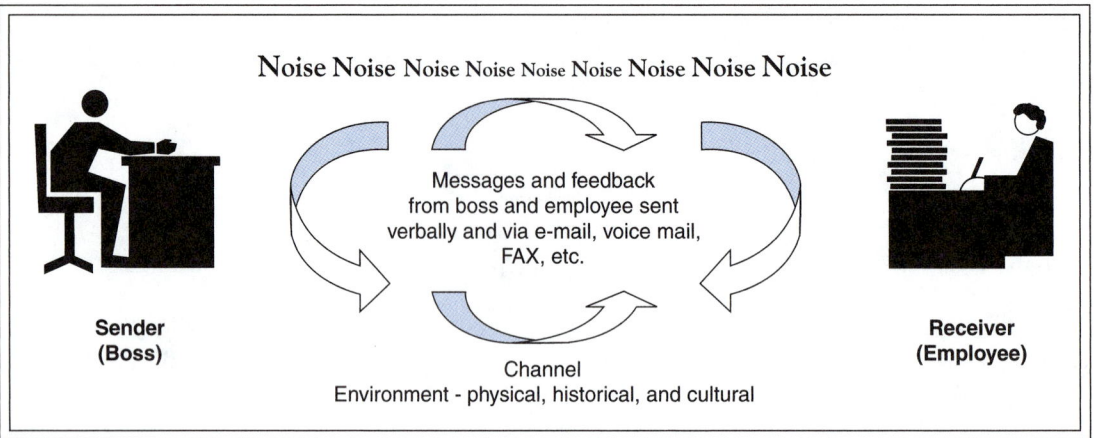

Figure 1.3
Current Model of Business Communication

the environment: loud talking from the next room, opening and closing of doors, or sudden announcements over a loudspeaker that disrupt a conversation. **Semantic noise** refers to differences people have for the meanings of words: misheard or misunderstood terms, a gender bias (e.g., saying "he" when referring to all managers or "she" when referring to all child-care givers), the perception of racial undertones (e.g., a fear or anxiety expressed as something "dark"), in-house or professional jargon, and culturally derived metaphors (such as the predominance of sports metaphors in North American business). **Hierarchical noise** refers to the shadings in meaning we attribute to a message based on a person's rank or status within an organization. For example, complaining to the customer service representative's supervisor rather than the customer service representative may make the customer feel that the message has been taken more seriously.

Feedback

Feedback is the activity of providing *senders and receivers with responses to their communication, ideas, and identities*. Initially, communication theorists viewed feedback in a very mechanical way. For example, a smile from our customer service representative could indicate acceptance of, and appreciation for, the customer's message. A frown could indicate confusion or disagreement. Quickly, however, communication researchers began to see the limitations of this either/or approach to discussing feedback. After all, a smile can be strategically deployed or faked. As researchers began studying the concept of feedback in business organizations, the complexity of the term grew.

Feedback affects communication in an organization in a number of ways. Beyond responding to the specific words and actions of a sender, feedback can bring to a conversation *broader business and cultural implications*. It can help maintain the status quo through responses such as "Because that's how we have always tracked sales." It can move a situation forward through responses such as "Actually, I don't know why we track sales this way. Did you use a different method in your last company?" It may initiate change by fostering openness: "Wow, that sounds like a great system. Could you develop a plan to transition our sales tracking using your method?"

Every exchange must be considered within context. If a company is lagging behind, feedback upholding the status quo might be considered negative. However, if a company has just undertaken a major change effort, confirming the status quo may be exactly what that company needs to do to remain successful. What might appear to be negative feedback in one situation might be positive in another.

Channels

A **channel** is *the thoroughfare a message takes from sender to receiver*. Channels have evolved from a simple choice between speaking and writing to complex choices from a myriad of personal and technological possibilities. Choosing the appropriate channel for communication influences the timing, reception, and understanding of a message. For example, our unhappy customer could choose to write a letter, appear in person, send an email, leave a voice message on an answering machine, make a posting to an Internet bulletin board, or call a media hot line. Each channel may reach a different audience and therefore elicit a different outcome. As a result, the choice of channel provides the customer—and the company—with varying levels of potential satisfaction and practical results.

Context

All communication occurs within an environment. Every environment includes a particular *physical situation*, a *cultural context*, and *at least two sources for communication history (the sender's and receiver's)*. Let's examine each of these influences in more detail.

Physical Situation

In the workplace, the physical situation comprises:

- Physical space, including "comfort levels" of temperature, humidity, and noise.
- Organization of the workspace, including placement of office furniture and displays of personal or professional items.
- Time and timing.

The *physical space* impacts communication partners and influences outcomes. Is the room large enough to accommodate everyone who was invited to a meeting? Are you discussing an intimate topic like raises or reprimands in an open office space? Is the room you are speaking in too crowded with furniture? Is the temperature too warm or too cold for comfort? Are there distractions caused by excessive noise?

As you can see, the size, location, organization, and comfort levels of the physical environment can make or break a deal, sidetrack negotiations, escalate conflict, or reduce the effectiveness of a presentation in a training program. If communication is impaired, or if distractions are present, people tend to focus on things other than what is being discussed or presented. For example, imagine that you are assigned to give a presentation to a group of potential clients. You spend weeks researching your group and honing your presentation. You book the "good" conference room two weeks in advance. The day of your presentation you walk into the conference room to find the space is being carpeted and painted. The only conference room you can secure is the room with the tattered chairs, the broken LCD panel, and a constant temperature of about 80 degrees. Chances are good that the condition of the room will negatively impact your feelings of confidence about the presentation as well as your audience's ability to perceive you, your company, and your product favorably.

The *organization of your workspace* can have an impact on perceptions of your identity, communication sensitivities, and professional competence. What does your workspace say about you? Is it a clean and neat area with well-organized shelves upon which are aligned carefully organized reference books and professional trade publications? Or is it a mess, complete with yesterday's half-eaten donut and long-cold cup of coffee? Does your desktop signal an organized approach to work, or is it the last resting-place of a myriad of personal objects, books, magazines, and various piles of junk? Have you decorated your walls with tasteful photographs and signs of professional accomplishments, or with torn-out pages from sports magazines and personal fitness guides? Are there displays of items that could be offensive to others, such as questionable cartoons or calendars, or photographs that advertise sexuality?

The display of personal and professional items in a workspace creates impressions of your personal and professional identity. People enter your workspace and take account of it as a reflection of your interests, accomplishments, and sensitivity to a variety of cultural and gendered issues. Many businesses prohibit the display of personal items such as pictures of loved ones and pets because they believe it detracts from the business context of the workspace. In recent years, most businesses have forbidden displays of suggestive sexual materials because they potentially constitute an actionable offense under sexual harassment laws. It is a good idea to become more conscious about the possible interpretation others may make of what you display in your workspace. Workspace displays are forms of nonverbal communication; they send clear messages about your understanding of the workplace culture that you are a part of. They reflect on your ability to interpret and participate in that culture.

Time and timing have dramatic effects on business and professional communication. As you undoubtedly know, some people are at their best in the morning, and others are night owls. Think about your own time preferences. Consider them when you plan a presentation or meeting or have to perform in an interview setting. Additionally, take into account the time and timing preferences of your audiences. Is it really a good idea to schedule that presentation right after the company lunch? Are meetings likely to accomplish more if they are scheduled on Monday or Friday afternoons? The influences of time and timing help create the atmosphere and environment for communication.

Cultural Context

Business and professional communication also occurs within a *cultural communication context:* the thoughts and feelings we have in a situation, the history between the communicators, and the relationship in which the communication occurs (Wood, 1996, p. 113). For example, our friend John took an executive position with the ABC organization, a small U.S. company located in the South. John is from Canada, where religion is rarely discussed or displayed at work. The company he works for frequently makes announcements about upcoming sales events, employee illnesses or hardships, and community needs, which are followed by the statement "Any prayers you would like to offer would be appreciated." Prayer is not a requirement of the job at John's company, yet it sets a *cultural context* for communication within his organization.

John's initial fears were that given the zeal of some religious organizations in the United States, he might have a difficult time adapting his communication to the workplace. As it turns out, he has been pleasantly surprised. While religion is certainly *a* contextual influence John encounters at work, it is not *the only* context that influences his communication within the organization (see Figure 1.4).

As a result of his experience at ABC, John's cultural context for talk about religion in his workplace has changed. He no longer views religious talk as an intrusion. He has even joked that a few times, when faced with particularly tough sales challenges, it was comforting to think about everyone back in the office pulling for him. He has begun to view the religious undertones as part of the organizational culture that reflects a caring team spirit.

John's example shows us that cultural contexts for communication *are not and should not be fixed.* As we grow and learn, as we gain insight and

Figure 1.4
Overlapping Contextual Influences That Inform a Conversation

knowledge from new experiences, people, and situations, the contexts that influence our communication experiences evolve.

Communication History

When we talk about **communication history,** we are referring to the interpersonal history between two or more communication partners. How long have you known one another? Where are you in your relationship? What has your combined experience with each other taught you about how each of you is likely to respond to situations? Have you had arguments or disagreements in the past? Are there topics you knowingly avoid? Are there issues on which you are likely to agree? What intellectual, social, and personal baggage does each of you bring to communication encounters?

Communication history can determine if you are open to the opinions and observations of a communication partner, or if you become defensive or closed-minded even before hearing what the other person has to say. Your shared communication history either creates a space for *potentially* open communication or closes the door to it. Yet with each encounter, both positive and negative, your shared history changes. If, for example, a supervisor has a history of never asking for input at a weekly meeting and suddenly does, the group's shared history is altered from that point on by that one significant event. Shared history shapes our communication and because of our communication is constantly being reshaped.

The Functions of Business and Professional Communication

Amber hurried down the hall, her arms full of papers, reports, and folders. She was nervous about her first meeting with her new team and she was determined to be ready. When she entered the conference room, she was relieved to find she was the first to arrive. Amber spent the next 15 minutes arranging her information on the table in front of her. She checked her watch and waited for the others. Right before 2:00, the members of Amber's new team began to enter the room. Most carried only a blank pad. Amber was amazed at how much better prepared she was than the other members of the team.

Janet, the team leader, began the meeting. She asked each team member to recap for Amber their assignment and the progress each team member had made. Amber immediately cut her off. "No need, Janet, I've read all of the progress reports from the past six months." She pulled out the folder and waved it to the group.

Janet smiled. "While I appreciate your efforts, I think you would benefit from hearing about the project firsthand from each team member."

Amber, not to be sidetracked, said, "Why don't I recap what I've read and you all can fill in any blanks? While I am sure you've all worked really hard on this project, I have a couple of ideas that might speed things along." Amber then launched into a 20-minute recap of what she had read.

When she finished, Janet smiled and said, "Thank you, Amber, for recapping all of the ideas we have already thought about and discarded for one reason or another. Now, Chad, would you begin filling Amber in on what wasn't in the memos and reports she read?"

Amber's face grew hot and red. She sank as far into the back of her chair as she possibly could. Wow had she read the memos wrong! She spent the rest of the meeting pretending to make notes and trying not to look at the rest of the team members. After the meeting she gathered up the materials in front of her and fled back to her cube.

Amber's unfortunate experience arose from a lack of understanding of the functions of business communication. The functions of business and professional communication are to:

- Organize tasks and people.
- Create identities.
- Engage in sense-making and interpretations of meanings.

Successful communicators realize that none of these functions occurs in a vacuum. They recognize that communication is a cumulative activity that builds understanding over time, rather than a snapshot that freezes understanding in place. Amber did not recognize these important functions of communication.

Organizing Tasks and People.

Everyone knows that a basic use for communication in the workplace is to convey the instructions needed to accomplish tasks. However, the need to bring people together to organize tasks and solve problems is critical for business communication success. Amber's careful preparation for the meeting showed she did not understand this function of communication. What Amber didn't understand is that in a business context, communication is used primarily *to organize tasks performed by people*. Or, to put it another way, communication in the workplace is *collaborative*. We have to organize tasks *with the help of other people*.

This has not always been the case. As you will learn in Chapter 2, the organization of work in most global organizations has changed from an individual to a *team-based model*. In part, this change is due to the communication influences brought about by advances in information technology, which increased the speed by which information could be organized and disseminated in and out of an organization. Technology also increased the amount of information that could be accessed. Together, these changes reduced the need to maintain many different levels of management and control of the information, as speedy and wide-ranging access to information "empowered" employees to make moment-to-moment decisions about their jobs. One major result of this influence of technology on the organization of work has been a new interest in group and team-based communication. Hence, individuals are seldom assigned to work alone. Companies today hire people to become team or group members, which means employees have to develop the skills associated with collaborative work and learning. In large part, this means altering the way we communicate.

Amber's example highlights what happens when we concentrate all of our communication efforts on creating meaning alone and ignore the experiences and needs of others. Amber's attempt at communication ignored everything that *wasn't* in the memos and reports she read. She ignored the team's experience. To be an effective team member at work, Amber needed to listen, ask questions, and *then* develop her ideas and present them.

Creating Identities

Your **identity** in the workplace is constructed out of how people see and respond to you (Eisenberg and Goodall, 2001). In effect, *identity is constructed out of your communication.* Identity consists of three interrelated interpretations of communication:

Organizational persona—who we are perceived as within the organization. This may be a function of position, status, rank, years of service, or role in a company.

Organizational credibility—whether we "do what we say we will do." This includes the values associated with being a trustworthy, honest, responsible, fair, and ethical person in the organization.

Organizational savvy—the ability a person has to successfully negotiate political and social boundaries in an organization. In some cases this includes knowing whom to talk to to get a job done. In other cases, it can mean the ability to gain new resources from unexpected sources.

Because she was a new team member, Amber's organizational persona was unknown. She had an opportunity to use her initial communication episodes to create the persona of a "team player," a "collaborative learner." Instead, her actions betrayed a team member who lacked organizational credibility and savvy. She was viewed after her first encounter with the team as a know-it-all, and it took months of hard work to prove that she could be a team player. In all, her communication choices seriously detracted from the identity she wanted to establish with her team.

Sense-Making and Interpretation

In addition to creating identities and accomplishing tasks, communication helps us make sense of an organization's culture and interpret the messages of co-workers, customers, and clients (Eisenberg and Goodall, 2001; Weick, 1996). **Interpretation** is the meaning we assign to messages. When we say **sense-making**, we are underscoring the idea that there is no one external reality that communication somehow "re-presents" (Hall, 1997). Instead, individual communicators construct versions of the realities they perceive and respond to based on their own past experiences, knowledge, feelings, needs, and expectations. We don't re-present reality in talk so much as we *represent a version of it*. Communication is the *representational bridge* that allows us to negotiate meanings, share interpretations, and collectively engage in productive, collaborative work.

When we say that employees make sense out of an *organization's culture*, we are saying that organizations are *very* complex symbolic environments. As you will learn in Chapter 2, **organizational culture** consists of the histories, habits, values, and rules for conduct that make working in a particular organization feel unique. From a communication perspective, this means that it takes a lot of collaboration and communication work to produce a shared sense of culture. Getting to that shared sense of culture requires a lot of communication that builds shared understandings and meanings. Add to this cultural context the uncertainties that always exist in any business setting, and you begin to get an idea why communication must be understood as an ongoing process of sense-making and interpretation that emerges from, and contributes to, an organization's culture.

Let's return to Amber's example. How could she have better made sense out of the culture she found herself working in? First, she should have been a much better *communication culture researcher*. Too often we find that students interested in the study of business and professional communication pay attention only to the strategies and skills they can use when they are going to engage in a conversation, work on a team, or make a presentation. But there is another, and very important, side to studying communication in this class. You can also acquire skills as a communication cultural researcher, specifically those skills that can help you become a more adept sense-maker and interpreter of organizational cultures. How can you learn to do that?

Researchers who study organizational cultures always begin by doing three things: (1) paying attention to the external environments (e.g., the organization of space and people, the displays in cubes and in work areas, the style of dress worn by employees, etc.); (2) listening to the internal talk of employees; and (3) asking questions about symbolic meanings when the meanings of expressions, sentiments, or actions are uncertain or their local interpretation is unclear. By developing and applying these communication cultural research skills, Amber would have had better information about her co-workers and the company.

Second, Amber made the mistake that too many workers new to a job also make. She failed to recognize *silence as an opportunity to listen*. By listening, Amber could have checked her understanding of the assignment, the team members' interpretations of it, their history with the project, and the interactions of her team members. By allowing her team members to speak, she may have also gained empathy for her co-workers and their efforts, which could have helped her make better communication choices. Also, by having an appropriate communication goal—that is, being a productive team member—Amber may have made a better first impression on her team members.

What Amber needs is a lesson in making choices, conscious communication choices. From our perspective, what Amber needs is a lesson in becoming a more *conscious* communicator.

> **Focus on Ethics**
>
> Did Janet handle Amber's introduction to the team ethically? An important component of ethical communication is to assist others by providing the information needed to make informed choices. Were there things that Janet could have done to ease Amber's first meeting with the team? How would you have handled Amber's first meeting differently?

Conscious Communication in the Workplace

One of the goals of this course is to make you a more *conscious* communicator. To become a conscious communicator you must be *strategic* in your formulation of messages and aware of the *ethical* and *business* consequences of delivering them. When we talk about **strategic communication,** we are referring to communication that is planned with specific audiences and intentions in mind.

Consciousness is the mental state that brings us together with others involved in a communication context. Being conscious means that we are at once "an observer, a perceiver, a knower, a thinker, and a potential actor" (Damasio, 1999, p. 10). To successfully engage in **conscious communication,** you need to *choose, create, coordinate,* and *deliver* your message. We will use the four-step Choose, Create, Coordinate, and Deliver **(CCCD)** process for conscious communication throughout the remainder of the book (see Figure 1.5). Let's look at each of these components in more detail.

Figure 1.5

The CCCD Process			
Choose a communication strategy	**Create** your message	**Coordinate** The communication episode or event	**Deliver** the message

Step 1: Choosing a Communication Goal

Choosing an effective communication goal, the object you hope to achieve, requires developing an awareness of the possible messages and interpretations of messages in any business situation. When we choose a goal, we analyze the possible outcomes of a communication situation. Different messages and different audiences require different communication goals. Goals are a blending of the *components* and the *functions* of communication designed to increase the likelihood of successful communication.

A goal that is appropriate for interpersonal communication might not be appropriate for a formal presentation. A goal that applies to an email, might be inappropriate in a team meeting. Let's look back at Amber's goal. Amber's goal was to show that she had reviewed the team's progress and had the answer to their problems. Was Amber successful? Might she have been more successful if she had started with the goal of becoming a good team member, or the goal of understanding the team's progress, rather than jumping straight to the goal of problem solving? Amber's embarrassment was a direct result of *not* practicing conscious communication. She did not make a conscious effort to choose a goal that took into account the collaborative nature of teamwork or the team's communication history. Moreover, she skipped the creating and coordinating steps, both integral parts of conscious communication, and jumped to the stage in the CCCD process of delivery. The result was negative for Amber and her team members.

Choosing a communication goal involves conducting a complete assessment of:

- Audience needs and expectations.
- Likely communication outcomes.
- The criteria against which you will measure your success.

Once you have chosen a goal, you can begin to create a message specifically with your goal and audience in mind.

Step 2: Creating the Message

Creating the message is the process of developing *a presentation plan* designed to reach a specific audience and carry out the strategy you developed in step 1. To a large extent, this part of the process is about *organizing* a message around a specific audience. You need to plan what you are going to say first, how to develop your ideas, and how to summarize and conclude your presentation. For example, in interpersonal situations you need to consider the purpose and scope of the conversation. In a meeting you would organize your talk based on an agenda. In a formal presentation you would use main points to support and guide the presentation.

To create a message, establish the agenda for a meeting, or plan a presentation you need to:

1. Develop a purpose for your talk (or a thesis statement for your presentation).
2. Determine the organization of your talking points (main points for a presentation).
3. Develop support for each of your talking points.
4. Craft effective introductory and concluding materials.

Once you have created your message, it is important to coordinate with other members of your team, department, or organization.

Step 3: Coordinating with Others

Conscious communication requires input from a variety of sources. It also requires a different way of thinking about success in organizations. The old model for success in business was the Lone Ranger model (James, 1996). The Lone Ranger would ride in on a white horse to save a department or organization from disaster, and then ride back out of town into the radiant sunset. The new model for success in organizations is more the Three Musketeers model: "all for one and one for all." For this collaborative process to work, you and the other members of your organization must *trust that you will keep each other informed*. It means that you must work to create an *inclusive* organizational community. To do this, you should:

- Assemble as much information as you can about how your agenda, plan, or position fits within the mission and goals of the organization.
- Communicate with other members of the organization (teams, departments, supervisors, and managers) your need for input and feedback.
- Respect the professional and personal boundaries of others.
- Adapt your message, episode, or event accordingly.

Coordinating is the act of bringing together everyone required to successfully deliver the message. Coordinating with others is an *ongoing* organizational activity and may in some cases take place concurrently with step 2: Choosing. For example, once you have determined your goals, outcomes, and criteria, you may need to check with other members of the team to ensure that any presentations representing the team reflect the team's goals. Or you may not have all the information you need to present an idea, so you may need to coordinate with other departments or team members to gather your information. As you coordinate information, you will be creating and revising your presentation.

Another important aspect of coordinating is checking to make sure that all the appropriate members of the organization are aware of the communication event. You should ensure that everyone knows where and when the event will be held. Coordinating also involves checking that all the necessary room and equipment reservations have been made. Now, you are ready to deliver your message.

Step 4: Delivering the Message

Your communication strategy is set. The research and analysis are complete. Your message is crafted. You have coordinated with other members of your team and outside departments. Now it is time to deliver your message. The final step in CCCD, **delivery,** is really the most crucial because in most organizations, the payoff is in the communication performance.

Three questions are typically raised about the delivery of a message:

1. How much should I practice my message prior to delivering it?
2. How can I improve my performance?
3. How can I maximize feedback to my performance?

As we move through the book, we will answer these questions and develop your understanding of the CCCD process. The CCCD process is designed to maximize your communication effectiveness in any business or professional situation. In Chapter 3 we provide a detailed examination of the CCCD process. In Chapters 4 through 13 we apply the CCCD to oral and written forms of communication in interpersonal, group or team, and public contexts.

Principles of Conscious Communication

One of the comments we often hear from beginning students in courses such as this one is "Why should I study communication? After all, I've been doing it all my life!" Our response has been that although almost everyone is fortunate enough to acquire an ability to communicate, not everyone learns how to communicate *effectively*. Still fewer people acquire the knowledge and skill to develop communication competencies specific to the workplace.

To learn about communication means more than simply "doing it." It also means to study it, to acquire knowledge about it. To study business and professional communication means to read and to discuss the important ideas that have shaped our most advanced understandings about this vital skill. After careful study, application of these understandings should help improve your skills. As a result of having successfully completed a course specifically designed to improve both your understanding and skills, you should be a more *conscious* communicator.

To help you begin our investigation of business and professional communication, and to help you begin to think more intelligently and consciously about communication in the workplace, we offer the following list of conscious communication principles.

Conscious communication is mindful.
Conscious communication displays awareness of communication as a process.
Conscious communication respects diversity.

Conscious communication is mindful. Communicating mindfully means that you take into consideration the needs and expectations of others and contexts (Damasio, 1999; Langer, 1989). Mindful communicators recognize that while it is important to use strategic communication to reach goals, it is equally important to reach business and professional goals ethically.

Conscious communication displays awareness of communication as a process. Although we use the term *episode* or *event* to describe an act of communication in the workplace, it is more accurate to think of communication as an ongoing, continuous process. One communication event leads into another, expanding the context of communication throughout an organization.

Conscious communication respects diversity. Sensitivity to others includes a profound awareness of **diversity:** cultural, gender, racial, religious, and socio-economic differences. To be a mindful communicator means to research and respond intelligently to those differences you encounter in the workplace.

Summary

Chapter 1 introduces the idea of conscious communication in the workplace. We began by exploring why communication is considered a "breakthrough skill" for the 21st century. We then discussed the components and the functions of communication in business and professional contexts. Next, we outlined and provided a conceptual overview of the CCCD process for improving communication at work. Finally, we provided a list of the principles of conscious communication in an effort to begin organizing your understanding of business and professional communication.

COMMUNICATING IN PROFESSIONAL CONTEXTS ONLINE

Use your **Goodall Connection CD-ROM** for quick access to the electronic study resources that accompany this text. Included on your CD-ROM is access to:

InfoTrac College Edition

The World Wide Web

A demo of **WebTutor** for *Communicating in Professional Contexts*

The **Communicating in Professional Contexts Website** at the Wadsworth Communication Cafe. The Communicating in Professional Contexts Website offers chapter by chapter learning objectives, activities, quizzes, and a digital glossary.

You can review and complete the following sections online at
http://www.wadsworth.com/communication_d/

What You Should Have Learned

Now that you have read Chapter 1, you should be able to:

- Discuss the relevance of studying business and professional communication.
- Provide a basic definition of communication in a business and professional context.
- Describe the phrase "breakthrough skills" and the relationship to communication.
- List and describe the components of the communication process.
- Describe the three major functions of business and professional communication.
- Outline the CCCD process and discuss how it might apply to a formal business presentation, a job interview, and the construction of a written memo.
- Discuss what is meant by "conscious communication" and describe its three principles.

Activities

The following activitiess can be completed online and, if requested, submitted to your instructor, under Student Resources, Activities for Chapter 1 at the Communicating in Professional Contexts Website at the Wadsworth Communication Café http://www.wadsworth.com/communication_d/.

1. Interview a manager, CEO, or business owner. Ask the person to detail his or her communication needs. Have the person rate the importance of interpersonal, organizational, team, speaking, written communication, and presentational skills for his or her employees. Describe the course you are taking. How important to the person's business are the skills you are developing?

2. Obtain a memo or report from an organization. This could be an email or memo from your workplace or something available on the Internet. If you use an email from an organization, be sure you have permission. Analyze the memo

or email using the information in this chapter. What clues did you find about the organization or writer's history and context? What cultural clues did you find? What did your analysis reveal?
3. Working with your classmates as a group, determine the communication strategy for the following scenario:

   Mary has worked hard for XYZ Corporation for five years. The last two years she has received outstanding performance appraisals by both her manager, Kim, and Kim's director, John. Each year, Mary was promised a raise the next year, but because of budget cuts the raise was put off until her next review. Mary likes her job and regularly goes above and beyond her job description. This year Mary was elated to be promoted not one, but two steps. A few days after her promotion, Kim called her into her office and told her once again, because of a budget freeze, she could not give Mary the raise to go along with her recent promotion. She told Mary she pleaded with her director, who in turn had "gone to bat" for Mary with the company president, who responded with a firm, "No." Mary likes her job, but she wants that raise. Given what you have learned in this chapter, what should Mary do to make her case?

Surfing the Net

Any sites referred to in the following activities are maintained under HyperContents for Chapter 1 at the Communicating in Professional Contexts Website.

1. It's not your father or mother's workplace anymore. Use InfoTrac College Edition or the World Wide Web (WWW) to create a list of five changes in the workplace over the last 10 to 15 years. Consider using search words like *global organizations*, *career development*, *multicultural management*, or *information technology*. Compare your list to those of your classmates. Organize the list to determine the top five to ten changes you can expect to deal with in the global workplace. How many of these changes are based on communication?

2. The introduction of teams, intercultural work groups, and telecommuting makes determining the context for communication more complex. Use InfoTrac College Edition or the WWW to develop a database of information for communicating in either a team or an intercultural work group or when telecommuting. Consider using search words like *intercultural communication*, *business communication*, *international business*, or *organizational change*.

Key Terms

CCCD *(15)*

channel *(7)*

choosing *(16)*

communication *(3)*

communication history *(10)*

conscious communication *(15)*

context *(7)*

coordinating *(17)*

creating *(16)*

delivery *(18)*

diversity *(19)*

electronically mediated messages *(3)*

feedback *(6)*

hierarchical noise *(6)*

identity *(13)* organizational culture *(14)* sender *(4)*
interpretation *(13)* organizational persona *(13)* sense-making *(13)*
message *(5)* organizational savvy *(13)* strategic communication *(15)*
noise *(5)* receiver *(5)*
organizational credibility *(13)* semantic noise *(6)*

Breakthrough Skill Development:
Building a Communication Profile

Do you have the communication skills you need to survive in a global economy? Do you regularly use email? Have you written memos or reports? Do you have specific research skills? How are your interpersonal skills? Are you prepared to communicate professionally? What are your strengths and weaknesses?

Office Team is one of the world's leaders in specialized administrative staffing, with over 200 offices internationally. They developed the following questionnaire to assess a candidate's ability to compete and communicate in the workplace in the year 2005 (*Canadian Manager*, 1999). The following questions will help *you* determine if you have the necessary "people" skills to be successful in the office of 2005 and beyond. For some of the questions, you may agree with more than one response. However, try to select the answer you agree with most. Circle your answers below, or you can complete the questionnaire online at http://www.wadsworth.com/communication_d/. Your total score is based on the number of questions you answer correctly.

The Questions

1. Your colleagues have been passed over for a promotion, and you've been informed that you got it. But the announcement date becomes delayed due to your supervisor's other priorities. In the meantime, there is growing speculation among the staff, and one of your co-workers asks if you've heard anything about it. What approach do you take?
    a. Tell the colleague that you got it, but ask that he or she be discreet about it.
    b. Wait it out until your supervisor is ready.
    c. Tell a few, select co-workers that you got it, but ask that they be discreet about it.
    d. Tell all co-workers involved.
    e. Tell your supervisor there is a growing discussion and you've been asked about it.

2. Your primary method of organizing work is to:
    a. Continually re-establish priorities as needed based on the requirements of the day.
    b. Complete yesterday's priority list before reviewing new assignments for the day.

c. Try as best you can to complete one project before accepting another one.
d. Prioritize each day's work and stick to it regardless of additional projects that may distract you.

3. Which one of the following statements best describes your beliefs or approach?
   a. I generally like to avoid conflict whenever possible.
   b. Allowing emotions to enter into business decisions is unavoidable.
   c. I'm good at logically thinking through a problem.
   d. Making a relatively quick decision is always better than waiting to make a decision.

4. Your supervisor has given you an assignment, but you're unfamiliar with certain aspects of the project in which others in the department have more experience. You:
   a. Spend whatever time necessary on your own, getting at least a cursory knowledge of the unknown areas.
   b. Seek the assistance of the other experts and, in turn, offer your expertise to them.
   c. Tell your supervisor up-front that you are not familiar with those aspects.
   d. Suggest to your supervisor that you handle only the familiar part.

5. Which one of the following statements best reflects your beliefs or approach?
   a. Success seems to come more easily to some people than others.
   b. If my closest friends and family agree on what's best for my career, I usually rely on their advice.
   c. My employer is in the best position to decide which career path is best for me.
   d. Career success is a direct result of my own efforts, not those of others.

6. The best way to manage people is to:
   a. Make it very clear that you're in charge.
   b. Solicit input from them before making major decisions.
   c. Share your expertise by offering your direct supervision to as many people as possible.
   d. Set your goals before you begin the project and communicate them loudly and clearly to the team before getting started.

7. Which one of the following statements best reflects your beliefs or approach?
   a. When managing a project, I like all the team members to remain on task with the original approach.
   b. People with greater seniority in a company are in the best position to generate useful ideas.
   c. When managing a project, I encourage people to share differing opinions.
   d. If the majority of people believe in a certain approach, it's probably the best one.

8. Which of the following best describes the ingredients of effective persuasion?
    a. Remaining steadfast in your beliefs and not wavering.
    b. Being forceful and vocal in your opinion.
    c. Being pleasant as much as possible.
    d. Having strong listening skills.
9. One of your closest friends is in a business that you rely on as one of several vendors. You inadvertently give a little more information to your friend than you give to the other vendors. You realize that you have now given her an unfair advantage. You:
    a. Explain to your friend that you shouldn't have released this information and ask her not to make it a factor in her bid.
    b. Take into consideration when evaluating the bids that your friend had more information.
    c. Give other vendors the same information and run the risk of appearing disorganized.
    d. Give information you did not give to your friend to other vendors so they also benefit.
10. Your supervisor praises you publicly on the results of a successful project. You received invaluable help on this particular assignment from a co-worker who wasn't named. You:
    a. Approach the co-worker later and apologize.
    b. Tell your boss that credit should also go to the co-worker.
    c. Weigh how important it is to bring up the co-worker's involvement.
    d. Write your co-worker a thank-you note.
11. Which statement most accurately reflects your beliefs?
    a. Writing will become less important due to technological advancements.
    b. Writing is a skill that is innate, not learned.
    c. An experienced writer uses large words and long sentences.
    d. An experienced writer tries to use fewer words.
12. Describe your verbal communication abilities.
    a. I'd rather walk on hot coals than speak to a large group, but I do fine one-on-one.
    b. I'm a much better oral communicator than writer.
    c. When I speak to a group, people seem to grasp my point quickly.
    d. I'm relatively talkative and not shy.
13. Which of the following best describes your approach to brainstorm meetings?
    a. I'm a risk-taker and generally don't like to "follow the pack" in my thinking.
    b. I'm good at building on the ideas of others.

Breakthrough Skills for the Global Workplace

     c. I've always implemented ideas well and had good follow-up.

     d. I'd rather offer a feasible, well-thought-out idea than just any suggestion.

14. Which of the following statements best reflects your beliefs or approach?

    a. I believe that my employer should provide me with the training I need.

    b. I often use the Internet to research information during nonbusiness hours.

    c. I believe that a person's college/university education will provide a comprehensive source of knowledge for the balance of his or her career.

    d. If I rely heavily on my supervisor's expertise, I'll get the best training.

15. Which one of the following best describes you or your beliefs?

    a. When the going gets tough, I often make an effort to reduce tension through laughter.

    b. Good-natured teasing of others creates a less tense environment and encourages camaraderie.

    c. People who succeed in most companies tend to take their work very seriously.

    d. I've always been a good joke-teller.

Answer Key

Each question was designed to test a particular *people* skill. The skill tested by each question is listed below.

1. Diplomacy/Discretion
2. Organization
3. Problem-solving abilities
4. Team-player skills
5. Accountability/Initiative
6. Leadership
7. Open-mindedness/Flexibility
8. Persuasion
9. Ethics
10. Honesty
11. Written communication
12. Verbal communication
13. Creativity
14. Educational interests
15. Humor

  1. Diplomacy/Discretion

     a. Sorry; your supervisor wasn't ready and should make the decision on timing.

     b. Problematic; your supervisor should be made aware of the staff's queries, as discussions and speculation will only grow.

c. Unfortunately, this could hurt the morale of others.
d. Very risky; it's your manager's responsibility, not yours.
e. Right! This is something your boss should be made aware of and be able to act on to everyone's benefit. In the 2005 office, you'll take a broader look at the company's overall welfare because you'll benefit more directly from it. Companies will offer such programs as performance-based pay and stock ownership to help retain highly skilled workers.

2. Organization
   a. Bingo! If new projects come in, you must evaluate their importance relative to existing priorities. In 2005, there will be more instant communication and more projects to prioritize, so this skill is crucial.
   b. Often tempting, but yesterday's work may have to wait if new projects are more urgent.
   c. Sorry; multitasking will be key in coming years—focusing on one assignment will be a luxury, rather than the norm.
   d. Oops! Such rigidity will keep you from attending to potentially more urgent projects.

3. Problem-Solving
   a. Who could blame you? But as interaction and communication levels increase, so will the potential for conflicts. Get ready to practice better conflict resolution skills.
   b. Sorry; in 2005, you'll have to put emotions aside. Your professional, analytical abilities will be put to the test.
   c. Way to go! You have the ingredients of someone who can think clearly and analytically, which is beneficial as the pace of business increases.
   d. Not necessarily; while speed and efficiency will be important attributes in 2005, you may need more time and information to evaluate the best course of action.

4. Team-Player Skills
   a. Not a bad choice—this demonstrates initiative. However, you could have worked in conjunction with the others in a team-oriented manner, saving time for the overall task.
   b. Correct! As we head toward 2005, the ability to approach and help team members will be valuable since productivity depends on continuous information exchange.
   c. Sorry; to find out what you'll need to know in the office of 2005, you'll be expected to show resourcefulness and initiative.
   d. Careful; you need to show your supervisors as well as your peers that you're a team player.

5. Accountability/Initiative
   a. Sorry; those who believe their success rides on factors beyond their control may need to change their thinking. In 2005, those who take charge of their careers will have the greatest number of opportunities.

Breakthrough Skills for the Global Workplace

b. A tough one; while you want to solicit input from those who care about you, your major career decisions should be based primarily on your own interests and goals. In 2005, being the CEO of your own career will be more important than ever.

c. Employers can help guide you, but the ultimate expert on your career growth and satisfaction is you.

d. Hurrah! Taking charge of your career, whether you're a full-time, part-time, or project worker, will bring the greatest challenge and financial rewards.

6. Leadership

    a. Proceed with caution! The future office environment won't allow for a command-and-control management style; employees want to contribute to making decisions and offer creative solutions.

    b. Right! Skilled employees will have many career options in 2005; they'll choose opportunities in which their ideas are heard. In an increasingly competitive business world, smart managers will encourage greater participation from team members.

    c. Sorry; while this may seem benevolent, this choice could indicate micro-managing technologies.

    d. Almost! While sharing your vision is an admirable management trait, allowing participation in setting goals is characteristic of a good leader.

7. Open Mindedness/Flexibility

    a. An understandable choice, but you may need to become less rigid and allow room for modification and improvements. In 2005, rapidly changing events will make flexibility a key attribute.

    b. Not necessarily; while more senior employees have experience on their side, ideas from more recent recruits or even consultants may provide valuable, fresh perspectives.

    c. Good! This approach will give you the best thinking from your team.

    d. Nice try; unfortunately, peer pressure can make some employees follow the path of least resistance, not always the most productive path.

8. Persuasion

    a. Careful; if you become too rigid in your arguments, the other individual may become defensive. You must show interest in the beliefs of others to create open lines of communication.

    b. Sorry. Intimidation or being more vocal will not convince people to see things your way; it could backfire.

    c. Being pleasant and courteous will certainly help your efforts, but listening carefully is an even more valuable skill in this instance.

    d. Right! The most persuasive people are those who have taken on the challenge of active listening to other individuals to best understand their perspective and motives. With increased business demands in 2005, you'll have less time to make your own case. Practice strong listening skills with co-workers and watch the results.

9. Ethics
    a. Caution; this may be naive, and you're not being fair to other vendors.
    b. Sorry; you're still not giving other vendors the full opportunity to compete fairly.
    c. Right! While this could be embarrassing, you'll know you've avoided giving preferential treatment to your friend. Ethics in business will remain critical in 2005.
    d. Problematic; if you give out different information, this still won't level the playing field.

10. Honesty
    a. A good try, but you're still accepting full credit.
    b. Excellent! Your honesty and sense of team play will be appreciated more than ever in 2005 as employees work more closely in teams and are given more autonomy to make critical judgment calls.
    c. Almost; you're moving in the right direction, but if you have doubts about whether something is ethical, chances are it is not, and you should take immediate steps to remedy the situation.
    d. A nice gesture, but you're still falling short of appropriately sharing the credit.

11. Written Communication
    a. Oops! There will be more emails than ever in 2005. Clear communication and good grammar will help you become more productive.
    b. Not really; with practice and initiative, you'll improve.
    c. Sorry; this may seem impressive, but good writers communicate clearly, not necessarily with big words.
    d. Terrific! Keeping your writing concise will make it easier to understand and will have a greater impact. As email becomes more pervasive in 2005, brevity will be valued; verbosity, counterproductive.

12. Verbal Communication
    a. Ouch! Time to practice speaking to groups of people. You might consider joining a Toastmasters group or looking for opportunities to give speeches at your company, volunteer group, class, or other venues.
    b. A good try, but the better answer would be that you can articulate your point clearly and effectively.
    c. Good! You're able to present a clear message orally, an invaluable trait in 2005 when you must think on your feet, whether in a small or large group or during a video conference.
    d. Close; you may have the necessary confidence to be a good verbal communicator, but making your point clearly and concisely is the next step.

13. Creativity
    a. You got it! In 2005, risk-takers with creative ideas will be highly valued as companies compete more fiercely to come to market with innovative products and services. Are you ready to make your contribution?

Breakthrough Skills for the Global Workplace

b. A step in the right direction, but innovative thinking will have to start with you.

c. Sounds good, but original thinking will take you far in 2005.

d. Sounds practical, but in 2005, you'll be highly valued for taking creative risks. Your thoughts may not be well-defined, but they could inspire or develop into outstanding ideas.

14. Educational Interests

a. Careful; companies in 2005 will invest more in training, but workers must take the initiative to constantly upgrade skills.

b. Yes! You demonstrated the thirst for knowledge that will make you marketable in 2005.

c. Close; a college education is certainly beneficial. But the most successful workers in 2005 will continually upgrade technical and "soft" skills.

d. Sorry, in 2005 you'll advance more quickly if you take it upon yourself to enhance your skills and knowledge, inside and outside of the office.

15. Humor

a. Good! You have an invaluable interpersonal skill that will help smooth tensions that may arise from an instant-information environment.

b. Sorry; humor at the expense of others is counterproductive.

c. Sounds like a valid concept, but one of the most important ingredients in career success is the ability to laugh at oneself, putting others at ease.

d. Great for parties, but joke-telling is not quite the same as light-heartedness that reduces stress in others and offers perspective on the big picture.

Scoring

Refer to the answer key above and add up your correct responses.

13–15 correct answers

Congratulations! Your outstanding people skills will be an important contributor to your career success in 2005.

10–12 correct answers

Great. You have solid "soft" skills that will facilitate your advancement in the office of the future.

6–9 correct answers

Pretty good, but your interpersonal and communication skills may need some work.

3–5 correct answers

Start concentrating on areas you are missing. You still have time!

0–3 correct answers

Now is the time to develop your people skills. Your career success will depend on it! Pay close attention to the information in this course that addresses these areas.

Your Communication Profile

Begin building your communication profile by collecting examples of good communication. These could be memos, reports, or emails you are particularly proud of. You could create a journal detailing conversations you have had that went particularly well. Think about communication events that went exactly as you hoped they would. Read interviews by people you respect or wish to emulate. What communication strategies do they use in their talk? How could you adapt those strategies?

Chapter Two

The Evolution of Communication in the Workplace

Reality isn't what it used to be."

—STEINER KVALE, *The Truth About Truth*

"It is no accident that most organizations learn poorly....*The way we have been taught to think and interact...create[s] fundamental learning disabilities."*

—PETER SENGE, *The Fifth Discipline*

We begin with the above quotations because they speak to the two most important ideas in this book. The first quotation captures the challenge of explaining communication in the workplace when the realities of the workplace, and our ideas about effective communication, are experiencing great change. The second quotation identifies the main causes of recent business and professional frustrations with managing and working in times of great change: how we've been (mis)taught to think and interact. This may seem like a negative way to introduce an otherwise positive chapter, but as you will see, the best way to deal with communication in organizations during times of great change is to teach people to be more conscious communicators and reframe the workplace as a learning organization.

In this chapter we explore how we have gotten to a time and place where "conscious communication" and "learning organization" sum up the best practices associated with success and productivity in the workplace. To prepare you to better understand these terms and practices, we want to revisit a parallel evolution of two lines of thought that dominated the 20th century: *theories of organization and management*, and *theories of organizational communication*. As a result of revisiting these theories, by the end of this chapter you will understand why and how this evolution has occurred. You will also see why "conscious communication" and the "learning organization" sum up a best-practices approach to business and professional communication.

To accomplish this task, this chapter is divided into sections that link theories of organization and management to theories of communication following a more or less concurrent historical timeline that begins in the Industrial Revolution and ends in the present day. Using the timeline shown in Figure 2.1, we walk you through the evolution of theories of management and how these theories influenced theories of business and professional communication.

If you are making an outline for this chapter, the following divisions should shape and inform your reading:

- Classical Management and Information Transfer
- Human Relations/Resources and Transactional Process
- Systems Thinking and Communication Networks
- Organizational Cultures and Power
- Organizational Narratives and Dialogue

Classical Management and Information Transfer

The classical period of management began at the height of the Industrial Revolution in the late 1800s and continued through the 1930s. The movement

Organizational and Communication Theory Timeline

Classical Period—	Human Relations—	Human Resources—	Systems Theory	Cultural Theory	Learning Organizations—
Scientific Management and Bureaucracy	Hawthorne Studies and Maslow's Hierarchy of Needs	Maslow's Hierarchy of Needs			Five Disciplines
1900	**1920**	**1940**	**1960**	**1980**	**2000**
Communication as Information Transfer		Communication as Transactional Process	Networks	Power / Organizational Narratives	Dialogue

Figure 2.1 Evolution of Organizational Management and Communication Theories

of people from the farm to the city and from the plow field to factory highlighted this period. As more and more people entered the workplace, factory owners and store managers began to explore new and different ways to organize and manage people (Eisenberg and Goodall, 2001).

If we looked back at organizational charts from this period, we would see charts that favor a strictly vertical, top-down arrangement. At the top is a board of directors; below is a president; below the president are a series of vice presidents; below the vice presidents are department managers; below them are the supervisors; and finally, at the very bottom of the chart, are the line workers. The term for this organization by rank and status is **hierarchy.**

Classical organizational structures assigned privileges according to one's rank and status in the organization. There were two important classical approaches to managing businesses and industries: *scientific management* and *bureaucracy* (Morgan, 1986). These two theories dominated the way organizations were structured and managed during the classical period.

Scientific Management

Scientific management, which emerged in the early 1900s, was defined by an engineer named Frederick Taylor (1913). Taylor believed management was a true science that should be governed by scientific principles, rules, and laws. He put forth the idea that factories and organizations should be operated as "efficient machines," modeled on the inner-workings of a well-made

Ford Assembly, March 1928 Hulton/Archive

mechanical clock. No doubt inspired by this image of "clockwork," he proposed that "time and motion" studies be conducted for every task in an organization. These studies encouraged business owners and managers to find "the one best way" (i.e., the shortest amount of time using the smallest amount of motion) to complete tasks. The results were used to establish standards for every job, to create an evaluation instrument that could be equally applied to every worker, and to reward (or punish) workers based on their production or performance. Tasks were divided into discrete, measurable units and workers were trained to perform only one task, thus making replacement of workers who were sick or injured relatively easy. Workers were seen as merely another replaceable part in the factory machine, and there was little, if any, room for learning or advancement. As Henry Ford, a proud scientific management enthusiast, once put it, "managers think; workers work."

But what did managers *think about* and *do*? During this same theoretical period, a Frenchman named Henri Fayol established the five functions of scientific management: planning, organizing, commanding [goal-setting], coordinating, and controlling [evaluating] (1949). According to Fayol, it was the manager's job to plan the work, organize tasks, set goals, coordinate work, and control the workforce. A person hired as a manager would be trained to perform these duties, and *only* these duties. There was no allowance for encouraging managers to learn how to do their jobs better, or even differently.

Scientific principles governed the management of a plant in pretty much the same authoritative, unchanging way that they were used to describe the movement of planets or the growing of soybeans. Certainly no thought was expended on "quality improvement" when it came to managerial tasks. A man (almost all the factory managers during this period in history were men) either knew how to do the job, or he didn't!

Although scientific management was, in principle, a good theory for organizing and managing repetitive tasks done in a mechanical environment, in practice it contributed to the dehumanization of the workplace. Because workers were considered replaceable parts in a relentless machine, they were often treated as less than human. Working conditions during this period were hard, labor laws were virtually nonexistent, and management decisions were the final word. Workers could be fired, hired, or reassigned based on their sex, race, religion, attitude, or relationships to other workers.

Bureaucracy

Although it might not seem so today, the creation of a **bureaucracy** was considered a more humane way of managing people in complex organizations. Max Weber, an observer of the rise of scientific management and a major sociological theorist of his day, saw bureaucracies as a means to overcome the problems of scientific management (1946). Weber believed that managed correctly, using a set of universalisms or standards of fairness, bureaucracies would stamp out the harsh, inequitable, and often deadly conditions that arose from poor scientific management (Perrow, 1986). According to Weber (Scott, 1990), an ideal bureaucracy must have a:

- Fixed division of labor.
- Hierarchy of work responsibilities and authority.
- Set of general operating rules that govern performance.
- Separation of the personal lives of employees from their professional lives.
- Selection process based on technical qualifications and equal treatment under the rules for operating the business.

Scientific management and bureaucracy both relied on strict top-down authority structures, centralized decision-making, and control of managerial power to govern the organization of work. What it left out was any concept that workers could learn to manage, managers could learn to become better at their jobs, or managers and workers could learn from each other if they communicated more equitably.

That would come later. In the meantime, let's examine the dominant theory of communication that shaped scientific management and bureaucracy.

Communication as Information Transfer

During the classical period, there was an implicit theory of communication that would later be termed the **information transfer model.** Visualize a pipeline through which information or messages pass. On one end of the pipeline is a "sender" and on the other end is a "receiver." What you have just pictured is a representation, or model, of communication that contains one or more of the following assumptions about information transfer (Axley, 1984):

- Language transfers thoughts and feelings from person to person.
- Speakers and writers insert thoughts and feelings into words.
- Words contain the thoughts and feelings.
- Listeners or readers extract the thoughts and feelings from the words (p. 429).

The information transfer model, while simplistic in its characterization of management and communication, nevertheless has had a lasting influence in bureaucracies worldwide. Moreover, academic interest in how people think and process information about task-oriented communication led to the development of sophisticated research programs aimed at explaining the gaps in this complex phenomenon. This research contributed to filling the gaps in the explanatory power of the information transfer model, which in turn created the questions that led to the emergence of human relation theories of management and a new perspective on communication in the workplace.

Human Relations/Resources and Transaction Process

Although the 1920s had been a period of extreme affluence and growth in America, the early 1930s quickly gave way to closed factories, massive migrations, and widespread poverty and unemployment. With little to lose, workers began to make demands for better working conditions, fairer wages, and equal treatment. Labor unions grew in popularity and power.

The poverty of the Great Depression eventually gave way to a new cycle of expansion and prosperity. Driven by the production demands of World War II, demands for fairer treatment of workers by managers sponsored by labor unions, and a desire among liberal-minded journalists, academics, and industrialists for a better way to get the job done, new theories of management emerged. These new theories of management grew out of what we now term the **human relations movement** (Eisenberg and Goodall, 2001).

What made it different? The human relations movement viewed employees less as *individual* replacement machine parts and more as sources of *group* information and skill that could be *developed* through training and education by the organization. Two ideas were key to this movement; they were contained in the *Hawthorne Studies* and *Maslow's Hierarchy of Needs*.

Hawthorne Studies

In the 1930s, Elton Mayo led a team of researchers to study the way people worked at Western Electric's Hawthorne Plant in Cicero, Illinois (Mayo, 1945). Using principles drawn from scientific management, Mayo was asked to conduct research in the plant to see if productivity improved when lighting conditions were altered. What he and his research team found surprised them. The changes in productivity they witnessed had nothing to do with the lighting, but everything to do with communication with and among the factory workers. In a nutshell, Mayo found that increased attention to the workers led to improved *morale*, which in turn improved productivity, a finding that became known as "the Hawthorne Effect." They also found that individuals are influenced by those around them, and those *group interactions* could have favorable effects on work.

These two insights became the basis for a gradual change from a strictly bureaucratic to a "human relations" approach to management. The core principles of the movement emphasized the:

- Importance of *open communication* and *supportive relations* between managers and employees.
- Need for managers to take into account employees' *feelings*.
- Need for managers to respond to the *developmental needs of workers*, which may be incongruent with formal hierarchies and task specialization.

Maslow's Hierarchy of Needs

During the 1940s and 1950s, a psychologist named Abraham Maslow developed the *Hierarchy of Needs* model to explain what *motivates* human behavior. The model represents a hierarchy of human needs that range from "lower order" needs such as food, clothing, and shelter, to "higher order" needs such as self-esteem and personal fulfillment ("self-actualization"). (See Figure 2.2.)

Maslow argued that to properly motivate employees required understanding what they were thinking about and aspiring to in their lives. Owners and managers began to understand that while a paycheck can help fulfill the lower-order needs, viewing workers as "human resources" by providing them with proper training and educational opportunities would help satisfy higher-order needs, thus making workers more productive.

Figure 2.2
Maslow's Hierarchy of Needs

Maslow's influence in managerial thinking cannot be overestimated. His work inspired other researchers to ask new questions about motivation and rewards, about the design and evaluation of performance, and about how "optimal performance" on the job might be accomplished. His work underscored the importance of what today we call "organizational learning" and "continuous improvement." He also set the academic stage for studies of "organizing for peak performance" (Eisenberg, 1990) that have led to very interesting insights about the necessary conditions for helping workers identify and meet challenges. In particular, Mihalyi Cziksentmihalyi's theory of "flow" (1990, 1997) suggests that peak performances are gained when workers feel motivated to do a job that is a little above their skill level, but have the training and resources to carry it out.

To understand how motivation, morale, and working in groups or teams are experienced at work, academics and professionals had to revise what they thought about "communication."

Communication as a Transactional Process

The **transactional process model** of communication emerged out of the failures of the scientific management and information transfer school to provide a model for motivation, morale, and teamwork. Specifically, after the Hawthorne studies, more attention was paid to the idea of communication as vital to manager/employee relations. As a result, clear hierarchical distinctions between bosses and workers were replaced with more equitable terms such as "senders" and "receivers." Additionally, these terms created an appreciation for how people at work perform those roles *simultaneously*.

According to the transactional process model:

- All persons are engaged in sending and receiving messages (Wenberg and Wilmot, 1973).
- Each person is constantly affecting the other (Wenberg and Wilmot, 1973).
- Feedback, particularly nonverbal feedback, is a vital source of information (Anderson, 1999).
- The person receiving a message, rather than the person sending the message, is the source of meaning (Axley, 1984).

Communication as a transactional process was the dominant communication model informing advances in human relations, human resources, and human potential approaches to organization and management. In an evolutionary sense, you can see how what was once a top-down, "command and control" perspective on business and professional talk gave way to a far more humane, and more complex, view of verbal and nonverbal communication. Three major areas of academic research and business practice benefited from this model:

- Interpersonal communication in the workplace
- Team communication
- Leadership

The transactional process model provides a useful, general approach to understanding interpersonal and team communication in the workplace, within which new findings are still being discovered and advances are still being made. However, new theories of organization, management, and communication were evolving that created yet another new way of thinking about communication in the workplace. Not only was verbal and nonverbal communication viewed as a management *function* or as a *component* of team effectiveness, but it also became more broadly associated with the process for *creating* the organization and becoming the substance of management. These new theories are called the systems and cultures approaches to organization and communication.

Systems Thinking and Communication Networks

Systems thinking is a theory of business organization that combines holism and interdependence. It views an organization as a system of interconnected individuals and teams. A major claim of systems thinking is that for one member of a team or organization to succeed, all members of the team or organization must succeed (Goodall and Eisenberg, 2001). These days, in the dawning of the 21st century, to call a company's interlocking webs of communication a "system" is to use a language that most business people readily accept and many understand. A system is a way to conceptualize the *dynamic set of relationships* that point to *a new kind of order*. This order is not one made of bureaucratic hierarchies and divisions of labor, but instead consists of *patterns of interaction* among the system's components (Farace, Monge, and Russell, 1977; Senge, 1991).

An *organizational system* is often envisioned metaphorically as a "family of relationships," in which the organization is equated with a family and each family member's communication has some effect on—is interconnected with—every other family member's understandings, meanings, and communication. The components of a system are (Eisenberg and Goodall, 2001):

- **Environment:** Organizations do not exist as isolated entities but as integral parts of the world.
- **Interdependence:** The organization, its environment, and the individuals and components within it are interrelated.
- **Goals:** What the system is organized to accomplish. Goals are negotiated between the individual components, with a large influence from the system's environment.
- **Feedback:** Feedback is an interconnected system of "loops" that connect communication and action. There are two kinds of feedback: *negative*, which corrects for deviations from the original goal, and *positive*, which finds new areas for growth and expansion.
- **Openness, order, and contingency:** These terms refer to the notion that there is no "one best way" to organize. To succeed, an organizational system must remain open and work within its environment, in an evolving and orderly way.

One of the major contributions to communication theory provided by systems thinking was the idea of *communication networks*. Another was the *contingent nature of decision-making*. A third was the importance of *feedback* to the health and resilience of the organizational system. Let's examine why these ideas were so powerful, and how they have influenced our business and professional communication.

The Links Between Systems Theory and Business and Professional Communication

There are three direct links between the *components* of an organizational system and *communication* in it: communication flow in networks, the contingent nature of decision-making (interdependence), and the importance of feedback to the health and resilience of the system. Each of these links has a direct impact on how we communicate and interpret meaning in the workplace.

Communication Flow in Networks

When an organization is viewed as a communication system, two patterns stand out. First, some communication flows into and through the organization according to *formal* chains of command and through established groups and teamwork. For example, because of the devaluing of currency in the Asian economy, U.S. stock exchanges reacted swiftly and strongly. The CFO of XYZ Corporation responded to this shift in the economic environment by asking each group leader or department head to analyze how this shift would affect their products and customers. Department or group leaders worked together to incorporate their analysis into future corporate directions, which they presented to the CFO at their monthly status meeting.

Second, some communication flows into and through the organization using *informal* or social patterns of routine interaction that are not prescribed or authorized by the organization in a formal way. Talk around the water cooler or impromptu discussions that occur in the employee lounge would be considered informal patterns of interaction. Together, these patterns teach us a lot about how messages are carried throughout an organization. For example, during the XYZ Corporation analysis, many employees and customers speculated on XYZ's ability to remain profitable. These conversations occurred over lunches, in parking lots, and during sales calls. Feedback from these informal interactions enlightened the formal discussion, providing decision-makers with additional sources of information. In turn, formal groups reported these concerns to their superiors, who engaged a consultant to help them through the period of potential crisis.

Contingent Nature of Decision-Making

As you can see from these examples, viewing communication flow through networks in a system reveals the ongoing, dynamic nature of interaction and feedback. It also reveals why companies use a contingent approach to decision-making. Rather than assume that once a decision has been made, the problem is solved, contingent decision-makers understand the constant need to revise decisions based on new information and ongoing analysis of the effects of past decisions. This pattern of interaction that informs decision-making is known as **interdependence.** One of its major outcomes is *organizational learning*.

(continued)

Feedback and the Health of a System

Maintaining open lines of communication is vital to the health and resilience of an organizational system. Open lines of communication ensure that feedback—both positive and negative (or corrective)—is available to make informed decisions and enhance the productivity of an organization. Lines of communication must remain open externally and internally. In the example above, the feedback received from customers was important for channeling customer concerns to the appropriate department and planning for communication back to the customer about future plans. One of the major outcomes of this kind of systems thinking has been the development and use of *continuous improvement* models to monitor the quality of the organization as well as its services or products.

Systems thinking has had a profound influence on theories of organization, management, and communication. Systems thinking is the core of Peter Senge's approach to using communication (in the form of dialogue) to build learning organizations (1994). But before we move into our discussion of conscious communication in learning organizations, we need to explain the influence of another powerful idea that also has had tremendous impact on our understanding of business and professional communication: *organizational cultures*.

Tips for Using Formal and Informal Networks Effectively

The systems perspective provides useful tips for communicating formally and informally in an organization. Let's examine ways you can use these concepts in your professional communication.

- Develop information and support contacts inside and outside of your workplace. Look for people who can help you plan the direction of your career, projects, and opportunities that you might have missed if you stayed within an organizational shell.
- Keep the lines of communication with your contacts open at all times. To do so, you need to listen carefully, respond quickly to requests, seek information when unsure, and give credit where credit is due.
- Understand that decisions in organizations are subject to change and revision. Don't stake out a position and refuse to change because you are relying on yesterday's information; tomorrow may require a shift in decision-making.

- Never assume your company operates in isolation. Keep up with current events, changes in technology and the global economy, and shifts in your industry that will affect your company.
- Understand that in business, change is healthy. For most people, this requires a shift in thinking: change is healthy and stagnation is unhealthy.
- Enter into all interactions from a conscious communication perspective. Be aware of the information value and potential effect of your communication on your identity, others' ability to act, and the organization's health and resilience.

Organizational Cultures, Communication, and Power

Organizational culture, like a system, implies an intricate, interconnected, and purposeful pattern or order. Unlike systems, however, a culture's pattern is drawn from the metaphors and language of "community," which implies:

- A *unique sense of place* that both unites and divides members (Louis, 1979).
- *Histories and visions* for the future, which may or may not be shared (Deal and Kennedy, 1982; Peters and Waterman, 1982).
- Locally-defined *customs, rituals, rules, rites, and procedures* (Pacanowsky and O'Donnell-Trujillo, 1983; Hofstede, 1983; Goodall, 1989).
- *Shared core values* that even when opposed by resistance factions are recognized to exist (Ouchi and Wilkins, 1985; Kotter and Heskett, 1992; Shockley-Zalabak and Morley, 1994).

The culture of the organization includes the way employees dress, how they speak to superiors, the items they display in their office or cubes, and more. Culture appears to consist of the behaviors, customs, habits, stories, routines, and other meaningful events and processes that organize people (Putnam and Pacanowsky, 1983). However, cultural researchers stress the importance of understanding that culture is not a "thing," but a "happening" (Pacanowsky, and O'Donnell-Trujillo, 1983).

Communication is the process by which culture is formed and transformed (Eisenberg and Goodall, 2001; Kellett, 1999). The cultural approach teaches us that communication *is* the culture. The verbal and nonverbal messages that arise from the organization's culture create the *meanings* of behavior, customs, habits, stories, routines, and the events and processes that organize and inform a group of people. As the anthropologist Clifford Geertz expresses it, "humans live in webs of meaning that we ourselves have spun" (1973).

Studying organizational cultures allows us to expand our business and professional communication knowledge to include an understanding of *power, organizational storytelling, personal narratives,* and *dialogue*. Let's examine each of these forms of contemporary business and professional communication.

The Influence of the Cultural Approach to Power

One of the advantages of the organizational culture approach to communication has been a new understanding of the role of communication in the creation of **power**—the sources of influence derived by an individual within an organization. In part, this new understanding of power was derived from looking critically at the advice about communication provided in previous models of organizing and managing (see Deetz, 1995; Conquergood, 1991; Conrad, 1991; Mumby, 1987). Before we can understand how the cultural approach challenged these theories of power, let's review how power functioned in previous models.

Classical Approach to Power

The classical approach to power provides what critics have labeled the *managerial view* of communication in organizations (Putnam and Pacanowsky, 1983). This means that our understanding of all communication practices, and especially of power, was rooted firmly in the idea that "rank has its privileges." Moreover, the expression of power was limited to structures created for, and functions carried out by, managers. French and Raven (1968) described the classic managerial forms of power:

Reward power: A supervisor can give a reward—such as a bonus, time off, or an award—based on compliance with a directive.

Coercive power: A boss has coercive power when employees perceive that negative things will happen if they don't comply with directives.

Referent power: A boss has referent power when employees do what is asked of them because they seek to emulate her or him.

Expert power: A boss has expert power when employees perceive a boss to have expert knowledge.

Legitimate power: A boss has power simply because of his or her position within the hierarchy. Employees perceive the position to be legitimately held and therefore comply with directives.

As you can see, there are times when each of these forms of power may be appropriate and useful. Power should be applied consciously and after a mindful examination of the outcome you hope to achieve.

The Human Relations Approach to Power

In the transactional process model, the idea of power shifts from the manager's position within the hierarchy to the *relationship between the manager and the employee*. The employee gains power, primarily by being encouraged to give feedback to the boss and to interpret his or her own meanings about the relationship and the work, and by negotiating with the organizational superior how, when, and with what resources the assigned work could be accomplished. The manager derives power from being more supportive, open, interested in the employees' feelings and thoughts, and trustworthy. Viewed this way, managers and employees use power *cooperatively*, and therefore more fairly.

The Systems Approach to Power

The systems perspective encourages us to see power less as a "thing" that organizational superiors "have" and subordinates "don't have" than as a *system of relationships* based only in part on an employee's status in the organizational hierarchy. Systems thinking helps us account for the available uses of power in everyday exchanges between and among equals (as well as between superiors and subordinates). For example, a lowly computer programmer with deep knowledge of an operating system has a lot of potential power in a company that requires that operating system to be in place and "up and running" to do business. If the system goes down, so do company profits. The programmer's power is held *in relation to* every other employee's ability to do his or her job. Concurrently, the programmer's success may well depend on the inputs about the computer system she or he receives from other employees. Viewed systemically, everyone has some available power relative to everyone else's available power.

Similarly, employees who are interpersonally close to, and whose information (e.g., feedback) is trusted by, their managers tend to be able to exert influence despite hierarchical differences. Quality of relationships and the perceived value of information mediate and often negate overt power as defined by rank and status. This principle also helps us understand the power of rumors and gossip in an organization. As sources of informal communication, rumors and gossip serve to balance power by directing and controlling information and feedback within a larger organizational system.

The Cultural Approach to Power

The cultural perspective assumes that there is a constant struggle for power in every organization (Deetz, 1995). In organizations, people vie for attention, resources, rewards, influence, and dignity. From a cultural perspective, people and groups holding power are described as "dominant," and others seeking power are labeled "resistant" (Goodall, 1990a; Scott, 1990). One major contribution of this perspective has been the study of power as it relates to, and is derived from, gender, racial, class, and sexual orientations in organizations.

Power and Difference   With the advent of the cultures perspective, the model for power expanded from *overt* hierarchy, information, and relationships to *covert* or hidden power (Conrad, 1983; Scott, 1990). Because of sociological research, power within companies came to be viewed in relation to power in societies. In societies marked by social and economic class divisions, where differences in opportunities and evaluations of one's abilities are often based on one's race, gender, or sexual orientation, the same patterns of influence and inequity are felt in businesses and professions. Furthermore, because sociologists and anthropologists teach us to see all cultures as localized sites of struggles between those who have power and those who don't, a new language of "resistance to domination" enters organizational analysis.

Power is now understood to occur "off-stage" as well as "on-stage" (Scott, 1990; Goodall; 1995), which means that the lines of power extend beyond face-to-face encounters, or even beyond the workplace. For example, disgruntled or alienated employees who feel wronged may turn their work worlds upside down, and therefore regain a sense of power and equity, by casting aspersions on their bosses. In the film *American Beauty* (1999), a character facing termination from his boring job in an advertising firm confronts his superior directly, turns the power equation inside out, and wins a large settlement. In real life, this is unlikely, as resistance to domination typically occurs off-stage. These off-stage performances may occur in break rooms, in comic asides performed behind the boss's back, in nasty emails to friends, in "work-hate narratives" (Goodall, 1995), and during after-work or weekend gatherings.

Power and Democracy Another way of understanding the cultural perspective on power is through the application of a cooperative (or democratic) model of influence. Although this is still the exception rather than the norm in business today, the concept bears examination. Stan Deetz created a model for power and democracy in the workplace using the "stakeholder organization" (1995), in which shared decision-making at every level is crucial to the success of the company. Deetz outlines four steps to create such a workplace (Eisenberg and Goodall, 2001, pp. 166–167):

1. *Create a workplace in which every member thinks and acts like an owner.* When power is shared for decision-making, stakeholders become more accountable to themselves, to each other, and to the society.

2. *The management of the work must be reintegrated with the doing of work.* Empowering stakeholders to have control over how they perform their own jobs eliminates the need for managers or supervisors. Power is thus shared among equals.

3. *Quality information must be widely distributed.* Information is power, and power in a stakeholder organization must be shared equally. Additionally, by encouraging stakeholders to share only "real" information, this model discourages the meaningless proliferation of memos, faxes, emails, letters, and newsletters that reinforce existing power hierarchies.

4. *Social structure should grow from the bottom rather than be reinforced from the top.* Power is vested in all of the stakeholders, who determine every aspect of their jobs and workplace instead of taking orders from people paid to oversee and direct the work.

Now that we have studied the idea of power in relation to cultural theories of organization, let's examine two of the ways communication functions in a cultural model: organizational narratives and dialogue.

Organizational Narratives and Dialogue

All of our experiences provide us with the raw materials to construct an ongoing "story of our lives" (Bochner, 1997; Goodall, 2000; Coles, 1989). Similarly, employees and managers in businesses and professions construct "organizational narratives" to recreate and retell the important events in their working lives (Boje, 1991, 1995; Mumby, 1987; Kellett, 1999).

Theorists have labeled this perspective the **narrative** view or paradigm (Bochner, 1994; Fisher, 1987). The essential idea behind the narrative paradigm is that, communicatively, *we live within the lines of the stories* we tell others about our jobs, our lives, and ourselves. These narratives do not simply *represent* our experiences; they also help *construct* them. Our identities, goals, values, and passions are derived from an ongoing narrative in which we figure as a central character. How we make sense of situations and others is largely determined by the ways in which we can use the plots and lessons of our ongoing stories to render "the new" within a context of "the old" (Weick, 1995).

Four uses of organizational narratives have been studied as forms of business and professional communication:

- **Organizational stories** (Mumby, 1987; Goodall, 1989; Boje, 1991): Individual accounts of the workplace that reveal how events occurred, problems were solved, heroes and heroines were created, legends were made, and "things are done around here." Some of these stories reveal how power works; for example, accounts of "how things are done around here" tend to repress alternative ways of doing things.
- **Work-hate narratives** (Goodall, 1995): Individual accounts of harms, misdeeds, or violence done to employees. These stories are often told to regain equity in a situation, but they sometimes forecast acts of revenge.
- **Narrative recovery technique** (Kellett, 1999): As a consulting tool, these stories are collected publicly from all employees in a particular department or area to "recover" the history of the organization from a personal perspective. The consultant uses key questions to prompt the narratives, including (a) what brought you to work here? (b) what are your personal joys and challenges? (c) have there been any turning points in your relationship to this company? (d) what vision do you have for your future here?

+ **Organizational change** (Ford and Ford, 1995; Kellett and Goodall, 1998; Kellett, 1999): Consultants, trainers, and managers all understand that productive change in organizations always *begins in conversations*. Because communication creates perceptions of reality as well as constitutes systems and cultures, communication is responsible for bringing into existence ideas for change. Stories about those conversations emerge as part of the shared history—myths, legends, turning points—of any organization or profession.

Dialogue

Conceptually, **dialogue** refers to *an ongoing, open, and dynamic process in which individual communicators have a balanced chance to speak and to be heard, and in which each person makes a conscious effort to understand and empathize with the perspective, experiences, and positions of the other* (Buber, 1985; Eisenberg and Goodall, 2001; Senge, 1991; Senge et al., 1994). The purposes of dialogue are to promote identity and community through empathetic understanding, to use communication to achieve mutual growth, and to search for meaningful patterns capable of effecting personal transformation and organizational change (Arnett and Cissna, 1996; Senge et al., 1994; Kellett and Dalton, 2001; Eisenberg and Goodall, 2001). As you can see, dialogue represents a unique and powerful form of communication.

H. L. Goodall (2000), working from an earlier Peter Senge (1991) model for describing types of communication, developed a continuum for conceptualizing a range of everyday forms of talk. These types of talk are:

+ Phatic Communion (e.g., routine exchanges of small talk).
+ Ordinary Conversation (e.g., discussion, gossip, or information exchange).
+ Skilled Conversation and Professional Communication (e.g., interviews, negotiations, conflict management, informative and persuasive presentations, team presentations, argumentation and debate).
+ Personal Narratives (e.g., stories).
+ Dialogue (deep conversation aimed at mutual growth that often requires risk-taking, creativity, and suspension of critical judgment).

As this continuum reveals, dialogue is the most advanced form of communication. Viewed from an organizational perspective, dialogue requires that equitable communication opportunities are afforded to all employees (Eisenberg and Goodall, 2001). However, merely having a right to speak doesn't adequately address the quality of talk that is exchanged during a dialogue.

The most *conscious* form of communication in an organization is dialogue. As you can see from Figure 2.3, the more conscious a communicator is of talk, the more open the exchange with the other person, the more dialogic the talk becomes. Let's examine the basis for this claim in greater detail.

Phatic Communication	Ordinary Communication	Skilled Talk	Personal Narratives	Dialogue
Routine, ritualized social talk	Exchanges of questions and responses, humor, ideas, and other forms of relational information	Interviews, negotiations, conflict management, presentational speaking, and teamwork	Autobiographical stories about the meaning of one's life experience	Creative, risk-taking, mutual quest for understanding and meaning

Figure 2.3
Communication Contiuum in a Learning Organization

Mindless Communication

Experience teaches us that we do not always behave mindfully at work or at home. Nor do we always behave in an ethical manner. In part, this is because many communication situations we face daily at work do not call for a lot of mental alertness or focused communicative activity. Communication researchers have termed these situations "phatic communion," or "small talk." In these situations, what is called for is not mindful, but "mindless" or automatic, often "scripted" responses (Greene, 1997; Goodall, 1996; Lodge, 1997).

Mindless communication—episodes of small talk or automatic talk—occurs most often in familiar situations. Why? Because when we are in familiar situations, speaking and listening to people we see every day, we often rely on past experiences, routines, rituals, or habits—what researchers call "scripted responses"—to guide our talk. We do not consciously select a strategy; we simply fall back on nonconscious routines we have used successfully. Below is a typical example of phatic communion:

SHAVONDA: Hi!
RICK: Hi.
SHAVONDA: So how are you?
RICK: Fine, and you?
SHAVONDA: Good.
RICK: So what's new in your department today?
SHAVONDA: Not much, and you?
RICK: The same. You know how it is. That's why they call it "work."
SHAVONDA: Yeah, I guess. Well, see you later.
RICK: Okay. See you.

Most of us repeat this form of small talk many times during an average day. Phatic communication is a necessary, although seldom sufficient, form of everyday business talk because it is a kind of social lubricant that encourages a surface level of collegiality and friendliness. Furthermore, cognitive researchers suggest that mindlessness is one way the brain conserves its energy for more challenging situations. In this way, "nonconscious behavior should not be viewed as an evil" (King and Sawyer, 1998, p. 334). By behaving "automatically," we make our mental energy available for other uses.

This is not to say that relying on phatic communion or small talk is a good thing. An overreliance on mindlessness diminishes our cognitive ability to develop new scripts or creative responses, and to otherwise *expand the repertoire* of available communication strategies we bring to new situations (Goodall, 1996). Communication ability is a skill, and like any skill, it requires practice. If all we do is rely on small talk and routine responses, we aren't using the full capacity of our communication potential. Nor are we getting much practice in developing the creative, mindful strategies that we need when phatic communion simply won't do. Nor are we always behaving ethically, because mindless activity does not allow for complex and difficult thoughts. This may help us account for why we inadvertently hurt others' feelings, or why we too often fail to appreciate how our routine actions have harmed or offended others. Finally, an overreliance on small talk probably encourages others to perceive us as friendly, but boring. For these reasons, success in business and professional communication is unlikely to occur when mindless communication dominates your everyday interactions.

Improving our conscious communication, becoming more mindful in business and professional contexts, should be a *major learning goal* for anyone planning an organizational career. Many of the more popular books giving advice for business communication success can be understood as reflections of the basic assumptions about conscious communication afforded by the cognitive perspective. For example, Stephen Covey's *The Seven Habits of Highly Effective People* (1990) advocates becoming more goal oriented, focused, and strategic in our dealings with others. Clearly, the knowledge and skills provided by this theoretical perspective on communication have direct relevance to developing important professional communication competencies. The next section discusses mindful, or more conscious, communication.

Mindful Communication

A mindful approach to talk enables us to view communication consciously, as a *mental* and *relational* activity that is both *purposeful* and *strategic*. We use our heads to come up with strategies that we encode into talk designed to help us achieve desirable ends with others. When we are conscious of our communication we become more *mindful* (Langer, 1990; Motley, 1992). **Mindful communication** requires:

- Analyzing communication situations.
- Thinking actively about possible communication choices available to us.
- Adapting our message to inform, amuse, persuade, or otherwise influence our listener or audience.
- Evaluating the feedback we receive as an indication of how successful we were in accomplishing our purpose.

But what if what is desirable for us might hurt someone else? Researchers suggest that cognitively based communication is, or at least should be, *ethical* (Langer, 1989). This is because we are *individually responsible* for our choices, our modes of adapting to listeners and audiences, and the outcomes of our actions. To become more conscious as communicators, which is to become more mindful and strategic in our dealings with others at work, should help us to become more ethical as well.

Focus on Ethics

Does communication qualify as mindful if you know your message will hurt someone? Are you responsible for the outcome if your goal is achieved? What responsibility do you have to others in the workplace if you know your communication might further your career but at the same time harm the career of another?

Research shows that we can expect mindful communication to occur in specific situations (Motley, 1992):

- *When there is a conflict between message goals.* For example, an employee may knock on a supervisor's door to ask permission to perform a task but also want to show the supervisor that he or she has taken the initiative to take on the task without being directed to do so. There is a conflict between the goals for the message—to demonstrate initiative or to ask permission.
- *When undesirable consequences are expected from the use of a particular message.* For example, a technical writer knows that she must inform the manager that his deadline will not be met. She also knows that he will not be pleased with this information and will likely blame her for not accomplishing the job. She thinks this will harm her career, but she also feels obligated to tell him the deadline will not be met.

- *During time delays between messages and mental processing difficulties, such as interpreting the meaning or intention of a message.* For example, two colleagues are having lunch together and one partner seems interested in taking the relationship, which until this time has been one of friendship and collegiality, to another, possibly romantic, level. The other partner pauses for a long time before answering her colleague's last statement about his "interest" in her. She is trying to figure out what he means. He is trying to figure out why she isn't answering him.
- *When communication situations are particularly troublesome or unique.* For example, a visiting computer engineer from Sweden arrives with gifts for the manager of a North American computer firm. The North American manager has no gifts to give in return and is clearly embarrassed. Both of them search for something to say to ease the situation.

The Next Step: Learning Organizations

Systems thinking and understanding organizational cultures revolutionized how we view organizations and communication. Until recently, however, these concepts were difficult to apply to the actual managing of, or communicating in, a company. Peter Senge and his associates (1991, 1995) have applied systems thinking to organizational cultures through the concept of a **learning organization**—an organization marked by conscious systems thinking and an ability to continually adapt communication to organizational, cultural, and individual changes.

The Five Disciplines

A learning organization is characterized by five "disciplines" (Senge, 1991) or characteristics:

- **Systems thinking:** Employees and managers understand the interconnectedness of communication between and among individuals and teams, as well as their connection to organizational structures and processes. Emphasis is placed on developing a common cultural language capable of generating conscious thought about how parts relate to wholes and vice versa. Openness, trust, commitment, and respect are the relational bases for knowledge and action, and a profound bias for change characterizes systems thinking.
- **Personal mastery:** The organization recognizes that individuals learn on and off the job, and continuous learning is a responsibility of all employees and managers. By valuing open communication, organizations encourage members to share what they have learned, even—perhaps especially—when it challenges or contradicts what is taken for granted or assumed within the company. Personal mastery is another way of conceptualizing

empowerment by emphasizing the need for continuous growth and renewal as vital to the individual and the organization.

- **Mental models:** Mental models are the images, assumptions, and stories that permeate the minds of the people working in an organization (Senge, 1991, p. 235). Communication represents and shares those models with others, and it connects the images, assumptions, and stories to the organization's mission and core values. Communication also helps identify similarities and differences in ways of conceiving of connections, allowing individuals to recognize gaps between their mental models and communication practices.
- **Shared vision:** It is one thing for a company to have a vision and mission; it is another thing for employees and managers to own and share it. Ownership of an organizational vision and mission requires shared communication built upon a foundation of trust, openness, empowerment, and honesty. Through communication, the vision and mission are driven into local practices.
- **Team learning:** The point of team learning is conscious, coordinated action that translates shared vision, mental models, and personal mastery into systems thinking and acting. When the team learns, so do the individual team members. When the individual team members learn, they have a responsibility to share what they have learned with the team.

Each of the above characteristics points to the need for more conscious systems-based thinking and culturally adapted communication. To adapt systems thinking to any business and professional context requires a commitment to learning and a desire for continuous improvement. Both of these goals require conscious communication practices.

Randolph Barker and Martin Camarata (1998, p. 445) offer a model of communication in creating and maintaining learning organizations (see Figure 2.4). The Barker and Camarata model shows that conscious communication is central in building a learning organization. As the environment becomes more complex and changing, relationships among individual employees and managers also become more complex and subject to change. Instead of relying on simplistic communication to guide understanding, what matters is mindful communication and dialogue.

Finally, this model shows how the preconditions of trust, commitment, and organizational support influence the organization–employee relationship, which in turn directly influences the ability of an organization to practice the five disciplines required to build a learning organization.

Dialogue and Learning Organizations

Senge and his colleagues at MIT are responsible for bringing the concept of dialogue to *practical* organizational applications. Senge realized that dialogue is the

Figure 2.4
The Role of Communication in Learning Organizations

Adapted from R. T. Barker and M. R. Camarata (1998).

```
                    simple/predictable        Environment         complex/changing
                    ←——————————————————————————————————————————→

    ┌──────────────────────┐    ┌──────────────────────┐    ┌──────────────────────┐         L
    │ Communication and    │    │ Communication and    │    │ Communication and    │         E
    │ preconditions of:    │    │ indicators of an     │    │ Senge's Five         │         A
    │                      │    │ organization-employee│    │ Disciplines:         │         R
    │   ❑ Trust            │ ⇒  │ relationship:        │ ⇒  │   ❑ Systems thinking │         N
    │                      │    │   ❑ Valuing the      │    │                      │         I
    │   ❑ Commitment       │    │     employee         │    │   ❑ Personal mastery │         N
    │                      │    │   ❑ Empowerment      │    │   ❑ Team mental      │         G
    │   ❑ Perceived        │    │   ❑ Employee         │    │     models           │         O
    │     organization     │    │     ownership and    │    │   ❑ Building shared  │         R
    │     support          │    │     acceptance of    │    │     vision           │         G
    │                      │    │     responsibility   │    │   ❑ Team learning    │         A
    └──────────────────────┘    └──────────────────────┘    └──────────────────────┘         N
                                                                                             I
     Mindless Communication   - - - - - - - - - - - - - -   Mindful Communication            Z
                    ←——————————————————————————————————————————→                             A
                    simple/predictable        Relationship        complex/changing            T
                                                                                             I
                                                                                             O
                                                                                             N
```

primary form of communication necessary to promote learning organizations (1991). Why? Because when individual communicators engage in dialogue, they are encouraged to *challenge existing sources of information, values, and beliefs* in ways that promote learning. They genuinely *listen to each other,* and because of that, they learn from others' experiences. They *speak from their hearts*, from their accumulated and often disparate experiences, rather than from the voice of their hierarchical position. They use their time together to *consciously construct* a more engaged, open, and respectful relationship.

It has probably occurred to you by now that *dialogue* and *learning organization* are terms that bring to life the ideas of organizations as systems and cultures. This is because:

- Dialogue in learning organizations recognizes the systemic powers of shared information and ongoing feedback.
- Dialogue, as the model for communication within an organization's culture, fosters more conscious forms of communication in everyday practices.
- Dialogue respects diversity and encourages ethical conduct in ways that promote mutual learning and productive change.
- Dialogue encourages participants in learning organizations to view their individual experiences as cultural information, and to realize that others' experiences within that same culture are likely to be distinctive,

different, and vital to a fuller appreciation of the culture, the work, and the environment.
- Dialogue in learning organizations promotes a balance between individuality and community. Taking a dialogic view of the role of communication in organizations encourages us to see talk as the moment-to-moment working out of the tension between individual needs for creativity and organizational constraints (Eisenberg and Goodall, 2001, p. 41).
- Dialogue in learning organizations values skilled talk and effective forms of communication at all levels, in all ways, each and every day.

Why We Learn About Theories of Communication

Our experiences teaching business and professional communication courses over the years have taught us that many students, when confronted early on in the term with material in a chapter such as this one, wonder *how it applies* to developing their communication skills? It is a fair question, and one that we will answer for you now.

Theories, to be practical, *must be applied.* You may have heard the expression, first coined by the mid-twentieth-century social scientist Kurt Lewin, that "nothing is so practical as a good theory." That statement is not just something an academic would say. It is a valuable expression that speaks to a profound human truth. A theory is best thought of as "intellectual equipment" (Burke, 1989), or as a tool to enhance our understanding. However, before you can apply a theory, or make it a part of your intellectual equipment, you have to develop an understanding of the theories that have guided our organizations.

By learning to think theoretically about communication in organizations, you acquire a language for describing and evaluating your personal experiences as a communicator at work. But you need to apply that language to your experiences in order to achieve the payoff. You have to incorporate what you have read into your everyday habits of mind. Use the theories as touchstones in your quest to understand the meanings of persons and things. Use them to become a more conscious, and more informed, communicator.

Summary

Chapter 2 explored the close connection between theories of organization and communication. During the classical period, the ideal organization was a factory built on the model of "clockwork." Theorists such as Frederick Taylor, Henri Fayol, and Max Weber, using the concepts of scientific management and bureaucracy, built organizational structures ready-made for top-down, information transfer models of communication. As these tight organizational structures and top-down approaches to communication were challenged by the effectiveness of simple human contact and a concern for workers' morale, human relations/resources and transactional process models gradually replaced them. As organizations became more complex, technological, and global, systems thinking emphasized the importance of communication networks as a way of understanding the role of groups and teams—and later, dialogue and learning—in creating and maintaining healthy and resilient systems.

Finally, renewed interest in the human side of enterprise revealed that communication was a cultural product, and that understanding an organization's culture afforded rich insights about everyday values, power, and the meaning of practices. Together, the concepts of systems thinking and organizational cultures combined to reveal that communication is both formative and transformative, and that attention to developing more conscious communicators was key to building learning organizations.

From these insights and histories we learned that all communication practices are important—from small talk to dialogue. However, the more skillful we become, the more conscious we become, the more likely we move toward practicing the values associated with building a learning organization through dialogue. We saw that the learning organization captures an idealized conception of communication at work capable of inspiring us to place greater value, and more directed skill development, on our daily communication understandings and practices.

COMMUNICATING IN PROFESSIONAL CONTEXTS ONLINE

Use your **Goodall Connection CD-ROM** for quick access to the electronic study resources that accompany this text. Included on your CD-ROM is access to:

InfoTrac College Edition

The World Wide Web

A demo of **WebTutor** for *Communicating in Professional Contexts*

The **Communicating in Professional Contexts Website** at the Wadsworth Communication Cafe. The Communicating in Professional Contexts Website offers chapter by chapter learning objectives, activities, quizzes, and a digital glossary.

You can review and complete the following sections online at
http://www.wadsworth.com/communication_d/

The Evolution of Communication in the Workplace

What You Should Have Learned

Now that you have read Chapter 2, you should be able to:

- Identify and define the two theories of management associated with the classical period of organizational management.
- Identify the communication theory that corresponds to the classical period.
- Identify and define the two studies associated with the human relations/resources period of organizational management theory.
- Identify the communication theory that corresponds to the human relations/resources period and the three areas of communication research that were derived from this period.
- Identify and define the components of a system.
- Distinguish between formal and informal networks.
- Define the term "organizational culture."
- Identify at least one theory of culture in organizations.
- Discuss the different approaches to power and how our thinking about power in organizations has evolved.
- Discuss organizational narratives and the types of research associated with them.
- Define and discuss dialogue.
- Discuss conscious communication to include providing the continuum for communication from mindless to mindful communication.
- Distinguish between mindless and mindful communication.
- Identify and discuss the five disciplines of a learning organization.
- Discuss the use of dialogue to build a learning organization.

Activities

The following activities can be completed online and, if requested, submitted to your instructor, under Student Resources, Activities for Chapter 2 at the Communicating in Professional Contexts Website at the Wadsworth Communication Café http://www.wadsworth.com/communication_d/.

1. Select a theory of organizational management. Describe the communication theory associated with the theory you selected. How are the theories linked? Link the tenets of the theory to your own organizational experiences.

2. Analyze a memorable conversation or dialogue from a current film. Look for points of theory described in the text. How does this exercise inform your understanding of the term "conscious communication"?

3. Working with your classmates as a group, select a theory discussed in this chapter that could help resolve the following situation:

John has recently joined your team. He does not share the team's goal or vision for completing the project required by your instructor. He shows up for meetings without being adequately prepared, and he doesn't talk unless directly spoken to. Every team meeting is a struggle to get John on board. Which theory best describes this situation? What does the theory suggest as an intervention? Given what you have learned in this chapter, what might you and your team members do? What theories informed your answer?

Surfing the Net

Any sites referred to in the following activities are maintained under HyperContents for Chapter 2 at the Communicating in Professional Contexts Website.

1. Organizational theories are the foundation for many of the management styles and practices you will experience in organizations. Select one of the theories discussed in this chapter and, using InfoTrac College Edition or the WWW, find an article from a major business journal or magazine that supports the theory you selected. For example, if you select bureaucracy as your theory, enter search words such as bureaucracy, Taylorism, or scientific management.

2. Enter the term "learning organization" as a keyword search on InfoTrac College Edition or the WWW. Search for organizations that use this terminology. Pick an organization from your search. How well has the organization you selected embraced the concept of a learning organization?

3. Go to the American Communication Association home page (http://www.uark.edu/~aca/). Click on the search engine for "organizational communication" and see what websites pop up. Cruise them for information that may be relevant to your assignments in this class and other classes.

4. Visit the Learning Organizations Home Page (http://www.bus.colorado.edu/faculty/larsen/learnorg.html). You will find many useful (and downloadable) articles on the origins and development of learning organizations, as well as some useful descriptions of organizational applications. You will also find links to other websites that deal with learning organizations. In particular, you should visit the Stanford Learning Organization Web and the Business Researcher's Interests: Organizational Learning and Knowledge Management.

Key Terms

bureaucracy *(35)*
dialogue *(48)*
environment *(40)*
goals *(40)*
hierarchy *(33)*
human relations movement *(36)*
interdependence *(40)*
information transfer model *(36)*
learning organization *(52)*

The Evolution of Communication in the Workplace

mental models *(53)*   organizational culture *(43)*   shared vision *(53)*
mindful communication *(51)*   personal mastery *(52)*   systems thinking *(52)*
mindless communication *(49)*   power *(44)*   team learning *(53)*
narrative *(47)*   scientific management *(33)*   transactional process model *(39)*

Breakthrough Skill Development:
Moving from Mindless to Mindful Communication

The next breakthrough skill offers a special challenge and opportunity for communication growth. *Spend an entire day communicating mindfully.* To do justice to this activity, you must:

- *Avoid mindless communication.* Refrain from answering questions in ritualistic, routine ways. Rather than asking, "How are you?" ask, "How did your interview go yesterday?"
- *Connect with each person you meet in a sincere and interested way.* Don't allow your mind to wander to others in the room, the things you need to do, what's happened to you in the past, or what you are going to have for lunch.
- *Don't give up.* When you find yourself communicating mindlessly, simply remind yourself of your goal and get back on track.
- *Communicate ethically.* Refrain from telling "little white lies" during your conscious communication.
- *Communicate authentically.* Do not just say things to please people if you don't mean them; speak your mind, from your heart.
- *Analyze each communication situation for the needs and expectations of others.* Think about possible communication choices before you speak. Adapt your communication to each listener or audience you encounter throughout the day.
- *Ask for and honestly evaluate the feedback you receive.* Use the feedback to determine how successful you were in accomplishing your purpose and as a source of corrective information capable of informing future communication choices.

Keep a journal of your "conscious communication day." Note the communication events that were conducted mindfully and those in which you lapsed into mindless communication. What did you learn from your experience?

Chapter Three

Preparing for Conscious Communication in the Workplace

Beth was not looking forward to Friday. She was scheduled to make an important presentation outlining a new advertising campaign to an important client. The audience included the client and members of his staff, her CEO, and three other people representing the creative, marketing, and finance departments of Beth's firm. Her talk was scheduled for 1:30 in the afternoon, right after her CEO—Regina—returned from what would undoubtedly be a big lunch with the client. Beth had 30 minutes available: 15 minutes for her presentation and the remainder for questions. At least, she mused, the whole thing would be over by 2 o'clock.

Beth wasn't nervous about her advertising skills. After all, she had graduated from a good school with a strong grade point average. She had completed two solid internships with major advertising firms. She had five years of creative experience and was now a member of an exciting new team. Since joining the firm, she had excelled at every task assigned to her. She was earning respect. She knew how to plan an advertising campaign, and she felt the work she had done on this project was probably her best work.

She was thrilled that her team decided she should make Friday's presentation. Their boss, Todd, the project director, who normally would make the presentation, had fallen ill and wouldn't be able to do it. When he called and asked the project creative team who should give the presentation, everyone agreed Beth should do it. Beth was energized by their confidence and she didn't want to let them down.

Beth had to find the best way to sell the client on this advertising campaign without giving away too many of the particulars. For one thing, while the broad strokes of the campaign were solid, many of the details had not yet been worked out. For another, it was a good idea to leave some areas of the campaign relatively undefined, so that the client would feel free to offer suggestions and feel as if he had a hand in the final design. The challenge, as Orin, one of Beth's team members, defined it, was "to create a presentation that was both strategic *and* ambiguous, that inspired confidence in their ability to deliver the campaign yet allowed for openness to ideas from the client."

Later that day, Beth received an email from Todd, who added another perspective:

> *The client will be entertaining bids from two other vendors, which is another good reason not to give away too many details. However, we have to sell him on the essentials—the message, our campaign strategy, the ability of our team to do the work creatively and on time, and the soundness of our budget estimates. You have to show him that selecting us to do this campaign is vital to his business success. That is really your task. Beth, we selected you to do this for us because we all have the utmost confidence in your skills. Call me after the presentation and let me hear about your—our—success.*

When she read this email, Beth found an important clue. She needed more information about the client's "business" needs. So far, she had concentrated on the *advertising* and *creative* needs of the client. Now, she needed to provide the client with a *business reason* for hiring her firm. Quickly, Beth was learning that audiences have multiple needs and expectations.

Beth appreciated Orin and Todd's views, but her own concerns were far more basic. From her perspective, the real issue was the *oral presentation* itself. How should it be organized? What should she say, and how should she say it? What visuals should be coordinated with her talk, and how could she maximize their influence? Another concern was how she could control the nervousness she always felt when speaking in front of people.

Beth hadn't given a formal speech since she was a sophomore in college. The project talks she had given in her advertising classes had been team presentations, and she had usually done the introductions or conclusions, leaving the heavier work of organizing the content to others. She had been hired for her present job in part because she was a "good communicator," but she felt she was far more effective one-on-one, or in a team, than giving a talk on her own. Now she sat facing her computer screen and didn't have a clue what to say or do.

Beth needed to get organized. But how? Then Beth remembered a presentation she had attended recently on conscious communication and a process for organizing communication. Maybe now was a good time to give it a try.

Organizing a Communication Event

As you learned in Chapter 2, "communication" is closely allied with "organization" (Weick, 1995). The activity of organizing is also a communication activity, and vice versa. Your communication organizes *possibilities* for meaning to occur. How well you organize—or *intentionally shape*—your communication has a lot to do with how successful you will be. This is because "order" also means "pattern," and as the communication theorist Gregory Bateson (1992) observes, "all communication is pattern recognition."

In its simplest form, the CCCD (choose, create, coordinate, and deliver) process introduced in Chapter 1 mirrors the "think before you speak" adage many of us heard from our parents. In a more complex form, the CCCD process provides you with a powerful tool for *organizing* interpersonal, team, group, presentational, and public communication episodes and events. Although each of the steps in CCCD applies to all of the contexts for communication, not every step needs to be completed in the same detail for each context. For example, when we are speaking to a co-worker about a project, it is necessary to choose our goal, create our strategy, coordinate our efforts, and deliver the message. However, we spend less time assessing the audience than we would if we were speaking to someone we didn't know or to a large group of people. Nor is it necessary to develop elaborate supporting materials or computer-assisted visual aids for a one-on-one talk with a colleague.

Throughout this chapter, we will use Beth's presentation to introduce the CCCD process. This allows us to illustrate how the process can be applied to organize a complex communication event. While the example in this chapter centers around a persuasive communication event, in subsequent chapters you will see how CCCD can be used as a general framework to improve the communication competence for any type of communication event. In the following chapters, we will illustrate how aspects of the CCCD process can be applied to interpersonal, group and team, public, mediated, and other types of presentational communication events.

But first, we will walk you through the CCCD process using Beth's presentation. Let's begin by reviewing the four steps in the CCCD process.

1. *Choose* a goal for your message based on an intelligent assessment of the business and professional culture, expectations and needs of audience members, possibilities for interpretation of your intended meaning, and likely outcomes.

2. *Create* a strategic and ethical plan for accomplishing your message goal with the targeted audience, which includes the verbal, nonverbal, and visual appeals.

3. *Coordinate* the event or episode with other persons who will have an influence on shaping a successful outcome.

4. *Deliver* your presentation after practicing it and gaining feedback on your performance.

We begin our discussion, with step 1, *Choosing a Goal for Your Message*.

Step 1: Choosing a Goal for Your Message

The first step in the CCCD process is *to establish a goal for your message*. To effectively define your goal, you must:

1. *Assess your audience.* Determine *who your listeners are* as well as their *needs and expectations*. Think about the reasons that your listeners will be helped if they accept your ideas. It is also a good idea to examine the ways in which they—or you—may be negatively affected if the communication episode doesn't go as planned.
2. *Generate outcomes.* Determine what you want your listeners to *know*, to *believe*, or to *do* as a result of your presentation.
3. *Establish criteria for measuring success.* Determine *how you will know if you have been successful* in attaining your goal.

In most business and professional settings, these tasks involve *interpreting information from a variety of sources*. Let's see how Beth accomplished each of these tasks.

Assessing Audience Needs and Expectations

When assessing the needs of the audience, many speakers mistakenly assume that *their* needs should be of utmost importance. Unfortunately, the **audience needs and expectations** and those of the speaker are rarely the same. Successful communicators recognize that while it is important to know what you *personally* expect to get out of giving a presentation, it is even more important to understand what your *listeners* should gain or expect to gain from it. After all, *listeners are our clients and customers* in business and professional communication environments. As in every other aspect of doing business, meeting the needs of our customers is a primary goal.

To meet her client's needs, as well as the expectations of her boss and coworkers, Beth should put herself in her client's shoes. She needs to *identify the reasons that the client would agree or disagree* with her presentation. To help her determine what these reasons might be, she should ask:

- What ideas and strategies have worked in the past with this particular audience? Has anyone in my firm dealt with this audience before? What can I learn from them?
- What reasons, authorities, examples, and "truths" does this audience regularly use to justify his position in reaching his goals? Is there some way to

gain access to past advertising campaigns used by this client, or statements the client has made about why he chose a particular campaign or firm?

+ What information can I gain from written or electronic sources to help me better understand our client? Are there recent publications in which the client is quoted or featured? Does the client's company maintain a Web site with useful information about their culture and values? Do I have friends or business contacts that might have valuable information? Can and should these be incorporated into my presentation?

Collecting this information can help Beth determine how the client might *comparatively evaluate* her campaign against any competitor. Once she comes up with the reasons the client may agree or disagree with her presentation, she can:

+ Create arguments within the presentation that satisfy the needs and expectations of the client.
+ Insert the client's reasoning and values or beliefs into the presentation.
+ Plan to articulate the information gained from research during the question-and-answer session.

While Beth is thinking through her presentation from the client's perspective, she also needs to consider what the client may see as *objections or potential problems* of the campaign. Here again, Beth should spend time coming up with the scenarios that could occur if the client doesn't accept her reasoning. She can use this information in one of two ways:

+ Offering a section toward the end of the presentation to articulate and overcome possible objections.
+ Including responses to objections in her question-and-answer session.

Thinking back on Todd's advice and the meeting with her team members, Beth identified *two distinct audiences* for her presentation: the *client* and the *members of her own firm*. Each would be coming to the presentation with very different needs and expectations.

To address the needs of her client, Beth decided (a) she must convince the client that her firm has a valuable idea for the advertising campaign, and (b) the initial presentation should allow for creative input from the client. If Beth's talk made it seem that their advertising company had it all figured out, this could suggest to the client that they were unwilling to listen to input or work with him on details.

To address the needs of her CEO and team members, Beth thought she must demonstrate the close working relationship between the client and the project team. She also must sell herself and her team as a friendly, open, cooperative group that knows their stuff. To do this, Beth would have to present herself as a professional and knowledgeable team player.

Beth created the following worksheet of Audience Needs and Expectations.

Step 1: CHOOSING A GOAL—Audience Needs and Expectations	
Audience	**Needs and Expectations**
Client	• Find an advertising firm that balances the creative needs of the project with the company's business needs (i.e., budget, time constraints, competition concerns). • Commit to a creative team that best represents the product, is open to ideas, and can work well with the company during this project.
Firm	• Sell the client on the concept of the campaign without giving away too many details. • Convince the client that the firm's message, strategy, team, and budget are better than the competitors' (without knowing the details of either competitor's campaign).
Beth	• Make a professional quality presentation within an advertising/sales environment by meeting the goals of the firm. • Satisfy and, if possible, favorably impress the boss and the other members of the firm by representing them successfully.

Determining the Possible Communication Outcomes

The **outcome** of a communication event is what you achieve as a result of speaking. Four general communication outcomes can be used to shape a goal statement for a business and professional presentation:

1. *Inform* listeners about an idea, process, or concept.
2. *Persuade* listeners to accept, purchase, value, or act on the information presented.
3. *Entertain* listeners.
4. *Build a business relationship* with listeners.

In some contexts, only one communication outcome will guide the preparation of the talk. Every day, people communicate with the goal to inform, *or* to persuade, *or* to entertain, *or* to build relationships. In other situations, there are multiple likely outcomes. For example, Beth knows that her job is to both *inform* and *persuade* her client, but she also realizes that her talk will be instrumental in *building a business relationship* between the client and the firm. This knowledge has direct implications for how Beth interprets her goal, organizes her presentation, assembles supporting materials, and answers questions.

Preparing for Conscious Communication in the Workplace

Beth also needs to determine what *her* communication outcome should be. Is she most interested in being seen by her client as a competent provider of information? As an effective sales person? As an informative and entertaining speaker? As the kind of person the client would want to work with on a project? Beth added an Outcomes column to her worksheet.

Step 1: CHOOSING A GOAL—Outcomes

Audience	Needs and Expectations	Outcomes
Client	• Find an advertising firm that balances the creative needs of the project with the company's business needs (i.e., budget, time constraints, competition concerns). • Commit to a creative team that best represents the product, is open to ideas, and can work well with the company during this project.	• *Inform* the client about the campaign concepts. • *Persuade* the client that the firm is better equipped to handle his advertising needs than the other firms he has investigated. • *Build* a business relationship that results in a commitment to Beth's firm.
Firm	• Sell the client on the concept of the campaign without giving away too many details. • Convince the client that the firm's message, strategy, team, and budget are better than the competitors' (without knowing the details of either competitor's campaign).	• *Persuade* team members and supervisor that Beth's ideas are based on solid research and creative efforts that present the best campaign possible. • *Build* on the team's relationship so they feel they have successfully met the client's creative and business needs. • *Inform* through feedback that Beth's presentation hit the mark.
Beth	• Make a professional quality presentation within an advertising/sales environment by meeting the goals of the firm. • Satisfy and, if possible, favorably impress the boss and the other members of the firm by representing them successfully.	• *Convince* Beth that she did the best job possible. • *Build* on her relationship with her team to successfully implement the ideas presented to the client.

After reviewing all the possible audiences, needs and expectations, and outcomes, Beth decided to focus on the second entry under her firm's needs and expectations: *Convince the client that the firm's message, strategy, team, and budget are better than the competitors' (without knowing the details of either competitor's campaign*). Beth believed that if she made this the main priority of her presentation, all the other outcomes would be met.

Establishing Criteria to Measure Success

Specifying **criteria** for measuring success means thinking about the desirable statements, behaviors, or actions that you want to receive from your audience during and after the presentation. Specifying these criteria will help you determine if you have reached your personal and business goals. It is also an excellent way *to learn* from a communication event or episode. By establishing criteria for an event and measuring the success of your communication against them, you learn how your communication may or may not have met the needs and expectations of your audience. As we saw in Chapters 1 and 2, positive and corrective feedback can and should help us to improve our communication skills.

What would Beth need to hear to know that she had provided the client with all the information he needed to make a decision? Or that she had made an effective presentation? Or that the client would be interested in pursuing a working relationship with her company? Learning to articulate these evaluative standards will help Beth reach her goal. She added a Criteria column to her worksheet.

Step 1: CHOOSING A GOAL — Criteria

Audience	Needs and Expectations	Outcomes	Criteria
Client	♦ Find an advertising firm that balances the creative needs of the project with the company's business needs (i.e., budget, time constraints, competition concerns). ♦ Commit to a creative team that best represents the product, is open to ideas, and can work well with the company during this project.	♦ *Inform* the client about the campaign concepts. ♦ *Persuade* the client that the firm is better equipped to handle his advertising needs than the other firms he has investigated. ♦ *Build a business relationship* that results in a commitment to Beth's firm.	♦ Shows interest in the ideas presented and favorably compares the concept to those presented at competing firms. ♦ Commends the firm on their ideas, teamwork, and attention to the client's needs. ♦ Agrees to the concept and is interested in discussing the terms set forth in the presentation.
Firm	♦ Sell the client on the concept of the campaign without giving away too many details.	♦ *Persuade* team members and supervisor that Beth's ideas are based on solid research and creative efforts that present the best campaign possible.	♦ The team nods and smiles throughout the presentation.

Step 1: CHOOSING A GOAL—Criteria *(continued)*			
Audience	**Needs and Expectations**	**Outcomes**	**Criteria**
Firm	• Convince the client that the firm's message, strategy, team, and budget are better than the competitors' (without knowing the details of either competitor's campaign).	• *Build on the team's relationship* so they feel they have successfully met the client's creative and business needs. • *Inform* through feedback that Beth's presentation hit the mark.	• The CEO supports Beth during the presentation, interjecting only to emphasize or clarify a point being made. • Her team congratulates her on her performance. • Her boss thanks her for her hard work.
Beth	• Make a professional quality presentation within an advertising/sales environment by meeting the goals of the firm. • Satisfy and, if possible, favorably impress the boss and the other members of the firm by representing them successfully.	• *Convince* Beth that she did the best job possible. • *Build on her relationship* with her team to successfully implement the ideas presented to the client.	• She is confident and calm throughout her presentation. • She walks away knowing she did a good job. • She doesn't second-guess her information, presentation, or ability.

To prepare for the first presentation in this class, we suggest making a worksheet like Beth's. Fill it out as you develop your presentation. Clearly defining your audience, outcomes, criteria, and goals will help you to be successful in class as well as in the workplace.

Step 2: Creating a Strategic and Ethical Message

The second step in the CCCD process is to *create the message*. To create a successful message capable of accomplishing the goals outlined in step 1, you must:

1. Determine the *thesis* of your message.
2. Determine the *organization of the main points* for the body of your talk.
3. *Support* each of your main points.
4. Create *transitions* for each of your main points.
5. Develop an *effective introduction and conclusion*.

Obviously, if you are communicating interpersonally, you may not need to write down your purpose, main points, supporting materials, transitions, and introduction and conclusion. However, you do need to *consider* each of these elements before you speak. Many professional communicators use the term "talking points" to refer to items organized for a one-on-one or group discussion. Communicating consciously requires you to be mindful of the process of communicating effectively with others in all communication contexts. Let's follow Beth through the process of creating her presentation.

Creating a Thesis Statement

Beth needed to turn her goals into a general thesis statement that would guide the development of the presentation. After reviewing her Step 1: Choosing a Goal worksheet, Beth wrote the following purpose on her Step 2: Creating the Message worksheet under *Purpose and Thesis Statement*.

Step 2: CREATING THE MESSAGE—Purpose			
Introduction			
Purpose and Thesis Statement	**Main Points**	**Support**	**Transitions**
• To provide compelling information about a new advertising campaign theme, strategy, and budget with the intention of persuading the client that the firm can do the best job.			
Conclusion			

The **purpose** is a general statement that defines the primary goal for your message. Beth's next step was to use the purpose to create her thesis statement. A **thesis statement** is a simple, declarative sentence that (a) introduces your audience to your message and (b) announces your intentions. In most business and professional contexts, the thesis statement *sets up expectations among listeners* that they will use to evaluate the effectiveness—and truthfulness—of your message. For this reason, it was vital that Beth not misrepresent herself or her goals for the presentation.

For example, because she wants the presentation to sufficiently motivate the client to sign a contract with her firm, she needed to focus on the *persuasive intent* of her presentation. But she also didn't want to overdo it. She wanted the client to buy her campaign because it met his needs and expectations, and because it would do a better job for him than other campaigns offered by her competitors.

Beth had to condense all of these thoughts and feelings into a simple, declarative sentence. To do this, she envisioned speaking directly to her client. Then she wrote on her worksheet what she would say to him one-on-one, as if they were engaged in a business conversation.

Step 2: CREATING THE MESSAGE—Thesis Statement			
Introduction			
Purpose and Thesis Statement	**Main Points**	**Support**	**Transitions**
◆ *To provide compelling information about a new advertising campaign theme, strategy, and budget with the intention of persuading the client that the firm can do the best job.* ◆ *I will present to you our concept that we believe will help you reach your product sales goals, and open your product to additional markets, while remaining within the budget guidelines you specified.*			
Conclusion			

Beth translated her informational and persuasive goals into a simple thesis designed to show how she plans to meet the listener's needs and expectations. Developing a clear and concise thesis statement will help Beth determine a preferred *organizational pattern* for the body of the presentation.

Determining the Main Points of the Message

Generally speaking, business and professional presentations contain between *two and four major points*. The number of points depends on the organization pattern that best accomplishes your purpose. However, research has demonstrated that if you use more than four main points, the chances are very good that listeners will forget some of them (Ehninger, 1974). Let's examine in more detail the relationship between your choice of organization pattern and the number of main points that best accomplishes it.

There are four basic organization patterns that can be used to structure a presentation:

- **Causal**—offering a cause and effect.
- **Problem–solution**—stating a problem and a solution.
- **Chronological**—detailing the sequence of events.
- **Topical**—outlining the main ideas surrounding the problem or issue.

Some thesis statements naturally lend themselves to *causal* or *problem–solution* reasoning. Others require a *chronological* sequence that provides a historical overview and development of an idea. Others suggest that a *logical series of topics* be presented to guide listeners' understanding (see Table 3.1).

Beth needed an organizational pattern that captured the major points she planned to cover. She considered using cause–effect, but drew a blank. Then she considered problem–solution. This pattern had merit because she could approach the development of her presentation as the solving of her client's problem: how to select an appropriate advertising campaign. But did this format allow her to present her ideas about the theme, or the implementation strategies, or even the budget? She decided it didn't. The chronological sequence also had appeal. She could use it to describe the evolution of her team's ideas about the proposed campaign, ending with a vision of how the client's sales would increase as a result of the advertisements. But on further reflection she rejected this pattern because she favored a softer sales approach, one that would allow the client to ask questions at the end. She wanted *his*

Table 3.1
Organizational Patterns for Messages

Basic Organizational Patterns

Two Main Points	Three Main Points	Four Main Points

• Causal Pattern
    Cause>>>Effect
• Problem–Solution
    Problem>>>Solution
	• Chronology
	    ◇ Past
	    ◇ Present
	    ◇ Future
		• Topical
		    ◇ Basic Idea
		    ◇ Implementation of the idea
		    ◇ Budget for implementation
		    ◇ How it all works

Preparing for Conscious Communication in the Workplace

vision, not hers, to be the last word. Finally, she chose the *topical* pattern because it would allow her to develop her ideas about the theme, the campaign, and the budget logically, from the customer's point of view.

Next, Beth developed a *preview* statement containing the best progression of her main points, as they evolved from her thesis statement. The preview prepares listeners for the informational content of the message by giving them advance notice of what they will be hearing. Using her topical pattern as a guide, she jotted down her main points.

Step 2: CREATING THE MESSAGE—Main Points

Introduction

Purpose and Thesis Statement	Main Points	Support	Transitions
✦ To provide compelling information about a new advertising campaign theme, strategy, and budget with the intention of persuading the client that the firm can do the best job. ✦ I will present to you our concept that we believe will help you reach your product sales goals, and open your product to additional markets, while remaining within the budget guidelines you specified.	✦ First, I will describe our concept and explain why we believe it will appeal to your target market. ✦ Second, I will provide a timeline of how we will implement the concept. ✦ Third, I will outline our proposed budget, which I'm sure you will find well within your prescribed parameters. ✦ Finally, I will answer any questions or discuss ideas you may have.		

Conclusion

Beth's work on her presentation thus far had produced a specific purpose and a general topical plan for accomplishing it. What Beth did was translate the topics she knew must be covered into a topical pattern that leads listeners *from an understanding of the information* (major points #1, #2, and #3) they will need to make a decision, *to a subtle persuasive appeal* (#4) for gaining the business. She felt the natural collaboration between presenter and client during a question-and-answer session provided her with the best opportunity to respond to specific needs and satisfy his expectations.

Her next task was *to expand on, and support, the main points in the body of her talk.* To accomplish this task she outlined the subpoints for each main point. She added these subpoints to her worksheet.

Step 2: CREATING THE MESSAGE—Subpoints

Introduction

Purpose and Thesis Statement	Main Points	Support	Transitions
◆ To provide compelling information about a new advertising campaign theme, strategy, and budget with the intention of persuading the client that the firm can do the best job. ◆ I will present to you our concept that we believe will help you reach your product sales goals, and open your product to additional markets, while remaining within the budget guidelines you specified.	◆ First, I will describe our concept and explain why we believe it will appeal to your target market. ◇ Concept ◇ Connection to target market ◆ Second, I will provide a timeline of how we will implement the concept. ◇ October–January ◇ February–April ◇ May–August ◆ Third, I will outline our proposed budget, which I'm sure you will find well within your prescribed parameters. ◇ Total budget ◇ Cost breakdowns by category ◇ Justification for budget ◆ Finally, I will answer any questions or discuss ideas you may have. ◇ Request for questions ◇ Request for business		

Conclusion

By outlining the subpoints derived from the main points in her speech, Beth knew exactly what additional information she needed to provide. She also began to see where in her presentation she would need to use supporting materials.

Developing Supporting Materials

Supporting materials *add interest, visual impact, and credibility to your message.* How many presentations, team meetings, or group discussions have you attended where the speaker droned on and on, mostly repeating the same main points over and over again? Is it any wonder that the audience's attention began to wander shortly after the speaker began talking? In today's high-tech, visually driven world, few people will sit still long enough to listen to anyone talk who isn't an incredibly captivating speaker, or who doesn't use interesting and engaging graphics to support the verbal message. In this section, we will discuss two types of support you can use to increase the impact of your message: *verbal support* and *visual support.* At the end of each subsection, we will review the types of support Beth selected for her presentation. We begin with verbal support.

Verbal Support

Often, business messages contain complex new ideas or concepts. Verbal support can make complicated messages or ideas clear. They can add punch to a message and credibility to concepts that might fall outside your audience's field of experience or expertise. There are four types of verbal supporting materials to use when developing the oral content of your message:

- Facts and statistics
- Testimony or authoritative sources
- Examples
- Narratives or personal stories

Facts and Statistics **Facts** are sources of *basic, empirically verifiable, information.* **Statistics** are *basic, empirically verifiable, numerical representations of information.* By "empirically verifiable," we mean that the statistics or statements represented as facts are drawn from credible sources and may be checked out by audience members. Facts and statistics have benefits and drawbacks. The benefits are that, if used effectively, facts and statistics offer quick, credible support for your message. The drawbacks are that facts and statistics are often overused, and as a result, people in business environments have developed the attitude that "you can find a statistic to support any position"—which, by and large, is true.

Nevertheless, facts and statistics *can* lend persuasive impact to your presentation if used effectively. To use facts and statistics effectively:

- Only use statistics from credible sources.
- Be sure that any statistics you use can be validated independently.

- Limit the use of statistics—don't use more than one or two facts or statistics for each main point.
- Tie your statistics to your audience—don't use a furnishing industry statistic in a talk about auto parts unless there is a direct and obvious connection.
- Use graphics to illustrate your statistics.

> **Focus on Ethics**
>
> You and a co-worker are asked to give a joint presentation. Your co-worker wants to use statistics that are inflated. You know the statistics will provide the audience with misinformation. What should you do?

Testimonies and Authoritative Sources   If appropriate to your topic and taken from a source recognizable to your audience, testimonies and authoritative quotations add instant credibility to your talk. Like facts and statistics, testimonies and authoritative sources reveal both benefits and drawbacks.

If the audience is familiar with the person offering the testimony, or believes the citation comes from a credible source, these forms of support may be very compelling. On the other hand, given the diverse views of most audiences, it may be difficult to locate a quotation from a source that has universal appeal. One person's idol—Bill Gates, Jesse Jackson, or Sandra Day O'Connor—may be the source of another person's disregard. In general, when using testimonies and authoritative sources:

- Only use quotes from sources your audience will find credible.
- Make sure the citation ties directly to your topic—don't name-drop simply for the sake of name-dropping.
- Cite only the information that is necessary to make your point—don't use a long confusing quote if only one sentence is all that is needed.
- Tie your citation to your audience—don't quote a furnishing industry executive in a talk to managers of auto parts stores unless there is a direct and obvious connection.

Examples and Narratives   Examples and narratives provide *memorable elaboration for main points and subpoints*. While extremely effective forms of support, they may require time to develop, a higher level of confidence and competence on the part of the speaker, and a close, personal identification between the listeners and the example or story used.

Presentational speakers using examples and stories often require additional rehearsal time to find the most effective method of phrasing, changes or modulations in tone of voice, and strategic uses of internal pauses. Used effectively, examples and narratives *humanize information* and *build rapport* between a speaker and audience.

Many speakers limit their use of personal stories or narratives to attention-gaining material for the introduction and leave-taking material for the conclusion. By contrast, examples can be effective when used throughout the talk, and they are particularly effective as support for the main points and subpoints in the body of a speech. To effectively use examples and personal narratives:

- Carefully choose examples and narratives with regard to the cultural, professional, gender, racial, and socio-economic considerations of your audience.
- Make sure the story or example is memorable (you may want to try it out on friends or co-workers prior to using it in a presentation).
- Try to use examples and stories that are fresh—that haven't been heard by the listeners before.

Beth had to determine *how much time she was willing to devote to each topic*. To make that decision, she considered—from the audience's perspective—how much verbal support each topic would require, and what specific types of support might do the best job. She reviewed her worksheet and added the following types of verbal support to each main point.

Step 2: CREATING THE MESSAGE—Forms of Support

Introduction

Purpose and Thesis Statement	Main Points	Support	Transitions
• *To provide compelling information about a new advertising campaign theme, strategy, and budget with the intention of persuading the client that the firm can do the best job.*	• *First, I will describe our concept and explain why we believe it will appeal to your target market.* ◇ *Concept* ◇ *Connection to target market*	• *Concept—Fact and examples* ◇ two examples of successful campaigns from the same target market • *Target Market—Statistics* ◇ current numbers representing the size of the market and target demographics	

(continued)

Step 2: CREATING THE MESSAGE—Forms of Support (continued)

Introduction			
Purpose and Thesis Statement	**Main Points**	**Support**	**Transitions**

♦ I will present to you our concept that we believe will help you reach your product sales goals, and open your product to additional markets, while remaining within the budget guidelines you specified.	♦ Second, I will provide a timeline of how we will implement the concept.
	   ◊ October–January
	   ◊ February–April
	   ◊ May–August
	♦ Third, I will outline our proposed budget, which I'm sure you will find well within your prescribed parameters.
	   ◊ Total budget
	   ◊ Cost breakdowns by category
	   ◊ Justification for budget
	♦ Finally, I will answer any questions or discuss ideas you may have.
	   ◊ Request for questions
	   ◊ Request for business
		♦ Timeline—Fact and examples
		   ◊ which media we will use and examples of how they will be used at each stage in the campaign
		♦ Budget—Statistics, authoritative sources, and examples
		   ◊ total budget—statistical breakdown
		   ◊ cost breakdown—statistical breakdown of each category and statements from clients illustrating the cost savings compared to other firms
		   ◊ justification—review examples for each phase and show quality vs. cost
		♦ Questions and request for business—Examples and personal narrative
		   ◊ review examples to illustrate points brought up during the question period
		   ◊ describe my experience with the firm, my clients, and why I think the concept and the firm are the best investment for the client	

Conclusion			

Visual Support

The old cliché, "a picture is worth a thousand words," is simply no longer true. We are *bombarded* daily with visual messages. In an average day, we see 3,500 advertisements, including commercials, billboards, print ads, brand names, and Web-page banners (Jhally, 1997). Only a few years ago, it was considered hip, cool, and cutting edge to enter a meeting, flip open your laptop, and begin a slide show presentation. Now, most business people have developed a "been there, done that" attitude to most presentational software special effects. Face it, words and pictures that morph, fade, and slide off a screen are interesting the first few times we witness them. After that, they may join the crowd in an already visually overloaded day.

However, having said that, there is still an important place for well-developed, relevant visual materials that are used to *support* a message. Visual supports range from traditional *flip charts, physical objects,* and *storyboards* to more advanced *slide show presentations, models,* and *demonstrations*. Each type of visual support should be understood in relation to its audience and context to make its use more effective. In Appendix A, the Visual Support Reference Guide, we provide a comprehensive list of the types of visual support, the appropriate audiences for them, do's and don'ts for display, and practical advice for using them.

Before selecting the type of visual support you will use, you should:

- *Determine the visual needs and professional expectations of your audience.* For example, engineers generally expect fairly technical visual support in the form of schematics or technical drawings, while a group of nurses would rather see live demonstrations of new techniques.
- *Preview the meeting or presentation location.* An engineers' meeting in a conference room wired for Internet hookups could easily use forms of computer technology to produce and display visual support.
- *Be aware of the time constraints.* A slide show that is well prepared and rehearsed may not add additional time constraints to your presentation. However, a presentation that depends heavily on the Internet must allow for Web pages that load slowly during peak hours of use and the likely impatience of the audience during those information display delays.
- *Determine the method that best adds visual quality, not quantity, to the message.* Showing a client the blueprints for every building ever designed by an architect may have less impact than showing one well-executed design, a model, and a picture of a building that is similar to the building needs expressed by the client.

Beth was lucky. She worked for a company and in an industry that afforded her the technology, and the knowledge, to create powerful visual messages to enhance her presentation. She decided to make use of both traditional and advanced types of support. To set the agenda for the presentation, lay out the main points and timeline for the campaign, and highlight the factual and statistical support of the talk, she would use a PowerPoint slide presentation. To showcase the concept, she would use traditional storyboards (large pieces of poster board with artwork representing each phase of the project). This would allow her to break up the visual portion of the presentation and avoid having her audience stare at the same projection screen for 30 minutes.

Beth now had most of the elements she needed for a strong presentation. This CCCD process was really making it easy to plan, organize, and develop her message. What was next?

Making Transitions

Transitions are devices that help audience members *listen* more effectively. Think of a transition as an internal signpost that provides *directions* to the audience members about (a) *upcoming changes* in the point being made, or (b) *internal movements in reasoning* that will occur in the speech. They may also serve as *previews/reviews* of material and as *internal summaries*. There are four types of listening problems created by the lack of a good transition:

1. Confusion can occur when *a speaker has moved to a new point* but the listener hears what is being said as support for the last main point.
2. Boredom can occur when the speaker *relies on the same device repeatedly*, such as "next."
3. Listeners will perceive speakers as less effective because of the *overuse of unplanned transition-fillers*, such as "okay," or "you know," or "well."
4. Listeners may become lost or disoriented in the message due to the *lack of a consistent reminder about the order* used to develop the ideas.

To avoid these problems, speakers make use of several types of transitional devices, as illustrated in Table 3.2. Beth realized that several places in her presentation called for effective transitions. She added them to her worksheet, being careful to *vary the type of transition*.

Beth was almost finished with her presentation worksheet. All that was left for her to accomplish was writing an introduction and conclusion.

Developing an Effective Introduction and Conclusion

Beginnings and endings in oral communication are uniquely interrelated. In part, this is due to the fact that structurally they surround the body of a talk, serving to preview and review its key points. Within the North American culture, we have learned to expect to hear in the ending of a presentation some reminder of what we heard during the beginning of it. A good presentation is circular; it returns to where it began, giving the audience a feeling of closure and completeness.

To accomplish this, the introduction and conclusion should wrap around the main points of the presentation by developing a complete thematic package. Occasionally, the theme for a presentation presents itself before the presentation is developed. More often, the theme evolves from the main points of the presentation, which is why we suggest writing the introduction and conclusion *last* rather than first.

Table 3.2 Types of Transitional Devices

When you need to:	Use this type of transition:
Introduce or preview topics in the speech	First, second, and third One, two, three A, B, C
Signal topic changes in cause–effect, problem–solution, and chronology patterns during the body of the speech	"Now that we have seen how X occurred, let's examine its influences on Y." "Now that we understand the problem, it is time to explore solutions." "The past has provided us with X. The present has given us Y. If you are like me, you are wondering what can the future hold?"
Offer extended explanations of key definitions or ideas	For example . . . To illustrate… Simply put… Allow me to clarify… In other words…
Alert listeners to spatial relationships	Think of the face on a clock. At one o'clock we see X; at four o'clock we find Y; at eight o'clock we locate Z. To the East… ; to the West… Alongside, behind, in front of, next to, below, above.
Remind your audience of your main points prior to moving to your recommendations	"We have seen that there are three causes of our problem. They are: 1___, which is caused by X; 2___, which is brought about by Y; and 3___, which is generated by Z. Now let's see what a solution should include and how we can work to implement it.

An effective introduction should be used to:
- *Gain the listener's or audience's attention.* There are many effective ways to gain the attention of the audience.
    - Ask an interesting question directly related to the theme of your speech.
    - Use a startling statement or an appropriate quotation.
    - Relate a personal experience that ties into the topic.
    - Tell a brief story that develops suspense or makes a humorous point.
    - Use a captivating or startling image.

Step 2: CREATING THE MESSAGE—Transitions

Introduction

Purpose and Thesis Statement	Main Points	Support	Transitions
◆ To provide compelling information about a new advertising campaign theme, strategy, and budget with the intention of persuading the client that the firm can do the best job. ◆ I will present to you our concept that we believe will help you reach your product sales goals, and open your product to additional markets, while remaining within the budget guidelines you specified.	◆ First, I will describe our concept and explain why we believe it will appeal to your target market. ◇ Concept ◇ Connection to target market ◆ Second, I will provide a timeline of how we will implement the concept. ◇ October–January ◇ February–April ◇ May–August ◆ Third, I will outline our proposed budget, which I'm sure you will find well within your prescribed parameters. ◇ Total budget ◇ Cost breakdowns by category ◇ Justification for budget ◆ Finally, I will answer any questions or discuss ideas you may have. ◇ Request for questions ◇ Request for business	◆ Concept—Fact and examples ◇ two examples of successful campaigns from the same target market ◆ Target Market—Statistics ◇ current numbers representing the size of the market and target demographics ◆ Timeline—Fact and examples ◇ which media we will use and examples of how they will be used at each stage in the campaign ◆ Budget—Statistics, authoritative sources, and examples ◇ total budget—statistical breakdown ◇ cost breakdown—statistical breakdown of each category and statements from clients illustrating the cost savings compared to other firms ◇ justification—review examples for each phase and show quality vs. cost ◆ Questions and request for business—Examples and personal narrative ◇ review examples to illustrate points brought up during the question period ◇ describe my experience with the firm, my clients, and why I think the concept and the firm are the best	◆ Introduction ◇ Preview the flow of the talk ◆ Concept ◇ Simply put, the concept will allow us to reach the target market by … ◆ Timeline ◇ Now that you have seen the concept, I would like to take a few minutes to discuss the timeline. ◆ Budget—Statistics, authoritative sources, and examples ◇ Of course, a timeline this rigorous requires an investment… ◆ Questions and request for business ◇ Review main points ◇ Return to introduction

Conclusion

- *State a thesis.* Explain in a clear and concise manner the topic of your presentation or the basis of your message.
- *Preview the main points in the body of the speech.* Outline the main points in your presentation using *signposts* to alert the audience or listener to topical divisions. For example: "First, I will discuss the concept we have developed. Second, I will discuss the timeframes associated with the concept. Third, I will go over the budget estimates associated with the project. Finally, I will answers any questions you might have."
- *Offer an inducement.* Explain to listeners what benefit will accrue to them—what will they *learn* that they don't already know or what they *will be able to do* that they can't already do—as a result of their participation in the speech.

Conclusions also have more than one function. Conclusions should:

- Review the main points in the body of the presentation.
- Provide a sense of closure by returning in some way to the *attention-gaining* device used in the beginning of the talk.

Beth thought about how to introduce her presentation. She knew her thesis and preview statements accomplished their business purpose, and she knew what inducement she could offer—the advertising campaign that would ensure the business success of this new product. What she didn't know was how to creatively grab her audience's attention. Until she had that firmly in mind, she also had no ending for her speech.

She decided to try out several approaches. Because the speech already included a lot of statistics and quotations from authorities, she ruled out these attention-gaining devices. She tried to put herself in the listener's position, and when she did so, she saw that what the presentation lacked was *variety*. Perhaps she should begin with a startling image? Perhaps some humor? No. The startling image might distract attention from the concept, and humor was always a bit risky with an unknown client. She remembered the CCCD speaker saying that for humor to be effective, she needed to understand the sense of humor of the client and try out the material on a similarly disposed listener beforehand. What if she and the client didn't agree on what was funny? Worse yet, what if she and the CEO of her firm didn't agree? That could be devastating to the whole presentation. You never get a second chance to make a good first impression!

She finally decided to use a personal story. As a fairly recent hire, she decided to use her experience trying to decide whether or not to accept a job with this company as a kind of comparison to how the client was deciding whether or not to buy this campaign. The central issues of company credibility, cultural and personal fit, how it would be to work with people on her team, and the value they placed on personal input were all likely issues for the client as well. Beth could begin and end the presentation on a personal level that might help sell the idea.

She added these entries to her worksheet.

Step 2: CREATING THE MESSAGE—Introduction and Conclusion

Introduction	
	♦ Personal narrative about choosing the company.
	♦ Statement of thesis.
	♦ Preview of main points.
	♦ After listening to my presentation, you will clearly see that our company has the ideas, the team, and the resources to make your product a success with teens across America.

Purpose and Thesis Statement	Main Points	Support	Transitions
♦ To provide compelling information about a new advertising campaign theme, strategy, and budget with the intention of persuading the client that the firm can do the best job. ♦ I will present to you our concept that we believe will help you reach your product sales goals, and open your product to additional markets, while remaining within the budget guidelines you specified.	♦ First, I will describe our concept and explain why we believe it will appeal to your target market. ◊ Concept ◊ Connection to target market ♦ Second, I will provide a timeline of how we will implement the concept. ◊ October–January ◊ February–April ◊ May–August ♦ Third, I will outline our proposed budget, which I'm sure you will find well within your prescribed parameters. ◊ Total budget ◊ Cost breakdowns by category ◊ Justification for budget ♦ Finally, I will answer any questions or discuss ideas you may have. ◊ Request for questions ◊ Request for business	♦ Concept—Fact and examples ◊ two examples of successful campaigns from the same target market ♦ Target Market—Statistics ◊ current numbers representing the size of the market and target demographics ♦ Timeline—Fact and examples ◊ which media we will use and examples of how they will be used at each stage in the campaign ♦ Budget—Statistics, authoritative sources, and examples ◊ total budget—statistical breakdown ◊ cost breakdown—statistical breakdown of each category and statements from clients illustrating the cost savings compared to other firms ◊ justification—review examples for each phase and show quality vs. cost ♦ Questions and request for business—Examples and personal narrative ◊ review examples to illustrate points brought up during the question period ◊ describe my experience with the firm, my clients, and why I think the concept and the firm are the best investment for the client	♦ Introduction ◊ Preview the flow of the talk ♦ Concept ◊ Simply put, the concept will allow us to reach the target market by … ♦ Timeline ◊ Now that you have seen the concept, I would like to take a few minutes to discuss the timeline. ♦ Budget—Statistics, authoritative sources, and examples ◊ Of course, a timeline this rigorous requires an investment… ♦ Questions and request for business ◊ Review main points ◊ Return to introduction

Step 2: CREATING THE MESSAGE—Introduction and Conclusion (*continued*)

Conclusion	✦ Review main points. ✦ Choosing an advertising firm is much like choosing a place of work. Because we will be working closely, it is important that you trust the people you work with, believe in their abilities, and find their ideas exciting and creative. I know I've found the right company; I'm sure you will feel the same.

When Beth was finished, she had a solid strategic plan for her presentation. She was excited about the meeting and confident she would do herself, her team, and her company proud. What a difference the CCCD process had made! Now she needed to meet with the other members of her team to ensure that *her message coordinated with their goals*.

Step 3: Coordinating with Others

Conscious communication is mindful of the needs and expectation of *others*. When we say "others," we are going beyond just the audience; we are talking about *everyone who might be impacted by the communication event*. Our friend Menyon, the director of technology for a large global apparel firm, made a statement that sums up the coordinating stage of conscious communication: "It doesn't matter if I am promoted, or if I look good, as long as the company can move ahead and meet its goals. As long as the company is moving ahead, I am moving ahead, because I own stock…have a stake in the company. My job is to ensure that *everyone has the information they need to keep the company moving ahead*."

Menyon's attitude epitomizes the Three Musketeer approach to communicating in organizations that we talked about in Chapter 1. She has learned that for a project to succeed is for her to succeed, and she can't do that by working alone and keeping information to herself. To be truly successful in today's business environment, Menyon has learned that she has to *provide information* to others who may be able to use it, gain from them *feedback*, and *coordinate* her communication efforts.

Also inherent in her statement is the recognition that communication is a process that moves a company forward. Without communication, Menyon's company, any company, would come to a grinding halt. Sharing what we know, what we are doing, what we think was said or heard, what direction we are taking on a big project or a group initiative, is vital for our growth as well as the growth of the company.

Coordinating our communication also allows us to gain vital insight (feedback) we cannot get working alone. Feedback tells us that we are on the right track and in sync with the goals and mission of the group, team, department, and company. It allows us to rehearse our message, to try it out on others *before* making a mistake. With corrective feedback, we learn to edit our errors, modify our information, and become more effective with others.

Coordinating also means making sure everyone who should be included in a communication event is notified of the event. It means asking for feedback from those who can help make a communication event successful. In Beth's case, this meant the other members of her team. Beth sent out an email asking her team members to attend a dry run of her presentation. She explained in the email that she was looking for feedback and wanted to catch any flaws before the client heard the presentation. After sending her email message, Beth looked over the presentation one last time and turned off the computer. She was really looking forward to getting some feedback tomorrow, but for now she needed a break from the project.

The next day, Beth arrived at the conference room 30 minutes early to set everything up and walk through her presentation once on her own. When her team members assembled, Beth began by telling them she was looking for feedback.

"I want to make sure that I have covered all the bases and that the presentation is solid," she said. "If *anything* is missing, please tell me."

"Like we wouldn't," someone said. Everyone in the room laughed.

Twenty minutes later, Beth sat down. "Well?" she asked. "What's the verdict?"

"Great job!" and "Nicely done" echoed from the group.

"Really fine job, Beth," Orin said. "But I do have a few notes I'd like to share."

"Great," Beth said, smiling. The group spent the next 45 minutes going over the notes Orin had made, polishing the presentation. When they were done, Beth really felt the presentation was the best it could be and thanked the team for their help.

Before she left that afternoon, she confirmed with the office coordinator that the room was booked for the next day and that all the standard arrangements for coffee, tea, and other refreshments were set. After running through the presentation a few more times that night, she would be ready.

Step 4: Delivering the Message

The payoff for a presentational event is the actual delivery of the speech in front of the intended audience. The first three components of the CCCD process ensure that you will have a professionally developed outline with strong supporting materials. These steps will help you develop an interesting, informative, and structured message that is appropriate for your audience and aligned with your personal goals. However, even the best message, with strong verbal and visual support and clear goals, will suffer if it is delivered poorly. The last component in the CCCD process—delivery—begins with your need to *practice*.

Practice, Practice, Practice

How many times have you listened to someone speak and felt that their message was good, but something was missing? Try as you might, you couldn't quite put your finger on it. Chances are good, what was missing was practice. Few of us are naturally eloquent. Fewer still feel really comfortable giving a speech without any preparation. Which is why practice is essential to delivering an effective message.

There are no research studies demonstrating an optimal amount of preparation and rehearsal time for presentations. However, most teachers of speech communication agree that the amount of practice time needed depends on:

- The amount of prior speaking experience.
- The number and complexity of presentational aids.
- Familiarity with the topic and audience.
- Confidence regarding speaking abilities.
- The degree of formality of the occasion or context.

Rehearsal of a message is not limited to presentational speaking. If you are meeting with a boss or a co-worker, take a few minutes *before* you talk to consider what you will say. Take into account your communication history, the norms of the organizational culture, and how your goals may or may not mesh well with his or hers. If you anticipate conflict, try out your message with someone who will give you honest feedback *before* you speak with your boss or co-worker.

In group or team meetings, think carefully *before* you interject. Think about *how* you will say what you want to say, keeping in mind the needs and expectations of your team members. Practice your message in your head, *before* you speak.

We have found that most people feel more confident if they practice a formal presentation at least three time before it is delivered. For important presentations (those that will get you noticed within an organization), you may want to practice more often, and before an audience of friends, spouse, or co-workers before you go public. This practice should be done with an outline or from limited notes (see Chapters 12 and 13 for an extended discussion). Each practice session should be *timed* (so that adjustments to the length of the speech can be made, if necessary), and the speaker should try to make less and less use of the outline or notes each time. As you acquire experience as a presenter, the amount of time you need to prepare will lessen, sometimes dramatically. But no professional we know presents an effective speech without some preparation.

Beth took this step seriously. Not only did she practice the presentation before her team members to gain their feedback, but she practiced again at home that evening. She knew that with a little extra practice she would feel confident the next day rather than nervous and anxious.

Practicing your presentation will help you achieve *four speaking characteristics* that make the difference between a good presentation and a great presentation. They are: fluency, naturalness, vivacity, and nonverbal competence. If you don't practice, your audience will immediately see that your talk lacks these characteristics. Let's look at each of these characteristics in more detail.

Fluency

Fluency refers to the *smooth or effortless articulation of a speech*. With practice, fluency naturally increases. You know what you intend to say, in what order, and as you practice, a comfortable speaking style emerges, helping you to sound more fluent. Practice helps you avoid saying "um," or "ah," or "like, you know," or any other form of speech that will make you appear less articulate. You will no longer connect sentences with "and" or "so." These speaking crutches go away and are replaced with natural vocal pauses, rather than stumbling for words and filling spaces with "and" or "uh."

Achieving fluency allows you to focus on the *flow of ideas* rather than on specific words. When you speak fluently, your message is clear and you deliver it smoothly and with confidence.

Naturalness

Naturalness refers to *an easy, genuine manner of speaking*. While your aim is not to recreate the Oprah Winfrey show, think about how natural she appears when speaking before a large audience. Natural speakers draw us into the message, making us feel a part of the presentation. They are fluent in their subject and comfortable talking about it.

Your aim should be to "be yourself." Avoid affectation; your attitude toward your audience should always be one of collaboration and equality, not superiority and distance. You should stand up straight, be precise yet poised, and reflect a positive, helpful posture toward your listeners. By analogy, think of how you speak with a group of friends or business colleagues in a public place.

Vivacity

Every day in boardrooms, conference rooms, and training facilities all across America, people are forced to sit and listen to seemingly endless streams of flat, lifeless, boring talk. **Vivacity** refers to the *energy and enthusiasm used when speaking*. High-energy speakers display a positive attitude toward their topics and their audiences, which has an infectious quality. This energy comes through in their enthusiasm for the subject and the opportunity to tell the audience about it.

However, do not confuse being vivacious with being *overly* emotional or *falsely* passionate. In most cases, audiences will reject the ideas of overly emotional or passionate speakers because they don't seem reasonable.

Nonverbal Competence

Nonverbal competence refers to the ability of a speaker to (a) maintain an appropriate level of *eye contact* with listeners, (b) use *gestures* without making them appear repetitive or redundant, (c) use purposeful *body movement*, particularly during verbal transitions in the speech, and (d) incorporate visual aids smoothly in the presentation. The more confident you become in the speaking of your speech, the more attention you can place on these aspects of effective delivery.

Practice helps you develop each of the characteristics described above. With ample practice, your delivery will be fluent, natural, vivacious, and competent. Your nonverbal cues will reflect a level of confidence and assurance that can only come when you feel confident and prepared.

How Beth Fared

After the client left, Beth's team members gave her a round of applause.

"Wow!" Orin said. "You really did well."

"Great job!" Todd said from the conference-room speaker phone. "I couldn't see the visuals, but I don't think I could have done a better job! I can finally get some rest and stop worrying about this account. Thanks, Beth."

Beth was thrilled with the results. The CCCD process worked just as the speaker said it would. The presentation she had dreaded provided her with an opportunity to help her team land an important new client. She knew she would never give another talk without using CCCD.

Summary

In this chapter, we introduced the CCCD process as the framework for developing conscious communication. We used Beth's example through the chapter to illustrate the four components of CCCD: Choose, Create, Coordinate, and Deliver. We briefly explained that while at first glance the CCCD process might seem a bit detailed for all types of communication events and episodes, in the following chapters we will show how you can apply CCCD to any type of communication event.

The discussion of CCCD in this chapter laid a foundation for the chapters to come. The use of the worksheets and the process Beth used to set communication goals, make choices, coordinate with team members, and deliver her message will reoccur to varying degrees throughout the book. Exposing you to these ideas early on in the text serves two purposes:

- You can begin to use the framework immediately, for your first presentation assignment in class.
- You have a firm grasp of the framework that informs the remainder of the chapters.

We will build on this framework in the remaining chapters to increase your understanding of what it takes to be a conscious communicator in the workplace. You will find that the CCCD process will work effectively for business and professional communication in the workplace, for both formal and informal speaking events.

COMMUNICATING IN PROFESSIONAL CONTEXTS ONLINE

Use your **Goodall Connection CD-ROM** for quick access to the electronic study resources that accompany this text. Included on your CD-ROM is access to:

InfoTrac College Edition

The World Wide Web

A demo of **WebTutor** for *Communicating in Professional Contexts*

The **Communicating in Professional Contexts Website** at the Wadsworth Communication Cafe. The Communicating in Professional Contexts Website offers chapter by chapter learning objectives, activities, quizzes, and a digital glossary.

You can review and complete the following sections online at
http://www.wadsworth.com/communication_d/

What You Should Have Learned

Now that you have read Chapter 3, you should be able to:

- List and explain the steps in the CCCD process.
- Discuss how the CCCD process reflects the principles of conscious communication.
- Use the CCCD worksheets to outline a basic presentation for your class.
- Provide feedback to others about their presentations using the CCCD process as your guide to what a professional presentation should include and accomplish.
- Explain how to choose communication goals.
- Explain why the body of a message should be created prior to the introduction and conclusion.
- Discuss why it is important to coordinate your communication event or episode with others prior to the actual delivery of it.
- Discuss strategies for improving delivery style and effectiveness.

Activities

The following activities can be completed online and, if requested, submitted to your instructor, under Student Resources, Activities for Chapter 3 at the Communicating in Professional Contexts Website at the Wadsworth Communication Café http://www.wadsworth.com/communication_d/.

1. Think about your class and instructor as an audience for your presentations. What needs and expectations do they have? How should their needs and expectations influence your choice of communication goals? Of communication content? Of style? Of delivery?

2. Compare what you have learned about writing outlines for papers in your English class with the advice given in this chapter about completing CCCD worksheets for an oral presentation. What are the similarities? What are the differences? What does this teach you about the relationship of oral to written style?

3. Think of an upcoming communication episode. Using the worksheets, devise a conscious communication plan. Try it out! What influences, if any, did the CCCD process have on your communication episode? How did CCCD improve your effectiveness?

Surfing the Net

Any sites referred to in the following activities are maintained under HyperContents for Chapter 3 at the Communicating in Professional Contexts Website.

1. Visit at least one website that specializes in oral communication. For example, you might try http://www.toastmasters.org. This site contains information on making effective oral presentations. What advice is given? How is that advice reflected in our CCCD process?

2. Visit http://www.eloquent.com. This is a site dedicated to providing audio and video transcripts of current business and professional speeches and presentations. You will notice that there are also some search features available, as well as outlines for some of the presentations. Use the CCCD system to critique one of the downloadable presentations available on this website.

Key Terms

audience needs and expectations *(64)*

causal pattern *(72)*

chronological pattern *(72)*

criteria *(68)*

facts *(75)*

fluency *(88)*

naturalness *(88)*

nonverbal competence *(89)*

outcome *(66)*

problem-solution pattern *(72)*

purpose *(70)*

statistics *(75)*

topical pattern *(72)*

transitions *(80)*

thesis statement *(70)*

vivacity *(88)*

Breakthrough Skill Development:
Completing the CCCD Worksheets

CCCD is a new and breakthrough process for organizing communication events. Now that you have been introduced to the process, you are ready to apply what you have learned. However, keep in mind that we will be building on and developing your skills throughout the course. In this skill-building exercise, we want you to begin using CCCD.

Using the CCCD worksheets (in Appendix A or online under Student Resources, Worksheets for Chapter 3 at the Communicating in Professional Contexts Website), prepare for your first in-class presentation. Your instructor will provide details on the assignment.

Critique at least one of your classmate's presentations using the CCCD worksheets as an evaluation guide. You can download a copy under Worksheets for Chapter 3 at the Communicating in Professional Contexts Website. Did the speaker complete all of the steps in the worksheets? For example, were the speaker's main points clearly defined? Did they tie into the speaker's stated thesis? Discuss your critique with the speaker. Help one another develop goals to improve your next speech.

Communicating in Professional Contexts In Action!

Communicating In Professional Contexts In Action! is available on your Goodall Connection CD-ROM and features an individual and group persuasive presentation and a dramatization of an interview discussed in Chapter 9. Improve your own presentation and interview skills by watching, listening to, critiquing and analyzing the scenarios featured on this program. After completing an analysis for each communication scenario and answering the questions provided, you can compare your work to our suggested responses. Now is a good time to test out your CD-ROM!

Chapter Four

Listening in the Workplace

Ben couldn't believe his boss was making him sit through a workshop on listening. "Listening of all things," he grumbled to himself. "What could you possibly learn about listening sitting in a workshop? This is such a waste of time!"

Ben thought about the pile of work on his desk, the three sales calls he had to make that afternoon, and the date he didn't want to be late for that evening. This "employee development" waste of time was going to set him back, way back.

"Hmmm," he mused, "maybe I can sneak out at the break and no one will notice."

Becoming a Conscious Listener

As we have seen in the previous chapters, often when we think we are communicating effectively, we may not be. This is equally true of **listening,** the process of *hearing and interpreting messages*. Listening is an integral part of the communication process. Think about it for a moment. How many of us truly listen? How many times has someone said to *you*, "You're not *listening* to me, are you?" One reason we haven't developed our listening skills is the fast pace of our culture. We don't seem to have time to listen; we are too busy talking, and if we aren't talking, we are formulating what we are going to say next.

Our failure to listen is also due to the lack of formal listening training we receive. Judith Pollack, president of Language at Work, describes the problem this way: "We spend 80 percent of our time communicating, but we only receive training in the speaking, reading and writing aspects. We *never* really receive training in listening, except at the hands of our teachers and parents" (Jones, p. 15, 1999). Patrice Johnson, director of Spectra Incorporated in New Orleans, emphasizes the importance of investing in listening training. She says, "I think listening is getting attention now because organizations don't have the luxury of redundancy. In the past, large dinosaur organizations had plenty of people to do rework, unnecessary work, and so forth. Failing to listen and the errors that it caused could be managed." (Salopek, 1999, p. 58). Now, however, many CEOs, training managers, and business owners think of listening as an important and crucial business skill.

Conscious listening, much like conscious communication, can be understood using a continuum (see Table 4.1). The continuum shows the spectrum of listening that ranges from hearing to conscious listening, or "listening to the whole," which emerges out of dialogue (Senge et al., 1994, p. 20). Let's look at the listening continuum in more detail.

Hearing

Hearing is the *passive and physical process of listening*. We may "hear" the words of a speaker, but we don't necessarily understand their meaning. Hearing is simply what happens when a message vibrates our eardrum and causes a signal to

Hearing	Informational Listening	Critical Listening	Self-Reflexive Listening	Conscious Listening
Listener processes a signal from a speaker.	Listener identifies the signal as words. Moves from hearing to listening.	Listener deliberates on what is said, exploring the logic, reason, and point of view of the speaker.	Listener reflects on how what is said applies to his or her life.	Listener becomes open to the speaker's point of view.

Mindless Listening. . . . . **Mindful Listening**

Table 4.1
Listening Continuum

move to the brain. At the physical level, our ability to listen can be affected by outside elements that may hamper our ability to hear, including noise and physical and technological diversions.

Noise

Imagine you are at a job fair in a crowded hotel conference room. You finally have the attention of the head of personnel for a company you have been trying to interview with for months. However, the noise in the room keeps you from hearing the hiring information you need to target your resume effectively. **Noise** is any sound that disrupts or interferes with the delivery of a message. Noise can cause a listener to become frustrated or confused, or to give up on the message altogether.

Physical Diversions

Have you ever tried to listen in a room that is too hot or too dark? A **physical diversion** is any physical element that disrupts or interferes with the delivery of a message. A few years ago we were asked to sit in on training sessions at a software development company. The head of training had received a number of complaints from trainees about the material and the trainers. The head of training changed the trainers, revised the materials, but still the complaints continued. Oddly enough, trainees only complained when the training was done at the home office. One hour into a training session there, we knew exactly why the trainees were complaining. The room where the training sessions were held was a medium gray color. The lights in the main part of the room were kept dim so that the trainees could see the large LCD screen at the front of the room. The temperature was a lulling 78 degrees. The problem wasn't the materials or the trainers. It was the room! The physical space lulled the trainees to sleep and kept them from listening or learning.

Technological Diversions

A **technological diversion** is any technological element that disrupts or interferes with the delivery of a message. How many times have you initiated a conversation, only to have the phone or doorbell ring? Because we work in a home office, this happens to us many times a day. After using "call waiting" for only two weeks, we called the phone company and canceled the service. This "revolution in the way people use the telephone" was distracting and annoying to our callers. Even if we did manage to keep the first caller on the line, by the time we returned to the call, our listener was distracted or frustrated and no longer focused on our message.

> ### Tips for Overcoming Blocks to Hearing
>
> 1. Hold conversations in spaces where noise is not a problem. If you are in a crowded or noisy space:
>   + Move to a quieter space, if possible.
>   + Make an appointment to call or see the person when you will be back in your office and can concentrate on the conversation. Be sure to secure the information you need to contact the person at a later date (phone number or email address).
> 2. Make adjustments to the physical space:
>   + Move closer to the front in dim rooms. Adjust the temperature.
>   + Hold the speaker or meeting manager accountable for the physical space. If you attend regular meetings in the same room and every week you fall asleep or freeze during the meeting, bring it to the attention of the person who arranged the meeting.
> 3. Be conscious of technological distractions:
>   + Don't take other calls, read your email, or open your mail while someone is talking to you. Give others your full attention.
>   + Be honest if someone begins a conversation during a time when you know you will be distracted. Tell the co-worker, "This is not a good time for us to talk. I am really distracted right now and will not be able to give you my full attention. Can we schedule another time to talk about this?"

"Okay," Ben thought. "That makes sense. Hearing is the physical part of listening. Noise and other things can block it. So what?"

Informational Listening

Informational listening describes the stage when a message *begins* to be interpreted by the listener. At this stage in the listening process, *we assign meaning to the words* we hear, and we listen for information. Many people conduct much

Figure 4.1
The Listening Cycle

of their business communication at this stage of the listening process, getting caught up in a cycle of listening and responding, without moving on to the next stage, critical listening (see Figure 4.1).

At this level, our ability to listen and gain information can be influenced by internal elements, such as cultural, gender, and language differences. Another factor that may interfere with listening is the communication history we have with the person speaking. Let's look at each of these in more detail.

Cultural Differences

Cultural differences affecting communication can include the slang used by a younger or older generation, the language and tonal accents used by another nationality or race, the regional differences in language style, and the jargon used by a certain profession or industry. All too often, we focus on the cultural differences of the speaker and forget to listen to the message itself. In business, where diverse cultures abound, this can become a serious communication problem.

Consider the situation of Rasheed, a highly qualified, motivated programmer at a software development company. Rasheed was new to the United States as well as to the company, but he churned out more lines of code than almost anyone else. When he spoke, however, his voice was barely above a whisper. In meetings, members of the development team would talk over one another, excitedly working through ideas. Rasheed struggled to be heard, but often he gave up out of frustration. He wasn't used to the team's raucous organizational culture. Unfortunately, the team was losing out on a valuable perspective on the project. After a few weeks, Rasheed confided his concerns to another team member, Sandra. She suggested to the team that Rasheed raise a manila folder whenever he had a point to make. The tactic worked well. Not only did the team listen more carefully to Rasheed, but they began to listen more carefully to each other.

Tips for Working with Non-Native Speakers

- Pick one member of the group or team as the liaison for the non-native speaker.
- Encourage the non-native employee to put comments, suggestions, or other input in writing. Generally, non-native speakers have a better command of the written language.
- Repeat sentences back to the speaker, clarifying your understanding, one sentence at a time.
- Be patient. It is just as frustrating for the non-native speaker as it is for you. Becoming frustrated or angry will heighten the speaker's anxiety, which will make it more difficult for you to understand one another.

Cultural barriers can also present themselves in less obvious ways. An older male boss may ignore the suggestions of a younger male employee simply because he thinks the younger man is too inexperienced to know what he is talking about. Even clothes can present cultural barriers to listening. When talking to a sales clerk, have you ever found yourself distracted by the clerk's multiple earrings, or choice of earring location? Have you found others distracted by *your* nonverbal presentation of self? How *you* look and present yourself in a business setting can distract from your ability to communicate, by impeding other's ability to listen.

Tips for Removing Cultural Barriers to Listening

- Mentally acknowledge nonverbal distraction before you begin a conversation. By making yourself aware of the distraction and acknowledging it, you reduce the interference it may cause.
- Concentrate on the words and meanings of the speaker rather than allowing yourself to become distracted.

> ✦ Acknowledge cultural differences. When dealing with someone significantly older or younger, realize that you are coming from very different positions, but you each have something to offer.

Gender Differences

We've all heard John Gray's statement, "Men are from Mars and women are from Venus." We know that studies of the differences in the way men and women communicate are numerous. However, understanding *why* men and women communicate differently can go a long way to explaining *how* men and women listen. Noted communication researcher Deborah Tannen explains the differences in the way men and women tend to communicate this way: "Men communicate to report and women communicate to build rapport" (Tannen, 1990).

Let's look at this statement from a *listening perspective*. If men are communicating to *report* knowledge, chances are good that they are not as attuned to receiving feedback or gathering additional information or viewpoints. Men in business often view communication as a simple process of *delivery*, as one-sided communication events intended to impart knowledge.

If women are communicating to build *rapport* (create mutual understanding), they are more receptive to feedback and responses of others. Women are generally considered *empathetic* listeners. They are affected not only by the words they hear, but also by the perceived feelings of the speaker. Openness to feedback and empathetic listening create a view of communication as *conversation*, as exchanges that are used to further *relationships*.

Gender differences also seem to occur in the way men and women process conversational cues. Women tend to use and process conversational cues like "Oh really," "Hmmm," and "That's interesting" as means of moving the conversation along. These cues signal they are listening and engaged. For men, these same cues may signal agreement or submission. Men often view such cues as prolonging a conversation when all that is needed is a quick decision. Women become frustrated by most men's inability to listen rather than react. Becoming aware of the gender differences in listening can help to overcome gender-related misunderstandings and frustrations in the workplace.

Tips for Overcoming Gender-Related Listening Differences

- Become aware of the differences in the way men and women tend to communicate and listen. Reading one of the books or articles on gender and communication suggested in the References will help you become more aware of these differences.
- Be sensitive to the differences in communication. Listen *carefully*, regardless of a person's gender.
- Use summaries and questions to ensure that you have heard what was said.
- Don't assume that conversational cues like "Hmmm" or "Uh-huh" signal agreement.

Language Differences

A Canadian friend of ours occasionally will say something that is absolutely clear to her, but not to us. These twists of language happen across generations, cultures, and industry groups. Often, language differences occur because an industry or generational group has given a new meaning to a word or phrase. For example, the Internet has introduced a new and evolving lexicon to the English language. The word "web," which to most people means something a spider uses to catch food, now can be used to refer to an intricate woven relationship between sites on the Internet. "Surfing," which once required water and a surfboard, now can mean looking for information or entertainment opportunities on the Internet.

> ## Tips for Surmounting Language Barriers
>
> + If you are in a meeting and cannot check your understanding of a term or phrase, write the phrase down. After the meeting, clarify the meaning with another team member or the person speaking.
> + If you are in a conversation and someone uses a phrase or term you don't understand, *ask for clarification*. Too often, people assume that asking for clarification will make them appear unsavvy or out of the loop. By not asking for clarification, you set yourself up to make mistakes or have future misunderstandings.
> + Keep your own jargon and language differences under control. Using the latest term might lead to miscommunication that costs you or your company time and money.

Communication History

Have you ever noticed that there are certain people you tune out *before* they begin to speak? Have you ever considered why you respond this way? Chances are it is because of your **communication history,** the cumulative record of communication events between the participants of a conversation.

Communication history can interfere with listening in many ways. For example, some people just seem to waste your time. Others want to talk about issues you have no interest or stake in. Some people have the communication style of a battering ram; they hammer their point home over and over again. Others communicate only to complain. Their communication evolves around negative messages about how much work they have to do, how unfair the company is, or how bad their personal relationships are. There are two distinct problems with these dysfunctional communication styles:

1. The speaker views the listener as a passive receptor who is there to absorb whatever message the speaker chooses to send.
2. The speaker assumes that talking is more powerful or important than listening.

As we will see later in this chapter, both of these positions weaken a speaker's ability to communicate effectively. Unfortunately, there are times in business when you *have* to communicate with these people to gain important information, which might mean wading through a certain amount of overload or negativity first.

> **Tips for Dealing with Communication History Barriers**
>
> + Begin any conversation by setting parameters. For example, "Gee, Mahoan, I'm sorry I can't talk. Hunter needs these figures for a meeting in 15 minutes."
> + Don't avoid someone who has information you need because of your past communication history. Acknowledge your history and ask for the information you need. For example, "I know we normally talk about your job when we meet, but today, I would like to focus on our project. If you need to talk about your job, we could schedule lunch later in the week."
> + If communication history or someone's communication style continues to block your ability to get information, find a new source for the information, or discuss the problem with your boss. Chances are, you are not the only one dealing with the problem, which might be affecting your entire team, the department, or the company.

"Not bad," thought Ben. "I can use some of these tips. Maybe this listening stuff even explains why I've had a hard time talking to some of the women in our sales group. I know I have at least two customers this will make a real difference with, especially Mr. Spencer. If I have to listen to his list of complaints about labor, manufacturing, and delivery problems again, I'll go nuts. Next time I call on him, I will begin by acknowledging his problems. Now I have a way of dealing more productively with him. Maybe I should stay after the break and find out what critical listening is."

Critical Listening

Many people get bogged down in the cycle of listening and responding. As communicators we are all skilled in phatic communion and informational exchanges; what we lack skill in is **critical listening**—the ability of a listener to deliberate on what is said by exploring the logic, reason, and point of view of the speaker. It is only when we reach the critical listening stage that we can begin to reflect on the credibility of the speaker, the message, and the motivation behind the talk. Before we can reflect on the impact a message has on us personally, we have to evaluate the qualities of the message.

Speaker Credibility

When we examine a speaker's credibility, we are evaluating the personal and professional qualifications a speaker brings to a communication event. The qualifications a speaker needs in an interpersonal communication event may be different from those required for a formal presentation. For example, if your boss, a 29-year-old with an MBA from the Wharton School of Business and no actual work experience, offers you advice on dealing with a client you have been working with for five years, how would you view her advice? However, if the advice came from an account executive who worked with the client for eight years before you took over the account, would you view the advice differently? On the other hand, if the MBA boss presented a workshop on a new way of creating a monthly sales report that saves time, would you respond more positively to her advice?

It is important to note that not all speakers are credible in every communication situation. Each situation, event, and speaker must be considered individually.

The Message

When we speak, it is important to back up what we say with support. When we listen, we are listening for the *supporting evidence* or *data* a speaker uses to add credibility to a message. You should listen for:

- *Facts and statistics*. Are the facts and statistics offered reliable? Do they come from respected sources? Do they support the speaker's claims, or have they simply been used for effect?
- *Examples*. Are the examples *clear* and *relevant*? Or have they been added to make the material seem more interesting? Do you recognize an example as something that holds true for the topic? Can you identify with the example?
- *Personal appeals*. Are the personal appeals used to gain your compliance appropriate for the message and the speaker? Are the appeals being used in place of a strong and clear factual appeal?

Motivation

Motivation is the force or reason that drives us toward an action. All talk is rooted in the motivation to reach a goal. For example, we may speak to take up a department's cause, support a program slated to be cut, or rouse a group to action. Even passing along task information is rooted in the need to ensure that a job gets done.

When you evaluate a speaker's motivation, you must listen for the speaker's stake in the message. What does the speaker *have to gain*? Is the speaker's motivation similar to yours? Or is the speaker acting from a selfish position?

When *you* speak, evaluate your own motivation. What do others hear you say when they listen to your message? Are your motivations appropriate for the message? Will you be perceived as working for the good of the team, or only for yourself?

> *After the break, Ben sat reflecting on what he had heard. He was beginning to understand why he had been the only one from his team chosen to attend the Listening in the Workplace workshop. He didn't like to admit it, but he could see that he had not been a very effective listener. He needed to make some changes, and this workshop was really going to help him do it.*

Self-Reflexive Listening

So far, our listener has:

- Heard what was said.
- Mined the message for useful information.
- Evaluated the credibility of the person speaking.

Now it is time to *reflect on the message*. **Self-reflexive listening**—listening for how what is said applies to a listener's life—allows us to integrate and then move beyond the first three stages of the listening process. By *reflecting* on what is said and how it will affect us, we move closer to conscious listening. When we listen self-reflexively, we are listening for the ways a message reflects our:

- identity at work
- personal goals
- understanding of an issue or problem
- sensitivity to the needs of others

Identity

When we listen self-reflexively, we hear and reflect on the meanings of *what others say about us*. Listening to what others say about us, our work, our values, and our work ethic provides us with an important insight into who we are in the workplace. The metaphors people use to describe us—"he's a real go-getter," "she's the brightest bulb in the accounting department," or "that's the toughest team I've ever had to work with"—create our work identity. How do people at work describe you? What are the adjectives commonly used when people talk about you or your work? Does this talk accurately reflect who you are or want to be in the workplace?

Personal Goals

Listening for the personal goals of the speaker gives us insight into the speaker's motivation. Listening self-reflexively allows us to think about *how our personal goals are aligned with those of the speaker*. Is this a person you want to do business with, or are the speaker's personal goals outside of your personal or ethical boundaries? Are your personal goals aligned in such a way that, together, you could bring about change or close a sale that you could not accomplish separately? Listening for personal goals helps you identify people who can help you succeed and those who do not share your ethical, moral, or business values.

Understanding

Listening self-reflexively provides you with an opportunity to evaluate how well you understand a person, problem, or situation. Too often in business situations, we are concerned with how well *other* people understand a problem. It is much easier to be critical of another's position without really evaluating *our own* understanding. Listening self-reflexively allows us to listen to the verbal cues that signal *our* understanding of a problem or situation. Cues from others, such as "I really think you are on the right track" or "I'm not sure you see the whole problem," signal how well we are grasping their message and intention.

Sensitivity

Listening with **sensitivity** means *taking into consideration the speaking differences* of your communication partners. Becoming a sensitive listener requires listening for, and awareness of, the differences that arise from racial, gender, cultural, socio-economic, and other factors that contribute to how we evaluate meanings and messages. It means that we are aware of how these differences affect our ability to listen and integrate the message into our thinking.

Conscious Listening

The final stage on the listening continuum is **conscious listening,** openly listening to the speaker's point of view that emerges out of dialogue. Conscious listening occurs when all of the communication partners involved in a communication episode or event listen for, and reflect on, how talk affects the whole group, team, or company. Peter Senge describes this conscious listening as the "deeper patterns of meaning that flow through a group…that build a subtle awareness of collective thought that profoundly transforms our experience of what is possible" (et al., 1994, p. 20).

Conscious listening transforms us from individuals into relational partners or a collective group moving forward *together*. Conscious listening, like dialogue, takes into account the *shared vision*, *goals*, and values of a relationship, group, team, or organization. Conscious listening results in new alternatives that we would not have seen had we not listened consciously.

Tips for Listening Consciously

- Stop talking. You cannot listen at any level if you are talking.
- Stop reacting. You cannot listen consciously if you are focusing on what you are going to say next.
- Listen for feelings. It is easier to be empathetic if you understand how someone feels. Rather than focusing on the content, take a minute to focus on the feelings of the speaker.
- Listen for cues about yourself. What is the listener saying about *you*? Does it ring true?

(continued)

- Listen for motivation. What is motivating the speaker to feel this way, react this way, take this position?
- Listen for intention. What does the speaker really want to happen as a result of having spoken?
- Listen for position. Is compromise possible, or is the speaker unmovable?
- Listen for benefits. How will this benefit you, your company, or your client?
- Recap what was said as calmly as possible. Use phrases like "I heard you say that…" or "It seems that you want…"
- Ask for confirmation. Ask questions such as "Do you feel I have a handle on the situation now that we've talked?"
- Suggest alternatives that work for both the individual and the whole. "We could ask Paula to reschedule the meeting so that you will have more time to prepare. Or we could tell the group that your report is preliminary because you were given the assignment yesterday, but they can begin to analyze the information. And let's go ahead and let everyone know your final report will be available on Friday."

Conscious listening is a vital business skill. It opens us to the views of others, presents possibilities we would not see if we didn't listen consciously, and creates a level of understanding in organizations that helps move your relationships, teamwork, and the organization forward. Now that we have a better understanding of listening in the workplace, let's look at listening with specific business contexts.

After the workshop, Ben stayed to talk with the speaker and to thank her for the information. He was amazed at how much there was to learn about listening, something he had obviously not been doing very well. Now he was determined to become a conscious listener in all his business and personal communication encounters.

The Importance of Listening in Business and Professional Contexts

Developing conscious listening skills should be a goal for anyone in business. In fact, there are many situations in business where we discover that listening is our job. How well we listen in these situations, the level at which we listen, and the outcome of our listening will all have a direct impact on our success in our chosen business or profession. This section addresses the role of listening in a few typical business situations.

Listening in Meetings

Meetings require a combination of listening skills. Although most of the listening we do in meetings is for information, it is also important that we follow the listening continuum up through critical, self-reflexive, and conscious listening. How well we listen can provide us with important information and an opportunity to share knowledge and receive feedback.

Tips for Listening in Meetings

- Set a positive example. Sit up, be quiet, and take notes. There is nothing worse than being in a class, meeting, or presentation with someone who whispers, squirms, talks, or is otherwise disruptive.
- Don't pass judgment. You will continue to encounter your share of boring, unorganized, or unskilled speakers. Your job, however, may depend on the *information* you get from the speaker. Listen for information; downplay the presentation style.
- Take good notes. Outline the speech or talk, using the CCCD components. Try to determine the speaker's:
    - Purpose
    - Thesis
    - Preview
    - Main points
    - Support
    - Conclusion
- If possible, review the material later with the speaker or other members of the audience to verify or modify what you heard.
- Follow up on any points that need clarification or action.

Listening in Conflict Situations

Listening in conflict situations requires well-developed listening skills. It also requires patience. Often, when we find ourselves in conflict situations, we become defensive. However, the conflict may be situational, not personal. We need to learn to listen to the speaker's reaction and feelings about the situation, rather than concentrate on our own anger, defensiveness, or need to counterattack.

Tips for Listening in Conflict Situations

- Relax and take a few deep breaths. Step back a few steps from the person who is speaking so that you gain control over your personal space. Stepping back physically can also help us to step back mentally.

(continued)

- Don't become defensive when the speaker focuses on you rather than on the situation. Keep *your* thoughts and words focused on the *situation,* not the person. Remember, not everyone knows how to listen consciously.
- Acknowledge the conflict. If you know in advance that a conflict is brewing, begin the conversation with, "I know we have different views. I would like to hear yours before we go any further. Then, please listen to what I have to say."
- Listen for areas of compromise. Most conflict resolution arises out of compromise, not consensus.
- Listen for signs of escalation of the conflict. If this happens, say, "I think we are becoming overly emotional. Perhaps we should meet later to discuss this."
- Recap what the speaker said. Show you were listening critically by recapping the speaker's motives, supports, and appeals. Show you were listening *self-reflexively* by acknowledging your role, from the speaker's perspective, in the conflict. Show you were listening consciously by pointing out the areas of compromise and alternatives for moving forward.

Listening to Complaints

One of the things Kanika disliked most about working for a company was the amount of time she had to spend listening to co-workers', managers', and clients' complaints and problems. Now that she works as an independent consultant, she finds she gets much more accomplished because she doesn't have a stream of people in her office every day that she has to listen to. Kanika's attitude might appear negative at first, but it is important to understand the difference between someone in the workplace who has a legitimate complaint and the chronic complainer who nibbles away at our time and energy.

Legitimate Complaints

Legitimate complaints are those that arise from clients, customers, or members of your organization that address specific issues or problems. These types of complaints should be listened to with care and handled quickly and efficiently. To handle a legitimate complaint:

1. Listen carefully. Allow the person to have his or her say.
2. Remain neutral. When listening to a complaint, keep in mind that the complaint is not an attack; it is a request for acknowledgment.
3. Listen empathetically. Think about how the situation or problem has affected the person.

4. Repeat the person's statement of the problem. Let the person know that you understand the problem or situation from their perspective.
5. Ask what the person would like to have happen.
6. Explain your position.
7. Follow up in any reasonable way to ensure the person's satisfaction.

Chronic Complainers

Chronic complainers complain about everything: the company, their manager, their assignments, and their co-workers. They rarely ever take action on a problem. Instead, they spend their time complaining. Listening to chronic complainers can zap our energy, create feelings of distrust toward group or team members or the organization, and take time away from important organizational activities.

Tips for Dealing with Chronic Complainers

- Acknowledge their complaint and their feelings about the situation.
- Explain that although you understand the situation must be frustrating, you cannot spend any more time discussing it.
- Offer positive actions the complainer can take to resolve the situation.
- When confronted by the complainer again, explain that you are in the middle of a task and now is not a good time to discuss the problem. After you refuse to listen to the complaints a few times, most complainers will get the message and either begin complaining to someone else or take action.

Listening When Asked for Help

Occasionally, whether you are a manager, co-worker, or team member, someone will come to you for help on a project or career advice. When this happens, listening is the most vital skill you can use to ensure you give the best help possible. How we listen can determine how well we understand the problem, the person's needs, and the feelings that may be contributing to the situation.

It is also important to understand what people expect from you. Are they looking for advice, a sounding board, a chance to vent, or the information they need to make an informed decision? Often, people will come to you for help and their words will say one thing, but what they want is something entirely different. Listening can help you pick up on the clues that are vital to understanding exactly what someone needs.

We have discussed the differences in communication styles between men and women. These differences also apply to the way men and women tend to approach requests for help. Men generally listen to the problem and then immediately provide a course of action. Women generally listen to the problem, ask questions, and ask how the speaker feels about what is happening. Women tend to be concerned about the feelings of the person asking for help, while men tend to be concerned with addressing the problem and moving on. There are benefits to each style; both genders can learn from one another.

When people ask for your help, you should:

1. Let them speak. Don't interrupt or offer quick solutions.
2. Ask them what form they want the help to take. Ask if they want advice, assistance, analysis, a solution, or simply your support.
3. Offer the help they ask for if you feel comfortable giving it.
4. Keep the conversation to yourself. When people ask you for help, they are doing so because they trust you. Don't abuse their trust by telling others about their request if it should be kept private.
5. Offer support after the conversation is over. Follow up with their request and see how they are doing.

Summary

Learning to be a conscious listener is important for two reasons: listening can help you avoid mistakes and misunderstandings, and it can help to move your business and professional relationships forward. Listening allows us to gather important information, empathize with co-workers and clients, gain a deeper understanding of situations, and reflect on our place within a specific communication context.

In this chapter, we discussed listening as a skill vital to the workplace. We introduced the conscious listening continuum and the types of listening: hearing, informational listening, critical listening, self-reflective listening, and conscious listening. While listening occurs in many forms, conscious listening is the form of listening we should all strive to do in our business and professional interactions. We also offered a number of tips for dealing with specific listening situations and contexts.

COMMUNICATING IN PROFESSIONAL CONTEXTS ONLINE

Use your **Goodall Connection CD-ROM** for quick access to the electronic study resources that accompany this text. Included on your CD-ROM is access to:

InfoTrac College Edition

Listening in the Workplace

The World Wide Web

A demo of **WebTutor** for *Communicating in Professional Contexts*

The **Communicating in Professional Contexts Website** at the Wadsworth Communication Cafe. The Communicating in Professional Contexts Website offers chapter by chapter learning objectives, activities, quizzes, and a digital glossary.

You can review and complete the following sections online at http://www.wadsworth.com/communication_d/

What You Should Have Learned

Now that you have read Chapter 4, you should be able to:

- Identify and define the five types of listening.
- Explain the conscious listening continuum and provide two important characteristics of each type of listening.
- Explain why listening is a skill that is vital to the workplace.
- Distinguish between hearing and listening.
- Describe possible blocks that may keep someone from hearing a message.
- Draw the listening cycle associated with informational listening.
- Describe the four barriers that may occur with informational listening.
- Describe the qualities you should evaluate when listening critically.
- Discuss the four components of self-reflexive listening.
- Explain conscious listening and why it is important in the workplace.
- Follow the tips for listening in meetings.
- Listen in conflict situations.
- Listen to legitimate complaints and handle chronic complainers.
- Listen when asked for help.

Activities

The following activities can be completed online and, if requested, submitted to your instructor, under Student Resources, Activities for Chapter 4 at the Communicating in Professional Contexts Website at the Wadsworth Communication Café http://www.wadsworth.com/communication_d/.

1. Spend an entire day focusing on your listening skills. Take the time, for each communication event you encounter, to go through each stage of listening. Listen for information, critically, self-reflexively, and finally consciously. Write down your listening experiences. What did you learn about yourself as a listener? What did you learn about conscious listening?

2. Evaluate a specific listening situation. What was the context? What were the speaker's motives? Was the speaker credible? What did the person want?
3. In your group, share an experience where either conscious listening or a lack of good listening skills had an impact on your personal or professional life. Ask your group members for feedback. What would they have done differently in the situation?

Surfing the Net

Any sites referred to in the following activities are maintained under HyperContents for Chapter 4 at the Communicating in Professional Contexts Website.

1. Track down one of the listening sites on the WWW. Share with your group or class some of the exercises you found on the site. For example, the International Listening Association at http://www.listen.org lists links to other sites, articles on listening, and listening exercises.
2. Enter the term "business communication, listening" as a keyword search on InfoTrac College Edition or the WWW. Search for articles that use this terminology. Pick an article from your search that discusses listening in a business context. How would you do in the organization or context discussed in the article?
3. Go to the American Communication Association home page at http://www.uark.edu/~aca/. Type "listening" into the search engine and see what websites pop up. Cruise these sites for information that may be relevant to your assignments in this class and other classes.

Key Terms

communication history *(101)*   informational listening *(96)*   physical diversion *(95)*

conscious listening *(105)*   listening *(94)*   self-reflexive listening *(104)*

critical listening *(102)*   motivation *(103)*   sensitivity *(105)*

hearing *(94)*   noise *(95)*   technological diversion *(96)*

Breakthrough Skill Development:
Moving from Mindless to Mindful Communication

Working in a group, complete the following exercise. This process allows you to work consciously through the exercise at an experiential level, and to work through the exercise again at an evaluative level.

The Process

1. Pick one member of the group to tell the story narrated below. (If your class is not working in groups, read the story to a friend and complete the remaining steps of the exercise.)
2. Go around the group and give each person three minutes to expand the story.

3. As each person speaks, listen to the personal narratives, facts, history, and other elements interjected into the story.
4. After the last person has spoken, leave the group without discussing the story further.
5. Write an essay describing what you heard and your listening experience. (See additional instructions below.)

The Story

Enrique was excited about his promotion to area sales manager at GHS. He had worked hard to reach his goal of becoming a sales director by age 30. The company was growing and expanding, which meant he had more opportunity ahead of him. Shortly after his promotion, the regional sales director, Hal, asked him to fly to the home office in Tampa for a regional sales meeting. The meeting would be on Monday; however, Hal wanted Enrique to fly in on Saturday so that he could go "golfing and hang out with the guys."

Later that day, when Enrique was talking to Mary, the area sales manager of another district, he mentioned that he was arriving in Tampa on Saturday. Mary asked why and Enrique told her Hal had invited him to go golfing. Mary…

Group member one speaks for three minutes, adding to the story.

Group member two speaks for three minutes, adding to the story.

Continue until all the group members have added to the story.

Your Essay

Outside of class, write a 3–5 page paper about your experience. How did gender, language, culture, and communication history affect what you heard? How did listening play a part in the development of the story?

Chapter Five

The Power of Verbal and Nonverbal Communication in the Workplace

Every morning, on his way to work, Lawrence listens to talk radio. He switches between a National Public Radio news-oriented format and a local talk show featuring a feisty pair of hosts who engage callers in a discussion of the "question of the day." Most mornings, the questions are about people's personal relationships or work relationships, and sometimes they are about personal relationships with co-workers. Lawrence finds the NPR broadcasts interesting and informative, but more often than not, he finds himself listening to the talk show because he believes it reveals "how people really are."

Lawrence considers himself a student of "how people really are." He studied psychology, sociology, and communication as an undergraduate at his state university and is now enrolled in a weekend MBA program. He is the assistant manager of human resources for a large bank, a job that allows him to combine his interest in people with his love of business. His favorite books are the self-help and motivational varieties, with a strong preference for those best-selling authors who talk about how to deal with people at work and in personal relationships.

Lawrence sees himself as a positive, empathetic, high-energy person who excels when working one-on-one with other employees, trying to help them solve work-related problems. He believes that he works well in small-group or team situations, where he can use his knowledge of people to bring out the best in them. Because of his experiences as a college debater, he feels very comfortable and confident in presentational speaking situations. All in all, Lawrence believes that he is a well-rounded communicator.

Lately, however, his sense of himself as a good communicator who can handle any situation has been challenged at work. Last week, he overheard some co-workers talking about him in unflattering terms. They described him as being a "person who is all flash and no real substance." They made fun of his positive attitude, his high levels of energy, and his always-present smile. One co-worker even joked about the way he dressed, calling his style "imitation GQ."

These comments stopped him cold in his tracks. Were they really talking about him? The more he overheard of their conversation, the clearer it was. Not only were they talking about him, but they were making fun of the way he spoke and dressed. He stood in the hallway, hidden from view, with a growing sense of anger mixed with fear that gradually gave way to an overall sense of embarrassment. He walked back to his office alone and shaken.

With all his study of "how people are," with all his confidence about his communication skills, he didn't know what to do. Should he charge back down the hall and make a scene? Pretend he hadn't heard them? Act cool, as if nothing of importance had occurred? Try to get even?

As he reflected on his experience, he decided to use it to his advantage. He apparently needed to rebuild his image at work. If he was being perceived as a shallow person—all flash and no substance—what could he do about it? Maybe his clothing was part of the problem. And his big smile. On the other hand, maybe it was the other people who had the problem. After all, what is so bad about being positive in your attitude at work? Or being well dressed? Or smiling? Why should he trust the opinions of people who talked badly about him behind his back?

The talk show he was listening to this morning featured the question: "What do your co-workers do that makes you nuts?" The first caller claimed that she wasn't being taken seriously by her co-workers. Lawrence turned up the volume. He listened for a while to her woes: she had good ideas, but other people stole them and she never got credit for the work she did. Within minutes, the hosts began imitating—cruelly, Lawrence thought—her high-pitched voice and her somewhat whiny conversation style. The caller became quiet and Lawrence felt a little sorry for her.

The second caller complained that co-workers were spreading rumors about him in his organization, but he was at a loss about what to do. He felt that if he denied the accusations, he would look guiltier. If he didn't say anything about them, he looked bad too. Lawrence nodded. The hosts asked what the rumors were about. The caller hemmed and hawed then finally admitted that the company was in the process of being bought out by a competitor. He was in charge of a department that was due to be downsized, and everyone thought he was negotiating a side deal with the new owners. "Well, are you?" asked one of the hosts. "Who, me?" came the reply. It was instantly apparent that the caller was not going to give a straight answer to the question—which probably meant, Lawrence mused, that the caller didn't give straight answers to any questions. That was his problem. His co-workers were spreading rumors because there was an absence of truth being told. Lawrence had seen it before.

The third caller reported that she was the victim of repeated sexual harassment at work, and that even though she had filed a complaint, nothing was being done about it. To make matters worse, everyone she worked with now gave her the silent treatment, as if she was the person who had done something wrong by reporting it. "Maybe they fear for their jobs if they associate with a whistle-blower," one of the hosts offered. "Yeah, maybe," the caller replied. "I'm thinking about quitting," she admitted. "Don't do that!" shouted one of the hosts. "You haven't done anything wrong!" The caller sighed loudly. "You know," she said, "it just shouldn't be like this. I wish I knew what to do." Lawrence, being well trained in dealing with sexual harassment issues, knew the woman was being unfairly treated and found himself aggravated that the human resource department at her company wasn't doing its job properly.

Finally, a woman called in to say that there was this nice guy at work, an assistant manager, who everyone was down on lately. They talked badly about him behind his back. They made fun of how he dressed, how he talked, and even the books he read. This angered her because she knew he was a dependable, hard worker who always had a smile on his face and a positive attitude toward his co-workers. She thought some of his co-workers were jealous of him because he was going back to school to get his MBA, which would mean he would eventually get a big raise and a promotion. She didn't know whether to tell him what was going on behind his back. She was also a bit ashamed that she hadn't said anything when people were slamming this guy.

Lawrence froze. He recognized the caller's voice. This person worked down the hall from him, in computer services. He had no doubt whom she was referring to. She was talking about him! He listened to this station because it revealed "how people really are." Now, what he was listening to was how he really was, at least as far as some others saw him.

As Lawrence turned onto the avenue where his office was located, the hosts were saying it was "too bad" co-workers were acting that way, but they had to wrap up the show. They encouraged the caller to "talk to the man." Then, in their talk-show wisdom, they summed up the complaints they had heard during this hour as proof that "the people we work with are basically the same people we went to high school with, only older, uglier, bolder, and meaner." This line was accompanied by the standard laugh track, and then the show ended.

But for Lawrence, the day was just beginning.

Communication of Self in the Workplace

In this chapter, we examine the relationship of communication to our work *identities* and the concept of *power*. As Lawrence learned, what we say and do in the presence of others largely determines who we are, or our *identities*. In turn, our identities determine how much *power* we have to influence others and outcomes. To develop positive identities and have influence at work, you need to understand the role verbal and nonverbal communication plays in how others see you. As you will learn, issues of identity and power are related to how *conscious* we are of our presentation of self in verbal and nonverbal communication situations.

Lawrence's experience shows us that other people's perceptions of our verbal and nonverbal communication create our identity at work. *Identity* is the response we get from others to what we say (verbal communication) and do (nonverbal communication) (Mead, 1934; Goodall, 1983; Wood, 1997). In this way, we are only partially in control of our identity at work. Those with whom we exchange verbal and nonverbal communication have a great deal of impact on our workplace identity. To gain more personal control over others' perceptions of our identity requires us to become more conscious of our communication.

How can we do that? By becoming more *aware* of the influence of our verbal and nonverbal communication in the workplace and choosing *strategies* for improving our image. Table 5.1 shows the connection between awareness and identity in the conscious communicator.

Developing Awareness in the Workplace

We need to *become more conscious of our overall verbal and nonverbal impact in the workplace*. We need to pay closer attention to our choice of words, selection

Verbal and Nonverbal Awareness Continuum

Unaware	Moderately Aware	Aware
Communicator uses: • unclear, ambiguous phrases. • no strategies for upward and downward communication. • exclusive, disconfirming messages. • unsupportive messages. • communication that detracts from professional credibility. • communication that displays little or no awareness of the relationship between power and words. • communication that displays no awareness of gender differences in talk.	Communicator: • uses a mixture of clear and ambiguous phrases. • attempts to apply upward and downward communication strategies. • uses a mixture of inclusive and exclusive messages. • attempts to use supportive messages. • uses communication that doesn't detract from professional credibility. • is aware of relationship between power and words. • applies knowledge of gender differences in talk.	Communicator uses: • clear, strategically unambiguous phrases. • strategies for upward and downward communication. • inclusive, affirming messages. • supportive messages. • conscious verbal communication that enhances professional credibility. • communication that demonstrates the relationship between words and power. • communication that displays a respect for the differences in the way men and women communicate.

Mindless . . . . Mindful

Table 5.1
Awareness Continuum

of behaviors, appearance, and style of dress. We need to actively seek out feedback from others to our communication in interviews, interpersonal exchanges, group and team meetings, and presentations. By showing others that we are interested in their responses to what we say and do, we encourage them to share information with us about our identity at work.

We also need to become better *monitors* of the influence our behaviors have on others. By **monitoring,** we mean two things:

- Checking the accuracy of your perceptions regarding how the messages you believe you sent were actually interpreted.
- Questioning the cultural and contextual factors that may lead to different perceptions about your communication.

Monitoring Our Assumptions About Communication

It may seem odd that we are often our own worst enemy when it comes to communicating mindfully at work. But the truth is that too often we operate mindlessly, allowing our stereotypes, cultural biases, assumptions about the meanings of words, and routine perceptual filters to control our daily communication at work.

Most of us operate mindlessly because we live as if *our assumptions about verbal and nonverbal meanings are essentially the right ones*. For example, we assume that we were reared the right way, that our religious and political beliefs are the right ones, and that our thoughts and feelings about what others say are justified. It is as if we assume that our life—which is also to say our culture, gender, age, socio-economic level, and race—is the center of the known universe, and that everything and everyone essentially revolves around us. The problem with this belief in our rightness is that it may lead us to treat others unfairly or create inequity in the workplace.

The Principle of Workplace Equity

Equity is the principle that we should be treated fairly by others and, in turn, should treat them fairly. Think of equity as the golden rule that governs the *choosing* and *creating* of verbal strategies for workplace communication.

The concept of equity is based on four key assumptions (Walster, Walster, and Bershied, 1978; Wilson, and Goodall, 1991):

1. *People work for rewards.* **Rewards** are what people derive from their work (money, identity, power, support, companionship, a skill set) in relation to what it costs them (physical labor, mental and emotional stress, free time, time away from family, subordinating personal goals, dealing with difficult people, harassment). When there is a balance between what they get out of going to work and what it costs them to be there, they feel a sense of equity. Some days are better than others, but overall there is a sense of fairness, of justice, of balance in their work lives.

2. *People seek empowerment.* When people believe they are being rewarded fairly for the job they do, they tend to do a good job and feel good about the work they perform. Workers who feel a sense of equity also tend to feel a sense of empowerment. **Empowerment** is the process of enabling and motivating employees, mainly by removing roadblocks, which builds feelings of personal effectiveness and control. When employees feel they are heard and their input is valuable, their performance improves. They actively seek better ways to perform tasks and get along with people because, in the end, what is good for the business is good for them.

3. *People become stressed when they feel they are being treated unfairly.* When people find themselves in a state of inequity, they become stressed. Inequity may be caused by unequal pay for doing the same job as others, unfair treatment by co-workers or bosses, or a sense that the company doesn't care about the welfare of the worker as much as the worker cares about the welfare of the company. The stress brought on by feelings of inequity impairs the job being done. The more inequity that is felt, the more stress is experienced, and the worse the job becomes.

4. *People experiencing stress will try to restore equity.* When people experience stress brought on by feelings of inequity, they will try to restore equity in one of three ways: (a) *seeking mental equity* (making excuses for the bad treatment, forgiving the wrongdoer, assuming an attitude of moral or intellectual superiority); (b) *seeking actual restitution* (doing less work, slowing down the work of others, stealing property); or (c) *seeking narrative equity* (talking badly about the workplace, engaging in gossip and rumors designed to lessen the influence of the perceived wrongdoer, telling "workhate" stories).

In many ways, the equity principle can be applied directly to choosing communication strategies in the workplace. Your overall goal should be to select strategies that encourage others to treat you equitably, and that demonstrate your interest in treating others equitably.

Making Conscious Choices About Verbal Communication

Making conscious choices about communication is a central way in which you can become a better workplace communicator. It also is a way to improve your communication skills at work. Why? Because most people's verbal communication at work can suffer from seven types of problems:

- A lack of clarity or a misuse of ambiguity.
- An inability to distinguish communication strategies for upward or downward communication in the organization.
- A failure to distinguish between inclusive (affirming) or exclusive (disconfirming) message strategies.
- A failure to distinguish supportive from nonsupportive messages.
- An inability to conceive of verbal communication as a way of enhancing professional credibility.
- Lack of awareness of the relationship of our words to power.
- Lack of awareness of gender differences in talk.

In the following sections we describe in more detail each of these challenges to verbal communication in the workplace.

Clarity and Ambiguity

Clarity means providing messages in the clearest, least ambiguous way. **Ambiguity** means expressing oneself in terms that are unclear or open to multiple interpretations. One of the most frequently given pieces of advice for the workplace is to communicate *clearly*. As you learned in Chapter 2, the underlying theory of communication informing this advice is the *information transfer* model. The idea, simply put, is that if a sender can find the clearest, least ambiguous way to say something, the chances are greater that the receiver will hear and understand it as it was intended. The problem with this conception of communication is that regardless of how clear the message may be, people still interpret the meanings of words differently.

Does this mean that clarity shouldn't be a goal of effective communication? Absolutely not. What it does mean is, even if you choose and plan a message that you think is clear, your audience may not hear exactly what you communicated. Assume that *miscommunication* is likely, and ask for feedback on what message your listener actually heard. When you behave this way, *you gain power over the meanings others attribute to your communication.*

Tips for Communicating Clearly

- *Clarify the received messages to avoid misunderstandings.* Have you ever missed a meeting because you wrote down the wrong date or time? You may have jotted down "Tuesday" under the assumption that it was *next* Tuesday, not *this* Tuesday, only to find that you were wrong. To avoid misunderstandings, check the accuracy of what you think you heard rather than assume you are right.

- *Avoid abstraction.* The goal should be to reduce possible misunderstandings by becoming more specific in your language usage. Instead of saying "We've got a problem; we need to talk," which may set off alarms for your co-workers, say instead "We have a problem with the email system this morning, so we'll need to call a meeting to exchange ideas about getting it fixed." Remember, the closer your language gets to representing the *specific* reality you are trying to describe, the less abstract it will be.

- *Be careful of your use of jargon.* Every organization, profession, age group, and culture develops its own verbal shorthand known as "jargon." Used inside of the group, these terms save time. Outside the group, these terms are often incomprehensible, which only increases the likelihood for misinterpretation or misunderstanding. One of the considerations you have any time you select a goal for a message is to adapt your language usage to the needs and expectations of your audience or listener.

- *Avoid the use of inflammatory language.* Too often we punctuate our workplace communication with expletives, harmful expressions, or words that demean the character, efforts, or abilities of others. When this happens, conflict often occurs. If it occurs during an ongoing conflict, the conflict tends to escalate.

- *Avoid cultural and gender biases in everyday speech.* Many of the words and expressions we use are culture specific, and very often our style of speaking (and listening) is gender specific. For example, the statement "That dog don't hunt" may communicate clearly in Alabama, but its meaning will

(continued)

probably be lost on someone from Japan. Similarly, gender and communication specialists often distinguish between men's tendency to communicate in a "reporting" style (e.g., "I'm just telling it like it is") and women's tendency to use a "rapport-building" style (Tannen, 1990). Taking gender and cultural differences into account is an important element of becoming a more mindful communicator in the workplace.

Upward and Downward Communication

A nationwide survey of employees who have changed jobs points to a correlation between employee turnover and supervisor relationships. The majority of those surveyed cited a bad supervisor, not low pay, as the main reason for job change (*Greensboro News and Record,* May 30, 2000). Our guess is that we would find poor communication skills at the core of the breakdown in the supervisor/employee relationship.

Although a number of organizations have flattened hierarchical structures and empowered employees, most companies still equate *hierarchical position* within a company with power. Put simply, the higher up you are on the organizational ladder in terms of title, position, seniority, or salary, the more authority you have to exert influence on those whose position is understood to be hierarchically lower. As you learned in Chapter 3, power that is associated with position in an organization is referred to as *legitimate* power.

In everyday communication, power among levels of legitimate authority in organizations is greatly influenced by choices made about the style and content of talk. This means that *how you choose to speak to organizational superiors* (anyone higher than you on the ladder) *and subordinates* (anyone lower than you on the ladder) *can determine how they respond to your identity, requests, directives, and commands.* Speech used with organizational superiors is called **upward communication.** In general, the following communication choices tend to enhance employees' power and identity with superiors.

- Balancing politeness with a clear task orientation.
- Balancing friendliness with respect and deference to authority.
- Balancing self-interest with company needs.
- Asking for feedback on the accomplishment of tasks.
- Avoiding sexist, racist, or classist remarks.

Speech used with organizational subordinates is called **downward communication.** In general, the following communication choices tend to enhance employees' power and identity with subordinates:

- Listening openly to employees' communication.

- Responding honestly to inquiries and requests.
- Asking for information prior to evaluating a situation or problem.
- Providing feedback on tasks.
- Avoiding sexist, racist, or classist remarks.
- Balancing personal and professional respect with a task orientation and accountability.

Inclusive and Exclusive Messages

Organizations are *cooperative* settings. To work usually means to work with other people, using communication to coordinate objectives and activities and to share meanings. For this reason, your identity at work is derived from generalized observations about how you deal with people. Are you open to the ideas of others? Do you seek feedback? Are you interested in what others think and feel about issues? Do you share credit (or blame)?

Evaluations such as these reflect what communication scholars refer to as "inclusive and exclusive" message strategies. The basic idea is that how you treat others at work is part of an overall goal you have for using talk in your life. In political terms, one way to conceive of the difference is to think about *democratic* versus *autocratic* strategies. **Inclusive message strategies** are democratic because they reveal your interest in fitting in with the group or business culture, taking into account the thoughts and feelings of others, soliciting contributions from others, and actively valuing differences in opinion as a way of maximizing the available information needed to carry out a task. Examples of inclusive strategies include:

- Actively coordinating your goals with co-workers' goals.
- Asking for and being willing to give feedback about tasks.
- Soliciting the opinions of others on a project.
- Avoiding seeking sole credit for good ideas or work.

By contrast, **exclusive message strategies** reveal an autocratic communication style. Exclusive strategies are revealed in a "me first" pattern of behavior. Examples of exclusive strategies include:

- Seeking individual credit for ideas or work.
- Requiring compliance from others.
- Attempting to forge close allegiances with selected others who can advance your personal goals or career (often without feeling any equitable obligations or sense of reciprocity).
- Pitting one group or person against another.
- Demonstrating a lack of interest in the opinions of others, particularly others whose opinions or background may be different from your own.

We *choose* to behave inclusively or exclusively. As a result, others evaluate our patterns of behavior accordingly. Those persons who reveal an inclusive pattern tend to find that others are willing to work with them to achieve goals, to affirm preferred identities, and to cooperate with them in order to accomplish tasks. They tend to be more integrated into formal and informal communication networks, thus improving their opportunities to gain and give feedback. They tend to be valued as team players by managers and co-workers. By contrast, persons who reveal an exclusive pattern tend to find themselves more isolated from others in the workplace, which often translates into feeling less connected to formal and informal networks. Because they are not interested in the opinions of others and do not seek feedback, they leave themselves, their motives, and their actions open to suspicion, misinterpretation, and criticism. As a result, those who use exclusive message strategies tend to have less influence in the workplace and less control over interpretations of their identities.

Confirming and Disconfirming Messages

People are sensitive to the responses others give to their talk. One way in which we monitor our work identities is by evaluating the responses we get as being either *confirming or disconfirming*. Confirming responses support and enhance the identities we seek; disconfirming messages deny or harm our identities. Examples of *confirming messages* include:

- "I appreciate the work you did on this project."
- "I think that is a great idea!"
- "You are a wonderful employee."

Using the equity principle discussed earlier, you can see how positive, confirming messages influence co-workers, subordinates, and superiors to reciprocate. Confirming messages may also inspire them to repeat exemplary performances, or even encourage them to believe they are capable of higher qualities of work. By contrast, disconfirming messages attack the very heart of workers. Examples of *disconfirming messages* include:

- "I can't believe anybody in this company would do such a stupid thing!"
- "This is incompetent work."
- "I'll never forget that you made this mistake."
- "I can't believe I ever trusted you to carry out this task."
- "You are a fool!"

Using the equity principle, you can see what is likely to happen when disconfirming messages are given to co-workers, subordinates, or superiors. There is a strong likelihood that the targeted individual will retaliate by seeking some form of restitution for the perceived harm done to her or his identity.

So how should you communicate verbally to persons who have made mistakes on the job? When engaging in corrective communication, it is important to *limit the discussion to the task and not attack the person*. Whenever possible, frame the error within a more general statement that affirms the worker's identity. In this way, you separate the mistake from the identity of the person who made it. In this way, you inspire others to see that you treat people fairly and responsibly on the job. As you can imagine, these verbal choices will also enhance perceptions of *your* identity.

That said, it is also sometimes the case that emotions get the best of us. When stressed, many people say or do things they later wish they hadn't. Another important form of verbal communication in any workplace is the *sincere apology*. Equity may be restored when a sincere apology is given.

Supportive Versus Nonsupportive Messages

Closely related to inclusive and confirming message strategies are the mindful goals of using communication to provide support for others. As we have pointed out, because the workplace is a cooperative setting, people value other people who try to support them. **Supportive messages** communicate concern and respect for others and indicate cooperation. Supportive messages include:

- Offering to help out on a project.
- Listening.
- Doing nice things for your co-workers.
- Showing respect for others' views and feelings as well as for the general condition of the workplace.
- Demonstrating concern for the welfare of co-workers.

By contrast, the use of nonsupportive messages is closely related to exclusive, disconfirming communication. **Nonsupportive messages** are associated with an inflated ego and self-centeredness. They communicate disrespect of others and a lack of cooperation. Nonsupportive messages include:

- Appearing aloof and behaving in a superior manner with co-workers.
- Refusing to be of assistance on a project when asked.
- Withholding information.
- Not listening.
- Disrespecting others and the condition of the workplace.
- Lacking concern for the welfare of co-workers.
- Not being a team player.

Individuals who choose to be supportive in their dealings with others at work tend to encourage others to treat them equitably in return. Individuals who behave in nonsupportive ways also encourage a sense of equity from others: unsupportive behavior tends to reap more unsupportive behavior. In terms of constructing an identity in the workplace, supportive messages tend to encourage others to affirm your identity and, at the same time, provide *corrective* feedback when necessary. After all, being supportive sometimes means pointing out ways that communication may be improved or errors corrected. In this way, support does not always mean affirmation. Supportive messages, however, go a long way toward encouraging others to help you obtain your goals.

Enhancing Personal and Professional Credibility

One of the first theorists of human communication, Aristotle, pointed out in his classic treatise *The Rhetoric* that the goal of all public talk should be the improvement of one's *character* with one's peers. Today, we label that goal for talk as the enhancement of personal and professional credibility.

Credibility refers to the *authority* and *trust* listeners or audiences give to speakers. If we believe that an individual is a good person, knowledgeable about a topic, and trustworthy, we tend to pay more attention to what he or she says. We also tend to be more easily influenced by the person. For this reason, advertisers promote their products with testimonies given by credible spokespersons. Today, credibility is often associated with celebrity, which may be a cultural by-product of living in a media-influenced age. However, the fact remains that we are persuaded most by those persons we find credible.

In the workplace, employees find that by developing their own personal and professional credibility they also influence others to affirm their identities. Credibility is a goal for communication that is enhanced by:

- Becoming *informed and knowledgeable about the work* assigned to you, which includes being an information resource for others and providing people with the information they need, when they need it.
- Behaving in a *trustworthy* manner by keeping secrets and confidences, looking for the good in situations and others, and not spreading gossip and rumors.
- Being *open, honest, and authentic* in your dealings with everyone.
- Demonstrating that you are *capable of being a friend* as well as a co-worker by showing humane respect, regard, and caring for others on the job.
- *Doing what you say you will do*, which means becoming reliable as a person and as a professional.
- Graciously *accepting criticism and corrective feedback from others*, and using these messages to improve your performance.
- *Accepting personal responsibility for your actions and not blaming others* for your problems, challenges, or mistakes.

Verbal Communication and Perceptions of Power

Communication is the basis for our identity, and it is also the source of our personal and professional **power.** Forms of *organizational and institutional* power are tied to one's status and hierarchical position at work. For example, a manager has the power to organize work teams, set objectives, and evaluate workers. Similarly, forms of *cultural* power are derived from an individual's wealth, perceived attractiveness, or family lineage.

But there is a form of power that is not tied to status or cultural hierarchies and that is directly related to communication. This is the *communication* power that refers to *the perception others have of your ability to use words and actions to obtain workplace results that would not have occurred otherwise.* In this way, communication power is a *rhetorical* or *narrative* quality that is attributed to you by listeners, audiences, co-workers, or managers because of what you say and do.

Gendered Talk

Research has shown that women and men can differ in the ways they tend to communicate, construct meanings, and derive implications or evaluations from communication (see Tannen, 1994; Wood, 1997, for review). For this reason, we say that all talk is "gendered." **Gendered talk** refers to the differences between the ways men and women tend to communicate.

Generalizing about gendered talk in the workplace is difficult. For every generalization there are clear exceptions to the rule. However, research studies have shown the following to be true (Wood, 1997):

- Women generally use talk to *build rapport* in relationships; men generally use talk to *make reports* to others.
- Women's style of talk tends to be more *expressive* (rich with words intended to deepen understanding and meaning); men's style tends to be more *instrumental* (clipped responses, intended to provide direction).
- Women's communication style tends to be more *tentative;* men's style tends to reflect more *certainty.*
- Women tend to use talk to *create and maintain relationships;* men tend to use talk to *gain control over situations and others.*

For reasons that should be clear from the above list of gendered differences, we suggest that women and men can improve their communication with each other in the workplace by meeting one another halfway. Here are some suggestions you might find helpful:

- Avoid the assumption that your intentions or meanings are clearly shared.
- Avoid talk that stereotypes another's talk or that connotes inferiority due to gender (e.g., "Only a woman would…" or "Guys always think…").

- Think about the gender implications of communication *prior* to speaking.
- Be willing to switch styles when the situation calls for it.

Your workplace identity is based on the responses you get from others to what you say and do. However, you can have some control over how others respond to you by making wise choices about message strategies designed to help you accomplish your personal and professional goals. By communicating inclusively and affirming others' identities and efforts, by showing support for others, by striving to become credible as a person and as a professional, by being more aware of cultural and gender biases in talk, you limit the possible negative responses others can make. You gain greater control over their perceptions of you, and of your chances of reaching your goals with their help.

Verbal Lie Detectors

Do you know when someone is telling the truth? Here are some tips that may help you detect when someone is trying to deceive you.

- Response time—the time between the end of a question and the start of a reply. Liars take longer and hesitate more.
- Distancing—not saying "I," but talking in the abstract (for example, liars might say, "One might believe...").
- Uneven speech—stuttering while trying to think through the lie. Liars might also suddenly talk quickly, attempting to make a sensitive subject appear less significant.
- Gap filling. Liars are too eager to fill in the gaps of conversation. Liars keep talking when it is unnecessary, as if a silence signifies that the other person does not believe them.
- Raised pitch. Liars raise their voice unnaturally. Instead of the pitch dropping at the end of a reply, it is lifted in the same way as asking a question.
- Message insecurity. Liars are unsure of their message, which leads to an increase in stuttering, slurring, and Freudian slips.

From Adrian Furnham, 1999, "Gesture Politics," *People Management*, 6, 52.

Nonverbal Communication and Perceptions of Meaning

Nonverbal communication is the natural counterpart of verbal communication. Nonverbal means "without words," and nonverbal communication refers to all of the resources beyond what you say that contribute to the meaning of a message. Unless you are physically removed from your listeners or audience (e.g., talking on the phone or using email), what is interpreted as meaningful in your interaction will be informed by what you say *and by how you look when you say it*. Researchers have found that about 65–70% of the social meaning of communication is conveyed nonverbally (Birdwistell, 1970; Philpott, 1983). Interestingly enough, researchers have also established that if there is a discrepancy between what you say and how you look when you say it, most listeners will believe your nonverbal actions over your verbal ones (Andersen, 1998).

In this section we want to examine the sources of nonverbal communication in business and professional contexts. Throughout our discussion, we want you to understand that while "actions speak louder than words," in most cases actions work with words to produce meanings. The discussion in this section centers around the nonverbal communication that is commonly accepted within corporate America. If you find yourself dealing with other cultures, you should familiarize yourself with the nonverbal expectations and taboos of those cultures.

Your Workspace

In Chapter 2 we discussed the importance of keeping your work area neat, free from clutter, and clean. We also stressed the importance of *artifacts*, the personal and professional items that mark a territory as our own. We encourage the use of artifacts that attest to your accomplishments—decorating your office space with diplomas, certificates, and awards. We discourage the display of personal items, and under no circumstances should you display anything that has suggestive sexual content. Our basic message is to treat your workspace as an *extension of your professional self*. Become conscious of the way your office area and artifacts *communicate* to others.

Tips for Creating the Optimal Workspace

- Keep displays of your personal life to a minimum. One family photograph is enough. Don't clutter your office with items that may suggest you'd rather be doing something else.
- Prominently display diplomas, awards, certificates, and other professional accomplishments.
- Clear your desk and empty your trash prior to leaving work for the day.
- Keep personal collections at home. Your workspace is not the area to show off your car magazines, beanie babies, McDonald's toys, or collection of cat photographs.
- Be aware of the messages you are sending when you display personal items in your workspace.

The books highlighted below will help you to create the optimal workspace. Putting time and effort into the appearance of your workspace sends a clear non-
(continued)

verbal message to those around you that you are in control and ready for whatever needs to be done.

Taming the Office Tiger by Barbara Hemphill (Kiplinger Books, 1996). This book is considered by many large companies, including 3M and Xerox, to be *the* book on organizing your workspace. *Taming* provides tips for managing a filing system, organizing your computer, using to-do lists, and knowing when to use piles. It also provides a list of essential tools for any office and tips for managing your voice mail.

Practical Feng Shui at Work by Simon Brown (Barnes & Noble Books, 1998). Feng Shui is based on the principal that everything has energy, and how you arrange your space either enhances or detracts from your energy. By positioning your desk and other materials in the optimal place, you can create an office that energizes you and helps you achieve your goals. Feng Shui also addresses issues like clutter, which practitioners believe saps your energy and ability to accomplish tasks and move forward.

Clothing and Personal Appearance

You've undoubtedly heard the expression "You never get a second chance to make a good first impression." But have you ever asked why that is true? The answer is that most humans make initial evaluations of each other based on stereotypes, and stereotypes are largely derived from the *size and shape of our bodies*, the *clothing* we wear, and their perceptions of our level of *physical attractiveness* (Andersen, 1998). Of course we know we should avoid stereotyping, and that evaluations made on the basis of stereotypes can be wrong, but the fact is that most of us engage in it routinely every day. There is no place in our lives where stereotyping is more evident that in the formation of initial impressions. According to uncertainty-reduction theory (Berger and Calabrese, 1975), nonverbal cues are read and interpreted against stereotypes to reduce the uncertainty in initial interactions. In other words, as tennis star Andre Agassi puts it, "image is everything."

What does research about personal appearance teach us? For one thing, our culture values and rewards people who are tall, physically fit, appropriately dressed, well groomed, and physically attractive (Andersen, 1998, p. 31). Anyone who has watched television commercials can attest to the fact that the sale of body-building equipment, makeup, perfumes and colognes, clothing and hair styles, beer, and even soft drinks is dependent on the success with which the ad communicates messages of success, popularity, and happiness. Commercials rarely stress the intrinsic worth of being healthy, fashionable, or fit (Jhally, 1997). We live in a postmodern world that glorifies images rather than substance.

In business and professional settings, the norms for our cultural ideals also apply. Every few years, one of the major TV news programs does a segment on job interviews. Invariably, these shows pit a physically fit, well-groomed, attractive, and well-dressed applicant against an overweight, sloppily dressed, unattractive, and unkempt applicant. Both applicants have resumes reflecting exactly the same work experience and qualifications. Not surprisingly, the attractive applicant is consistently hired. The unattractive applicant is treated rudely and is rejected on the basis of appearance. Noted communication theorist Peter Andersen points out that "appearances can be deceiving, but that fact is almost beside the point. A communication perspective recognizes that subjective impressions by receivers are all that really matter" (1998, p. 31).

What should you do to "dress for success" on the job? Ethnographic studies have shown the advantages of researching the physical appearance, clothing, and hairstyles associated with people doing the job you are applying for (Goodall, 1989; Goodall and Phillips, 1985). Before applying for a position with a firm, ask for a company tour. Pay attention to how people dress. Ask yourself if your appearance and clothing choices are a match for this organization. In most cases you will find that human resource people and managers tend to hire people who fit the attitude, appearance, and style of their company (Wilson and Goodall, 1991). Even in the "business casual" workplace, there are limits; going beyond those limits may send the wrong signal.

Once you are on the job, become more conscious of how your clothing choices fit into the norms of the organization. Unless you are interested in making a personal statement (perhaps at some risk to your career), it is a good idea to opt for a look that doesn't attract too much attention. As a headhunter once explained it to us, "I tell my clients that the most subversive people in any organization tend to be the most conservatively dressed. That way they can be subversive without looking like revolutionaries. The difference is whether they really want to change things, or just look like they do."

Tips for Dressing Successfully in the Workplace

- Never dress noticeably better than your boss or your peers. Your boss may wonder if you are moonlighting or after his or her job. Your peers may feel you are trying to show them up.
- Savvy business people understand that for men, casual dress means khakis or, depending on the organization, nice jeans with a nice golf shirt. Women have a harder time achieving a "business casual" look. Women

(continued)

should dress down on business casual days and achieve a casual look without trying to look like "one of the boys." Avoid tight jeans, shorts, and other apparel that works against your ability to be taken professionally.

+ Jewelry should be kept to a minimum for men and women. Too much jewelry can be distracting and, in some cases, physically limiting. The wrong kind of jewelry can alienate people. The reality is that everything in the competitive workplace counts. Our goal here is to simply make you aware.

Voice

The human voice is a powerful instrument of meaning. Learn to listen critically to how you speak, and monitor the match between your vocal characteristics and the attitude, intention, or emotion you want to convey. Such monitoring is vital to communication effectiveness.

How many times have you heard or used the expression "It's not *what* you said; it's *how* you said it"? What came across was not the words that were spoken, but an *interpretation* of the words derived primarily from the sound of the voice, or what communication theorists call *paralanguage*. Paralanguage is a powerful form of nonverbal communication because it conveys to listeners a communicator's *attitude, intentions,* and *emotions*. Consider the following list of sources of paralanguage in light of your own experiences responding to the meaning of others.

+ *Pitch* (is the sound of the voice high or low?)
+ *Tempo* (is the message delivered rapidly or slowly?)
+ *Intensity* (what words are vocally accented, or spoken softly or with particular emphasis?)
+ *Range* (the ability of the speaker to vary the pitch, tempo, and intensity of what is expressed verbally)
+ *Resonance* (richness or weakness of tone)
+ *Volume* (the loudness or softness of the voice)
+ *Articulation* (the precision with which words are spoken)
+ *Rhythm* (the relative flow and punctuation of the voice)
+ *Pause* (the frequency and duration of silences between words, phrases, sentences)
+ *Dysfluency* (is the message punctuated by expressions such as "er," "um," "you know," and "like"?)

Overall, these sources of paralanguage tell us a lot about the attitudes, intentions, and emotions we use to construct what we call the *meaning* of a message. Consider, for example, how we determine if someone is enthusiastic about a project or nervous about doing a presentation. Or whether someone we asked to carry out instructions will actually do so. In all of these cases, our evaluation is based on:

- Articulation and tempo of the voice.
- Relative authoritative resonance we hear.
- Smoothness or interruptions in flow present in the rhythm of delivery.
- Too many or not enough pauses.

How we speak shapes how others interpret our messages.

There is a *caveat*. Although all of us believe we can evaluate a person's voice with great accuracy, there are important *cultural* and *gender* differences that have been revealed by research. For instance, men who use a wide vocal range and often vary their pitch may be perceived as feminine and aesthetically inclined, whereas women using a similar pattern are perceived as dynamic and extroverted (Richmond and McCroskey, 1995). Similarly, some women and many members of the X-generation tend to tag their sentences with vocal inflections ("uptalk") that render a declarative statement into a question. For example, "I'm having lunch with Paul? We'll talk about the project?" may be intended as two statements of fact when the vocal cues suggest they are two questions.

Body Movement, Facial Expressions, and Eye Contact

The study of body movement, including facial expressions, eye contact, and gestures, is known as **kinesics.** The specific study of the eyes as a source of communication is called **oculesics.** Together, these forms of nonverbal communication dominate the research literature and provide interesting and useful resources for the conscious communicator in business and professional settings.

Of all of the forms of nonverbal expression, the most important source of information is the *face*, and especially, the *eyes*. Research shows that we seldom manifest distinct or recognizable facial expressions when we are alone (Kraut and Johnson, 1979). But the face becomes expressive when we are with other people, and humans have learned to be very attentive to even small differences in facial expression and eye contact.

We also learn how to *manage* our true feelings using our facial expressions. Researchers have shown that as we mature, we learn to "manage facial affect" by deploying five "display rules" (Andersen, Andersen, and Landgraf, 1985; Ekman, 1978; Bugental, 1982). Those display rules are (from Andersen, 1998, p. 36):

- *Simulation*: showing feelings when we have no feelings.
- *Intensification*: showing more feelings than we actually have.
- *Neutralization or inhibition*: showing no feelings.

- *Deintensification or miniaturization*: showing less feeling than we actually have.
- *Masking*: covering a feeling with an expression of a feeling we are not actually experiencing.

Children do not learn to manifest these display rules until preschool or during their elementary years. Mastery of them doesn't occur until adulthood.

One of the negative consequences associated with failing to express our true feelings is an increase in adverse psychological reactions, feelings of stress, and disease (Buck, 1979). In the workplace, we limit the ability of others to respond when we limit our nonverbal cues. By managing our facial cues, we are depriving others of valuable communication information.

The *eyes* provide the clearest case of meaning associated with nonverbal communication. Why? Because when we talk to each other, we tend to locate the other person's self right behind the eyes. We establish eye contact to make contact with others. According to research (Kendon, 1967), eye contact performs eight potential nonverbal actions:

1. Regulates interaction by signaling turn-taking.
2. Monitors interaction by receiving information from others.
3. Signals cognitive activity because eye contact is typically broken when individuals are thinking about complex issues.
4. Expresses involvement in the interaction.
5. Reveals intimidation through intensive staring, particularly when combined with negative facial expressions.
6. Reveals flirtation.
7. Reveals attentiveness.
8. Displays the level of participative immediacy of listener involvement and attention.

Benefits of Making Eye Contact

There are seven benefits to making good eye contact. Eye contact:

1. *Inspires trust.* Looking people in the eye instantly inspires trust. Would you make a major purchase from a salesperson who didn't look you in the eye?
2. *Automatically gains confidence.* Hold a firm gaze and you will be perceived as being more businesslike, more serious, and more self-assured.
3. *Buys you time.* If you've lost your train of thought, or if you don't know what to say next, or if you've been caught off guard, eye focus is your best

weapon of defense. You'll seem deep in thought—even a bit mysterious—but can use a pause to collect your thoughts, take a deep breath, and plan your next move.

4. *Quietly keeps control.* If people in a meeting are ignoring you, talking over you, or otherwise usurping control, use eye contact to redirect them. Simply stop speaking and fix your eyes on them until they notice you (and they will). Be sure to keep a neutral expression so you don't come across as a sour-faced schoolteacher scolding pupils. Once you've regained control, hold it.

5. *Deftly wields power.* Who isn't drawn in by a silent person with a strong gaze? If your eyes aren't focused on a person, you may be giving up power. Are you silent and looking down? You may be viewed as bored or subservient. Are you looking away or out the window? You may be seen as a daydreamer.

6. *Effectively stifles stage fright.* When you focus your eyes on one person at a time for varying lengths of time, you instantly reduce a large audience to a series of one-on-one conversations.

7. *Effortlessly puts others at ease.* People on the receiving end of good eye contact benefit as well. You can help others feel at ease and open up.

Adapted from Guiliano (1999).

Researchers have also discovered that the eyes communicate through pupil dilation. Our pupils dilate (enlarge) when we are aroused, interested, or attracted to another person (Andersen, Todd-Mancillas, and DiClemente, 1980). Most people are relatively unconscious of this signal and in many cases attribute positive responses to something else—a pleasant facial expression or a nice smile.

Eye movement is a controversial area of nonverbal communication research because results have been inconsistent. However, there is a general belief that the eyes move right or left during cognitive activity, and there is a tendency, at least in males, to move the eyes to the left when employing visual or spatial right-hemisphere thought, and to look right when employing linguistic cognition.

In business and professional settings, just as in everyday life, facial expression and eye contact communicate potentially useful information about ourselves and others. In our experience as consultants, we often find that people who display positive, affirming, and inclusive facial expressions and who maintain eye contact tend to win allies and attain a reputation for being good to work with, or for. They are perceived as being easy to be around, and the general nonverbal message they seem to be sending is one of openness to, and interest in, others. How do they do this? In our experience, they are skilled in:

- Maintaining eye contact with listeners, and using eye contact as a source of information about the emotional responses of others.
- Using positive, affirming head nods to indicate listening to as well as appreciating the information being shared.
- Smiling easily and genuinely.

We tend to believe that the eyes are the source of truth about character and intention. Given that chronic liars tend to be very good at maintaining eye contact while telling lies, this is probably not as good an indicator of character as we believe it is. We also believe that smiles and affirming head nods are signs of interest, attention, and respect. However, in other cultures, such as Asian cultures, head nods merely mean that a message is being heard, not necessarily agreed with. These differences suggest that easy generalizations are probably not warranted. Nevertheless, becoming a more conscious communicator means monitoring your own and others' facial expressions and eye contact. It is important to become aware of the nonverbal messages you may be sending others with your face, eyes, and body. To do well in business and professional settings, you need to be mindful of the potential meaning of these nonverbal messages at least as much as you are mindful of your own and others' verbal content. You must also be mindful of cultural and gender differences that may affect your verbal and nonverbal communications with others.

Nonverbal Lie Detectors

Just as there are verbal indicators that you are being less than truthful, nonverbal cues may give you away. Check your nonverbal behavior for:

- Too much squirming. If you shift around in your seat, you are signaling your desire not to be there.
- Too much, rather than too little, eye contact. Liars tend to overcompensate.
- Micro-expressions—flickers of surprise, hurt, or anger that are difficult to detect.
- An increase in comfort gestures. These often take the form of self-touching, particularly around the nose and mouth.

From Adrian Furnham, 1999, "Gesture Politics," People Management, 5, 53.

Personal Space

Proxemics is the study of interpersonal space and distance (Andersen, 1998). What do we know about the relationship of nonverbal communication to spatial relationships? Researchers have identified three broad categories of meaning: territoriality, crowding and density, and personal space.

Territoriality

Humans are territorial creatures. Think about your desk in a classroom, or your room in your residence. How do you feel when someone invades your space? What do you do about it? Researchers have found that we use nonverbal communication to signal our *boundaries*, or markers of the edges of our territories (Sommer, 1969). We may leave our books or clothes on chairs or in rooms, or we may place backpacks on tables. In dating relationships, partners often leave behind personal items as if to signal to others that they are currently occupying this space, and perhaps to ward off potential intruders.

Crowding and Density

It has become a cultural cliché to say "I need my space." But in fact, research shows very clearly that this is true. When we feel crowded—in classrooms, rock concerts, or offices—we tend to become measurably stressed. In extreme cases of crowding, people have been shown to become pathological and engage in criminal conduct.

Personal Space

As we walk through life, we feel that we own a certain degree of space around us at all times. We call this area our **personal space,** and research indicates that we feel violated, uneasy, stressed, and potentially violent if anyone other than an intimate encroaches on it (Hall, 1968; Anderson, 1999). Our sense of the extent of our personal space varies from culture to culture. (What a Canadian thinks is close may seem distant to someone from Turkey.) Hall (1968) maintained that in North America we have four "zones of interaction":

+ *Intimate zone*—from the edge of our skin to about 18 inches away from our bodies. We only allow into this zone close friends, intimates, and family members.
+ *Casual or personal zone*—from about 18 inches to 4 feet away from our bodies. This is the space we reserve for most conversations and social engagements with friends and family members.
+ *Social-consulting zone*—from 4 to 8 feet. This is the zone we reserve for most business transactions with shop clerks and sales personnel, and with teachers, ministers, lawyers, and other professionals. This is also the zone we use most often in team or group meetings and with anyone with whom we want to signal a "business-only" relationship.
+ *Public zone*—8 feet and beyond. This space is reserved for public speakers, celebrities, and executives.

Most people regard these distances as almost sacred. This means that we protect them, and we regard invasions of them to be culturally, if not personally, offensive. For persons interested in becoming more conscious of their business and professional communication, it is wise to keep these distances in mind.

Touching

The study of touching as a form of nonverbal communication is called **haptics.** Researchers (Heslin, 1974) have identified five basic types of touching behavior, which we have organized below from least to most intimate.

- *Functional-professional.* This is the form of touching that we expect from physicians, massage therapists, coaches, tailors, hairstylists, and other professionals who must invade our personal space and lay hands on us to do their jobs.
- *Social-polite.* The handshake is the most obvious example of this form of casual, yet meaningful, touching. Other forms include the social hug and the pat on the back, or placing a hand momentarily on the forearm of another person.
- *Friendship-warmth.* This category ranges from the outer limits of social-polite touching to the edge of love-intimacy touching, and for this reason it is the most common and most ambiguous in our culture. As Andersen puts it "too much touch or touch that is too intimate conveys love or sexual interest, whereas too little touch may suggest coldness and unfriendliness and arrest the chance for relational escalation" (1998, p. 47).
- *Love-intimacy.* This is touching we reserve for those closest to us, and research indicates that it is unique to each person. Usually, this touching is nonsexual, but it may become sexual with the appropriate partner in the right setting. Studies show that when this type of touching occurs, the result is "increased psychological closeness and warmth" (Andersen, 1998, p. 47).
- *Sexually arousing.* This is the most personal and most intimate form of touching shared by humans. Research indicates that it is also the most arousing and most anxiety-producing form of human contact. For this reason, it requires "mutual consent, a high level of attraction, and a desire to stimulate and be stimulated by one's partner" (Andersen, 1998, p. 47).

As with other forms of nonverbal behavior in the workplace, it is important to become aware of the messages that may be communicated by touching. As a conscious communicator, you must be mindful of the potential meaning of such nonverbal messages.

Harassment and Communication in the Workplace

Thus far in this chapter we have been concerned with functional forms of verbal and nonverbal interaction. In this section we describe a *dysfunctional* form of communication that is all too common in the workplace: harassment. The Equal Employment Opportunity Commission (EEOC) tracks the following forms of harassment and workplace discrimination: race, sex, national origin, religion, age, and disabilities. Based on EEOC guidelines, harassment includes:

- Slurs about sex, race, religion, ethnicity, or disabilities.
- Offensive or derogatory remarks.
- Verbal or physical conduct that creates an intimidating, hostile, or offensive work environment.
- Creating conditions that interfere with the individual's work performance.

In the remainder of this section, we will concentrate on sexual harassment, a form of harassment that is prevalent in the workplace. Much of the information and many of the tips provided in this section can be applied to the other forms of harassment listed above.

What Is Sexual Harassment?

In the context of the workplace, **sexual harassment** is any form of sexually explicit verbal or nonverbal communication that interferes with someone's work. The Civil Rights Act of 1964, additional legislation in Congress, and federal, state, and local court decisions have addressed two types of sexual harassment:

- **Quid pro quo** ("this for that"): harassment based on the threat of retaliation or promise of workplace favoritism or promotion in exchange for dating or sexual favors. In recent years, this principle has been interpreted to refer to suggestions and innuendoes as well as explicit quid pro quo comments.
- **Hostile work environment:** harassment derived from sexually explicit verbal or nonverbal communication that interferes with someone's work or that is perceived as intimidating or offensive. It is important to note that the behavior doesn't have to be *intentional* to create or contribute to a hostile work environment. Off-hand remarks or casual displays of sexually explicit materials count. So do remarks that the sender may think of as "compliments."

Sexual harassment can occur between persons of the same sex as well as persons of the opposite sex. Although usually associated with the negative behavior and activities of men in the workplace, it may also be litigated when men are the alleged victims and women are the alleged perpetrators. The Equal Employment Opportunity Commission reports that, between 1990 and 1996, formal sexual harassment complaints jumped 150% (see http:www.eeoc.gov/stats/harass.html). Sexual harassment has become so pervasive in North American society that many for-profit and nonprofit companies, as well as most government agencies and schools, have implemented policies, mandatory seminars, and workshops to train employees in how to recognize and prevent it.

Sexual harassment, while clearly recognized as a problem in North American organizations and culture, is not viewed similarly in other cultures. Latin and Mediterranean cultures, for example, do not regulate physical contact or suggestive language usage in the workplace. Because of such differences, many intercultural misunderstandings in the workplace can occur. As we've pointed out already in this chapter, it is a good idea to understand that our assumptions about the rightness of our communication acts are largely *culturally* derived.

How Can Harassment Be Avoided?

The best defense against a sexual harassment charge is to carefully monitor your own verbal and nonverbal communication. Be courteous and polite at all times.

Take other employees' feelings into consideration when you speak to them. Recognize that women and men often respond differently to comments about appearance, suggestions about behavior or attitudes, and sources of humor.

Do not engage in sexual commentary, jokes, or banter about others' appearance or clothing. Do not bring sexually explicit photographs, magazines, objects, or calendars to your workspace. Around people you know to be especially sensitive to issues of harassment, be especially careful about your conduct. Trying to excuse yourself for an offensive statement or gesture is embarrassing and hurtful to your credibility at work; losing your job or having to spend months in litigation is far more damaging to your sense of self and career.

We all share an obligation to make the workplace a safe and productive environment for everyone. Toward this end, avoiding verbal and nonverbal communication likely to be perceived as offensive is the *only right thing to do*.

What Should You Do If You Are a Victim of Harassment?

Even though there are laws against sexual harassment, knowing exactly what you should do when you feel victimized is not always easy. One of the common problems experienced by harassment victims is the belief that either nothing will be done about it, or that saying anything about it may cost them their job (Claire, 1998). Unfortunately, both of these scenarios can occur. The machinery of the judiciary is often slow, and victims of harassment may be forced to spend months or years in court trying to gain a settlement.

This does not mean you are defenseless. Nor does it mean that you should keep quiet about harassment. What you should do is be conscious of the steps the courts have determined a victim of harassment should pursue. They are:

1. *Confront the harasser and ask him or her to stop the offensive behavior.* This advice is often the hardest to follow. If you fear the harasser, consider writing her or him a letter expressing your concerns or asking a friend to intervene on your behalf. However, it is vital to confront the person with the charge and to document the outcome. Failure to do so can result in a less viable legal position.

2. *Keep a diary in which you record the dates, times, and places of offensive or harassing actions.* In many cases, simply informing a harasser about the problem is enough to stop unwarranted comments or actions. However, if it persists, it is important to record, in as much detail as possible, further incidences of harassment. You are establishing a pattern of harassment, which is much harder for the harasser to defend against in court.

3. *Complain about the harasser within the channels prescribed for such action by the policies of your employer.* Become familiar with the policies regarding employee appeals in your organization. Follow them to the letter. Most companies ask that complaints against employees be made to a supervisor, who may then channel them to a personnel committee, union, or mediator for resolution. It is also important to decide what actions you want

taken on your behalf. Will you be satisfied if the harasser stops harassing you? Or do you feel that additional remedies are required—a public apology, a job transfer, coverage of medical expenses?

4. *File a legal complaint with the federal EEOC or with your state agency for workplace discrimination.* You are entitled to file a complaint and to legal representation. For persons who elect to pursue this option, it is a good idea to schedule a meeting with an EEOC representative to discuss your case.

Sexual harassment is a crime. It is very serious business. It doesn't matter to the courts how you may personally feel about it, or whether your words were intended to offend or be complimentary, or how other people may have responded to similar jokes, suggestions, or touching. Being labeled as a convicted harasser will likely have lifetime negative consequences. Think carefully about these consequences *before* you engage in any activity that may be perceived as potentially harassing.

Summary

This chapter explored the dimensions of verbal and nonverbal communication at work. We began by detailing the relationships among verbal communication, identity, and power. In these sections we focused on how important it is to engage in conscious decisions about verbal behavior, to monitor the effect of one's choices on others, and to be receptive to feedback about verbal communication. We then turned our attention to nonverbal communication. In these sections we focused on the powerful influences nonverbal actions have on the interpretation of meanings. We concluded this chapter with a discussion of sexual harassment as a special form of dysfunctional communication involving both verbal and nonverbal components.

COMMUNICATING IN PROFESSIONAL CONTEXTS ONLINE

Use your **Goodall Connection CD-ROM** for quick access to the electronic study resources that accompany this text. Included on your CD-ROM is access to:

InfoTrac College Edition

The World Wide Web

A demo of **WebTutor** for *Communicating in Professional Contexts*

The **Communicating in Professional Contexts Website** at the Wadsworth Communication Café. The Communicating in Professional Contexts Website offers chapter by chapter learning objectives, activities, quizzes, and a digital glossary.

The Power of Verbal and Nonverbal Communication in the Workplace

You can review and complete the following sections online at
http://www.wadsworth.com/communication_d/.

What You Should Have Learned

Now that you have read Chapter 5, you should be able to:

- Discuss how we make conscious decisions about verbal and nonverbal communication in the workplace.
- Discuss the role of monitoring in conscious communication.
- Discuss the principle of workplace equity.
- Describe the difference between upward and downward communication.
- Explain the differences between inclusive and exclusive messages.
- Discuss the differences between supportive and nonsupportive messages.
- Explain how we can use verbal and nonverbal communication to enhance personal and professional credibility.
- Describe a few types of verbal power displays.
- Discuss the differences in the ways men and women tend to communicate.
- List the types of nonverbal communication that may occur in the workplace.
- Discuss the impact of clothing and personal appearance on our professional identity.
- Discuss how eye contact affects our nonverbal communication.
- Discuss proxemics and why the concept of personal space is important to communication in the workplace.
- Discuss haptics and the types of touch that are appropriate and inappropriate in the workplace.
- Discuss the two types of sexual harassment recognized by the courts.
- Discuss ways to avoid sexual harassment.
- Describe what to do if you are a victim of sexual harassment.

Activities

The following activities can be completed online and, if requested, submitted to your instructor, under Student Resources, Activities for Chapter 5 at the Communicating in Professional Contexts Website at the Wadsworth Communication Café http://www.wadsworth.com/communication_d/.

1. Look at the area of your dorm room or apartment you use for studying, or your office, cube, or desk where you work. What nonverbal messages does your workspace send out? Are they the messages you want others to receive? Investigate the references in this book or go to the bookstore to find

resources to help you get your work area in shape. Ask for books on clutter, Feng Shui, organizing, or space management.

2. Briefly, write about a communication event that had a significant nonverbal component. The event you choose can be placed in either a professional or educational setting. What was memorable about the encounter? Did your behavior help or impair your ability to resolve the situation? What would you do differently now that you have read this chapter?

3. Spend a day of conscious, positive communication with the following goals in mind: clarity, inclusion, supportiveness. As you go through the day, be aware of how you use power and gender in your talk. Write a short essay about your experience. What did you notice? Did people respond to you differently? How did you feel at the end of your positive communication day?

Surfing the Net

Any sites referred to in the following activities are maintained under HyperContents for Chapter 5 at the Communicating in Professional Contexts Website.

1. Write a sexual harassment policy for a fictitious company. When you have finished, go to InfoTrac College Edition or the WWW and find examples of real policies. What did you leave out? What would be the result of using your policy?

2. Using the search engine on InfoTrac College Edition or the WWW, type in "gestures" as a keyword search. Look for information on offensive gestures. These could be gestures other cultures find offensive or gestures that could be considered harassing. Pick one of the resources you located and summarize the information for your class or group. Include the Web address so that your classmates can use the resource in the future.

3. Use InfoTrac College Edition or the WWW to find information on "dressing for success" for the workplace. Create a shopping list of the items that you need to dress for success. Keep in mind the type of work you will be doing and the culture you will be working in.

Key Terms

ambiguity *(120)*	hostile work environment *(140)*	proxemics *(136)*
clarity *(120)*	inclusive message strategies *(123)*	quid pro quo *(140)*
downward communication *(123)*	kinesics *(133)*	rewards *(119)*
empowerment *(119)*	monitoring *(118)*	sexual harassment *(140)*
equity *(119)*	nonsupportive messages *(125)*	supportive messages *(125)*
exclusive message strategies *(123)*	oculesics *(133)*	upward communication *(122)*
gendered talk *(127)*	personal space *(137)*	
haptics *(138)*	power *(127)*	

Breakthrough Skill:
Dealing Ethically with Verbal and Nonverbal Communication Diversity

As a professional, you will be called upon to attend meetings of professional groups or civic organizations. These groups provide us with opportunities to network, gain information about our profession or industry, and practice our communication skills.

Attend either individually or with your group a meeting of your local Toastmasters organization (or you may choose to attend another civic or professional meeting). You can use the Internet to locate meeting times and places in your community (for example, the Toastmasters International Website is http://toastmasters.org).

This is your opportunity to be a "fly on the wall." Carefully watch the public and interpersonal communication events that occur during the meeting. What verbal and nonverbal cues did you notice people using to deal with communication diversity? How did males and females differ? What cues were used to deal with cultural diversity? How did the older members of the group communicate with the younger members of the group? What cues did you find yourself using?

Take two examples from the meeting and apply the information in this chapter to the examples. How would those participating in the communication event you selected have benefited from what you have learned? Discuss your experience with the class.

Chapter Six

Information Technology and Conscious Communication

Jen's morning routine always starts out with turning on her computer. Then, while waiting for the start-up program to run, she checks her phone messages. She has learned to appreciate callers who keep their messages short and to the point. It drives her crazy when callers drone on and on, forgetting to give a return phone number or name, then requesting she call them right back.

By the time Jen finishes the chore of voice mail, her computer is up and running, and it is time to check her email messages. This morning, at least three are flagged with red exclamation marks, meaning that they are urgent. But experience has taught her that maybe one is actually important and the other two really aren't urgent at all. She'd like to give the sender the benefit of the doubt and assume he or she simply forgot to turn off the "high priority" option. Chances are, though, the urgent messages are from someone who figured that she would check the urgent messages first, thus improving her or his chances of getting a quick response.

As Jen finishes reading the urgent emails, Shakira pops her head into Jen's cubicle and announces, "Meeting in five minutes, Jen. Be sure to bring your Palm Pilot." Five minutes! What should she do first? Answer the urgent phone messages, or the urgent emails? And what about the remaining messages in her inbox?

When Jen picks up her Palm Pilot—the electronic, personal digital assistant (PDA) that the company encourages employees to use for making notes and linking with word processing and calendar programs to save time and hopefully money— she realizes that she has begun to resent it and the other forms of technology invading her life. These days, her Palm Pilot, email, cell phone, desktop computer, and voice mail ensure that she is never very far from communication with co-workers, clients, suppliers, friends, and family. Heading out the door, she thinks, "Welcome to another day in information technology hell."

This chapter is about information technology and conscious communication in the workplace. Our aim is to help you begin thinking about information technology as a communication tool and improve the way you use it. To begin, we ask you to imagine yourself as Jen. Given how much your life is probably already shaped by some of the same kinds of pressures and challenges of information technology that she faces, this shouldn't be too hard. Now imagine that your aim in reading this chapter is to *gain more control over your time* by making better use of technology to communicate in the workplace. Accordingly, we will focus on *improving the results* you get from initiating and responding to technologically mediated messages.

We begin by framing our discussion of technology as an extension of what you have already learned about the relationship of communication to *power*, to *gender*, and to *systems and cultures of organization*. We move on to a brief discussion of the types of information technologies currently in use in organizations, and our conscious communication approach to making better decisions about using them. We then offer a practical section on doing Web-based research.

We conclude this chapter with some words of advice about how much technology you need, and how much information about technology you really need to know.

Information Technology and Communication

We want to begin our exploration of information technology with an intriguing thesis developed by an information scientist named Dan Lacy (1995). According to Lacy, if world history is viewed from a communication perspective, the societies that communicated information the *farthest and the fastest* gained *power* and dominated each era.

For example, consider our human evolution as communicators from, as Lacy puts it, "grunts to gigabytes." Among our ancient ancestors, hunters who could gesture and grunt in ways that gained the cooperation of other hunters were able to pool their resources, hunt larger game, and better organize themselves for survival. Similarly, we can see how the invention of the Phoenician alphabet and rules for grammatical usage led to the dominance of the Phoenicians in their epoch and to the later ancient Greek construction of a system of logical reasoning. In turn, these advances led to the systematization of rules for conduct and laws for societies.

Power and the domination of a given society were not solely gained, nor maintained, by peaceful means. Roman generals and Chinese warlords used messengers to hand-deliver plans for attack to their armies, thus greatly contributing to their ability to coordinate battles. The printing press, radio, television, computers, and satellites have significantly improved the widespread distribution of information and the speed with which it can travel, and they have affected what nations or multinational corporations control our destinies. As Lacy puts it, the nation or company that can send messages the farthest and the fastest *wins*.

The Downside to Information Technology

One downside to Lacy's worldview is that there are losers in every era, those people, nations, or companies who cannot compete. They fall behind in their ability to access and process important information. They do not *learn* at the speed and from the diverse cultural sources required to maintain current knowledge and skills. These days, because information is a commodity of primary value in a global economy, the effects of falling behind in information technology have never been greater, or potentially more devastating. As Barnet and Cavanaugh (1994) expressed it, we are rapidly becoming a world made up of Global North and Global South, where those in the northern hemisphere have access to information technology and economic resources for the development and deployment of information, and those in the southern hemisphere don't. Companies with well-developed information technology systems and the economic resources to train people to use them become more powerful, and those who rely on outdated modes of accessing and processing information find they can no longer compete.

Our hope for the future is that those of us in the Global North who are privileged to have access to information technologies and economic resources will find ways to build new bridges to those societies who are less fortunate. Such humane gestures are unlikely in business, however, as global competitiveness works against any form of altruism.

But even if humane gestures triumph, simply providing the technology is unlikely to be enough. We must also provide intelligent ways of deciding what technologies are needed to carry out meaningful tasks, and what technologies are less useful or merely redundant. We must combine our ability to provide material resources with better instruction about becoming more conscious, and more ethical, in our business and professional uses of those resources. To do that means acquiring a new perspective on the relationship of *information technology* to business and professional *communication*.

Revising Our Approach to Information Technology

Do you ever feel controlled by technology? Like Jen, do you sometimes feel overwhelmed by the sheer number of messages you have to respond to? By the pressure to respond to all of them? Do these concerns interfere with your desire and your ability to respond to those messages *thoughtfully*?

When organizations provide employees with information technology resources—pagers, answering systems, computers, etc., as well as the training to use them—they do so because they believe they are empowering their workers to organize and manage work on the workers' own schedules. What they seldom realize is that they may also be contributing to the employee's sense of **information overload.** When too many forms of communication intersect at one time, we have difficulty making decisions and responding.

Of course, in a success-oriented, individualist culture such as ours, making these resources available also carries with it the implicit message that you should never *not* be working. In a television commercial for an investment-banking firm, this point is driven home. In the commercial, a police officer pulls over a car and, upon discovering the identity of its driver, suggests that instead of playing golf this afternoon, the driver should go back to the office. Why? Because last year, the driver was only in the top 10, not the top 5, of all investment bankers. The policeman pulls the golf bag out of the back seat of the car and returns to his patrol car, leaving the driver somewhat bewildered but obviously guilty. *Guilty.* Of what crime? Of not working when he *could have been.*

Increasingly, we have given up more and more of our leisure time for the allure, as well as the demands, of work. This is one reason often cited by women for leaving organizational life in order to pursue alternative careers that give them more time for themselves and their families (*Utne Reader*, 1997). Working out of the home often affords more time, and more control over the demands made on them, than does working in a company. But for some women and men opting for a work life constructed out of a home office, this often only means trading the intrusions of information technologies at work for those that now reside in the home office.

Information Technology and Gender Differences

We have learned in previous chapters that there tend to be significant differences between women and men when it comes to communication. But for a long time, researchers did not see a correlation between gender differences and perceptions or uses of information technology. Recently, however, important new questions have been asked that highlight how gender differences can be used to better understand decisions about information technology in the workplace (Geffen and Straub, 1997; Matheson, 1991; Witmer and Katzman, 1997).

Gender differences impact the introduction and diffusion of information technologies. Women tend to experience greater levels of anxiety than men do when it comes to implementing new information technologies, and user-friendliness is a larger issue for women than for men. But women tend to adopt characteristic masculine usage patterns once the technology is in place (Matheson, 1991; Geffen and Straub, 1997, p. 397).

Women tend to place information technology within a social context. They have a greater need for "a technological medium to convey 'the presence' of the communicator—her feelings and thoughts" (Geffen and Straub, 1997, p. 397). Women tend to want to express themselves in a medium that allows for greater elaboration of their reasons and feelings, whereas men tend to focus primarily on the instrumental function of mediated speech.

Men and women perceive the modes of communication differently; for example, women tend to perceive email communication as less useful than men do (Tannen, 1994b; Gefen and Straub, 1997). Women and men may have differing perceptions of the "social presence" of email. More misunderstandings may take place between women and men who communicate via email due to the different perceptions of the social meaning of words used in that technological context. This may help explain why women tend to use more graphic accents (e.g., smiles, frowns) in email than men do (Witmer and Katzman, 1997).

Organizations planning to introduce new or updated information technologies should *take into account gender differences*. Additionally, men and women should learn to recognize that differences in gender may significantly *influence perceptions of meaning associated with email*, as well as other forms of mediated speech. Marketing specialists make use of this research when putting together focus groups designed to help implement new technologies in the workplace or provide feedback to systems and software designers about user impact and usage.

Information Technology and Conscious Communication

How can we better think about, make decisions about, and use the rich information technology resources available to us? In an informal, ethnographic study conducted for this text, we considered the types of personalities typically associated with usage patterns in organizations we've consulted with. The results are displayed in Figure 6.1.

As Figure 6.1 shows, there are a range of usage patterns for information technologies based in part on the preferences for communication mode and in part by personality. At the left side of the continuum we represent those persons who are least likely to use or respond to technology: "Luddites." A **Luddite** is a person who refuses to adapt to new forms of technology. (The term comes from workers in 19th-century England who destroyed machines that they thought would threaten their employment.) Typically, people who fail to adapt to technological advances fall behind in their ability to compete successfully, so Luddite behavior is not a good choice for people who work in a business and professional environment.

In the middle of the continuum, we represent a range of users—from the compulsive personality through the employee who just tries to cope day in and day out with information overload. Employees in the middle of the continuum may try to limit the time they send and receive mediated messages, thus

LUDDITE Refuses or ignores technology	COMPULSIVE Receives and processes compulsively	RITUALIZED Receives and processes at set times during the day	COPING Tries to use technology as adjunct to communication	CONSCIOUS COMMUNICATION CHOICES:
Employee receives but does not process or respond to most electronic messages.	Employee always online or using cell phone to detriment or neglect of human contact.	Employee will receive and respond to messages *only* at prescribed times.	Employee thinks about the best channel for messages but doesn't always follow through.	Employee profoundly aware of the influences of channel on the meaning of a message.

Mindless Technological Domination - - - - - Mindful Technological Power

Figure 6.1
Conscious Communication and Technology Continuum

risking being thought rigid. Or they may try to make better-informed decisions about channels for exchanging messages but are not always able to carry through on their decisions. As you can see, the more conscious you become as a communicator, the less willing you are to allow information technologies to control your time or the *channels* you use to create, maintain, or change relationships with others.

On the far right of the continuum, you see those persons who make conscious decisions about which technology to use for maximum communication effectiveness with minimal intrusion on their lives. To become a mindful, more conscious user of communication channels means adapting our thinking about selecting appropriate channels and considering likely outcomes when selecting technology. Conscious users of technology understand the need to include relational and contextual information when communicating using technology. To reduce the possibility of misunderstanding in communication with co-workers or clients, mindful communicators may limit the amount of information shared via email and phone messages, and they may make more time for personal contact.

Ideally, the more conscious you become of the influences of technology with respect to what we know about communication on business and professional relationships, the more power you gain to define how and when you will select and use technology. When used wisely, technology is a catalyst for change. Robert H. Buckman, vice chairman of Buckman Laboratories International, states:

> *If you want to change your company, radically increase the span of communication for each individual. Let each person use a computer to communicate with anybody in the company—or anywhere else in the world—without any barriers, real or imagined.*

> *When you change a person's span of communication, you also change their span of influence—you expand their power. The more you allow each person to grow in terms of information and power, the more you grow the entire organization. (1997)*

In the following section, we provide advice about using technology to change your span of communication.

Types of Information Technologies

Huber (1990) uses two broad categories to define types of communication technologies currently available to organizations:

1. *Computer-assisted communication technologies*, including forms of image transmission (e.g., facsimile, image modems, video conference), electronic and voice mail, and computer networks.
2. *Computer-assisted decision-aiding technologies*, including online management information systems, information retrieval databases, and expert systems or programs.

In the following sections, we will describe the first type of technology, which deals directly with communication. We will discuss how to make informed communication decisions about using specific types of technology and provide tips to increase your mediated communication efficiency.

Computer-Assisted Communication Technologies

As little as 20 years ago, technology was not a word that was part of the daily lexicon, and desktop computers were considered a luxury. However, fax (facsimile) machines and phone systems were beginning to dominate offices as high-tech business solutions. Today, fax machines, while still widely used, are considered old technology. Many people use the fax as a last resort when a "hard-copy signature" is required or if the intended recipient of the message doesn't have email software that allows attachments.

As modems became faster, PCs more prevalent, and email more sophisticated, sending documents via email became an important business solution. Now, it is becoming commonplace to attend meetings by sitting in front of your "computer cam" and sharing information across a computer network with team members located hundreds, even thousands of miles away. Now that you have read Chapter 4, it should be clear how important it is, in many professional contexts, to have the ability to see the person sending the email or attending a meeting electronically. These images provide real-time clues to meanings and the context of verbal feedback. In addition, high-technology and scientific firms often use videocams to facilitate communication among members of a diverse and multilingual workforce.

Video conferencing, while becoming increasingly more widespread, has yet to catch on the way its creators had hoped. In part this is because people prefer face-to-face contact (Long, 1987), and in part it is because there are often time delays in message transmission, making the exchanges seem artificial in ways that interfere with communication.

In all of these applications, more informed choices about implementing and using technology can be made by following these conscious communication principles:

- The quality of the image is likely to convey an impression about the credibility of the sender as well as the importance of the message. Choose images that are high quality and that represent the best interests of you and your company.
- Ask whether or not anything of value is gained by using image-based transmissions of messages. For example, if diversity of your workforce means that people who do not share a common language are going to be asked to communicate, will the availability of facial images facilitate shared meaning?

Electronic and Voice Mail Systems

Voice answering systems, pagers, and emails are routinely used by almost everyone who interacts in a business and professional environment. However, not as many people are aware of how to make decisions about the communication dimensions of these channels for communication. In the story at the beginning of the chapter, Jen was unhappy when a voice message was overly long and didn't supply a name or return phone number. She also was displeased when she saw "urgent" markers by email messages that she had learned from experience were probably not urgent at all.

Making clear and conscious choices about how and when to use voice mail and email will ensure that your message is well received and acted upon. Abusing voice mail and email leaves your messages to the mercy of the delete button. Below, we offer tips for using voice mail and email effectively.

Tips for Using Voice Mail and Email

Using Voice Mail

Voice mail is any message left on a telephone answering system. Think of voice mail as a rough equivalent to a business memo.

- Be clear and concise.
- Give relevant information such as the date and time of the communication, and the name of the sender and intended receiver.

- Limit the message to two or three sentences. If additional information or clarification is needed, the receiver can call you back.
- Include the specific date and time a response is required, if necessary.
- Do not ramble or mix information or purposes.

Using Email

Email is electronic mail transmitted to or from your computer almost instantaneously anywhere in the world. Think of email as a virtual conversation rather than a long essay.

- Use short, concise statements that offer opportunities for feedback.
- Follow the assumption that each partner to an email will have at least one turn in the conversation to make a point or respond to the other person's information.
- Don't cry wolf. Don't mark every email message *urgent*. Eventually, your audience will catch on and stop reading your email.
- Invite follow-up in the form of person-to-person contact, letters, or a phone call, so that the communication partners can facilitate more detailed exchanges.
- Convey emotion. If a posted message appears to have ambiguous meanings or if it could cause an unwanted emotional response, use an "emoticon" to signal the mood or effect intended. For example, a smiley face [:)] after a sentence may signal humorous intent; a wink and smile [;)] can indicate "this is just between us," or a sense of irony; a frown [:( ] can indicate displeasure or unhappiness.
- Have easily recognized participants. Attaching a "signature file" to your emails helps recipients locate you via other communication channels—phone, fax, physical address, and virtual address via email, home page, or Web site.

What Email Is and What It Is Not

- *It isn't a novel; it is a business message.* Emails should be concise and to the point. This should help eliminate the need for follow-up phone calls or other emails to clarify what you meant.
- *It isn't a fight; it's a form of public communication.* Avoid "flaming" others with critical comments, slurs, or negative personal comments. If you have a problem with someone, resolve the problem *in person*.
- *It isn't junk mail; it's email.* Avoid sending unsolicited emails by making sure that the content is likely to be of value to the recipient. "Spam" (the Internet term for junk mail) is seldom appreciated and, after the first one from a particular source, is usually deleted unread.

(continued)

♦ It isn't a private love letter; it's a public document. There is no such thing as private email. Even if the message is deleted, it can be accessed from the hard drive or network system. For this reason, think of everything that you send as potentially readable by your boss.

Computer Networks

Computer **networks** are two or more computers that are connected either locally (within a company or building) or widely (across different geographic locations) by cable, phone lines, or satellite. Unlike email and voice mail, computer networks do not facilitate direct communication. Instead, these forms of technology are indirect facilitators of communication. Local Area Networks (LANS), Wide Area Networks (WANS), and the Internet, all facilitate the communication process. These forms of technology allow us to access files, email, the World Wide Web, and documents stored in another computer, in another room, or even in another part of the world. Perhaps the biggest impact networks have had on business and professional communication is **telecommuting:** working from your home or other remote location, away from your company's primary location, but connected by telephone, fax, and computer.

Telecommuting, commuting to work along the information superhighway, has created a number of communication challenges. How do you communicate, build relationships, deal with conflict, or solve problems with members of a team that have never met face to face? While telecommuting has certain advantages (freedom over your time and empowerment to do work your own way), the disadvantages (feeling cut off from everyday organizational life, lack of person-to-person contact, uncertainty about your place in the organization's culture) are only now being addressed from a communication perspective.

Virtual communities, where participation in the issues of the day can be more democratic and more deliberative, are springing up on the Internet and within organizations to address the feelings of isolation often associated with telecommuting. These communities bring together like-minded people or members of a team to work through problems, share ideas, and resolve conflict.

An interesting off-shoot of these communities is the **netiquette** that has emerged from their interaction. Netiquette is the term used to describe appropriate manners when participating in online discussions. The basic rule is to "think before you type and lurk before you leap" (Trenholm, 2000, p. 323). Netiquette encourages community members to:

♦ Use appropriate entry and exit rules.
♦ Check FAQs (Frequently Asked Questions) that are posted on the Web site, to avoid redundant questions.
♦ Avoid "flaming" others when you disagree with them.

Email and Chatroom Shorthand

FWIW—For what it's worth
FUBAR—Fouled up beyond all recognition
GD&R—Grinning, ducking, and running (after a snide remark)
GTG—Got to go
INAL—I'm not a lawyer (but...)
IDK—I don't know
IMHO—In my humble opinion
IYKWIM—If you know what I mean
IYKWIMAITYD—If you know what I mean and I think you do
LOL—Laughing out loud
OTF—On the floor
OTOH—On the other hand
PMFJI—Pardon me for jumping in (a polite way to get into a running discussion)
PMJI—Pardon my jumping in
RTFM—Read the "fascinating" material (usually in anger)
POS—Parent over shoulder
TIA—Thanks in advance
TPTB—The powers that be
TTFN—Ta-ta for now
ROTFL—Rolling on the floor laughing
RSN—Real soon now
SOHF—Sense of humor failure
SWALK—Sealed with a loving kiss
SPAM—Stupid person's advertisement
WRT—With respect to
WYSIWYG—What you see is what you get
YMMV—Your mileage may vary
YWIA—You're welcome in advance

Jim DeBrosse, Cox News Service, reprinted in Greensboro News and Record, *September 24, 1999.*

Video Conferencing

Often, you will find yourself assigned to a work team or group whose members may not work in the same city, state, or even country. In many cases, virtual teams rely on **video conferencing** to hold meetings or present ideas. In video conferencing, two or more participants at different sites conduct a conference by using computer networks, or audio and video equipment. With the cost of travel increasing every day, many companies are finding that video conferencing is an economical answer for providing long-distance training or bringing a company spread across many time zones together for company meetings.

However, without planning and practice, video conferencing can be confusing and intimidating. Using CCCD (choose, create, coordinate, and deliver) to plan the components of your presentation and adding in elements for video conferencing will help ensure your success. The tips below were developed with help from Diane Howard's work on video conferencing. Howard teaches students and professionals how to present information in a video conference environment.

Tips for Video Conferencing

Before You Begin

1. Reserve the video conference facilities for the day of your presentation and for one or two practice sessions if necessary.
2. Learn to use the equipment. Ask the technology support person at your company to go over all the equipment with you. Ask questions and be sure you understand how everything works. Ask someone who frequently uses the equipment to attend your practice session and give you advice for using the equipment more efficiently.
3. Determine your potential audience in advance. If possible, find out the names of those attending the conference and their affiliations.
4. Keep in mind that video conferencing is a visual medium. Therefore, *you become a visual aid.* Wear bright colors that project well on screen. Keep your hair, jewelry, and other accessories simple so they do not distract your audience. Make sure the room you are presenting in is free of visual clutter.

When Conferencing

1. Present an agenda for the meeting. This could be on a PowerPoint slide, or you could email the agenda to your audience in advance.
2. Vary the images on the screen: you, a PowerPoint presentation, back to you, other members of the team at your location (this is possible if you have a camera person at your facility or if there are multiple cameras in the room), back to you.
3. Use body language that is confident, energetic, and engaging. Just because you are speaking into a camera doesn't mean there is no audience.
4. Look into the camera! Don't forget that there are people watching. Don't walk out of camera range and continue to talk while your audience stares at a blank screen.
5. Adjust your speech and movement for the time lag that may occur between you and the remote audience. Speak more slowly than normal. Enunciate carefully. Vary the quality of your voice so that your presentation isn't flat or boring.

Information Technology and Conscious Communication

News You Can Use: Doing Web-Based Research

In addition to opening up opportunities for telecommuting and networking, another major advantage of the Internet is that it provides us with access to information quickly and relatively painlessly. However, one disadvantage is that finding and distinguishing quality information from all the rest of the stuff that is out there can be very time consuming and frustrating. In this section we want to recommend ways of using the Internet that can help you to distinguish among qualities of information available on websites. All of the websites we include are maintained and updated under Student Resources, HyperContents for Chapter 6 at the Communicating in Professional Contexts Website at the Wadsworth Communication Café http://www.wadsworth.com/communication_d/. First, some general guidelines:

- *Check out your school's library for information about search engines that are unique to your institution.* Librarians are usually the most up-to-date professionals to consult when it comes to doing research on the Internet. Many universities sponsor collaborative Internet-based research programs that allow users to electronically search professional journals, magazines, newspapers, and reference sources. In some cases, users can print entire articles and abstracts from these sources at no charge.

- *Use your school's home page to begin navigating the Internet.* Most universities and colleges in North America sponsor websites with practical links to libraries, research institutions, academic departments, and alumni and student organizations. These sites provide useful search advice and help the novice user become acquainted with what the Internet can offer.

- *Contact the Communication Institute for Online Research (CIOS) to begin your research project.* Go to http://www.cios.org/ and follow the links. This is a very easy-to-use, impressive site designed for students.

Next, we want to offer advice about finding valuable information that is posted on websites:

- The best, official information in any field of study or profession is likely to be found on the home pages of the professional organization's website. Check out the National Communication Association (http://www.natcom.org/) or the Academy of Management (http://www.aom.pace.edu/). The American Communication Association website (www.uark.edu/~aca) offers an online journal and comprehensive links to research sites associated with the communication field. For an interesting, eclectic resource, check out the Western Connecticut State University site at http://www.wcsu.ctstateu.edu/~wiss/online.htm.

- Bulletin boards and discussion groups provide formal and informal sources of information, and many sponsor archives that can be searched with keywords or topics. For comprehensive listings of available groups, see http://www.tile.net/ and http://groups.yahoo.com.

- Popular information relevant to any field of study can usually be found on the websites for commercial magazines and newspapers. They often sponsor archives that are searchable. For a good example, check out the *New York Times* online (http://www.nytimes.com/), or *Business Week* magazine (http://www.businessweek.com/), or Microsoft's online magazine *Slate* (http://www.slate.com/).

- Individual home pages can be unreliable as sources for information, but some are unique, artistic, or alternative resources. You can access them by either knowing the electronic address of the home page, or by using an Internet search engine.

- Information on any topic can be found through search engines such as Yahoo, Excite, Netscape, AltaVista, GoTo.Com, InfoSeek, or Ask Jeeves. Our personal favorite is Ask Jeeves (http://www.askjeeves.com/) because you can type in your question in natural language and the engine will provide several alternative interpretations of the meaning of your wording, each with its own set of links.

Surfing the Net for Information: A Practical Guide

1. Access a search engine and type in the most succinct keywords that you think identify the sites you want to visit. The sites will appear in a rank order determined by your keywords and the search engine's evaluators. For example, let's assume you want to find up-to-date information on ecommerce. One possible source of information is trade magazines with sites on the Internet. For our purposes, let's say you want to visit *Business Week* online. Type in "Business Week Magazine."

2. Once the relevant sites are identified, click on the site you want to visit. If the site contains a lot of graphics, it may take a while to appear on your computer screen. The *Business Week* site is professionally created, so they limit graphic content on the home page to small items that load fairly quickly. In a few seconds, you will see the entire page. Links generally appear in blue or as underlined text. To explore a topic, click on a link. Or you can use the search engine for the site to locate ecommerce information within the *Business Week* archives.

3. Let's say that a story on ecommerce is available on the *Business Week* home page. When you click the link, it takes you to Intel Corporation's site about starting ecommerce companies, complete with stories from start-ups. On the Intel site, a link at the bottom of the page takes you to a list of other information resources about ecommerce.

4. **Bookmark** the site you found. Bookmarking allows you to save the site address for future reference. Click the *Bookmarks* button on the toolbar at the top of your Web browser. Clicking the *Bookmarks* button while you are on a particular Web page automatically prompts you to add the bookmark to a folder. The next time you want to visit this site, click on the *Bookmarks* button, find the name of the Intel or *Business Week* site, and click on it.

How Much Technology Do I Need?

Often, when consulting, we encounter people who do not have the technological skills to keep up with the changes in their industry. Their lack of skills is frustrating for them, their colleagues, and their customers. However, we also regularly encounter the "techno geek," the person who has every gadget, software program, and electronic toy ever made. Sitting with a techno geek in a meeting can be quite painful as the person attempts to juggle a pager, cell phone, laptop, PDA, and other devices. As with most areas of our life, there needs to be a balance.

In our experience, the most successful users of technology are those who *pick a few tools that are appropriate for their jobs and become very proficient with the tools they selected*. What does this mean exactly? We will use ourselves as an example. We are writers. We write books, and we write articles. When we do consulting, we write reports and analyses for our clients. Many of our writing projects require graphics and special layouts and design. We also need to keep in touch with our clients on a regular basis, so we need voice mail and email.

To accomplish our tasks, we have become very proficient in using Microsoft Word, Pagemaker, a number of graphics programs, Microsoft Outlook, and the Internet. Because one of us travels to client sites and prefers to be mobile, she primarily uses a laptop. Because one of us primarily works in an office at school or at home, he prefers a desktop computer. We don't do extensive calculations, need spreadsheets, or require extensive database support. Therefore, we have not invested time or money in this type of software. However, we keep the versions of the software we do use current and our skills with them up to date.

How much and what type of technology you need depends on several factors:

- *Your business or profession*. Why spend hours or weeks learning a piece of software that you will never use? Find out which software is commonly used in your chosen field and learn it, now. If you are in accounting, you will need to be proficient with spreadsheet software. If you are a cartologist (map maker), you will need to know CAD CAM software. Learning the software now ensures that you will be able to communicate your ideas in the proper format when you need to.

- *Standards set by your industry*. Each industry differs slightly on the specific types of hardware and software that are used. For example, Word Perfect has evolved as the word processing package preferred by lawyers. It is equipped with templates and standard phrases that assist with the creation of legal forms and documents. Graphic artists and designers almost exclusively use MacIntosh computers. Microsoft Word is widely preferred in business environments. These standards have evolved over time and are slow to change. Stick with the technology that is the standard in your industry.

♦ *Amount of time you are willing to invest in learning.* "Continuous learning," "life-long learning," and "learning organizations" are phrases you will hear again and again throughout your business or professional life. There is no area of that life where these terms are more relevant than the area of technology. Technology changes every day, and it is difficult to keep up with the changes in software, hardware, and networking. Invest in and learn only those technologies you are willing to continuously use and keep up to date.

Summary

This chapter served as an introduction to technology and communication in the workplace. As we proceed through the book, we will introduce software programs and skills that are used for specific types of communication. We believe it is important to understand how technology impacts your communication in the workplace. To foster that understanding, we looked at the ways technology is used in business and professional settings and offered tips for using technology more efficiently.

COMMUNICATING IN PROFESSIONAL CONTEXTS ONLINE

Use your **Goodall Connection CD-ROM** for quick access to the electronic study resources that accompany this text. Included on your CD-ROM is access to:

InfoTrac College Edition

The World Wide Web

A demo of **WebTutor** for *Communicating in Professional Contexts*

The **Communicating in Professional Contexts Website** at the Wadsworth Communication Café. The Communicating in Professional Contexts Website offers chapter by chapter learning objectives, activities, quizzes, and a digital glossary.

You can review and complete the following sections online at
http://www.wadsworth.com/communication_d/

What You Should Have Learned

After reading Chapter 6, you should be able to:

- Provide a brief history of the evolution of technology in the workplace.
- Describe the downside to technology.
- Discuss the gender differences associated with technology.
- Explain how we can use technology consciously.
- Describe the relationship between power and spans of communication.
- Describe the two types of information technology.
- Discuss the advantages and disadvantages of telecommuting.
- Provide tips for using voice mail and email effectively.
- Discuss virtual communities and their use in the workplace.
- Walk through the process for doing Web-based research, including providing sites that you could use.
- Discuss the three elements used to decide how much technology you need in your chosen field.

Activities

The following activities can be completed online and, if requested, submitted to your instructor, under Student Resources, Activities for Chapter 6 at the Communicating in Professional Contexts Website at the Wadsworth Communication Café http://www.wadsworth.com/communication_d/.

1. You have to set up an important meeting for your group. The meeting will be Monday, October 25, in Conference Room 7 at 9:00. Each participant needs to be prepared to give a brief update on his or her progress. At the end of the meeting, you will be giving Dension, the foreign exchange student assigned to your group, a going-away party. Write an email that includes the above information.

2. You consistently receive voice mail messages from Carl that are incoherent. Whenever Carl calls, he mumbles, forgets to leave complete information, or rambles on about three or four unrelated topics. How do you address the problem with Carl?

3. You are one of the first in your department chosen for the new telecommuting project. You are excited about the prospect of working at home but are concerned that you may be overlooked for future promotions or special projects. What steps can you take to ensure that you remain a part of the company culture?

Surfing the Net

Any sites referred to in the following activities are maintained under HyperContents for Chapter 6 at the Communicating in Professional Contexts Website.

1. Your boss asked you to find information about a competitor. You need to research the company on the WWW. The company's name is InvoiceLink. Use the Internet to provide your boss with information about the company's products and history.

2. You are desperately looking for a new job. You have tried Barron's and other professional newspapers and have networked with everyone you know, to no avail. Yesterday, someone mentioned using the employment bulletin boards on the Internet. Use the Internet to find the job descriptions for five jobs in your chosen field. You can use sites like the Monster Board (http://monster.com) or Career Builder (http://careerbuilder.com).

3. Go to http://www.netlingo.com on the Internet. Familiarize yourself with the terms listed on the site. Pick three terms that you have not heard before but that you think are terms you and your classmates should know to be computer literate in the workplace. Share the terms and their definitions with your class or group.

Key Terms

bookmark *(160)*

email *(155)*

information overload *(150)*

Luddite *(151)*

netiquette *(156)*

networks *(156)*

telecommuting *(156)*

video conferencing *(157)*

virtual communities *(156)*

voice mail *(154)*

Breakthrough Skill:
Recognizing the Importance of Technology in the Workplace

We have talked about technology as an important communication tool that creates a span of communication. For this breakthrough skill development, we would like you to begin investigating the technology associated with your profession or chosen career. What software products are the standards in your industry? What computer skills do you need in order to communicate your ideas effectively? What is the learning curve associated with these skills? What steps would you have to take to become proficient?

Create a technology plan that includes:

- The type of software.
- Your current level of proficiency.

- The learning curve to reach the level of proficiency that is standard for your industry.
- The steps you need to take to learn the product.
- The classes or training available either through your current job, at your school, or at community colleges or training locations in your city.
- The benefits of learning the software now vs. waiting until you are beginning a job or looking for a job in your field.
- The costs involved in becoming a proficient user of the technology.
- The cost involved if you *don't* learn the technology.

Chapter Seven

Exploring Interpersonal Communication

As Jose sat listening to Marie, the human resource representative for Murry, Howel, and Frintz, he was amazed at how lucky he was to find a position with this company. Not only did they have great benefits; they had this incredible program for new employees. Rather than make them sit through boring presentations on the company's 401K or medical plans, they were teaching him skills he could actually use, before he even set foot into his new department.

Marie explained that their workshop would be organized around a process called CCCD, which would teach them how to choose productive communication goals, create appropriate messages, coordinate within relational communities, and deliver messages in ways that would build and strengthen their professional interpersonal relationships. Marie told them that, by the end of the workshop, everyone would have developed skills to help them succeed interpersonally in the workplace. Jose was so impressed with Marie's easy communication style and her message, he was eager to hear more.

Choosing: Strategies and Ethics for Relational Development at Work

Choosing is the process of defining the strategies and goals for your interpersonal behavior. However, before we can begin choosing strategies, it is important to look at how we use talk to create relationships with others at work. What is the "work" of talk in building professional relationships?

In a practical sense, the "creating" stage of relational communication is about how we make decisions that will guide our choices of words and actions with others in the workplace. From first impressions to last good-byes, the work we do to manage our relationships involves *balancing strategies for obtaining our goals with the ethical dimensions of workplace conduct*. This begins with first impressions.

First Impressions

How do we form first impressions of people? The term we use to describe this complex process is **perception.** Perception refers to how we process and interpret cues from a person's outward appearance, voice, and language usage.

How does perception work? According to cognitive psychologists and communication scholars (see Andersen, 1993), we use **schemata,** or mental pattern recognition plans, that "help us identify and organize incoming information" (Trenholm, 2000, p. 50). Sarah Trenholm, a communication scholar, suggests that we use three basic patterns to develop first impressions: person prototypes, personal constructs, and scripts.

Person Prototypes

We tend to characterize individuals by their physical and behavioral resemblance to an existing category of person. These categories are **person prototypes.** In everyday usage, we call person prototypes *stereotypes*. For example, we can recognize "student," "college professor," "politician," "business person," "cowboy," "artist," or "evangelist." If you can quickly form a mental representation of a type of person, you are relying on the person prototype schema.

Although stereotypes help us identify people by their relationship to our idealized images of a role or category, they also encourage us to ignore or miss important details that separate uniqueness among individuals from categorical generalizations. Because person prototypes form a basis for first impressions, they also influence how we choose to communicate with others. We tend to seek out contact with people who fit stereotypes we associate with positive images and roles, and we avoid contact with people we associate—fairly or unfairly—with negative images and roles. While it is true that you should "never judge a book by its cover," we often do.

Personal Constructs

If stereotypes represent basic patterns of person and role definition, **personal constructs** may be thought of as representing *specific evaluations we make of others based on our assessment of their personal communication habits and behaviors*. For example, we tend to evaluate others as being "hard charging" or "easygoing," as "neat and clean" or "sloppy," as "nice" or "mean."

The important thing to remember about personal constructs is that they are *our personal preferences*. Of the wide variety of clues we can pay attention to, each of us typically uses only a few to figure out others. For this reason, two people may meet a third person and come away from the interaction with different interpretations of the third person's identity and behavior.

> Marie asked the workshop group to think about five people they worked closely with on their previous job. Then they had to write the names of those five people on a piece of paper. After each name, they had to write down a series of adjectives to describe the person. Jose wrote:
>
> Kathryn—senior VP, hard-working, feminist, rigid
> Larry—account executive, sharp dresser, witty
> Eric—director of finance, bottom-line, heartless, athletic
> Rod—support staff, young, useless, trouble, slacker, black clothes
> Vikki—project leader, smart, team leader, motivating
>
> Marie asked the group to think about what their lists indicated about their personal constructs. "Do you tend to classify people by their physical or psychological characteristics? By their clothing? By their sense of humor?" she asked. Then Marie said to the group, "How might you do if others used these same personal constructs to evaluate you?"
>
> Jose noticed the first thing he wrote down was the person's job title. "I wonder," he thought, "what does it say about me that I think of everyone as who they are on the

organizational chart first, before anything else? Maybe I should get to know people first, before labeling them."

Scripts

First impressions often occur during phatic communion. **Phatic communion** is the patterned sequences of talk that we use every day. Another term for phatic communion is **scripts.** Scripts allow us to behave effortlessly, mindlessly, while we appear to be engaged in a conversation. Because we know how to act during a scripted performance, we tend to evaluate others based on their compliance with—or alteration from—our preferred lines in the script. However, we need to be careful about applying our script to others and thereby denying them opportunities for creativity and uniqueness of expression. To counter this powerful influence, we need to become more mindful during these scripted performances.

> Marie asked the group to think about their scripts. Jose had to laugh when he thought about where he previously worked. He always found it funny that, every day, his co-workers walked through the office saying "Hi, how are you?" to everybody, knowing full well no one cared. And, he thought, "I am as guilty as the next person."
>
> "As you can see," Marie said, "first impressions are a natural part of how we acquire general information about others, but also, because they are drawn from stereotypes, personal preferences, and scripts, they have the potential to be unreliable. It is a good idea to remember these things when forming a first impression of someone else."
>
> Then Marie asked the group, "What can you do to make a better first impression? What strategic choices can enhance your presentation of self to others in a business or professional setting?"

Several strategic choices enhance the impression we make during our first encounters with others. When meeting someone for the first time:

- Establish eye contact, smile, and offer a firm handshake.
- Speak clearly and avoid using nicknames during initial encounters. This holds true whether you are introducing yourself or someone else.
- Listen carefully for the other person's name when being introduced. Repeat the name to yourself a couple of times or use a mimetic device to remember the name. For example, you can remember someone named McDonald if you think of the restaurant chain or the children's song.
- Listen carefully to what is being said and respond clearly and succinctly when asked questions. Maintain a positive business attitude.
- Have a sense of humor. Smile and be pleasant.
- Maintain an appropriate social distance during the interaction. Do not be a close talker. Keep space between you and the other person.
- Exchange business cards for future contact, if appropriate.
- Leave when the conversation is over; professional people have work to do.

Establishing Expectations and Boundaries

Although first impressions set the patterns of communication, how we construct our relationships is heavily dependent upon how we interpret the contexts and boundaries surrounding a communication event. To complicate things further, these interpretations are influenced by our experience, which in turn defines our expectations, which in turn limit our communication because of the limits of those *perceived boundaries*. In many ways, our ability or failure to communicate effectively in interpersonal communication events is a vicious circle. (See Figure 7.1.)

> When Marie asked for volunteers for a demonstration, Jose raised his hand. Marie then took Jose aside and gave him a card with the details of a communication event on it. Jose would be playing the role of the director of a large department who was meeting a new employee. When the employee introduced himself, Jose was supposed to give him a complete brush off.
>
> Jose sat down at the desk in the front of the room while Marie instructed the other volunteer, Max, about his role. Marie gave Max a card with his script and told him to pretend he was knocking on a door and then begin.
>
> "Hi, I am Max, the new tax accountant. HR told me you were expecting me. I'm really excited about being here," Max read from his card.
>
> "Who? Oh, yeah. Look, I don't have time to show you around today. Lydia sits right outside the door in the first cube on the left. She can show you around and introduce you to the tax team lead." Jose then turned around and acted as if he was working on a computer.
>
> Max walked back to his seat looking dejected.
>
> "Max," Marie said, "how did that make you feel?"

Figure 7.1
The Cycle of Interpersonal Communication

"I didn't like him at all. If that had been a real situation, I would have thought I'd made a huge mistake coming to this company," Max said.

"Yeah," said Jose. "I can't imagine how he would feel the next time he ran into me. How could you trust anyone who acted that way?"

"Exactly," Marie said. "It would take a long time for Max to feel comfortable. Even if Jose's behavior was an anomaly, this first interaction would taint every encounter Max had with him thereafter."

Expectations and boundaries have an effect on peer relationships in the workplace. Research suggests that we use three general categories to define peer relationships at work (Fritz, 1997; Kram and Isabella, 1985).

- *Information peers:* people of more or less equal status with us but with whom we share low levels of trust and disclosure, little emotional support, and little personal feedback.
- *Collegial peers:* people of more or less equal status with us and with whom we share a moderate level of trust, disclosure, and expressions of self. For example, with these peers we may engage in "career strategizing, job-related feedback, friendship, some information sharing, confirmation, and emotional support" (Fritz, p. 30).
- *Special peers:* people of more or less equal status with us and with whom we share high levels of disclosure, intimacy, and confirmation. With our special peers, we feel free to express ourselves fully, openly, and directly.

Our perceptions of the people we work with, and our responses to them, may be limited by the peer category we place them in. For example, we have a higher level of self-disclosure with collegial peers than we have with information peers, and our highest level of self-disclosure is reserved for the people we consider our special peers.

Organizational relationships are also limited by rules, policies, and cultures (Gilsdorf, 1998).

- **Rules:** taken-for-granted assumptions and formal pronouncements about proper communication between and among employees.
- **Policies:** explicitly developed guidelines regarding conduct in the workplace. Often these guidelines are stated in a company's policies and procedures manual.
- **Cultures:** evolved standards for communication practices that may be unique to the organization and must be acquired through observation and experience.

"In addition to boundaries," Marie told the group, "organizational relationships are also limited by rules, policies, and cultures. Rules can be stated or just taken for granted. In our company, for example, it's taken for granted that humor flows among peers but rarely between employees and superiors. But we routinely hold meetings in

which the CEO must appear before all employees and answer any question honestly. This has become an important part of our organizational culture."

Marie took this opportunity to give everyone a copy of the company's policies and procedures manual. She suggested that they read the manual that evening and make a list of any questions they had. The HR director would spend an hour or so going over their questions the next day. She described the manual as the basis for shared policy and procedure understanding within the organization.

Behaving Ethically

Knowing that organizational relationships are defined by expectations and limited by boundaries, policies, rules, and cultures can help you become more strategic and ethical in your selection of communication practices. You improve *strategic* skills by focusing communication goals on what individuals can fairly provide, and by being mindful of the limits that operate within your relationship. You improve *ethical* skills by communicating within these established boundaries.

Although it may appear obvious that relationships in the workplace—and the workplace itself—should be governed by conscious ethical decision-making, the fact is that the harsh realities of a global marketplace often place the ethical interests *against* the business interests of organizations. There are numerous examples of companies that, when faced with a choice between making a profit and doing the right thing, have chosen the bottom line. Tobacco company executives, for example, have admitted they knew the health risks associated with cigarette smoking, yet they continued to cover them up.

However, public vigilance via the Internet, combined with investigative reports from responsible journalists, has encouraged more ethical conduct from organizations. Furthermore, "whistleblowers" (Redding, 1993) have been more willing to speak out publicly about unethical, immoral, and illegal business activities.

After the break, Jose was ready to hear more about strategic choices for relational development in the workplace. Marie brought up the topic of ethics.

"Let's look at the relational level of ethical conduct and decision-making in the workplace," she said. "Much of our ethical understanding is based in an organization's culture and values. For example, in the film Glenn Gary, Glenn Ross, *the sales representatives in a company openly use unethical practices with customers that mirror the treatment they receive from their own management. The employees dish out to the customers what the managers have dished out to them."*

Marie mentioned another example. "In the film Working Girl, *the main character expresses her belief that misrepresenting herself to her superiors was justified in her company because she was being forced to play by rules she had no hand in making. Was her behavior unethical? Perhaps, but watching the film, you see that the character is working within the boundaries set by the organization culture."*

A number of Web sites have popped up that are devoted to personal accounts of ill treatment of employees. These sites provide employees strategies for whistleblowing and for overturning sources of corporate hierarchy and domination (see http://www.temp24-7.com/LIVE/issue/current/home_frames.html). The question is, are their recommendations ethical?

Unfortunately, ethical decisions are seldom easy. This is because "doing the right thing" often depends on where you are standing in relation to an issue or problem. For example, the main character in the film *Working Girl* engages in what many would consider unethical conduct, but she sees her choices as necessary because women from working-class backgrounds have limits placed on their opportunities in American corporate life. The maniacal sales manager in *Glenn Gary, Glenn Ross* believes harsh methods are required to motivate a sales force because his own job depends on their performance. As some economic philosophers—such as Milton Friedman—have pointed out, if the point of running a business is to make money for investors, then shouldn't our ethical code be derived solely from that primary objective? If so, wouldn't any decision that reduced profits for investors be considered an *unethical* decision?

Ethical decision-making and conduct can be rendered even more problematic on a global economic scale because an organization's cultural values may also be shaped by national norms. For example, North American firms often complain that they are disadvantaged when dealing with companies from nations that allow—and even encourage—the payment of bribes or the giving of expensive gifts to enhance business opportunities. On the global stage, what may seem obvious and ethical in one culture may well be illegal or unethical in another. Is it better to lose business while maintaining high ethical standards, or to compromise those standards by paying bribes and giving gifts that may enhance profits?

Communication ethicists point out that when arguments about ethical conduct are reduced to "the ends justify the means" reasoning, what people fail to acknowledge is Gandhi's truth: "means are ends in the making." The "ethical urgency" that ought to be used to guide decisions about conduct is, therefore, *that you don't know how things are going to turn out* (Bracci, 1999). In *Working Girl*, the main character's decisions may seem acceptable because of how things turned out for her, but in everyday business life, we don't know how things are going to turn out. We should, therefore, make decisions about ethical conduct based on what the consequence of behaving this way is likely to be.

To do that, we need to build our ethical practices on a solid foundation of core communication values. Ethical communication practices begin with an organization's need to clarify its underlying workplace values within the context of national norms and practices. For example, research indicates that in North American business culture, there are a number of most desirable organizational values associated with ethical communication practices (Harshman and Harshman, 1999, p. 30):

- Trust one another.
- Treat each other with respect.
- Recognize the value of each individual.
- Keep your word; do what you say you will do.
- Tell the truth; be honest with others.
- Act with integrity.
- Be open to change.
- Risk failing in order to get better.
- Learn; try new ideas.

The above list of productive organizational values reinforces the central notion that relational ethics are part and parcel of our everyday communication in organizations. *There is no communication event or episode that does not reflect an ethical attitude or stance, or a strategic decision that cannot be informed by a conscious consideration of its ethical implications.* For this reason, the National Communication Association has adopted the following ethics code.

NCA Credo for Ethical Communication

Adopted November 6, 1999

Questions of right and wrong arise whenever people communicate. Ethical communication is fundamental to responsible thinking, decision-making, and the development of relationships and communities within and across contexts, cultures, channels, and media. Moreover, ethical communication enhances human worth and dignity by fostering truthfulness, fairness, responsibility, personal integrity, and respect for self and others. We believe that unethical communication threatens the quality of all communication and consequently the well-being of individuals and the society in which we live. Therefore we, the members of the National Communication Association, endorse and are committed to practicing the following principles of ethical communication.

We advocate truthfulness, accuracy, honesty, and reason as essential to the integrity of communication.

We endorse freedom of expression, diversity of perspective, and tolerance of dissent to achieve the informed and responsible decision-making fundamental to a civil society.

We strive to understand and respect other communicators before evaluating and responding to their messages.

We promote access to communication resources and opportunities as necessary to fulfill human potential and contribute to the well-being of families, communities, and society.

> We promote communication climates of caring and mutual understanding that respect the unique needs and characteristics of individual communicators.
> We condemn communication that degrades individuals and humanity through distortion, intimidation, coercion, and violence and through the expression of intolerance and hatred.
> We are committed to the courageous expression of personal convictions in pursuit of fairness and justice.
> We advocate sharing information, opinions, and feelings when facing significant choices while also respecting privacy and confidentiality.
> We accept responsibility for the short- and long-term consequences for our own communication and expect the same of others.

Balancing strategies for creating effective relationships at work with the appropriate ethical standards is a constant challenge for all communicators. In our view, learning to think of ethical conduct in terms of likely relational outcomes rather than solely as an "ends-means" justification is a good way to practice conscious ethical conduct. These principles hold true whether you are communicating face to face, in a conference call, or over the Internet.

"If you are ever in doubt about whether some action is ethical," Marie told her workshop group, "you can always fall back on the Golden Rule: Do unto others as you would have them do unto you. It is simple, but it works."

Creating: Messages That Reflect Self, Other, and Context

"Now we are ready to move on to the second step in the CCCD process—creating goal-oriented messages that are adapted to the needs and expectations of others within specific contexts," Marie told the group. "Anyone want to guess how we go about doing that?"

"We just talk and hope for the best?" Jose said. The others laughed.

"No," said Marie. "We use tools that help us create a message that meets the needs of our audience within a specific context. For the next hour, I will describe both the intellectual and practical tools you need to use to create strategic and ethical messages in workplace relationships. Let's begin with equity."

To create strategic messages in the workplace, we make use of the following concepts:

✦ equity
✦ self-disclosure

- risk-taking
- feedback
- dialectics
- dialogue
- conflict resolution

Equity: Principles of Everyday Exchange

In Chapter 5 we introduced the idea of equity as a principle that guides most workplace interactions. We defined equity as the principle that we should be treated fairly by others and in turn should treat them fairly. We asked you to think of equity as the golden rule governing the *choosing* and *creating* of verbal strategies for workplace communication.

To refresh your memory, let's reexamine the four key assumptions that inform equity theory (Walster, Walster, and Bershied, 1978; Wilson, and Goodall, 1991):

- *People work for rewards.* We all attempt to maximize our outcomes. In relationships at work, we try to obtain our personal, social, and professional goals by gaining the cooperation and support of others.
- *People seek equity.* We all want a sense of fairness and justice to guide our relationships with others.
- *People become stressed when they feel they are being treated unfairly.* If we find ourselves in an inequitable relationship, we feel tension, stress, frustration, or even anger. We cannot overcome these ill feelings until we restore equity in the relationship.
- *People experiencing stress will try to restore equity.* We may restore equity mentally, socially, or physically.

As you can see, the equity principle can be applied directly to choosing communication strategies in the workplace. Your overall goal should be to select ethical strategies that encourage others to treat you equitably and that demonstrate your interest in treating others equitably. When you do so, you uphold the principle of *reciprocity*.

Sources of inequity in workplace relationships include:

- Lying, cheating, or stealing.
- Misrepresenting yourself, your goals, or your methods.
- Not speaking up for a colleague who is wrongly accused or held accountable for something that isn't her or his fault.
- Not supporting the work of someone who regularly supports you.
- Allowing someone else to pick up the check for lunch or dinner without offering to do the same for them next time.

- Failing to volunteer to help someone meet a deadline even though this person has volunteered to help you in the past.
- Failing to personally disclose your feelings about an issue or idea after you have asked someone else to disclose their personal feelings.
- Being chronically late for meetings and events.
- Trying to claim credit for work done by a group or team.
- Ingratiating yourself with superiors at the expense of others with whom you work.
- Withholding information from others that may benefit them.
- Spreading rumors or gossip about others.
- Telling someone else's secrets.

Once we recognize equity as a powerful tool for building rewarding professional and business relationships, we can tip the scale toward ethical and equitable behavior. We can also use this new knowledge of equity as a way of evaluating and critiquing our own and other's communication choices.

"Have you ever found yourself sitting in a meeting and listening to someone who was describing their recent surgery in frightening detail?" Marie asked.

"Yes!" said Jose. *"I seem to be a magnet for people who want to tell me things I really don't want to know. I don't tell other people personal things about myself. Why do other people feel that they can tell me anything about themselves?"*

"Is it that you dislike hearing about other people's personal life, or is it that you feel a lack of equity? If you aren't disclosing and others are, possibly you feel that things are out of balance," Marie offered.

"Hmmm. I never really thought about it like that," Jose said.

Self-Disclosure and Risk-Taking

George Caspar Homans (1961) proposed that all human relationships can be partially understood as *exchanges of goods, services, sentiments, and time*. These exchanges should ideally be *equitable*, as relative value for goods, services, and sentiments is always understood between people as something that should be fairly traded, and the amount of time one person puts into a relationship is generally understood to need to be reciprocated by the other partner.

Given this theoretical framework, self-disclosure and risk-taking have *commodity value* in workplace relationships:

- If I offer disclosures about myself to you, I expect that you will, in return, disclose about yourself to me.
- If I take risks in our relationship, I am also encouraging you to take risks in our relationship.

As if guided by a marketplace metaphor, we "trade commodities" in our relationship. We understand the values we attach to those commodities. We operate under a principle of reciprocity and equity in making those trades or exchanges.

However, it is important to point out that self-disclosure and risk-taking—while potentially powerful resources for building close, personal relationships—can create risks in business and professional relationships. **Self-disclosure** means providing personal information within a conversation. Telling your co-workers the intimate details of your life provides them with ways of understanding how your personal history informs and shapes your workplace identity. It also provides information to people who may not have your best interests in mind. Imagine, for a moment, if the details of your most reckless behavior on a weekend or vacation became common knowledge at work. You now have a rough analogue for how disclosures of personal information can become sources of risky information in the workplace. Before you disclose, think about whether or not you really want your co-workers, and your superiors, to know these things about you. Chances are you probably don't.

Tips for Monitoring Disclosures

Your Disclosures

- Only disclose personal information to people you know well and trust. Remember: Trust must be earned.
- Before you disclose something, stop and think about how information you disclose might be used.
- *Never* disclose personal information to anyone who may use it against you.
- Never disclose anything that may be interpreted by others as potentially damaging to your reputation or character, nor encourage others to. This includes all potentially illegal, immoral, or unethical conduct, no matter how it was motivated, how funny it was, or what the outcome may have been.
- Don't disclose information someone told you in confidence.

Responding to Disclosures

- Keep in mind, you are not a licensed therapist or counselor. If people who need emotional support begin disclosing unwanted or troubling information to you, the best thing you can do for them is help them find their way to a trained professional.
- If someone you work with begins disclosing personal information at a level you are not comfortable with, say "I'm sorry, but there are some things about you I'd rather not know." Or "While I sympathize with your situation, I would like to keep our relationship on a professional level."
- Remember that self-disclosure is expected to be reciprocal. If others disclose information about themselves to you, they will expect you to disclose information about yourself to them.

When communicating in the global workplace, you should bear in mind that people from other cultures may be uncomfortable with the level of self-disclosure and risk-taking that many North Americans routinely offer. Your goal when creating messages should be to *adapt* your talk to the needs and expectations of others.

Asking For and Giving Feedback

Feedback means providing others with an evaluation of the effectiveness of their actions. Feedback is a valuable source of information that allows communicators to adjust their talk to situations and to other people. Skilled communicators seek out feedback because it provides them with an evaluation of how well their messages achieved their goals, what modifications may need to be made, and what they may want to consider doing to become more effective. Asking for feedback is an important tool for the development of your communication skills.

Giving feedback, however, can be problematic. Not everyone wants feedback. This may be because most people are simply not skilled in providing good feedback, so our reaction to feedback tends to be negative.

Research by Trenholm and Jensen (1992) suggests the following five rules for giving feedback:

- *Own your own message.* Use the pronoun "I" to begin statements that evaluate the performance of others. Avoid using generalizations such as "everyone thinks" or "we all know" to preface your remarks. As long as you make it clear that *you* are the one providing the feedback, you are showing ownership (and responsibility) for what you say.

- *Avoid apologizing for your feelings.* Don't preface feedback with a disclaimer such as "It might just be me, but I thought what you said in the meeting was ill-timed." This sort of disclaimer gives the impression that you are apologizing for the feedback, or that *you* are the one at fault, not the person to whom you are offering the feedback. You are also downplaying the corrective effect of the message, which may be counterproductive. Say what you mean. Notice how different the impression would be if the sentence started "I thought what you said in the meeting was ill-timed."

- *Make your message specific and behavioral.* Don't mask your feedback by being vague or ambiguous. The idea is to give someone useful information about their communication. To do that means specifying precisely what behaviors are being targeted. Focus on behaviors that may be modified or changed rather than on general mental states or attitudes. For example, you could say "You didn't return my call yesterday and as a result I didn't get the information I needed to finish the budget report." This kind of statement explains the behavior that caused the problem and opens up possibilities for a discussion of what needs to be done in the future.

- *Verbal and nonverbal behaviors while giving feedback should support one another.* Avoid trying to smile while expressing frustration, anger, or resentment because the message your expression gives may be quite different from what you say. As we pointed out in Chapter 5, when there is a discrepancy between nonverbal and verbal messages, we tend to believe the nonverbal.

- *Avoid evaluating and interpreting your communication partner unless he or she asks you to.* Useful feedback avoids promoting defensiveness. Unsolicited feedback can easily be viewed as criticism, thereby encouraging your partner to become defensive or to argue against what you are offering.

"Feedback," Marie explained, "is essential to personal, team, and organizational learning. It provides us with valuable information about the processes and outcomes of our communication, which is to say about our choices for strategic and ethical messages."

"You know," said Jose, "now that you've explained it, I understand why people often don't respond the way I had hoped when I try to help them. It wasn't necessarily that I was trying to give them feedback; it was the way I was giving the feedback."

"Yeah," said Max, "and I think I will be able to think differently about people giving me feedback in the future. Maybe this will even help with my wife." Everyone laughed.

"Within any work group, and even in a marriage," Marie said with a smile, "how we learn from feedback will be a guide to how open others are likely to be with us in the future. When we combine all the elements we have discussed so far, we are moving closer to a dialectical approach to interpersonal communication or dialogue. Let's take a quick break and then talk about these concepts."

Dialectics and Dialogue

A **dialectic** generally refers to the interaction of two arguments that are by nature oppositional. The term *relational dialectics* (Rawlins, 1984; Baxter, 1988; Baxter and Montgomery, 1996) refers to the interaction of two opposing arguments or forces—called *tensions*—operating within the boundaries of the same relationship. Interpersonal researchers have identified three primary sources of relational dialectics:

- *Autonomy-togetherness dialectic.* To be in a relationship often means to spend time and to share information together. However, no matter how much you enjoy spending time with another person, sometimes you just want or need to be by yourself.
- *Novelty-predictability dialectic.* All relationships form patterns. In time, these patterns become predictable. Because relationships are at least in part predictable, they can be safe, comfortable, and serve as islands of sanity in an otherwise stressed world. However, we also want our relationships to be novel, to offer excitement, adventure, and opportunities to experience and learn from new places, persons, and things.
- *Expressive-protective dialectic.* This dialectical tension informs how we make decisions about sharing information about ourselves with our relational partners and co-workers. There are times when we freely disclose, and there are times when we prefer not to share what we consider private.

With all of these sources of dialectical complexity operating in our relationships, how can we make space for dialogue? More importantly, how do we make space for talk within the autonomous, predictable, and protective environments of the workplace?

Dialogue is communication that focuses on mutuality and relational growth rather than on self-interest. Dialogue is "more concerned with discovering than with disclosing, more interested in access than in domination" (Anderson, Cissna, and Arnett, 1994, p. 2). Peter Kellett (1999) has applied the idea of relational dialectics to creating dialogue in organizations.

- *Focus on mutuality.* Both partners to a dialogue should use the experience to learn and to grow; both communicators should consciously try to help the other person.
- *Discover rather than disclose.* Communicators should ask questions aimed at improving understanding of the other's position, standpoint, and perspective. Avoid unnecessary self-disclosures that deflect attention from mutual growth.
- *Be more interested in access than domination.* Communicators should avoid strategies designed to one-up or demean the perspective offered by the other person. Each person should remain open to differences of opinion, values, and beliefs. The exchange of talk should be aimed at uncovering those differences for the purpose of mutual understanding and growth.

"The key word here," Marie said, "is growth. Our company encourages dialogue that helps us to grow individually within our jobs, and as an organization. When you are faced with a confrontational situation, you should focus on: How will this situation help me to grow?"

"That's good long-term advice," Jose said. "But what do you do when you have a real problem with somebody?"

"I won't kid you; we aren't perfect," Marie replied. "Conflict occurs here. Let's talk about some ways to work through conflict when it does occur. Often, we find that workplace conflict occurs when two people have incompatible goals," Marie explained. "For example, consider how you feel when you want to attend a professional advancement seminar, but your boss schedules a mandatory taskforce meeting during that week. Such conflicts are normal in the operation of any business and can usually be resolved by both partners engaging in a problem-solving session aimed at negotiating a creative solution. Can anyone think of possible solutions for this scenario?"

"Maybe I could provide my boss with input in advance that could be used at the taskforce meeting," said Max.

"That's a possibility, said Marie. "Anyone else?"

"Maybe I could take a break from the seminar and do a conference call during the taskforce meeting. That way, I wouldn't miss out on either," said Jose.

"That might work as well. The point is that you and your boss get together with the goal of solving the problem," said Marie. "But as we all know, not all conflicts are so easily worked out. Before we discuss more ways to work through conflict, let's look at some less desirable strategies many of us tend to use."

Working Through Relational Conflict

Conflict refers to the feelings or perceptions of imbalance that arise in a relational setting. A number of strategies help us temporarily avoid or postpone a confrontation, but they will not help resolve the conflict (from D. Johnson, 1993, pp. 205–207):

- *Withdrawing:* walking away, changing the subject, or ignoring the conflict.
- *Accommodating:* giving in immediately simply to end the conflict.
- *Compromising:* giving up part of what you want in exchange for your communication partner also giving up part of what he or she wants.
- *Avoiding or postponing:* failing to engage in communication designed to address the conflict, or suggesting that the conflict be addressed later.

While each of the above strategies may be appropriate in a given context, each provides a less than optimal way of working through the conflict. For example, by withdrawing, avoiding, or postponing conflict, relational partners may build up resentments that surface in other situations. By accommodating and compromising, relational partners may create an imbalance in their relationship that influences other aspects of their talk and work. Of all the strategies available to us to work through a conflict, *only a problem-solving dialogue stands a good chance of producing a win-win situation.*

That said, it is also true that "conflicts experienced in organizations are often related to deeper processes" (Kellett and Dalton, 2001). For example, conflicts can be based on deeper systems of meaning related to the politics in an organization (Cheney, 1995), differing perceptions of "the reality" of an issue that inform competing values and narratives (Mumby, 1993), or deeper organizational processes and themes (Smith and Eisenberg, 1987). To get at these systemic or cultural conflicts, it is helpful to ask the following questions (from Kellett and Dalton, 2001):

- *Where does the conflict come from?* Who and what is producing the disagreement? Is there a history of disagreements between the communicators?
- *How is it being managed?* Who avoids it, and who wants to engage in it? What goals are being sought by the participants?
- *How do other people react to the conflict?* Is it perceived as "something new" or "nothing new"? What negative work-related consequences can be associated with the conflict? What personal consequences follow from it?
- *How does it affect key organizational functions?* How does the conflict influence productivity? How does it influence openness? Honesty? Learning? Dialogue?
- *How does it manifest systemically in other organizational practices?* Are stress levels higher for those with similar conflicts? Are discussions routed around these key participants? Is there a loss of potential important feedback? Are denial and blaming strategies spread to other conflicts? If the conflict is gender, class, or race based, are other work relationships negatively impacted? How?

Conflict is often described as a *neutral* organizational term (Eisenberg and Goodall, 2001). This is because some level of conflict is natural to all group and team-based activities (Fisher, 1984) and because conflict, when properly managed, can lead to productive, insightful, and creative learning opportunities (Goodall, 1990). Managing a conflict requires admitting you have one, and then being willing to work through it using a problem-solving approach. By contrast, conflicts that are hidden, repressed, avoided, or denied tend to build resentment and frustration, as well as create additional problems within the organization.

Coordinating: Making Relational Communities Work

"Now that we've developed skills for creating positive, effective messages," Marie said, "it is time to talk about the third component of CCCD—coordinating. When we work in organizations, we are constantly coordinating with others. In order to coordinate our communication effectively, we need to become more aware of the goals, needs and expectations, schedules, and informational concerns of others. For the next hour or so, we will examine some of the major influences on relational management in the workplace, including differences brought about by culture and gender."

Negotiation of Cultural Differences

Today's global workplace poses new challenges for communicators and for educators. As Lovitt and Goswami (1999) point out, until very recently most textbooks and training tools for multinational business environments stressed the importance of learning as much as possible about other cultures. This included studying the history, politics, religion, economic structure, education, linguistics, and technology of a culture, as well as the "do's and taboos" of communicating with persons representing that culture. More recent research (Scollon and Scollon, 1995; Perkins, 1999) indicates that only certain cultural factors, such as "ideology, face systems, forms of discourse, and socialization" (Scollon and Scollon, p. 126), actually influence business and professional communication. Moreover, shared similarities in language usage and standards for evaluating communication among professional categories—engineers, accountants, technical writers, technicians—may outweigh other cultural factors (Webb and Keene, 1999).

The important thing to remember is that learning about other cultures is a good way to build a repertoire of intercultural and cross-cultural communication skills as well as to show respect and appreciation for those other cultures. While educating oneself about world cultures is a rich enough subject to last a lifetime, there are some practical ways to begin exploring how cultural differences may influence communication. With this goal in mind, we like to begin with a basic difference between *individualist* and *collectivist* cultures (Triandis et al., 1988).

Individualist cultures, such as the dominant culture of the United States, revere the individual person and expect individuals "to make their own decisions, develop their own opinions, solve their own problems, have their own things, and, in general, learn to view the world from the point of view of the self" (Samovar, Porter, and Jain, 1991, pp. 73–74). Persons in individualist cultures value democratic relationships and are less influenced by status or hierarchy when dealing with each other. *Collectivist cultures*, such as the dominant culture of China, revere the common good over self-interest, value group and family identity over individual achievement, and tend to respect vertical status hierarchies. As you can well imagine, relationships between representatives of these distinct cultures could be very difficult. However, some of the negative influences of these cultural differences can be significantly reduced by each partner learning more about the communication rules and cultural norms of the other person. Table 7.1 outlines several rules or strategies for collectivist-individualist interaction.

Arthur Bell (1992), Jurgen Bolten (1999), and Judi Brownell (1999) build on the work of Triandis and others to suggest that when persons from different cultures interact, a "third" or "transaction" culture is created. Bell elaborates:

> When you and your own cultural background come into contact with persons of another culture, something new emerges—a middle ground, called a "transaction culture." In this new middle ground, sensitive and often unstated rules and understandings guide behavior. That is, if a member of Culture A interacts with a member of Culture B, neither the cultural rules of A nor those of B are the sole guide for behavior. Instead a mixed set of rules—middle Culture C—develops for the purposes of the interaction.
>
> For example, consider the cultural rules that would guide a business conversation between you and a manager from Japan. You would not speak and act entirely as you would when conversing with American co-workers, nor would the Japanese manager hold fast to Japanese conversational rules and behaviors. Both of you would consciously and subconsciously bend your own cultural habits and assumptions to accommodate the communication needs of the others. (pp. 452–453)

Negotiation of Gender Differences

Women and men exhibit generalizable differences in communication styles. Confusion about these styles can interfere with the message. Learning to coordinate your communication style with that of the opposite gender can help you to negotiate a successful outcome.

Women tend to use what Deborah Tannen calls a "rapport-building" style, whereas men tend to use a "report-making" style. These differences in style, as well as differences in language and meaning, contribute to relational communication challenges in the workplace. For example, the fact that men tend

Rules Collectivists Should Follow When Interacting with Individualists	Rules Individualists Should Follow When Interacting with Collectivists
1. Don't expect to be able to predict an individualist's attitudes and behavior on the basis of group affiliations. Although this works in your country, individuals have their own ideas.	1. Expect collectivists to abide by the norms, roles, and obligations of their groups. If group membership changes, expect members' values and personal styles to change as well.
2. Don't be put off when individualists take pride in personal achievement, and do not be too modest yourself.	2. Do not disclose personal information unless asked. Feel free, however, to disclose your age and salary.
3. Expect individualists to be less emotionally involved in group affiliation than is the norm for you. Do not interpret this as coldness or as a personal defect.	3. Do not criticize collectivists or openly refuse their requests. Expect them to be more sensitive to loss of face than you are.
4. Do not expect persuasive arguments that emphasize cooperation and conflict avoidance to be as effective as they are in your culture. Do not be offended by arguments that emphasize personal rewards and costs.	4. Persuasive arguments based on authority appeals or on the good of the group will be more effective than those based on personal rewards.
5. Do not interpret initial friendliness as a signal of intimacy or commitment. Expect relationships to be good-natured but superficial and fleeting according to your own standards.	5. Spend a great deal of time getting to know others. Be patient, expect delays, and do not adhere to a rigid timetable.
6. Pay attention to written contracts. They are considered binding.	6. Do not be surprised if plans are changed after everything was seemingly agreed upon. Do not be surprised if negotiations take a lot longer than you consider necessary.
7. Do not expect to be respected because of your position, age, sex, or status. Do not be surprised if individualists lack respect for authority figures.	7. Let others know your social position, job title, and rank. A collectivist has a strong need to place you in an appropriate niche in the social hierarchy.
8. Expect individualists to be upset by nepotism, bribery, and other behaviors that give in-group members an advantage over others.	8. Gift giving is important, but do not expect to be paid back immediately.
9. Do not expect to receive as much as you would in your own country. After initial orientation, you may be left to do things on your own.	9. Remember that for collectivists, family and social relationships are extremely important. Expect collectivists to take time off from work for family matters.
10. Do not expect an individualist to work well in groups.	10. Do not expect to be afforded as much privacy as you may be used to.

From Harry C. Triandis, Richard Briskin, and C. Harry Hui, "Cross-Cultural Training Across the Individualism-Collectivism Divide," *International Journal of Intercultural Relations 12* (1988), pp. 269–298.

Table 7.1
Rules for Collectivist-Individualist Interaction

to interrupt women speakers may be explained by research findings, but research findings should not be used to excuse this form of rude behavior. Similarly, the fact that women tend to use more *qualifiers* ("I think maybe," "I guess," "maybe just a little bit," "kind of"), *disclaimers* ("It might be beside the point, but," "Don't get upset with me, but"), and *tag questions* (e.g., "You know?")

should not diminish the need users of such weak syntax have to more carefully monitor their speech.

Another relational challenge occurs because not all women and men adhere to these gross stereotypes. Some women are report oriented, and some men are rapport oriented. Some men use annoying tag questions, and some women routinely interrupt anyone who happens to be speaking. Simply categorizing individuals by these general findings can be very misleading. Labeling a pattern as a "genderlect" (a gender dialect) may help us to understand these differences, but it doesn't necessarily help people communicate more effectively with each other.

Most communication scholars agree that the single most important skill for us to develop is *flexibility* (Wood, 1997; Tannen, 1994; Trenholm, 2000). When we become aware of the way we talk and effective strategies for communication, we begin to override the automatic impulses we have and replace bad communication habits with habits that will serve us better in the workplace (Tannen, 1990, p. 95). Doing this makes us more mindful communicators.

"In other words," Marie explained, "to communicate effectively across cultures and genders requires both partners to be somewhat knowledgeable about each other's culture and communication rules, but also able to suspend the rigidity of them. We need to become more conscious, mindful communicators. Part of being mindful is learning how to deliver your message. Delivery is the fourth step in the CCCD process."

Jose glanced quickly at his notes and the outline of the CCCD process. "Choose, create, coordinate, deliver," he repeated to himself.

"We can view delivery in two ways," Marie continued. "Delivery can be dramatistic or pragmatic. Let's spend a few minutes looking at both forms of delivery and how we can take a mindful approach to delivering interpersonal messages."

Delivering: Improving Relationships at Work

Delivery of interpersonal messages can be viewed as *dramatistic* or *pragmatic* (Eisenburg and Goodall, 2001). Viewed dramatistically, all relationships are cultural performances, and the delivery of your communication role in those performances is central to the ongoing story, or narrative, of the workplace. Viewed pragmatically, how well we learn to adapt our communication to the needs and expectations of relational partners will determine the quality of those relationships and our levels of satisfaction within them. Either way, skill in building relationships at work means becoming mindful of our continuous need to learn from those relationships and to improve them.

To become a more mindful communicator in workplace relationships, we recommend that you:

- Become more conscious of your goals for communicating with others, and their goals for communicating with you.

- Recognize that communication has consequences. Avoid mindless talk, careless comments, gossip, rumors, sexual banter, and innuendoes.
- Always be mindful of the equity principle in workplace relationships. Always be conscious of the exchanges and commodity values that operate within them.
- Accept responsibility for your own communication in relationships. Own what you say and do.
- Be open to feedback from others. Use the feedback to improve your relational performance.
- Accept conflict as a natural part of any human relationship. When it occurs, try to use problem-solving to resolve it, but recognize that not all conflicts are resolvable.
- Treat others with respect and honesty. Take into account the ethical dimensions of your decisions and the influence those actions may have on your relationships and communities.
- Be mindful of cultural and gendered differences in relationships.
- Use communication to build flexibility and freedom into the ways we interact with each other.
- Always be on the lookout for ways to improve your communication with others. Never stop learning.

"Okay," said Marie, "that's it! Now you are all ready to go into the workplace and develop healthy, productive, mindful relationships. Right?"

"I don't know if I can change all my bad relationship habits overnight," Jose said, "but you have certainly taught me a lot about relationships in a short period of time. I know that I will spend a lot more time thinking about what I am going to say and how I am going to say it than I did in the past."

"Yeah," said Max. "Just having CCCD to fall back on will help me to organize what I am going to say, especially in difficult situations. Thanks, Marie."

Summary

In this chapter, you learned how you could use CCCD to organize interpersonal communication. We examined the process of choosing strategies that further goals while communicating ethically. We also examined how important first impressions are and leaned ways to improve the impressions we give and monitor those presented by others. This was followed with a discussion of expectations and boundaries and how reliant we are on these elements to help us define interpersonal situations and our responses to them.

Throughout this section, we discussed the ethics of interpersonal communication. By listing the ethical practices we believe are important in the workplace, we laid a foundation for developing ethical responses in the workplace. We discussed tools for creating messages that are ethical while maintaining equity in relationships, and we learned to balance self-disclosure in our communication.

We discussed dialectics in the workplace and ways to use dialogue to resolve issues of dialectics. In our discussion of conflict, we talked about the typical responses to conflict and provided a list of questions designed to help you manage conflict in the workplace.

We then discussed how cultural and gender differences affect coordinating a message in the workplace. Finally, we discussed delivery of a message as a way to improve work relationships. The goal of this chapter was to help you communicate more effectively in your personal relationships in the workplace.

COMMUNICATING IN PROFESSIONAL CONTEXTS ONLINE

Use your **Goodall Connection CD-ROM** for quick access to the electronic study resources that accompany this text. Included on your CD-ROM is access to:

InfoTrac College Edition

The World Wide Web

A demo of **WebTutor** for *Communicating in Professional Contexts*

The **Communicating in Professional Contexts Website** at the Wadsworth Communication Café. The Communicating in Professional Contexts Website offers chapter by chapter learning objectives, activities, quizzes, and a digital glossary.

You can review and complete the following sections online at
http://www.wadsworth.com/communication_d/

What You Should Have Learned

After reading this chapter, you should be able to:
- Explain the importance of first impressions.
- Discuss how person prototypes and personal constructs affect your first impressions.
- Explain how scripts undermine opportunities for creative or unique expression.

- Use information about expectations and boundaries to improve your relationships.
- Explain how rules, policies, and culture impact our communication.
- Discuss the importance of communicating ethically.
- List ways that we can communicate ethically.
- Define equity and how it is applied in the workplace.
- List sources of inequity in the workplace.
- Discuss how risk-taking and self-disclosure enhance communication.
- Explain the concept of feedback and how it can be used to improve communication.
- Discuss the concepts of dialectics and dialogue.
- List negative reactions to conflict.
- Discuss how conflict can be handled in the workplace.
- Explain how we can adjust our message delivery for cultural or gender differences.

Activities

The following activities can be completed online and, if requested, submitted to your instructor, under Student Resources, Activities for Chapter 7 at the Communicating in Professional Contexts Website at the Wadsworth Communication Café http://www.wadsworth.com/communication_d/.

1. Think about a communication situation you recently experienced that resulted in unresolved conflict. How did you handle the situation? Based on the conflict section in this chapter, how could you have handled the situation differently? Write a narrative of the situation, using what you have learned.

2. Ask the members of your group, friends, or peers at work to describe their first impression of you. Make a list of the words that recurred in the descriptions. Is this the impression you want to project? Develop a plan for changing the first impression that others form of you.

3. In your group, have each person disclose something about himself or herself that the group didn't previously know. Be careful about what you disclose. Reread the section on disclosure and think carefully about what you want this group to know about you. How did the disclosures change your impression of your group members? Was the information disclosed appropriate? Why? Has your impression of each group member grown more or less favorable? Discuss the nuances of disclosure in your group.

Exploring Interpersonal Communication

Surfing the Net

Any sites referred to in the following activities are maintained under HyperContents for Chapter 7 at the Communicating in Professional Contexts Website.

1. Go to the Conflict Resolution Resource Center website at http://www.conflict-resolution.net/index.cfm. Click on the *Articles* link. Select one of the articles from the site. Read the article and summarize it for your group. Share the information on conflict with your group members.

2. In the search engine of one of the online bookstores (Amazon.com or BarnesandNoble.com), enter the term "business ethics." Pursue the books that are listed. Read the summaries of the books. Consider reading one of the books from the list to enhance your knowledge of workplace ethics.

3. Review your recent email. Think about how you are using self-disclosure in an email setting. Is your self-disclosure equitable? Or do others disclose considerably more or less than you do? What can you do to make your electronic disclosure more equitable?

Key Terms

conflict *(183)*

cultures *(171)*

dialectic *(181)*

dialogue *(181)*

feedback *(179)*

perception *(167)*

person prototypes *(167)*

personal constructs *(168)*

phatic communion *(169)*

policies *(171)*

rules *(171)*

schemata *(167)*

scripts *(169)*

self-disclosure *(178)*

Breakthrough Skill:
Providing Valuable Feedback

Have each group member prepare a three-minute talk about themselves. Keep in mind the principles of CCCD covered in this and the preceding chapters. In your group, take turns giving your talk. Refer to the Communicating in Professional Contexts Website at the Wadsworth Communication Café http://www.wadsworth.com/communication_d/ for copies of the CCCD worksheets. Each member of the group should give feedback to at least one other person. Your feedback should:

- Use the word "I" so that you own your message.
- Avoid apologies.
- Be specific.
- Avoid conflicting verbal and nonverbal behaviors.

This exercise is designed to prepare you for the group and presentation exercises to come.

Chapter Eight

Interviewing and Conscious Communication

Ling sat at his desk, surprised at how much better he felt now that he had contracted with a consultant to help him staff the new technical writing department that he was responsible for developing. As director of customer service for Bilin.com, an Internet start-up, Ling handled everything that "impacted customers both internally and externally." Two weeks ago, he found out this included the documentation, online help, and training materials required for the various software systems Bilin.com develops and uses. The problem was, Ling didn't know anything about writing documentation or hiring technical writers.

Carmen, the head of the quality assurance group, soon came to the rescue. In her previous job at a different company, Carmen had worked with a technical communication consultant who helped her define and staff the documentation and training group there. She gave Ling the consultant's name and number and suggested he give Valerie a call.

Now, sitting at his desk a week later, Ling thought about his meeting with Valerie, the consultant he had just hired. "What a strange interview," Ling thought. "I feel like I was the one being interviewed! I have to get better at this now that I have all this responsibility."

On the way back to her office, Valerie thought about her newest consulting job. She was excited to be working for a smaller company again, doing what she did best—hiring and training writers and building a department. Yet she could tell from her meeting with Ling that this was going to be a lot of work. Ling didn't have a clue about interviewing, the job requirements for technical writers or trainers, the requirements for a documentation department, the components of a documentation set, or anything else that would be needed to get the department up and running. That was the downside. The upside was that Ling seemed to be a nice, easygoing guy who didn't mind admitting what he didn't know and didn't try to snow Valerie. He was honest about his inability to hire and develop a writing staff on his own. He had been very up front about the budget and staffing resources that were available. Valerie found that honesty a big plus.

Conducting Conscious Interviews

Conscious interviewing assumes there is *a back-and-forth, give-give exchange of ideas, questions, and information on the part of the interviewer and interviewee.* In many ways, watching a good interview is like watching a good tennis match. Each participant is responsible for upholding his or her end of the game. Each must return information in order for the interview to continue. The worst interviews happen when one or both participants drop the ball. Game over. Nobody wins.

Interrogation	Persuasive or sales interview	Informational interview or focus groups	Employment interview	CONSCIOUS COMMUNICATION CHOICES:
Interviewee is grilled about a grievance filed by a customer or a co-worker. Typically one-sided and biased.	Interviewer appeals to the values and needs of the interviewee to make a convincing pitch or appeal. Typically one-sided, can be manipulative.	Employee will receive and respond to messages *only* at prescribed times.	Employee thinks about the best channel for messages but doesn't always follow through.	Give and take of information by participants who are informed and goal oriented.

Mindless Interviewing - - - - - Mindful Interviewing

Figure 8.1
Conscious Communication and Interviewing Continuum

In this chapter, we will follow Ling and Valerie to demonstrate how conscious communication works when we conduct interviews. We will also examine how the CCCD process works in a variety of interviewing contexts. While the main example is that of an employment interview, other examples, tips, and questions will be presented to explore the different types of interviewing you may encounter in the workplace. The basic types are indicated in the conscious communication and interviewing continuum provided in Figure 8.1.

Before you begin an interviewing process, it is important to identify the type of interview you are conducting. Are you trying to fill a position, solve a problem, or gather information? Let's examine the types of interviews in more detail.

Interrogation

From the perspective of the conscious communication continuum, with its scale of mindless to mindful communication, the most mindless form of interviewing is **interrogation.** An interrogation is a one-sided interview that usually concentrates on the negative aspects of a situation or an employee's behavior. Although interrogation may sound ominous and out of character in the business world, you might be surprised how often managers interrogate rather than interview employees when there is a problem. While there may be a rare occasion when an interrogation would bring results, we don't recommend using this technique if your goal is to build rapport, gain information, or develop consensus.

Persuasive or Sales Interviews

At its core, a **persuasive interview** is a sales call. Most people recognize it as such. How many times have you been sitting home in the evening and received

Interviewing and Conscious Communication

a call from a telemarketer who first apologizes for disturbing you and then rushes to inform you "This is not a sales call; I only want to ask you a few questions." The first time you hear this pitch you think, sure, I can answer a few questions, but then you find yourself listening to a 10-minute sales pitch. The persuasive or sales interview is usually one-sided and can be manipulative.

Performance Reviews

A **performance review** is a review or critique of an employee's work and job performance. Performance reviews are designed to give employees feedback on their performance, reward good performance, set expectations for improvement, and solve any problems that an employer thinks may be inhibiting good job performance. While they are often classified as interviews, rarely are performance appraisals conducted in the give-give manner of a true interview. Nor should they be. The performance review is the employer's, manager's, or team leader's opportunity to let employees know how they are doing. While there should always be room for a brief period of question and answer, the format for a performance review should be that the manager imparts most of the information, and the employee listens and takes notes. After the employee has had an opportunity to evaluate the information provided in the review, the employee should be allowed to offer additional information or evidence, if necessary.

Tips for Performance Reviews

Employer

Before the Review

- Ask for a written evaluation from the employee of his or her performance.
- Carefully read the employee's evaluation *before* you complete your evaluation.
- Review (if a record exists) the employee's past two performance reviews.
- Outline the areas of the employee's performance that exceeded expectations, met expectations, and fell short of expectations for the appraisal period.
- Indicate areas that have fallen below expectations over the past two review periods.
- Outline a course of action for the employee to follow that will meet expectations.
- Document the course of action in a memo for both you and the employee to sign.

During the Review

- Present the evaluation to the employee beginning with areas that exceeded expectations, followed by those that met expectations, and ending with those that were below expectations.
- Keep the focus on the employee's job performance and team and group interactions.
- Avoid making vague references to the employee's "attitude" or other subjective references.

Employee

Before the Review

- Prepare a written evaluation of your work prior to the manager's evaluation.
- If you are not asked for a self-evaluation, check with your manager two weeks before your review date and request the opportunity to provide a self-evaluation.
- In your evaluation, give an honest assessment of your performance. Include the areas where you believe you went above and beyond the requirements of the job and the areas where you need improvement.
- Outline goals for the next review cycle. The goals you outline should reflect your individual and team goals.
- Submit a well-thought-out, well-reasoned, organized appraisal of your work.

During the Review

- Listen, listen, listen. By now, your manager knows what you think. Listen carefully to everything he or she has to say.
- Take notes.
- Be gracious when given praise or high marks for doing well.
- Acknowledge areas you know need improvement.
- Ask for a period to reflect on and respond to areas that may be in dispute.

Employer

During the Review (continued)

- Present the course of action for improvement.
- Ask the employee if he or she has questions.
- Offer the employee a brief period to think about the evaluation and respond either in writing or in person.
- Ask the employee to sign the review memo documenting the course of action. Indicate that you will expect the memo to be signed by the employee by a specific date and that nonresponse on the part of the employee indicates agreement with the memo as is.

After the Review

- Follow up on the memo if the employee has not signed it by the date specified.
- Continue to document problems as they arise, but don't harp on problems that have been discussed and solved.
- Praise the employee for changes and progress made.
- Follow up with additional reviews as needed at three-month intervals.

Employee

During the Review (continued)

- Walk away from the review without being defensive, negative, or closed to suggestions offered by your manager.

After the Review

- Spend some time honestly thinking about your review.
- Don't talk about the review with co-workers or vent only your side to friends and family.
- Submit a well-thought-out, well-reasoned, organized assessment of your review if you believe any areas were unfair.
- Indicate areas of agreement and areas that seem unfair or too harsh. Suggest ways to remedy the disagreement. Indicate that you are willing to work on your performance as well as working toward an amicable conclusion.
- Give your manager an opportunity to respond.

Information Interviews or Focus Groups

A person, group, or organization uses an **information interview** to gather *specific* information, further understanding, or test a concept or idea. Information interviews can take the form of exit interviews, legal investigations, medical histories, surveys and polls, news interviews, research interviews, or personal or organizational histories. A **focus group** is a group assembled to help explore an idea or test a product or concept.

Information interviews can be one-on-one or with a group:

- one-on-one—for example, a team leader interviewing an employee who has quit to determine if there were problems on the team (this is also referred to as an exit interview), a doctor interviewing a patient about an illness, or a sales manager interviewing a customer about changes to a product.
- with a group—for example, focus groups used to explore a new Internet concept, or professional groups polled at a meeting about regulatory changes.

The goal, the purpose of the interview, the persons interviewed, and the limits of the interview should be clearly defined *before* the interview begins. Information interviews that stray beyond these set limits are rarely effective and can be frustrating for the persons being interviewed.

Tips for Information Interviews

Interviewer

- Determine the purpose of the interview.
- Conduct any research necessary to familiarize yourself with the interview subject.
- Set clear goals for the interview.
- Create limits for the interview, including the number of participants, the questions to be asked, and the timeframe for the interview.
- Select participants for the interview who have knowledge of or experience with the subject.
- Develop a clear structure for the interview.
- Prepare the interviewees by explaining the process you will use for conducting the interview.
- Follow up with a thank-you email, phone call, or note. Or, if appropriate, send the interviewee a thank-you gift.
- Prepare the final report.
- Present the final report.

Interviewee

- Confirm the purpose of and the process for the interview before the interview begins, if the interviewer does not provide an orientation.
- Think carefully about your answer before speaking.
- Don't elaborate unless you are asked to.

Interviewing and Conscious Communication

> - Don't be an interview hog. If you are a member of a focus group, don't always be the first to speak. The interviewer is interested in everyone's opinion.
> - Don't try to be funny or entertaining. Focus groups are expensive to conduct, and interviewers will not appreciate wasting time.
> - Don't attempt to bias the other members of the group. Each member of a focus group is selected to provide a balanced view of the product, concept, or service under investigation. It is not your job to sway the members of the group to your side.

Employment Interviews

Employment interviews are the most common forms of interviews. Many of you have already experienced an employment interview or you soon will be. The purpose of an employment interview is to create a match between employee and employer that meets all or most of the goals each party brings to the table. Which means that the participants must do the following:

- Spend time clearly defining their goals and expectations prior to the interview.
- Be honest about their goals and expectations to ensure a good fit.
- Approach the interview from an informed position that allows information to flow back and forth.
- Make an informed choice based on all the available information.

The goal of an employment interview should never be to "find a warm body to fill the position" or to "get a job, any job." If these are the goals, the outcomes will surely be dismal for both parties. The remainder of this chapter focuses on using the CCCD process to conduct an employment interview.

Choosing: Setting the Parameters for the Interview

Successful employment interviews are governed by a number of parameters. Valerie knew this, and before she and Ling could proceed, she needed to lay out those parameters for him. She explained each of the pieces that had to come together before they could interview the first applicant. The main pieces were goals and job descriptions.

- *Goals:* the goals help you determine the qualifications you are looking for and other factors such as the number of team members required, the job title for each position, and the mix of team members.
- *Job descriptions:* the job description helps you tailor the skills set and experience to the specific job—for example, the number of years of

experience a person must have, the specific tools required, or the types of experience a person must have.

These elements allow you to develop a framework for a positive and productive interview for you and the applicants.

Setting the Goals for the Interview

If you are the interviewer, an obvious goal is to find the best-qualified person to fill the position. However, you may also find that a number of secondary goals, once identified, will help you narrow the field of applicants and result in a better fit for your organization. For example, are you looking for a spit-and-polish professional or someone who is more a khaki pant and golf shirt type? Do most of your team members have four-year or graduate degrees, or is the team a mix of interns and technical and degreed people? What qualities do you or your team members value most—hard work, a sense of humor, creativity? What have previous team members lacked that kept them from fitting into either the team or the corporate culture? These are the types of questions we will examine during the choosing phase of interviewing.

Valerie learned about conscious interviewing in an article she read and in a workshop she attended at a Society for Technical Communication (STC) conference. She began reflecting on the goals she had for the technical writer interviews she would soon conduct. They were:

1. Help Ling identify the qualities he is looking for in a writer that go beyond having the skills needed to do the work.

2. Educate Ling about the process of writing and the required knowledge base.

3. Find a manager and writing team that can work well together within the given culture.

Valerie then sent Ling an email (see following page).
After reflecting on Valerie's goals, Ling replied, listing the goals he had in mind. (See email on page 202.)

Valerie and Ling met a few days later to narrow down the goals for the interviews. The first goal they identified was to fill four positions: documentation and training team leader, technical writer, curriculum development specialist, and trainer/curriculum development specialist. For each of the positions, they identified additional goals.

1. Documentation and Training Team Leader: must have the ability to hire and develop team members, manage documentation and training projects, and be an enthusiastic spokesperson for the team within the organization.

2. Technical Writer: must have a solid history of technical writing within a software environment, must have a wide skill set, must be a self-starter who has demonstrated high levels of responsibility on previous projects.

Interviewing and Conscious Communication

```
Our meeting                                          _ □ ×
File  Edit  View  Insert  Format  Tools  Compose  Help
Send

     To: lling@bilin.com
     Cc: < click here to enter carbon copy recipients >
    Bcc: < click here to enter blind carbon copy recipients >
Subject: Our meeting

Arial        10   B  I  U

Ling,
I am very excited about our new project. I am looking forward to working with you to help you
staff the technical writing group at Bilin. I will begin drafting job descriptions in the next few
days and forwarding them to you for review. For now, I have prepared a list of my personal goals
for the interviews.

    • Educate Ling about the writing process and the required knowledge base.

    • Help Ling identify the qualities he is looking for in a team member that go beyond the
      writing skills.

    • Find a manager and writing team that works well together within the given culture.

Please take a minute to review them and add yours to the list. I would like for us to both start
from the same set of goals.

Thanks!
Valerie
```

3. Curriculum Development Specialist: must have a solid history of curriculum development within a software environment, must be able to work closely with the technical writer to develop training materials that work with the documentation set.
4. Trainer/Curriculum Development Specialist: must have an excellent training style, must have a solid history of curriculum development within a software environment, and must be able to work closely with the technical writer to develop training materials that work with the documentation set.

Developing a Job Description

Large corporations usually develop detailed **job descriptions** that minutely specify all of the individual duties and responsibilities that make up a particular job. Smaller companies like Ling's may not go into such detail. A job description for an open position usually includes experience and education requirements and the salary range for the position. This brief description is the basis for the job announcement that will appear in print ads or online job boards. These

> **Your message**
>
> To: valerie@triad.com
> Cc: < click here to enter carbon copy recipients >
> Bcc: < click here to enter blind carbon copy recipients >
> Subject: Your message
>
> Valerie,
>
> Thank you for responding to our meeting so quickly. I have reviewed the goals you set and agree with them. I have also included a few of my own.
>
> - Determine the qualities needed in a good Documentation and Training team leader.
> - Find team members that are excited about developing a new department within an Internet start-up framework.
>
> Back to you,
>
> Ling

job announcements or brief job descriptions set the basis for the interviewing questions and allow potential applicants to determine if there is an initial match with the company.

Valerie and Ling carefully scripted each job description to identify the broad qualities they were looking for. Valerie suggested they concentrate their efforts initially on the team leader's position. This would allow them to hire the team leader and have the team leader participate in hiring the other members of the team.

Just as the resume is the first impression you have of a job applicant, the job description you place in the newspaper and trade publications or on the Internet is the first impression prospective employees have of the job and your company. When you write a job description for a job announcement, you should:

- Keep the description as short but informative as possible.
- Provide a list of at least three qualifications for the position.
- Identify the city and state the job is located in. Online job banks allow users to search by city and state. Not providing this information may narrow your pool of candidates. Providing this information may help eliminate applicants who will not relocate to your area.
- Provide a clear contact for the applicant along with contact information. If you are using an online job bank, be sure to provide an email address. If you

don't want to use your own email address, have your company establish an email address that is used specifically for job applications—for example: applications@bilin.com.

Using these guidelines, Valerie and Ling developed the following job description for the documentation and training team leader position:

Job Title: Documentation and Training Team Leader

Description: Internet start-up located in Greensboro, NC, looking for enthusiastic individual to join our growing company. We are seeking a team leader with 5–7 years of team, leadership, and knowledge-based experience. The D&T team leader will be responsible for hiring, leading, and developing a team of 5–7 writers, curriculum developers, and trainers. Primary responsibilities will be to determine the documentation and training set and schedule for each release, schedule training for new clients, provide ongoing internal training for the organization, and manage the training facility.

Send resumes to: applications@bilin.com. Please put D&T leader in the subject line.

Once they had the job description, they had to decide where to place the announcement. They had a number of options, each of which had advantages and disadvantages. A few of the options they considered are described below. (You can also go to these sources to look for job announcements.)

Local Newspapers

An ad in the local paper typically limits the applicants to the delivery area of the paper. The advantage of this option is that you will receive applications from people living in the immediate area who will not have to arrange a move to take the job, which means less lag time and no moving expenses. Also, this is a relatively inexpensive option for placing announcements. A disadvantage is that you may not live in an area where there is a large number of qualified people in your industry, which means that you may be choosing from a limited number of applicants.

University Career Placement Centers

Career placement centers are a great place to locate entry-level and experienced applicants who have returned to college to pursue a degree. Concentrating on colleges in your area ensures that the applicants will be readily available for interviews or accepting a position without racking up expensive travel costs.

Professional Associations and Trade Publications

Organizations like the Society for Technical Communication, the Internet Developers Association, the International Television Association, and the

American Academy of Audiologists all provide job databanks that help pair job applicants with organizations. The advantage of placing an announcement with a professional organization is that you are targeting a very specific group of people with very specific skills. The disadvantage is that chances are slim the person you find will be located in your city, which means you may have to pay moving expenses for higher-level positions.

Online Job Databanks

Online services like www.job-hunt.org, www.careerbuilder.com, www.monster.com, www.jobbankusa.com provide a wide range of announcement opportunities. Some of the online services serve a specific industry or profession. For example, www.brainbuzz.com concentrates specifically on placing network engineers and developers. The cost for placing an announcement with an online databank varies. The advantages are that you reach a broad range of potential applicants very quickly. In many cases, as soon as you hit the Enter key on the form, the job announcement is online. The disadvantage is the same as with professional organizations and trade publications; the ideal candidate may not live in your area.

Head Hunters

This is the most expensive option for filling a position. You are essentially paying someone to screen potential applicants. While this option can save you a tremendous amount of time, it is very expensive. Head hunters often charge as much as 25–30% of the salary if they place someone with your company.

Valerie and Ling examined all their options and decided to place an ad in the local paper and with the online job databanks of the Society for Technical Communication and American Society for Training and Development. While they were waiting for resumes, they turned their concentration to the questions for the interview.

Creating: Scripting the Interview

Good interviews set participants at ease and provide a flow for information between participants. This type of interview seldom takes place without a well-established interview plan or script. An **interview script** is a plan of questions used for the interview.

An interview script should contain questions that accomplish the goals listed on page 205.

Once the general script is created, it is important to realize that the script will need to be adapted to each individual interviewee. This type of interview is called a semi-structured interview. The interview script establishes the main

Sample Interview Script

Establish rapport	These questions should put the interviewee at ease and break the ice. Examples are: ✦ How was your flight? ✦ Did you have trouble finding us?
Define the interviewee's experience	These questions arise from the cover letter, resume, and references. Examples are: ✦ I see that you majored in communication. How has your major prepared you for this job? ✦ Tell us a little about your current position? ✦ What are two things about your current job that you find challenging? ✦ What are two things about your current job that you dislike? ✦ What has been your biggest accomplishment at your current position? ✦ What will you miss most about the company you work for? ✦ Of all the jobs you have had, which has been the best fit and why?
Clarify the requirements for the position.	These questions zero in on the requirements for the position. Examples are: ✦ This position requires hiring and developing a team of writers and trainers. How would you go about doing that? ✦ In this position, you will be required to manage a team. What qualities do you think are important in a team environment? ✦ As a manager, you will be required to report the progress of your team. How do you feel about providing regular status reports? ✦ An important function of this position is liaison to other teams. What skills do you have that will facilitate this function? ✦ How would this position further your career goals?
Present the organization	These questions open a discussion of the organization. Examples are: ✦ What do you know about Bilin.com? ✦ How do you feel about working for an Internet start-up, coming from such an established company? ✦ Bilin is a small, young company and we can't offer the benefits some organizations can. Is that a problem? ✦ We have just signed three major contracts, which has tripled our deliverables overnight. To meet our schedules, we know that we have to work extremely long hours. Is there anything to prevent you from working long weeks when necessary?
Provide closure	These questions signal the interview is ending and allow for a final opportunity to clarify information. Examples are: ✦ Do you have any additional questions? ✦ If offered the position, when could you start?

questions that will be asked within each segment of the interview, but it leaves the interview process open for follow-up and response questions. See the sample on page 207.

Ethical Interviewing

The interview script should not contain questions that are illegal or should not be asked in a job interview. It should also not ask questions that require an interviewee to justify his or her race, religion, marital status, age, sex, or sexual orientation. The chart on the following page describes some of the questions you can and can't ask. Valerie and Ling used this structure to develop the questions they would use in the D&T team leader interviews.

Coordinating: Setting Up the Interview

Interviews should not occur in a vacuum. When a team member is hired for an organization, he or she will work with people throughout the organization. It is important that new hires fit within the organizational culture and meet the expectations of those outside as well as inside the group. Ling and Valerie knew that they would need to include others in the interview process. They decided to include the following managers.

- Quality Assurance Manager, Carmen—Valerie emphasized the relationship the D&T team would need to have with QA. She decided that including Carmen in the interview process would be a good way to start this relationship.
- Implementation Manager, Tom—Ling suggested that training and implementation would follow each other closely and that the training team might need technical support from the implementation team.
- Human Resource Manager, Keisha—Company protocol required Keisha to be included as part of the interview process.

After determining who would be included in the interviewing process, they came up with the following interview schedule.

Ling: Welcome and orientation—10 minutes

Ling and Valerie: First question session—45 minutes

Carmen: QA question session—30 minutes

Tom: Implementation question session—30 minutes

Keisha: HR question session—30 minutes

Ling: Follow-up questions and closing—20 minutes

With the interview plan and schedule in place, they were ready to begin interviews. Now all they needed were the resumes.

Interviewing and Conscious Communication

Ethical Interviewing

Topic	What you can't ask	What you can ask
Martial Status	Are you married? How long have you been married? Are you divorced? Are you single? Do you go by your maiden name? Does you husband (or wife) mind you traveling?	This position requires a good bit of travel. Is there any reason you cannot travel? Have you ever used another name for any reason?
Children	How many children do you have? How old are your children? Is day care a problem for you?	Our company has an excellent onsite day care program. Would you like to visit the day care center?
Citizenship	Are you a US citizen? What country were you born in? How long have you lived in the United States? Do you have a green card?	Do you speak any languages other than English? Your Arabic is very good. How long have you spoken the language? Our company requires employees to provide proof of citizenship or legal work papers after they are hired. Will this be a problem?
Race	You have the nicest eyes. Are you Oriental?	There are no questions in this area that are appropriate.
Age	How old are you? When did you finish high school? I love getting my AARP discount. Have you applied for your card yet?	There are aspects of this job that require the operator to be over 18. Can you provide proof of age?
Physical Attributes	How long have you had a weight problem? Do you find it difficult to carry out functions of your current job?	This position requires a lot of physical activity. Do you have a handicap or physical condition that would keep you from performing any part of the job? Do you have any physical liabilities that may require special equipment or accommodations?
Military Service	Have you ever served in the military?	I see, when you were in the Navy, you were a telecommunications expert. How do you think these skills apply to this position?
Criminal Record	Have you ever committed a crime? Have you ever been arrested for anything?	Have you been convicted of a felony? Before you answer, I need to inform you that the information you provide may disqualify you for this position.

Delivering: Ready, Set, Interview

After Ling began to receive responses to the job posting, he and Valerie set up a time to meet and go over the resumes. Ling was eager to hire someone and wanted the team leader in place within three weeks. Valerie was concerned that things might not happen as quickly as Ling hoped they would. She cautioned Ling to look for the best-qualified candidate who was a good fit for the company and had the right attitude. Having spent years hiring writers and trainers, Valerie knew this could be a difficult and time-consuming process. The good news was that from the resumes, they had identified five good candidates for the position. The problem was, Ling's budget would only allow them to bring in three candidates to interview for the team leader's position. They decided to conduct phone interviews to screen the candidates and narrow down the field.

Conducting Phone (Screening) Interviews

Phone interviews are an excellent way of narrowing down the possible candidates for a job. From a phone interview, you can get a general idea of the personality, energy level, and knowledge base of an individual. However, you cannot see the person.

Ling and Valerie decided to start with Anna, whose strong resume highlighted her 12 years of documentation and training experience. She currently worked as part of a D&T team that, on paper, appeared similar to the team Ling hoped to develop. Ling placed her at the top of the list. Valerie, however, had a couple of reservations. Anna's job experience appeared complete, yet she had changed jobs frequently in the past seven years. Missing from her skill set were some software products that Valerie thought were key for the position. They set up a phone interview with Anna for 2:00 the next day.

Ling and Valerie met in the conference room and dialed Anna's number, using the speaker-phone option on the conference room telephone so that they both could hear Anna and speak to her. Anna answered the phone, saying "Hello" in a soft voice.

"Anna, I am here with Valerie, our consultant," Ling said, after introducing himself.

"Hi, Anna," Valerie said.

"Hi," Anna said softly.

Ling jumped right in asking Anna about the information on her resume and the duties of her current job. Anna answered each of his questions completely, but very softly. A couple of times, Ling had to ask her to speak up or repeat what she had said.

Valerie asked Anna about some of the software she used on various projects and then asked her about software she didn't see on Anna's resume. Anna explained that most of her positions had used the same software over the years and she really didn't need additional tools. She felt that sticking to what she had always used was more efficient.

Interviewing and Conscious Communication

Ling then addressed the issue of job changes. Anna explained that she had worked in the textile industry and been downsized a couple of times. She then found a job with a company that made machine engines. She was doing technical writing, but the work was very limiting, and she felt she was writing the same thing over and over, that she was stuck. So after only 13 months in her current position, she was looking again. She was very eager to find a position with a growing company in a growing industry.

Ling thanked Anna and told her they would be in touch. After hanging up, Ling asked Valerie what she thought.

"Well, I'm not sure if she doesn't like talking on the phone or if she is always that timid, but I found listening to her very trying. I can't believe you had to ask her to speak up four times. What did you think?" Valerie asked.

"I hate to say it, but I knew after the first four questions that she wasn't going to work out," said Ling.

Tips for Phone Interviews

1. Make sure that there are no distractions when you conduct or participate in a phone interview.
    + Reserve a conference room so that you will not be interrupted.
    + Have the interviewer call you at home, rather than try to have the conversation at work.
    + Turn off call waiting! The last thing you want to do is ask the interviewer to hold while you answer another call.
2. Speak clearly and loudly enough to be heard, especially if the call is being conducted over a conference phone.
3. Wait until each speaker finishes before beginning to speak. Answer all questions completely.
4. Clarify any questions you don't understand.
5. Smile. When you smile, your voice is more confident and friendly.

Summary

This chapter examined the different types of interviews and the uses for each. It also introduced the concept of conscious interviewing and used the employment interview as an example of how we can implement conscious interviews, primarily from the interviewer's perspective. We also followed Ling and Valerie through the process of developing goals, a job description, and an interview script. The chapter went over the importance of asking questions that are fair and nonintrusive but that elicit the information needed to qualify a candidate for a position. Finally, we discussed phone interviews. The next chapter examines the interviewing process from the interviewee's perspective.

COMMUNICATING IN PROFESSIONAL CONTEXTS ONLINE

Use your **Goodall Connection CD-ROM** for quick access to the electronic study resources that accompany this text. Included on your CD-ROM is access to:

InfoTrac College Edition

The World Wide Web

A demo of **WebTutor** for *Communicating in Professional Contexts*

The **Communicating in Professional Contexts Website** at the Wadsworth Communication Café. The Communicating in Professional Contexts Website offers chapter by chapter learning objectives, activities, quizzes, and a digital glossary.

You can review and complete the following sections online at http://www.wadsworth.com/communication_d/

What You Should Have Learned

After reading this chapter, you should be able to:

- Describe the major types of interviews.
- Discuss the difference between a mindful and mindless interview.
- List the steps in conducting a performance review.
- Discuss the do's and don'ts for information interviews.
- Discuss the choices that need to be made for a conscious employment interview.
- Create a job description.
- Set goals for an interview.
- Create a script for the interview.
- Establish an interview schedule.
- Conduct a phone interview.

Activities

The following activities can be completed online and, if requested, submitted to your instructor, under Student Resources, Activities for Chapter 8 at the Communicating in Professional Contexts Website at the Wadsworth Communication Café http://www.wadsworth.com/communication_d/.

1. Write a job description for your current job or a job you had previously. If you haven't had a job, write a job description for your ideal job.
2. Write an interview script for the job description you wrote in Activity 1.
3. In pairs, answer the interview questions for the job description and interview script. Or have a friend ask you the interview questions.

Surfing the Net

Any sites referred to in the following activities are maintained under HyperContents for Chapter 8 at the Communicating in Professional Contexts Website.

1. Enter the word *interview* in your search engine. Our search resulted in 114,625 hits. Scroll through the list of sites. Open some of the online interviewing sites and browse. Two of the sites we found were http://www.careercc.com and http://www.ukans.edu/cwis/units/com2/via.
2. Narrow the search by entering *interview questions* in the search engine. Open a few of the sites with interview questions. Print out the questions you find. Could you answer these questions? If not, begin to develop answers to the typical interview questions you find.
3. Search for a website that represents a professional organization associated with your major. Scroll through the job listings.

Key Terms

employment interview *(199)*
focus group *(198)*
information interview *(198)*
interrogation *(194)*
interview script *(205)*
job description *(202)*
performance review *(195)*
persuasive interview *(194)*

Breakthrough Skill:
Handling Team Interviews

Often, you will be asked to conduct an interview with two or more people. Let's consider the following scenario:

Ling and Valerie ask Tom, the implementation manager, to sit in on an interview with a prospective employee. The applicant, Jan Chin, is a young Asian American woman who is very qualified for the position. During the interview, Tom asks questions that are both illegal and inappropriate, many having nothing to do with Jan's ability to perform the job. Which of the following should Ling and Valerie do?

a. Ignore Tom and continue the interview.
b. Apologize for Tom, make excuses about how hard he has been working, and continue the interview.
c. Stop the interview, ask Tom to leave, and continue the interview.
d. Stop the interview, leave the room with Tom and ask him not to return, then continue the interview without him.

After the interview, which of the following should Ling and Valerie do?

a. Forget about what happened.
b. Confront Tom about his behavior during the interview.
c. Speak to Tom and then Tom's boss about his behavior.
d. Bring up your concerns with the human resource manager.

Select the answer you think is the best action for each situation. Write an explanation for your choices. Discuss your choices with the class or within your group.

Chapter Nine

The Job Search and Conscious Communication

Shannon was excited about the process of looking for a new job. After working as a technical writer for eight years, she finally finished her graduate degree and wanted to advance in her profession. While she liked the people she was working with, she didn't think she was being given all the responsibility she could handle. In the four years at her current job, she had performed every duty within her department. In the last year, she had planned and coordinated the writing and delivery of documentation for a number of high-profile clients. She had developed and delivered a number of training courses. She had even done the job of her boss, Lisa, the documentation and training manager, while Lisa was on maternity leave.

When Lisa returned to work, she praised Shannon for doing a great job. They both knew that Shannon was ready for more responsibility, but it was clear that no management positions would be opening up in the company. So Shannon decided to look for a new job.

Conducting a Conscious Job Search

Every day, people across the country look for jobs. Some will accept the first job they are offered. Some will accept a job that they aren't thrilled about, but they figure it's better than what they are doing now. Some will search for a job consciously and find a *great* job.

What makes the difference between the person who takes the first job offered and the person who finds a great job? The conscious job search. In this chapter, we will outline the process for conducting a conscious job search, including preparing for and participating in an interview. But first, look at the job search continuum in Figure 9.1 to see the difference between mindless and mindful job searches.

Before beginning the job search and interview process, it is important to identify the type of position you are looking for. Are you looking for a man-

Figure 9.1
Conscious Communication and Job Seeking Continuum

Idle job seeker	Interested job seeker	Focused job seeker	Conscious job seeker	CONSCIOUS COMMUNICATION CHOICES:
Job seeker goes through databanks or the newspapers, sees an interesting job and sends out a stock resume.	Job seeker finds a job announcement, changes the resume to target the job, sends resume.	Job seeker researches possible jobs, narrows list to positions he or she really wants, targets resume, sends.	Researches jobs, narrows possibilities, researches the company, targets the resume, dresses for the interview, asks the right questions, gets the job.	Job seeker is in control of the job search, seeks the information necessary to target the resume and interview, accepts the position that is right for him or her.

Mindless Job Seeking - - - - - Mindful Job Seeking

agement position or a trainee job? Do you want flexible hours? Are you hoping to travel? The first step in the conscious job search is to set your job goals.

Choosing: Setting Your Job Goals

The choosing process helps you set the parameters of your job search. Before you write your resume, apply for a position, or set an appointment for a job interview, you must set **job goals.** Job goals can be expressed as the type of position you want and the outcomes you want from your employment. You can start by identifying the following elements.

- types of positions you would enjoy
- benefits you expect from a position
- your salary requirements
- types of employers you would like to work for
- types of industries you would like to work in
- lifestyle you expect from the position

Job Research

The research stage is crucial for finding not only a job, but the *right* job. Without research, you are not aware of the job possibilities available or the limitations and benefits of a particular position. How do you know which job is right for you? How do you know which company will be a good fit? How do you begin a conscious job search? How do you set clear job goals? The first step is research. However, this crucial step in the job search process is often overlooked by most job seekers. What can research do?

- *Focus or broaden the types of jobs you are applying for.* Often, seasoned job seekers will continue to apply for the same job over and over, simply because "that is what I do." Rather than do some research to find related jobs or a similar job in a related industry that might be more fulfilling and interesting, they continue to do the same old thing; only the company actually changes. The flip side of this is the new job seeker who attempts to apply for anything and everything without a lot of thought for the duties, responsibilities, or salary associated with a particular job. Research helps you focus on the types of jobs that you want to do, eliminating those that don't fit your expectations.

- *Provide you with important job parameters.* Knowing important parameters like the educational and experience requirements, associated salaries, and travel requirements for a particular type of job will save you the time of applying for jobs you are under- and overqualified for and will keep you from omitting crucial elements from your resume.

- *Help you identify potential industries and employers.* Often, job seekers fail to target industries and employers that may offer great job opportunities.

Research helps you identify industries or employers you may not have realized need your services.

- *Help you define what you can contribute to a specific company.* The bottom line with interviewers is, "What can you do?" At the core of this question is "How will you make my job and life easier?" Without research, you cannot sell yourself to a prospective employer.
- *Impress an interviewer.* Interviewers are impressed when you take the time to research their company. Speaking intelligently about a company's products and services shows interviewers that you are interested in not just a job, but a job with *their* company.

How do you begin? There are a number of starting places for job research:

- The Internet—to find job boards, view a company's Web site, view online profiles and prospectuses, locate news articles, consult professional organizations.
- Company employees—to gather insider information on an organization.
- Company tours—to gather information on work habits, dress code, and departmental interaction.
- Friends and relatives—to gather an insider's perspective.
- Campus recruitment office—to determine the success rate of other grads who have been placed with a particular company or to research and schedule appointments with companies who are interviewing on campus.

You can use one or more of these tools to effectively research possible jobs.

Internet Research

The Internet has revolutionized the job search process. Using the Internet, you can search for job openings, research the company and key employees working for an organization, gather details about the products or services an organization provides, locate resumes targeted to a particular industry or specialty, and determine if you and the company are a good fit.

First, consult a few of the hundreds of job boards that have sprung up on the Internet. Some of these boards offer a wide variety of jobs that cut across a variety of industries, including medical, technical, high-tech, retail, and other types of jobs. Other job boards offer postings specific to a particular industry. For example, a number of job boards provide listings for high-tech development positions. Within the high-tech distinction, there are boards that list jobs only for JAVA programmers.

Company Employees

Company employees are a valuable source of information. If you know someone working in a company or industry you would like to work for, give him or her a call. Take the employee to lunch and ask questions about the company. Some areas to ask about are:

- organizational structure
- departmental ties, conflicts, and strengths
- work environment
- company future
- dress codes

However, when talking with current company employees, it is important to keep in mind that you are gaining one person's perspective. It may be necessary to balance what is said with the other information you gather about the company.

Company Tours

Company tours are often available at large companies like CNN, BMW, and Warner Brothers. Even some smaller companies like Ben and Jerry's Ice Cream offer daily tours. These public tours can be very useful for gathering information about an organization to help you determine if this is a place where you want to work. While on a tour, pay close attention to the interaction of employees, the dress code, and the working environment.

If a public tour is not offered, you might call the human resource department and ask for a tour of the organization. You can explain that you are interested in the company as a possible employer. Many organizations will not provide a tour, however, because the nature of their products or services is private. For example, many banking and financial institutions would view a request for a tour with suspicion and would deny your request.

Friends and Relatives

Many of us know someone working for exactly the company we want to work for. Or we may live in a city or town where there are only one or two large companies. Friends and relatives working in these companies can be a wealth of knowledge about the company, industry, and people we might be working with.

Campus Recruitment Office

The campus recruitment office can be an excellent source of information about prospective employers, dressing for an interview, targeting resumes, and more. College students looking for a job should visit their college recruitment office at least once. The college recruitment office may be able to put you in touch with alumni working for a company that you might be considering.

A number of Shannon's friends worked as technical writers across the country. Over the past few months, she had been querying them about their jobs. The happiest among them, Jen, was working for an Internet company in Seattle. She loved the fast pace and change the company was always going through. Also, Jen was always being asked to do things that, while writing related, weren't strictly writing tasks.

Shannon decided to track down the job boards that listed jobs for technical writers and managers in the high-tech area. She scrolled through the technical communication listings on MonsterBoard.com and the job board at the Web site of the Society for Technical Communication (STC). There were a number of job listings that Shannon was more than qualified for, but Shannon was looking for more than a repeat of her current position. She was looking for a job that would allow her to grow her career.

These are the job goals Shannon set:

- to work for an Internet company
- to find a management position
- to work with both documentation and training

Scrolling through the STC job board, she noticed a listing for a documentation and training team leader. The job description seemed to be just what she was looking for.

Job Title:	**Documentation and Training Team Leader**
Description:	Internet start-up located in Greensboro, NC, looking for enthusiastic individual to join our growing company. We are seeking a Documentation and Training team leader with 5–7 years of team, leadership, and knowledge-based experience. The D&T team leader will be responsible for hiring, leading, and developing a team of 5–7 writers, curriculum developers, and trainers. Primary responsibilities will be to determine the documentation and training set and schedule for each release, schedule training for new clients, provide ongoing internal training for the organization, and manage the training facility.
Contact:	Send resumes to **applications@bilin.com**. Please put D&T leader in the subject line.

< back >　　　　　　　　　　　　　　　　　　　　　**< next >**

Shannon printed a copy of the job description. She was interested in finding out more about the company listing the job. In this case, the listing included the company name. Many of the listings she read didn't have a company name or contact, which would have made additional research difficult until she received a response from a letter of inquiry.

Hint

If a job listing does not list the company name or contact information, but the job sounds interesting, send a general inquiry letter or email. This allows you to elicit more information from the company before sending a resume. For example:

Hello!

   I just finished reading your posting on MonsterBoard.com. I am very interested in the position you posted. However, I would like more information before submitting my resume. Any additional information you could provide about the position and the company would be greatly appreciated.

Sincerely,
Shannon Green

Shannon entered "bilin.com" in the search field on her Web browser and hit Enter. A number of possible matches were returned. A couple of the entries were articles that detailed the company's plans to go public later that year. One entry was for the company's Web site. She decided to check out the Web site first. After clicking through the site and reading about the company's products and services, Shannon was getting excited about the job. The Web site was laid out really well, but the writing definitely needed help. The products were interesting, something lacking in her current position. Best of all, Bilin was an Internet-based company, an area Shannon really hoped to get into.

Next, Shannon read through the articles she downloaded from her search. Most of what she read was very positive. Bilin.com started as a business-to-consumer company but recently made the jump to business-to-business. While their entrance in the business-to-business market came late in the game, the lack of competitors in this area had not really hurt them. One article announced a partnership with two large companies, which analysts said would help with their upcoming initial public offering (IPO). The final article listed Bilin.com as one of the best Internet start-ups to work for.

Sold! Shannon couldn't wait to structure her resume for Bilin.com.

Creating: Putting Together a Winning Resume

Let's start this section with a personal story. After Sandra finished her graduate program, she decided to stay at home with our son Nic. Four years later, after Nic started school, Sandra found that she had a good bit of free time and little to fill it. One afternoon, Bud came home ranting about how difficult it was to get a job and how his students were really struggling in the slow job market. Sandra challenged his point of view and boldly said, "Oh come on! I could get a job tomorrow if I wanted, and I've been staying at home with a child for the last four years." Of course Bud took Sandra up on her challenge. He dared her to find a job in the current market.

A few days later, Bud brought Sandra a job announcement from the Internet. The job announcement was for a consulting firm located in Tampa, Florida, that was looking for someone to develop documentation and training materials for a client in South Carolina.

Sandra researched the company, targeted her resume, wrote a snazzy cover letter explaining her absence from the job market, and faxed the resume to the number on the announcement. The next day, exactly one day later, the president of the company called Sandra. He loved her cover letter and resume. Sandra's past experience spoke for itself, but he was also impressed that she clearly understood the changes that had occurred in the marketplace and that she was equipped to adjust to those changes. He informed Sandra that although the project manager in South Carolina was looking for a technical writer for a specific customer, *he* was looking for someone to develop a documentation and training department for the entire organization. This was something, according to Sandra's resume, she had done in the past. Would she like the job? The salary and stock participation blew her away, and best of all, she could work from home. She immediately accepted the job.

We are telling you this story for two reasons:

- Bad resumes get thrown in the trash; good resumes will get you an interview; great resumes can make an important lasting impression.
- Resumes *can* open doors you may not know exist within an organization.

Selecting the Format

A **resume** is a formal statement of who you are. It is part autobiography, part work history, and part sales presentation. The primary goal of a resume and cover letter is to *compel the reader to call you for an interview.* If you currently have resumes out and you aren't receiving calls for interviews, revise your resume immediately.

Years ago, before computers were so widely available, we would spend hours on our resumes, have professionals review them, and pay to have the final resume typeset. We would get 20 or 30 copies printed and send it out. Not anymore. Now, because computers and high-quality printers are so prevalent, there is no excuse for *not* tailoring a resume to a specific job or employer. Even job seekers with little or no experience will benefit from tailoring their resumes. Tailoring the resume may require you to:

- Change the format based on the type of industry or organization you are applying to. For example, a technical writer applying to an engineering firm might use a traditional format; however, that same writer might use a contemporary format for an Internet firm, and an artistic format to apply for a position at a new magazine.
- Highlight accomplishments that match the job requirements.

- Change the language of the resume to match the jargon of the industry you are applying to.
- Change the tone of the resume from informal to formal, based on the type of industry you are applying to.

Consider the following resumes Shannon could have used for the positions she found in her search.

Traditional Format

The traditional format is very conservative and straightforward. It is the least creative resume style. This format should be used for very conservative organizations like law firms, banks, accounting companies, and other professional organizations.

Shannon Green

790 Snowgoose Cove
Middletown, MD 25678
210-555-5555
sgreen@middletown.com

Goal: To find a writing position with an established engineering firm that allows me to use my experience and education to the fullest.

Education

1993–1996	Master of Science in Communication from the University of Maryland.
1989–1993	Bachelor of Arts in English from Maryland State.

Work Experience

May 1996–current *Senior Technical Writer*	Computer Consultants, Inc. Middletown, MD 25678
	Duties include developing documentation, online help, and training materials for a variety of companies. Work required learning a number of custom software packages and developing custom materials.
June 1993–May 1996 *Technical Writer*	First Bank of Maryland Middletown, MD 25678
	Duties included developing documentation, online help, and training materials for teller software packages.
June 1990–June 1993 *Work Study*	The Graduate School Maryland State
	Duties included preparing graduate student packages for prospective graduate students and editing master's theses.

References available upon request.

Contemporary Format

The contemporary format leans toward the conservative, but it allows for the writer to include accomplishments that are worth mentioning. This format works

---

Shannon Green

Home
790 Snowgoose Cove
Middletown, MD 25678
210-555-5555
sgreen@middletown.com

Business
Computer Consultants, Inc.
Middletown, MD 25678
210-555-5552, ext. 789
shannon.green@ccinc.com

Goal: To find a writing position with a growing Internet company that allows me to grow and develop my skills and move into a management position.

Professional Experience

May 1996–current
Senior Technical Writer

Computer Consultants, Inc.
Middletown, MD 25678

Duties include developing documentation, online help, and training materials for a variety of companies.

Accomplishments:

Learned over 35 software packages in the last four years to develop customer documentation and training. Guided the development and delivery for the last nine projects including: selecting the writing and training team, developing the project plan, assigning the resources, and delivering documentation and training. Each project was delivered on time and within budget.

Received five outstanding reviews and pay raises over the last four years.

June 1993–May 1996
Technical Writer

First Bank of Maryland
Middletown, MD 25678

Duties included developing documentation, online help, and training materials for teller software packages.

Accomplishments:

Received TIP (Team Initiative and Performance) award from three separate branches for the training I wrote.

June 1990–June 1993
Work Study

The Graduate School
Maryland State

Duties included preparing graduate student packages for prospective graduate students and editing master's theses.

Accomplishments:

Asked to remain on in a full-time position after graduation.

Education

1993–1996   Master of Science in Communication from the University of Maryland. GPA 4.0
1989–1993   Bachelor of Arts in English from Maryland State. GPA 3.8

References available upon request.

well for managers or those who wish to move into a management position. This is also a good resume for advertising, marketing, and high-tech professionals.

Artistic Format

The artistic format is used by job seekers who need to display their creative or individual talents. It allows the writer to highlight talents or creative ability

---

Shannon Green

Home
790 Snowgoose Cove
Middletown, MD 25678
210-555-5555
sgreen@middletown.com

Business
Computer Consultants, Inc.
Middletown, MD 25678
210-555-5552, ext. 789
shannon.green@ccinc.com

Goal: To find a writing position that allows me to mix my creative talents and professional expertise.
Agent: Marilyn Timmons, 17000 Park Avenue, New York, NY 10028.

Writing Competitions and Awards

New York Literary Magazine May 2000	Juried Award, Short Story Competition
Maryland Writing Contest December 1999	Juried Award, Short Story Competition
Coyote Journal June 1999	Judges Award, Short Story Category

Books and Publications

I currently have one book, *Tales From My Heart,* and three short stories with my agent.

Professional Experience

May 1996–current *Marketing Writer*	**Computer Consultants, Inc.** Middletown, MD 25678
	Duties include writing and editing the company newsletter and marketing and public relation articles for a variety of business and trade publications.
Senior Technical Writer	Developed documentation, online help, and training materials for a variety of companies.
June 1993–May 1996 *Technical Writer*	**First Bank of Maryland** Middletown, MD 25678
	Duties included developing documentation, online help, and training materials for teller software packages.
June 1990–June 1993 *Work Study*	**The Graduate School** Maryland State
	Duties included preparing graduate student packages for prospective graduate students and editing master's theses.

Education

1993–1996	Master of Science in Communication from the University of Maryland. GPA 4.0
1989–1993	Bachelor of Arts in English from Maryland State. GPA 3.8

References available upon request.

that may be difficult to fit into a traditional or modified format. This format works well for artists, musicians, and actors who need to showcase their creative side.

> ## Two Words Never to Use on a Resume
>
> *Entry level.* These words activate red flags and sirens for those who are in charge of the screening process. You will be screened, never to be heard from again. Avoid using these two words, not only on your resume, but also in your job search language, written and spoken. Companies are not looking for entry-level employees. They are looking for employees who can contribute to the growth and development of the organization.
>
> *Adapted from Job Search Info at www.collegegrad.com (2000).*

Shannon decided to use the contemporary format for her resume. She liked the fact that it highlighted her work experience and her accomplishments, something she felt would be important to a fast-growing Internet company. Now, all she had to do was write a cover letter.

She reread the job description and highlighted the phrases she wanted to focus on in her cover letter. She knew that if she could tie her experience to these highlighted phrases, she could get an interview with Bilin.com.

Job Title:	**Documentation and Training Team Leader**
Description:	Internet start-up located in Greensboro, NC, looking for enthusiastic individual to join our growing company. We are seeking a Documentation and Training team leader with 5–7 years of team leadership, and knowledge-based experience. The D&T team leader will be responsible for hiring, leading, and developing a team of 5–7 writers, curriculum developers, and trainers. Primary responsibilities will be to determine the documentation and training set and schedule for each release, schedule training for new clients, provide ongoing internal training for the organization, and manage the training facility.
Contact:	Send resumes to **applications@bilin.com.** Please put D&T leader in the subject line.

< back >   **< next >**

Writing a Compelling Cover Letter

The cover letter Shannon crafted—after many many drafts—is shown below.

Documentation and Training Team Leader

To: applications@bilin.com
Cc:
Subject: Documentation and Training Team Leader
Attach: Shannon Green Resume.doc (19.0 KB)

Hello!

After reading your posting on the STC job board, I knew I had to submit my resume. I have been considering a chance since receiving my masters degree a few months ago. The job you posted resonated closely with many of the goals I have established for myself.

I am a motivated and experienced technical writer with <mark>over ten years of experience</mark>. For the past four years, I have worked for a consulting company <mark>creating documentation and training materials</mark> for a variety of companies and industries, developing a broad range of writing knowledge. I have led a number of project development teams and I know how to motivate writers and trainers. I have developed <mark>documentation and training sets for both internal and external training audiences, determined schedules, and managed training facilities for a number of clients</mark>.

I am looking for a position with a fast-growing company. I enjoy the change and challenge that are part of the Internet experience. I am looking forward to discussing my qualifications with you. You can contact me at the above email address or the phone numbers listed on my resume.

Sincerely,

Shannon Green

Look carefully at the phrases highlighted in the cover letter. Compare those to the phrases highlighted in the job description. Notice anything? Shannon worked the phrases from the job description into the cover letter. The phrases give her cover letter punch. The letter is written specifically for Bilin.com. Just as the resume is customized, so is the cover letter, using the keywords and phrases from the job description.

Recently, we did an Internet search on the word *resume*. The search returned 931,539 hits. That's almost a million Web sites with information about resumes. Here are a few of the sites we found:

www.resumenet.com—a site that allows you to publish your resume online and teaches you how to polish your resume.

www.jobweb.org—a guide that helps you write a resume by showing you sample resumes.

www.instamatch.com—a site that displays thousands of professional resumes.

Before you begin your resume, look at the resumes and cover letters contained on these sites. Borrow the best formats, wording, and styles you find. You don't have to reinvent the wheel. Just make sure that whatever you borrow is appropriate for the type of job you are applying for.

Tips for Submitting Resumes and Cover Letters

In this age of Internet and high-tech job searches, you have some decisions to make about how you submit resumes and cover letters. This can be a delicate call for some positions and organizations. Here are a few things to keep in mind.

- Conservative or traditional organizations (law, accounting, large established organizations with a long history): Submit your resume by mail, on good-quality cream-colored paper, using a traditional layout. Use a matching, legal-size envelope. Do not handwrite the envelope. Use a typewriter or printer to print the return address and mailing address on the envelope.
- High-tech, Internet, and progressive organizations: Submit your resume via email. In most fast-paced organizations, managers are email, not snail-mail, oriented. Your resume may sit unopened on the manager's desk while someone else's resume is read immediately.
- Artistic and creative organizations: Submit your cover letter, resume, and supporting materials by mail, unless your supporting materials are contained in files that can be sent over the Internet.

Be sure that the method of submission matches the type of organization and the job posting. If you are applying to a conservative organization that provides only an email address, by all means use email. However, if the company provides only a mailing address, don't go to the company Web site to find an email address for that company.

Finally, if you are interested in a position with a company but haven't found a specific job listing for that company, go to the company Web site. Look for the manager whose department or area best fits your needs. Often, company Web sites list key managers and their email addresses. Submit a cover letter and resume to that manager via email.

Coordinating: Preparing for the Interview

"Ling," Valerie said, "I have a resume I want you to look at."

Ling groaned. "Do I have to? So far we've seen 15 great resumes, but when we talk to these people, they aren't anything like their resumes."

"Why don't I give this one a call and do a screening?" Valerie offered. "If I think she's worth it, then we'll bring her in."

"Fine," Ling said. "If you like her, set something up for Monday and coordinate it with the interviewing team."

"No problem."

The Job Search and Conscious Communication

Valerie hoped Shannon would interview better than the last two candidates. When she returned to her office, she decided to call Shannon to set up a phone interview. She could send an email, but she had a good feeling about Shannon and wanted to speak to her as soon as possible.

"Shannon, this is Valerie Shaw with Bilin.com. We received your resume and I would like to set up a time to conduct a phone interview."

"That would be great," Shannon said. "I was hoping I would hear from you. When would you like to do the interview?"

"Well, I know I called your work number and this is probably not a good time. Is there a time either later today or tomorrow that we could talk for an hour or so?"

"Sure," said Shannon. "I picked up clients at the airport this morning at 6:30, so I planned to leave a bit early. Could I call you around four o'clock eastern time?"

"That would be great," Valerie replied. "I am looking forward to talking to you. But let me call you. Will you be at your home number?"

"Yes," Shannon said. "Do you have that number?"

"Sure do," said Valerie. "I'll talk to you in a few hours."

"Thanks for calling," said Shannon. "I'm really eager to hear more about the job and the company. Bye."

"Bye," Valerie said, smiling. Even in that short exchange, she heard an enthusiasm and ease she hadn't heard in the other candidates.

Participating in a Phone Interview

As Shannon drove home, she made a mental list of the things she needed to have in front of her for the interview. She needed her cover letter and resume, the job description, and she thought she ought to have the company's Web site up so she could refer to it at some point. When she got home, she arranged all the things she needed on her desk and got comfortable. She turned off call waiting and put a "Do not disturb" note on her apartment door.

Meanwhile, Valerie was preparing for the interview too. She also had a copy of the cover letter, resume, and job description in front of her. She had copies of the other interviewees' resumes as well. She had underlined the areas on each resume that had not rung true during the interviews. At exactly four o'clock, she dialed Shannon's number.

Shannon answered after the second ring. She didn't want to appear too excited, even if she was.

"Hello," she said.

"Hi, this is Valerie. I hope you didn't have to rush too much to get home."

"No, no problem. I have really been looking forward to this," Shannon said.

After an hour and 15 minutes of one of the best phone interviews Valerie had ever participated in, she started wrapping things up.

"Shannon, I would like to bring you in for an interview. I know it is already Wednesday and this is short notice, but we need to fill this position quickly. Could you fly down on Sunday evening and interview on Monday?"

"Let me look at my Palm Pilot and see what I have next week. Can you hold for just a second?" Shannon asked.

"Sure," Valerie said. "Take your time."

A few seconds later, Shannon said, "I think I can make that work. I do have a meeting Monday afternoon, but I can reschedule it."

"Great. I will have Keisha, our human resource manager, give you a call first thing in the morning. She will handle your travel arrangements and interview schedule. Do you have any questions for me?" Valerie asked.

"Yes, a few. Who will I be interviewing with? And what is your company dress code?"

"You will be interviewing with myself; Ling, the director of customer support; Carmen, the quality assurance manager; Tom, the implementation manager; and Keisha, the human resource manager. It will be a busy day. As far as the dress code, as long as you don't show up in a bathing suit, I think you will be okay." Valerie laughed. "This is an Internet company, populated by programmers, so you are bound to see everything from shorts and flipflops to the salespeople in business suits. I would suggest something in between and comfortable."

"Thanks, that helps," Shannon said, smiling.

"Anything else?" Valerie asked.

"No, I think that does it." Shannon was really excited about her interview. "I'm really looking forward to meeting you in person."

"Me too," Valerie said. "This has been great! If you have any questions, please don't hesitate to call or email me. I emailed my contact information to you while we were wrapping up."

"Thanks," Shannon said. "I'll see you Monday."

Valerie hung up and immediately sent Keisha an email asking her to arrange Shannon's interview. She then left Ling a voice mail:

"Ling, it's Valerie. I just got off the phone with Shannon Green and she's great! I think you are going to really be pleased. I set up her interview for Monday and I've already emailed Keisha to get the ball rolling. I have a strong feeling about this candidate, so I'm going to call the people she listed as references. We should meet on Monday at 7:30 to review her information before the interview. Bye."

Arranging the In-Person Interview

The next morning, Shannon received a call from Keisha, the human resource manager for Bilin.com.

The Job Search and Conscious Communication

"Shannon, this is Keisha. Valerie asked me to give you a call and work out the details for your interview," Keisha said.

Shannon would fly out of Baltimore at 6:00 on Sunday and arrive in Greensboro at 7:42. She would be staying at the Greensboro Hilton. The Hilton had an airport shuttle, there were a number of restaurants close by for dinner Sunday evening, and it was only a couple of blocks from the office. At 8:30, Valerie and Ling would meet her in the lobby for breakfast. Keisha would send her the itinerary for the rest of the day via email. Her flight home would leave at 5:30 that evening, and Valerie would take her to the airport.

"Any questions?" Keisha asked.

"Actually, I was hoping to be able to see a little of the city. I've done a good bit of research on the company, and I'm impressed. But the location will have a lot to do with my decision, should I be offered a job. Would it be possible for me to fly in on Saturday so I will have a chance to look around?" Shannon was a little nervous about asking, but she didn't want to take a job without seeing the city, and Valerie had indicated they would need an answer quickly.

"Sure! If you came on Saturday, we can save money on the airfare, so I can get you a rental car. Let me check the flights for Saturday and I'll call you right back."

An hour later, Shannon had received the final itinerary from Keisha by email. Her flight would leave on Saturday at 9:00, and she would be in Greensboro before lunch. Keisha had arranged for a realtor to meet her for lunch and drive her around for the afternoon. Sunday, she was on her own. She immediately started surfing the net for information on Greensboro.

Tips for Arranging Interviews

- Be flexible, but not foolish. Make sure you are comfortable with the schedule, accommodations, and travel arrangements. If you don't think the schedule allows you adequate travel time, say so. If you are uncomfortable with the accommodations, say so. You cannot be at your best for an interview if you didn't sleep the night before or if you haven't eaten because the schedule didn't leave time for lunch.

- Be understanding, but not gullible. Occasionally, you will encounter a small company or a start-up that will ask you to pay for your travel and they will reimburse you later. If you can afford to pay, you really want the job, and you can afford not to be paid back, say yes. If you can't, ask if other arrangements are possible. Explain that, while you are really interested in the position and the company, you are not in the position to finance the trip. In most cases, the company will work something out. Be sure that you keep all your receipts so that you will have a record of your expenses later.

(continued)

> + Make reasonable, not ridiculous requests. If you are a vegetarian, ask the human resource person if there is a vegetarian restaurant near the hotel. Don't ask for a suite, a luxury car, or a first-class seat on the plane unless you are interviewing for a CEO position.

Dressing for Success in the Internet Age

The rules used to be so easy. Wear a conservative blue or gray suit. If you are a man, wear a conservative tie. If you are a woman, wear hose and pumps. These days, however, you might be sitting across the table from someone in khakis and a golf shirt, or jeans and a Hawaiian shirt, so you might feel a bit uncomfortable in a stiff business suit. How do you know what to wear? Ask! Just as Shannon asked Valerie, you should ask either the person arranging the interview or call the human resource department. Explain that you are going to be interviewing and with which department, and ask about the dress code. Then, use common sense. Does that mean you can wear jeans and a Hawaiian shirt if you know that's how the interviewer dresses? No! It means you should dress less conservatively, but still remain professional. Follow the same rules as with the cover letters and resumes: conservative company, conservative dress; progressive company, lean toward business casual.

The chart below shows some of the basic do's and don'ts for creating a positive appearance at a job interview.

Do	Don't
+ match your level of dress to the type of company you are interviewing with.	+ wear heavy cologne or perfume.
+ wear conservative clothes for interviews with conservative companies; wear professional clothes for all other interviews.	+ wear distracting jewelry.
	+ chew gum, smoke, or eat during the interview.
+ have your hair cut before the interview in an attractive simple style.	+ wear heavy makeup.
	+ wear extremely high heels.
+ make sure your nails are well groomed; people notice the small things.	
+ carry a professional briefcase or portfolio.	

Delivering: Practicing and Being Interviewed

On Saturday, Shannon flew to Greensboro. She met with the realtor and looked at a few apartments, condominiums, and townhouses. By the end of the day, she had found exactly the right loft apartment in the downtown area, should she be offered the job.

Sunday, she ate brunch and drove around the city on her own. She liked what she saw. Now it was time to go back to the hotel and practice her interview.

In her hotel room, Shannon set up her laptop and connected to the Internet. She had always done well in interviews, but she wanted to brush up so she would be prepared for tomorrow. She entered the word interviewing in the search field. The search retrieved 114,625 Web sites. Two looked promising: Strategic Interviewing Tips at www.connectme.com and Interviewing Tips at www.executechjobs.com. She scrolled through the sites to pick up as many tips as she could. One of the things she came across was information on the different styles of interviewing: informal and formal.

Interview Styles

Interviews can be conducted in either an informal or formal style. To be on the safe side, you need to practice for both styles.

Informal Interviews

In an **informal interview,** the questions will be unstructured and will cover a wide variety of topics. Informal interviews make use of **open questions**—questions that require more than yes or no responses and that allow you a good bit of room to discuss your experience or perspective.

The advantages to this type of interview are that it allows you to showcase your experience, expound on your accomplishments, display your personality, and display your ability to speak clearly and confidently. The disadvantages are that people who are not confident speaking off the cuff may have a difficult time. The interviewee bears most of the responsibility for informal interviews, which means you have to have something to say. Otherwise the interview doesn't tend to be very fruitful.

Formal Interviews

Formal interviews are structured and center on questions designed to gather specific information. These interviews tend to be tightly scripted in advance. They frequently make use of **closed questions**—questions that require specific, concrete answers and that provide little opportunity to elaborate.

The advantages of the formal interview are that it works well for interviewers who don't know a great deal about interviewing. It allows the interviewer to learn from the interviewee without giving away how little he or she knows about the interview area. The disadvantage is that a formal interview don't allow the interviewer to get to know the interviewee. It provides a very flat, one-sided view of the interviewee.

In a formal interview, you might be asked questions like these:

- This position requires a good bit of travel. Is travel a problem for you?
- How many days of work did you miss last year?
- Do you have plans to return to school?
- Will relocating be a problem?
- We are a much smaller company than you have been working for. Have you thought about how that might affect your plans for promotions?

Practicing the Interview

To ensure that you don't have problems knowing what to say during an interview, practice responding to the following questions and prompts. Most of them are the kinds of open questions you would be asked in an informal interview. Some of Shannon's practice answers are included.

- *Tell me about yourself.* Keep your answer focused on the job and the interview. Plan an answer to this question in advance. The interviewer is not interested in your family, friends, hobbies, or dog unless these things somehow relate to the position you are applying for. Stick to the details of your resume and focus on your college courses and work experience. Find a theme that unites the decisions you have made into a cohesive plan, ending with why you decided to apply for this position.

Shannon thought about this question and came up with the following answer:

"I really enjoy my work. I have always believed it is important to do something you really enjoy, and I enjoy technical communication. I like working on a variety of projects with a lot of different people. I am best when I have a lot of irons in the fire, which this position seems to require. And I work really well in a team environment."

- **How did you decide to enter your current field of employment?** Few people grow up knowing what they want to be, and some never make a clear and conscious choice to major in something in college. However, you don't want a prospective employer to think that you just fell into your current job or that you only selected your career because you could make a lot of money or because your parents told you to become an accountant.

Okay, Shannon thought, this one is easy:

"I took a communication class my freshman year and immediately knew I wanted to be in communications. When I was a junior, I interned at a software company and worked in the documentation and training department. By the end of my internship, I knew that was what I was going to do."

- **Where do you want to be in five years?** Refrain from saying, "I want your job." Do, however, map a future plan that includes realistic, achievable goals without outwardly threatening the interviewer.

Shannon found this a tough question. After a good bit of thought, she decided on:

"I've been giving this a lot of thought lately and I know that my next position will greatly influence my plan. I know that I am ready for a leadership position. I am very eager to develop a department and watch it grow—which I think will keep me busy for at least five years. Beyond that, I have thought about consulting, but I think I need at least five more years of corporate experience first."

- **Why do you want to leave your current job?** This is a big red-flag question. The interviewer is looking for problems you might have with co-workers, your boss, authority figures, or an ability to do the job. Focus on the opportunities associated with the position you are interviewing for, rather than the disappointments of your current position. Do not, under any circumstances, knock your current employer.

This question is a trick question, Shannon thought. If I'm completely honest, I could come off looking like a disgruntled employee. I will keep this one short and sweet:

"Until six months ago, I was very happy in my current position. Then my manager, Lisa, went on maternity leave and I was charged with managing the department while she was gone. I found the new responsibilities challenging but extremely rewarding, and the department performed really well during that period. When Lisa returned, I realized that it was time for me to begin looking for a leadership position."

- *Describe your dream job.* Most of us have dreams of being paid to write the great American novel or an award-winning screenplay. Is that what your prospective employer is looking for? No! Nor should you say, "This is my dream job," if you are applying for a training or junior management position. Keep your answer focused on a logical career path for the position you are applying for.
- *Why do you want to work for us?* Here is where your research pays off. Let the interviewer know you have researched the company.

Okay, Shannon thought; this one I know:

"I am really impressed with the customers Bilin.com has attracted with the business-to-business product lines. I think I could learn a lot working with these types of clients. Also, the fact that Employment Inc. named Bilin.com as one of the top 25 companies to work for was very impressive."

- *Why should I hire you?* If you paint yourself as someone who can do anything and knows everything, you run the risk of being a big letdown if you get the job. That is, if the interviewer doesn't view your answer as a huge ego trip. When answering this question, be confident and keep your answer focused on your job and education.

I know why they should hire me. This is a piece of cake, Shannon thought.

"I am very motivated. I enjoy my work and work well with almost everyone. I have the project leadership skills you are looking for and the knowledge base the job requires. I'm ready for the work that is in front of whoever takes this position."

- *What are your greatest strengths and weaknesses?* The trick with this question is to be modest about your strengths and to turn a weakness into a plus.

This one Shannon was ready for:

"I strive to accomplish all of my assignments on time and within budget. Doing this often requires that I go beyond what is expected, and I expect those around me to do the same. Occasionally, I will find myself overworked rather than confront a team member who isn't pitching in as they should."

- *What makes you a good leader?* Try to avoid clichés or trite phrases. Make your answer concrete, and focus on actual experiences.

Shannon decided to focus on the certification program she helped develop.

"Recently, I was asked to lead a team tasked with developing a new certification program for our installation teams. After the first installation team received their certification, I got an email from the company president thanking me for putting the program together so quickly and informing me that the last installation was the smoothest we have ever had."

- *Do you have any questions?* Begin by focusing on the position and the fit within the organization. After a few questions about the organization, you can ask a few questions about salary and benefits. However, don't delve too deeply into this area until you are offered the job.

Being Interviewed

Ling began the interview.

Ling: "What do you think about Greensboro?"

Shannon: "From what I've seen, I really like it. I was surprised at the number of parks and how green everything is. I was also really pleased by the variety of housing choices."

Ling: "Would leaving Maryland be difficult for you? I see from your resume that you went to college in Maryland and then remained in the state. You must have deep ties to the area."

Shannon: "Actually, I am an Army brat. I've lived in Maryland longer than I've lived anywhere in my life. Moving, changing towns, and making a life in a different place has always been something I do easily."

Valerie: "Tell Ling a little about your current position. I know we have already covered a good bit of this, but I would like him to hear it from you."

Shannon: "I am currently a senior technical writer. But that title doesn't really do my duties justice. We have a philosophy that everything flows from documentation. Which means that the documentation and online help should be the basis for the training. When a client goes through training, we refer back to the online help and documentation, so we are constantly reinforcing both. When the client returns to their office, they know where to get the answers to their question in the documentation, online help, or training materials. Using this philosophy, we have reduced support calls by 82%.

"Because everything flows from the documentation, I am often in the position of team leader. I bring together the documentation writers, the curriculum developers, and the trainers for each project. I am responsible for the schedules, the resources, the deliveries, and the training classes."

Ling: "Sounds like you have your hands full. What are two things about your current job that you find challenging?"

Shannon: "The most challenging thing about my job is leading the project team. Often, people we hire come from very different environments from ours, and occasionally we will have a case where a trainer or curriculum developer wants to run the show. It is my job to explain the department philosophy and keep that vision on track. At the same time, I strive to recognize each person's contribution to the project.

"I also find the variety of clients we work with challenging. Each customer is a bit different, as is each delivery. That keeps me interested and learning."

Ling: "What are two things about your current job that you dislike?"

Shannon: "One of the reasons I am looking for a new position is the lack of room for growth. It is both a curse and a blessing having a great, competent boss. However, I don't see the department or the organization expanding anytime soon.

"There is also a bit of resistance to new ideas and technology. I have introduced a number of ideas for distance training, upgrading our current computer-based training, and creating Web-based online help, but most of these ideas have fallen flat. I feel that I keep growing and learning, but I can't seem to apply many of these skills in my current position."

Valerie: "What has been your biggest accomplishment at your current position?"

Shannon: "My biggest accomplishment was stepping in for my boss, Lisa, during her maternity leave. I kept the projects on track and developed new projects without our department missing a beat. I took a lot of pride in how seamlessly we operated while she was on leave. I attribute a good bit of this to how well she trained me and prepared me to assume a leadership role."

Ling: "What will you miss most about the company you work for?"

Shannon: "I will miss the people I work with. We have a great team and we work really well together. I helped hire a number of the people I work with, so I feel very connected to them."

Ling: "Interesting that you mentioned hiring people. This position requires hiring and developing a team of writers and trainers. How would you go about doing that?"

Shannon: "I think working with Valerie is a very smart move. She will help make this part of the job a lot easier. I would continue to tap the STC and training and development Web sites, and I would attend the local STC meetings to see if anyone within the organization is actively looking for a new position. This has been a great source of networking for us. I would have to investigate it further, but I would imagine that the Raleigh-Durham Research Triangle area has a very strong STC organization, so I would attend one of their meetings as well.

"When hiring trainers, it is important to do interviews and to have them do some stand-up training. We have avoided some potential mistakes this way. Some of the applicants with great resumes were not so great in front of the classroom.

"Finally, I would work the Internet job boards for both groups. A lot of people are putting their resumes out, and even though it is time-consuming up front, it can save time in the long run."

Ling: "In this position, you will be required to manage a team. What qualities do you think are important in a team environment?"

Shannon: "I think it is important that even though you are working in a team environment, every one needs to feel that their contributions are important. You have to maintain a balance between the needs of the team and the needs of the individuals on the team. Team members need to understand the goals and direction of the team and use their individual talents to help the team succeed. It is the team leader's job to give them the resources to ensure that happens."

Ling: "Okay, I'm a stickler for knowing what is going on. I like status reports, but right now I have two team leaders that hate doing them. As a team leader, you will be required to report the progress of your team. How do you feel about providing regular status reports?"

Shannon: "What I do with my current manager is to meet with her on Monday and Thursday. We go over what has been accomplished in the past week and what we will be working on in the next week. We work through any problems, issues, and snags. After the status meeting, I send her an email recapping what we have discussed. How would that work?"

Ling: "That sounds good. I have been trying different things and this mixes an informal reporting process with something formal I can use for my own status reports."

Valerie: "As the documentation and training team leader, you would be the liaison to other teams. What skills do you have that would facilitate this function?"

Shannon: "As a communication specialist, I understand the need for gathering and disseminating information. I am good at targeting the information people need and what I need to do my job. I have a real belief in sharing information. I think it makes everyone's life and job easier."

Ling: "How would this position further your career goals?"

Shannon: "Well, as I've said, I am looking for a position that will allow me to use the leadership skills I've developed in my current position. I am ready for this type of challenge and feel strongly that it is the next logical step in my career."

Ling: "What do you know about Bilin.com?"

Shannon: "I've done a good bit of research on the company through articles on the Internet, and I have spent a good bit of time looking at your Web site. What I don't know is what it is like to work for Bilin.com and what challenges face the company. Can you tell me a bit about that?"

Ling: "I'm glad you asked. Our public image is that of a growing organization rocketing to the top of the Internet dotcoms, and to some extent, that is true. Organizationally, we are a group of mostly nice people who want to see this company succeed at the highest level. Overall we have a lot of fun, work really hard, and have our fingers crossed most of the time. In the next year, we have to grow up. Right now, we are still a small company. We need a formal training program, we need to deliver solid documentation and online help, we need to develop the support area, and we need to deliver what we promise to our customers. If you ask someone else, you will get a different answer, but to me, these are the things that are important."

Valerie: "How do you feel about working for an Internet start-up, coming from such an established company?"

Shannon: "I'm excited about it. In some ways, I feel that I've missed out by staying with a more traditional company. I think it would be exciting and challenging."

Ling: "Bilin is a small, young company and we can't offer the benefits some organizations can. Is that a problem?"

Shannon: "To be honest, I would need to know more about what you do and don't offer. I need to have a medical plan, but dental isn't as important. I would like to *participate in some form of retirement through a 401K or profit sharing, but being vested in a stock option plan would certainly offset a 401K. Can you tell me more about the benefits?"*

Ling: "I could, but I'm sure I would leave something out. Keisha has a presentation planned for you later today. Can we table this until then?"

Shannon: "Sure. I may have additional questions by then."

Valerie: "We have just signed three major contracts, which has tripled our deliverables overnight. To meet our schedules, we need to hire someone as quickly as possible. If offered the job, when could you start?"

Shannon: "I could start in a week. I would need at least a week to move and wrap things up in Maryland."

Ling: "Sounds great! Do you have any additional questions?"

Shannon: "Yes. Can you tell me a little about who I will be interviewing with the rest of the day?"

Throughout the day, everyone was impressed with Shannon. By the end of the day, Ling had gotten back in touch with everyone and was drafting an offer letter when Valerie brought Shannon by Ling's office to wrap up.

"Hi! How is it going?" Ling asked.

"Great! Everyone is so nice. Thanks for giving me the opportunity to come down and meet everyone," Shannon said.

"I'm so glad to hear it. I need to meet with Keisha and work out the details, but I would like to have a formal offer for you by tomorrow," Ling said, smiling. "If we can work out the details, could you start the first of next month? That gives you two and a half weeks to wrap things up in Maryland."

"Wow! I knew you were in a hurry, but I didn't expect you to make a decision this quickly. Yes, if everything works out, I'm sure I could start on the first. Thanks!"

Sitting on the plane a few hours later, Shannon couldn't believe how her life had changed in just a weekend. She couldn't wait to get home and see if Ling had emailed her the offer letter. She needed to send Ling and Valerie a thank-you note. She also had to plan her conversation with Lisa. She was glad she had spent so much time planning and preparing for her interview. It had certainly paid off.

Summary

In this chapter, we followed Shannon through the process of conducting a conscious job search. We discussed the elements of a conscious search and applied the CCCD process to seeking a job. We began with choosing job goals. Without setting clear goals, chances are you will end up in a position that isn't right for you. We also emphasized how important research is in the job search process. We walked through the process of conducting research on the Internet, through company employees and tours, through friends and family, and through your campus recruitment office.

We then concentrated on the process of creating a resume. We reviewed the formats you can use for a resume and when to use each type. We talked about using the words from the job description when you are creating your resume and cover letter.

In the section on coordinating, we provided tips for participating in a phone interview. We also talked about how to coordinate the travel arrangements for out-of-town interviews and how to decide what you will wear on your interview.

The delivery section explained the differences between informal and formal interviews. We emphasized how important it is to practice before you go for an interview. We also provided possible answers to standard interviewing questions. Finally, we walked through a typical interview, providing you with a script you can use to prepare for future interviews.

COMMUNICATING IN PROFESSIONAL CONTEXTS ONLINE

Use your **Goodall Connection CD-ROM** for quick access to the electronic study resources that accompany this text. Included on your CD-ROM is access to:

InfoTrac College Edition

The World Wide Web

A demo of **WebTutor** for *Communicating in Professional Contexts*

The **Communicating in Professional Contexts Website** at the Wadsworth Communication Café. The Communicating in Professional Contexts Website offers chapter by chapter learning objectives, activities, quizzes, and a digital glossary.

You can review and complete the following sections online at http://www.wadsworth.com/communication_d/

What You Should Have Learned

After reading this chapter, you should be able to:

- Establish goals for your next job.
- Conduct research on possible jobs, potential companies, and career information.

- Use a job description to create a resume and cover letter.
- Select the appropriate format for your resume.
- Select the appropriate format for submitting your resume.
- Participate in a phone interview.
- Make arrangements for out-of-town interviews.
- Select the appropriate clothing for an interview.
- Use the practice interview questions to structure answers for an interview.
- Do well during an in-person Interview.

Activities

The following activities can be completed online and, if requested, submitted to your instructor, under Student Resources, Activities for Chapter 9 at the Communicating in Professional Contexts Website at the Wadsworth Communication Café http://www.wadsworth.com/communication_d/.

1. Find a job description for a job you might be interested in. Develop a resume that is geared toward the job description.
2. Review the questions listed in the section on "Practicing for the Interview." Prepare answers for five of the questions.
3. Go to the college recruitment office at your school. Ask about the services they offer. Look at the current list of corporate job openings. Select three job announcements that fit your career goals.

Surfing the Net

Any sites referred to in the following activities are maintained under HyperContents for Chapter 9 at the Communicating in Professional Contexts Website.

1. Select a company you may want to interview with at some point. Research the company on the Internet. Write about what you found.
2. In an Internet search engine, enter the professional title for a job you might want. Review the information you find. What are the professional requirements, starting salary, and career track for the position you selected?
3. Go to the Quintessential Careers website http://www.quintcareers.com/dress_for_success.html. Read the article "When Job-Hunting: Dress for Success." Review your wardrobe. Are you ready for an interview? Make a list of the items you need to dress for success.

Key Terms

closed questions *(232)* **informal interview** *(232)* **open questions** *(232)*
formal interview *(232)* **job goals** *(215)* **resume** *(220)*

Breakthrough Skill:
Developing a Smooth Interview Style

A smooth interviewing style can only come with practice. This exercise is designed to give you control over the interviewing situation so that you can concentrate on developing a confident interview style.

1. Select a job description you would like to interview for.
2. Using the job description, prepare a resume and a cover letter.
3. Prepare an interview script (you may use the questions provided in Chapters 8 and 9).
4. Prepare the answers for your questions.
5. Select a group or class member to interview you.
6. Provide the group or class member with the interview script (do not include the answers you have prepared).
7. Schedule the interview.
8. Have the group or class member conduct the interview.
9. Ask the group or class member to critique your performance using the following criteria.
    - Did I provide adequate answers to the questions?
    - Did I show knowledge of and enthusiasm for the position I selected?
    - Was I sincere?
    - Did my answers reflect the practice I have done?
    - Was I confident?
    - Would you hire me?

    If possible, you should:
    - Practice your answers at least three times before the interview.
    - Dress as you would for an actual interview.
    - Have the interview video-taped so that you can review your own performance.

Communicating in Professional Contexts In Action!

Communicating In Professional Contexts In Action! is available on your Goodall Connection CD-ROM and features model presentations and a dramatization of Shannon's interview discussed on pages 235–238 of this chapter. Improve your own interview skills by watching, listening to, critiquing and analyzing the scenario featured on this program. After completing an interview analysis and answering the questions provided, you can compare your work to our suggested responses.

Chapter Ten

Communicating in Groups and Teams

Shannon was excited about the opportunity to lead a team. However, now that she was finally a team leader, she was a bit overwhelmed. She knew she needed help getting things off to a good start, so she called her mentor, Pam, who had been her first supervisor and had always given her good advice. Pam had more than 20 years of experience in documentation and training, and she had won numerous leadership awards.

"Shannon, it is about time!" Pam said after Shannon described her new position.

"Thanks, Pam. I am really excited and I know I can do this job. But I have a few questions. What do I do first to make sure this team works together well and we accomplish our goals?"

"I'll give you the process I use when I work with a new team," said Pam. "First, you have to choose strategies for leadership, group participation, and selecting group members. Then, you create a vision, goals, and objectives and develop a process for problem solving that will guide your team. Next, you need strategies for coordinating the team's activities with those of other teams in the organization. Finally, you have to deliver. If you can do these things, you can create a successful team."

"That's all? Wow, I'll have that done by tomorrow," Shannon said jokingly. "It sounds like I have a lot of work ahead of me."

"You do," said Pam, "but I know you'll do fine. And you can call me anytime you need help."

"Thanks," said Shannon. "I'm sure I'll take you up on that!"

Conscious Communication in Groups and Teams

In the workplace, a **team** is defined as a group of individuals who share a unifying goal. During the last 10 years, organizations have begun to use teams to surmount communication problems in organizations and bring people together. Many of these teams were put in place as organizations downsized and hierarchies were flattened. Teams allow organizations to eliminate middle managers who come between the goals and vision of the organization and those ultimately responsible for implementing those goals and carrying out the organization's vision. However, many organizations simply lumped people together, called those groups teams, and provided them with little or no team training. The result was in many cases dismal. As you can see from the continuum in Figure 10.1, simply applying the label *team* does not a team make.

The more people get together in groups and teams, the more opportunities there are for misunderstanding and miscommunication. As the number of group members increases, so too does the likelihood of conflict. Individuals may clash over conflicting goals for the group, differences in preferred methods and strategies for carrying out the group's work, and disagreements about

Group of individuals	Group in name only	Collaborative group	Team	CONSCIOUS COMMUNICATION CHOICES:
People who come together occasionally to pass information. Members have a laissez-faire attitude, individual orientation, lack of initiative and no responsibility for group success.	Members are thrown together with little orientation or clear purpose. Main function of the group is meetings. After group work is done, members return to their individual jobs or departments.	Group members disagree over conflicting goals for the group, cite differences in preferred methods or strategies for carrying out the group's work, but use collaboration and conflict to move the group forward.	Members share a unifying goal. The team succeeds through shared knowledge, diversity of experiences, and collaborative energy. Members realize their individual success depends on the synergy of the team.	Give and take of information by participants who are informed and goal oriented.

Mindless Groups/Teams - - - - - Mindful Groups/Teams

Figure 10.1
Conscious Communication and Group/Team Communication Continuum

perceived individual realities. The results can be stress, boredom, and frustration that seldom provide the necessary environment for effective or creative group communication. Add to these frustrations the reality that one team's priorities are often not the priority of another team within the organization and you have the potential for organizational chaos. Effective, conscious communication can help bring order to the chaotic environment in which many teams function.

Team communication, depicted at the far right of the continuum in Figure 10.1, occurs when a team achieves **synergy,** the stage at which people are truly working together. A synergized team recognizes that shared knowledge, diversity of experiences, and collaborative energy provide the team with a powerful resource. When tackling a business or professional problem, what makes the difference between a group and a team are mindful communication processes and practices that improve the likelihood of success for everyone involved.

As you will see, the CCCD process offers an opportunity to develop the components of conscious communication necessary for a successful team experience. In this chapter, we will follow Shannon as she builds the Documentation and Training Team at Bilin.com. After reading and studying the material in these sections, you should have a blueprint for communicating with others in groups and teams. However, for the purposes of this discussion, we will focus on teams as the most conscious form of group communication.

Choosing: Strategies for Organizing Teams

Shannon needed to establish some strategies for organizing her D&T team. She knew that many of the frustrations that are inherent in team participation could be avoided through conscious communication. Specifically, team experiences improve when the members choose productive strategies for organizing team activities. Successful teams:

- develop effective leadership strategies
- outline strategies for team participation
- develop criteria for the selection of team members
- practice adaptive communication skills such as behavioral flexibility
- create collaboratively stated goals and objectives for group work

In the remainder of this section, we will discuss the first four strategies listed above. In the next section, we will talk about creating goals and objectives.

Developing Effective Leadership Strategies

At its most basic level, leadership in groups refers to a set of managerial functions (Barnard, 1938; Gouran, 1970; Hirokawa, 1992). For example, in most business and professional group meetings, the most senior member of the group—the person highest up in the organizational hierarchy—is thought of as "the leader" and is responsible for carrying out managerial tasks. Tasks might include scheduling meetings or sending weekly status reports to an executive team. As important as these management functions are to a group's success, leadership does not end with them. In fact, the real power of leadership emerges from the leader's ability to manage the communication of the group. In many ways, it is this attention to the communication of members that allows a group to develop the synergy needed to become a team.

How can a team leader manage the communication of the group? Let's take a look at the basic strategies and how each is used to create synergy within a team.

Initiating Discussions

A team leader recognizes when the team needs to communicate and initiates the discussions needed to move the team forward. The team leader's role is to help team members make sense out of the organization's vision, objectives, and activities. The team leader knows that by sharing knowledge and information, the team will make decisions that are based on the experience and collaborative efforts of the team.

Providing Information

A team leader must be a conduit for information. A team cannot function in isolation from other teams or other units of the organization. To be a conduit, the team leader has to learn to listen to the myriad of conversations (verbal and electronic) that flow within an organization and transfer from them the information that is needed by the team to make good decisions.

Seeking Information

An effective team leader recognizes when the team needs additional information to make decisions or move a project forward. The first component to seeking information is asking the right questions. A team leader must learn to ask team members what they need to succeed. An effective team leader helps team members identify the sources for additional information and, if necessary, arranges access to those sources.

Consensus Building

While a good team leader recognizes that teams are made up of individuals, he or she is also aware that to move forward, the team must move forward together. It is the task of the team leader to build understanding among team members. Whether in meetings or through other means of communication, a team leader should ask the team members for points of agreement. The team leader then uses those points of consensus to develop a plan, which moves the team forward.

Giving Assignments

An important function of the team leader is to give the team members assignments. Too often, team leaders expect team members to instinctively know what they should do. Without direction, team members may step on each other's toes or go off in directions that may not help the team as a whole. Team leaders can ask for volunteers for assignments that don't require the skills of a specific team member, but ultimately, it is up to the team leader to ensure that the team stays on task and accomplishes their goals.

Clarifying Goals

A **goal** is a concrete, achievable end. **Objectives** are the tasks required to reach a goal. Effective team leaders understand that often team members are working on a number of projects and possibly on a number of teams simultaneously. It is the team leader's responsibility to help team members prioritize their goals and tasks and keep projects on track. Team leaders should seek ways to move the team forward by having regular meetings with each *individual* team member and asking what that person requires to accomplish her or his goals.

Summarizing and Evaluating

A team cannot succeed within an organization without someone who will report the progress of the team to outside members. A team leader keeps other teams and the executive team apprised of the team's progress. In their reports, team leaders should provide outside members with an evaluation of the team's progress. They should also identify any additional resources that might be required and any dates associated with the team's project.

Celebrating Success

An often overlooked but important function of a team leader is knowing when to celebrate success. Team leaders need to recognize both individual and team success and celebrate it. Celebration may come in the form of a congratulatory email, an announcement at a team or organization meeting, or a party to celebrate completing a project. However the celebrations occur, it is important that they take place and that team members feel appreciated for their work.

Phrases Leaders Shouldn't Use

The phrases listed below kill participation and creativity. Team leaders should go beyond pat negative phrases to those that encourage participation and solutions.

1. That's not the way we do things here.
2. We tried that once before.
3. I don't think that will work.
4. We don't have the resources.
5. Don't you think that's more trouble than it is worth?
6. Please just stick to your job; I'll worry about everything else.
7. Let's just keep doing things the way we always have.
8. We've never gotten any cooperation, buy-in, or help from that department, so why try now?
9. Because I said so.
10. That will cause me way too much work, so forget it!

Participation

Choosing strategies for participation is another way to improve mindful team communication practices. Participation refers to what you contribute to the team effort and how you conduct yourself as a team member. One way to become a more mindful team participant is to learn from the mistakes your fellow team members make. Another way to improve your participation is by asking yourself the following questions.

- What does the team expect from me?
- How can I best serve the team?

- Do I have any promises or commitments to the team I haven't fulfilled?
- Is there any reason I cannot succeed?
- Is there information I need?
- Is there any way that I can help other members of the team?

We want to underscore the importance of effective team participation. Toward that end, we stress a number of behaviors that contribute to effective participation:

- Be fully committed to the team and its work, and remind yourself of this commitment regularly.
- Prepare for dialogue on specific topics by thinking about the contributions you can make in meetings, informal team discussions, and email conversations.
- Prepare a list of personal goals for any team meeting that may serve as your personal guide to assessing your performance and the team's progress.
- Listen carefully, and without interruptions, to the contributions of others.
- Provide verbal and nonverbal feedback to members of the team.
- Ask relevant questions publicly rather than keeping them to yourself or sharing them only in private with a co-worker.
- Be willing to adapt your behavior to the needs and expectations of *individualized* others; avoid stereotypical evaluations of others.
- Avoid taking comments personally or engaging in personal attacks on other team members and thereby contributing to negative conflict.
- Be willing to share personal opinions and stories as well as offer sound evidence to support your arguments.
- Be willing to participate fully in team traditions, rites, and rituals.
- Help the team stay on task by avoiding commentary that leads them astray.
- Trust the team process and the members of the team.

As you can see from the above listed characteristics of effective leadership and participation, the coordination of personal goals and attitudes with communication strategies and behaviors increases the conscious effort you put into teamwork. Coordinating your communication with the team's vision and goals is essential to group success. Equally important is the selection of team members.

Selection of Team Members

Choosing the most appropriate individuals for a team is associated with the team's success (Eisenberg, 1990; Bennis, 1999). Unless individuals understand why they were chosen for a team assignment, and recognize that they have good reasons to participate and contribute to a team, chances are they will feel that their time as a team member is wasted.

In part, the success of a team is due to what researchers have come to label **jamming** (Eisenberg, 1990), a term borrowed from musicians. Jamming means engaging in a spontaneous, energetic group session. It refers to the positive energies (and fun) that emerge from total group coordination when every individual has a role to play in the team as well as a chance to demonstrate individual skills. The result is usually that the performance of the whole group improves, sometimes dramatically. However, as most musicians recognize, jamming requires that the group members have *about the same skill levels*. "Stars" detract from team play by intimidating those with less skill, and persons who have little skill have a difficult time working at the team's level, which everyone notices. The selection of team members should be accomplished with regard to similar skill levels.

However, Warren Bennis (1999) argues that good leaders in organizations view teams as places where talented individuals can develop new understandings and skills. Part of the team process is a learning process. For this reason, you want to select individuals for team membership based not only on what you know they can contribute, but also for the synergistic power of the group to help further their organizational learning abilities and their ability to be flexible. In other words, select team members who will mix well with the other members of the team.

Adaptive Skills

Team communication is different from group communication because of the level of collaboration and cooperation. This increase in cooperation occurs when team members develop what researchers call "adaptive skills" (Phillips, Pedersen, and Wood, 1990; Goodall, 1990). **Adaptive skill** refers to the ability of team members to adapt their behaviors to the needs and expectations of others. Adaptive communication skills involve *behavioral flexibility,* which consists of the following mindful processes (Goodall, 1990, pp. 133–134).

- Developing a *repertoire of self-presentations* that can be used to formulate appropriate responses to situations and to others.
- Serving as an example of effective *collaborative* communication for others by actively demonstrating your desire to work well with others, by showing patience with emergent ideas, by actively listening and responding to the ideas and suggestions of others, and by complementing the work and contributions of group members.
- Accepting the *legitimacy and honesty of others' self-presentations* by learning to expect and adapt to displays of diversity in meeting behavior, by not allowing personal conflicts or past performances to interfere with your ability to share information productively, and by staying on task.

All of these knowledge and skill areas provide parameters for task-oriented talk to be shared among team members. They provide a foundation for meeting management because they demonstrate to team members the need to stay on task and on schedule, working together toward a common goal.

Creating: Defining the Goals and Strategies for a Team

Teams succeed when they have clearly stated goals and commonly perceived objectives. Team members feel more ownership of the team's goals and objectives when they participate in defining them. Shannon had a clear idea of what Ling and the senior management team expected from her team; however, she believed it was important that the team develop a team vision and set of objectives together. She decided to have an off-site kick-off meeting to formally introduce the team members to each other and define the vision and objectives for the team.

Shannon knew that, in organizations, the terms shared vision and kick-off meetings often are met with groans. She had delivered this response herself many times. In the past, team leaders, HR directors, and company owners, with the best intentions, forced her to participate in visioning or kick-off meetings that fell short of everyone's expectations. The leader would stand in front of the group and deliver a speech about how this experience was going to be different. Then, everyone would be asked to participate in "team-building exercises," many of which Shannon and the other participants had done before. Finally, they all would be served ice cream and sent back to their work stations. A week later, the participants would receive a memo that contained the vision statement. Rarely, thought Shannon, does the vision reflect the output from the visioning exercises or the input from the participants.

"This time," Shannon thought, "it is going to be different. I need this team to understand that their participation is key to our success. I need to organize the kick-off meeting to ensure we accomplish our goals. I need an agenda."

Agendas

Because so much of the business of a meeting is dedicated to sharing information, creating and managing an **agenda** is central to the success of any meeting. An agenda is a functional document that should include the date, time, and place of the meeting and a speaking assignment or role for any participant who is responsible for a specific area of the agenda. It should be organized chronologically, moving the talk from issues that remain to be resolved from previous meetings, to current topics, to assignments for the next briefing. Figure 10.2 provides an example of the agenda Shannon sent out announcing the kick-off meeting of the Documentation and Training Team.

Figure 10.2
Sample Agenda

> **Documentation and Training Team Kick-off Meeting**
>
> *Date:* 14 December 2001
> *Time:* 9:00 A.M.–1:00 P.M.
> *Place:* Inveress Conference Center—Pine Room
>
> ### Agenda
>
> Opening Remarks
> Introduction of Team Members
> Discussion of Management Team Vision and Stated Objectives
> The D&T Vision Within the Vision
> Lunch

The purpose of the kick-off meeting was to introduce the team members to one another and develop a vision and objectives for the D&T team based on the company vision and objectives. Shannon began to think about each of the agenda items and how she would accomplish each item during the meeting. She then drafted a plan for each item on her agenda:

Opening remarks	Short, 5-minute welcome and personal introduction. *Use CCCD to organize this part.*
Introduction of team members	Ask each team member to interview one other team member and then introduce the member to the team.
Discussion of management team vision and stated objectives	Read the Bilin.com Vision and Objectives Statement. Ask Ling to attend this portion of the meeting so he can address any questions the team might have.
The D&T vision within the vision	Use the exercise from Peter Senge's *The Fifth Discipline* for creating a team vision.

Creating a Shared Vision

Within the context of an organization, a shared **vision** refers to the overall, far-reaching idea of what a team or organization should accomplish and the values that should inform those accomplishments. To help her team members develop their own vision for the team, Shannon adapted an exercise outlined in Peter Senge's book *The Fifth Discipline* (1994, p. 337). Her version is reproduced below.

The D&T Vision

Step 1: The Vision of the Future

It is five years from today's date and you have, marvelously enough, created the organization you most want to create. Now it is your job, as a team, to describe it—as if you were able to see it, realistically around you. Consider these questions one by one, painting an ever-clearer shared vision of your future organization.

Make sure each member of the team has an opportunity to comment on each of the questions. Note the main points on a whiteboard that everyone in the group can see:

1. Who are the *stakeholders* associated with our team? (Remember we are five years in the future.) How do we work with each stakeholder group? How do we produce value for them?
2. What are the most influential trends in our industry?
3. What is our image in the marketplace? How do we compete?
4. What is our unique contribution to the marketplace? What is the impact of our work on other teams, the organization, and our customers?
5. How do we make money?
6. What does our team look like? How does our team interact with other teams in the organization?
7. How do we handle good times? How do we handle hard times?
8. In what ways is our organization a great place to work?
9. What are our values? How do people treat each other? How are people recognized?
10. How do we know that the future of our team is secure? What have we done to ensure its future for ourselves?
11. What is our team's role in the organization?

After you answer each question above, ask:
How will we measure our progress?

Step 2: Current Reality

Now come back to the current year and look at the organization as it is today.

(continued)

12. What are the critical forces that allow us to succeed?
13. Who are the current stakeholders today—both inside and outside the organization? What changes do we perceive taking place among our stakeholders?
14. What are the most influential trends in our industry today?
15. What aspects of our team will empower people? What aspects of our team may disempower people?
16. How is the company's Vision and Objectives Statement currently used by other teams?
17. What do we know that we need to know? What don't we know that we need to know?

Step 3: Creating the Vision

Underline the key words in each answer. Did any words reoccur in the answers? Highlight these words. Make a list of the main themes that emerge from the answers. Draft a vision that incorporates the main themes and key words that you identified from the answers.

Shannon was pleased with how well things were going. The introductions went smoothly, and even though the process of introducing each other was a bit cheesy, it had helped break the ice and put everyone at ease. The discussion of the company's Vision and Objectives Statement also went well. Ling did a great job of facilitating the questions without attempting to impose a vision on the group. So far, everyone seemed eager to participate.

After a short break, Shannon discussed the visioning exercise she had planned for the team. She provided each team member with a copy of the instructions and questions that would guide the process.

After two hours of work, the team agreed on the following vision statement:

The Documentation and Training Team will provide our stakeholders with *task-oriented documentation* and *training materials* that together *solve problems, facilitate learning,* and *reduce customer uncertainty*. Meeting this goal will *increase customer confidence, reduce support needs,* and *add significant pre- and post-sales value to our products.*

Shannon was thrilled! The clear agenda and organization plan allowed her team to create a shared vision that would unify the team. She praised the group for their hard work. She tasked each team member to come up with 1-year, 6-month, and 3-month objectives based on the team's vision. She asked that the team members submit their objectives to her by the following Wednesday.

"We will discuss the objectives on Thursday at our status meeting," Shannon said. "We will use your objectives to draft the objectives that will guide the group in the short and long term. Thanks for your enthusiasm and creativity. I think we are off to a great start. Let's eat!"

Coordinating: Establishing a Creative Environment for Team Problem Solving

A few weeks after the kick-off meeting, Shannon was faced with a dilemma. Two of the company's sales teams had promised training to two different customers the same week. Neither sales team wanted to back off their commitment. Shannon's team would have to come up with a solution. Frustrated, Shannon called her mentor, Pam.

"How are things?" Pam asked.

"Really good," said Shannon. "We had a kick-off meeting a few weeks ago that was very successful. We came up with a vision statement and objectives that we are using to frame our projects. But I have another question."

"Sure," Pam said. "What's up?"

"How do you go about solving problems or planning detailed projects?" Shannon asked.

"Good question," Pam said. "I have found that in order to keep all the projects my team is responsible for moving forward, we have to be creative. However, to do this, I had to create an environment that would allow team members to offer creative ideas and solutions in a structured way. I also had to recognize that we were working under certain organizational constraints."

"Like what?" asked Shannon.

"Well, budgets for one. And time constraints. There never seems to be enough time to finish a project. Another big constraint is priorities, which of course are always changing. Oh, and let's not forget a lack of resources. Should I go on?" Pam laughed.

"No," said Shannon, "I get the picture."

"You have to balance the creative solutions of the team with the constraints of the organization," Pam said.

"How?" Shannon asked.

"Well," said Pam, "You have to establish an environment that can unleash the creative energy of your team members. But you have to be creative within the constraints that your company places on you. You also have to coordinate your team's activities with the activities of other teams."

Coordinating with Other Teams

In Chapter 7, Exploring Interpersonal Communication, we discussed how individuals within an organization should interact. We added to that foundation, at the beginning of this chapter, by providing the communication skills that should be developed by leaders and participants of teams. In this section, we will look at problem-solving skills that can be used within and across teams to coordinate problem-solving efforts within an organization.

Often in organizations, a major communication breakdown occurs when teams must solve problems that affect more than one team. While team members may do a relatively good job of communicating within their team, if needs, expectations, resource requirements, information, and deadlines are not being passed from one team to another, one or more teams may be set up for failure.

How do we make cross-team endeavors successful? One way is by encouraging teams to look for creative solutions to problems when they occur. **Creativity** results from giving people the freedom to explore alternatives beyond the traditional ways of doing things. However, too often, giving a team license for creativity is interpreted as freeing the team from the natural constraints inherent in any organization. **Constraints** are restrictions or limits, which in an organization may result from factors such as limited resources, time, or money. Charged with finding a creative solution to a problem, a team might feel free to suspend the need for a written agenda, abandon order in the discussions, or ignore the vision or objectives of the organization or team. Unfortunately, this type of creativity usually doesn't yield productive results.

Without a framework for sharing talk, throughout the organization, creativity is unlikely. Organizational theorists such as David Bohm (1980) point out that creativity actually exists because of constraints, and that both forces are necessary to produce innovation and change. Just as an artist works with the constraints of her or his materials, budget, and available time, so do problem-solving or planning teams work within the constraints of their own imaginations, budgets that have been given to them, and a projected deadline. Yet the artist still manages to produce great art, and problem-solving groups come up with interesting, if not unique, solutions. How does this happen?

Coordinating the Problem-Solving Process

Successful planning and problem-solving begins with a commonly shared understanding among team members about *problem-solving processes*. One of the oldest and most reliable methods for solving problems of any kind is the scientific method. For this reason, researchers and theorists of small-group and team behavior have long advocated adapting the scientific method to human problem solving (Dewey, 1912; Phillips, Pedersen, and Wood, 1979; Goodall, 1990). When applied in a business or professional setting, the problem-solving process consists of eight steps:

1. Understanding the charge
2. Phrasing the question
3. Fact-finding
4. Establishing criteria for a solution
5. Generating alternative solutions
6. Testing each alternative solution against the criteria
7. Formulating a solution
8. Presenting the solution

Each of these steps is more fully discussed below.

Step 1: Understanding the Charge

What must the team accomplish? To understand their charge, the team must outline the problem to be solved. The team should determine:

- What is the nature of the problem?
- Who is involved?
- What is each person's stake in the problem and solution?
- What resources (financial, material, technological, and human) are currently available?
- What are the deadlines?

When Shannon's D&T team assembled in the conference room to discuss their scheduling problem, Shannon asked the team to answer the questions above. Their responses are shown below.

What is the nature of the problem?	The sales teams scheduled two clients for training in the same week.
Who is involved?	The sales teams, the D&T team, and both clients.
What is their stake in the problem and solution?	The sales teams' credibility. Our reputation as being "team players." The clients' trust that we, as an organization, will deliver what we say we will.
What resources (financial, material, technological, and human) are currently available?	We currently have the human resources to teach classes for both clients; however, we don't have the classroom facilities. If we have to secure off-site training facilities, we will have to ask for a budget increase to cover the rental costs.
What are the deadlines?	We need to have a solution by the end of the week.

Step 2: Phrasing the Question

Once the problem has been outlined, the team should determine the issues that will guide the remainder of the team's decision-making. To accomplish this goal, the team must *phrase the issue as a question*, which will be used to guide all future interactions. Keep in mind:

- The wording should be clear.
- The wording shapes the outcome and possible solutions.
- The wording should reflect what is important or relevant for solving the problem.

The D&T team wrote and rewrote their issue question a couple of times and finally settled on:

Can we, given our existing resources, provide quality training to both clients in the same week?

Step 3: Fact-finding

To answer the question phrased in the second step of this process, the team must collect and organize as much relevant information about the issue as possible.

Communicating in Groups and Teams

In order to collect the necessary information, the team must be willing to share information among team members and with other members of the organization. There are three areas of fact and questions associated with each that the team should investigate:

- *Background.* What decisions were made and by whom that led to the current situation? Has this problem arisen in the past? If so, how was it resolved? Was the resolution considered successful?
- *Current state of the problem.* Who are the people involved who have information about the problem? What possible solutions do they have to offer? Is there anything we don't know that they might be able to tell us?
- *Possible outcomes.* What are the customer's expectations? What are the organization's expectations? What are the team's expectations?

The D&T team's responses are provided below.

Step 4: Establishing Criteria for a Solution

Establishing criteria against which to measure possible solutions ensures that the team will settle on the solution that comes closest to meeting the needs

Background ◆ What decisions were made and by whom that led to the current situation? ◆ Has this problem arisen in the past? If so, how was it resolved? ◆ Was the resolution considered successful?	Two separate sales teams promised training to two separate customers for the same week. This is the first time we have encountered this problem, so we don't have an historical solution.
Current State of the Problem ◆ Who are the people involved who have information about the problem? ◆ What possible solutions do they have to offer? ◆ Is there anything we don't know that they might be able to tell us?	The sales teams, our group, and the clients. Each sales team wants the other to renege on their promise. We don't know if there are any other dates that might be acceptable for either client.
Possible Outcomes ◆ What are the customers' expectations? ◆ What are the organization's expectations? ◆ What are the team's expectations?	The customers' expectations are that we will provide training when we promised. The organization's expectations are that we find a solution for delivering training. The team's expectations are that the sales teams learn a valuable lesson from this situation and no one promises training for specific dates without first consulting with the D&T team.

of all the stakeholders. After the facts have been determined, and before a solution is articulated, the group needs to establish the standards that will be used to assess, evaluate, and test possible alternative solutions. To do this, the group should articulate an ideal solution that answers the following questions:

- What would the ideal solution look like?
- What might it include?
- How would it impact the stakeholders?
- What resources are necessary to implement the solution?

The D&T team developed the following responses.

What would the ideal solution look like?	The ideal solution would be one that provides both clients with training without making it seem as if we cannot live up to our promises.
What might it include?	It might include incentives for either client to accept a flexible training solution.
How would it impact the stakeholders?	It would provide all the stakeholders involved a positive solution.
What resources are necessary to implement the solution?	A meeting with the sales teams, phone calls to the clients, and the D&T time to work through possible solutions.

Step 5: Generating Alternative Solutions

The goal of this step is to create as many possible alternative solutions as the team can think of. Generally, the team will use a brainstorming technique to accomplish this purpose, and team members should articulate alternatives without interrupting the flow of talk with comments or criticism. A number of software packages are designed to facilitate the brainstorming process.

The D&T team generated the following alternatives during their brainstorming session (see Figure 10.3):

Tips for Brainstorming

- Write down everything. The beginnings of a solution may lie within a thought or idea.
- Don't criticize anyone's ideas. There are no bad ideas.

- Keep going until the team is completely out of ideas.
- Link or stream ideas to encourage creative, unique thinking. For example, one team member may say "classes," which leads to "new scheduling options," and the next may say "staggered classes," to which a third might add "joint membership."
- After brainstorming, use clustering to group ideas together.

Figure 10.3
Brainstorming Results

[Diagram: "Overlapping Training Dates" in center, with four options: Joint training, Move the dates for one client, Offer discounts for flexibility, Offer both clients a train-the-trainer option]

Step 6: Testing Each Alternative Solution Against the Criteria

The team should expose each alternative to the criteria posed in the fourth step of the problem-solving process. When doing so, the team should fairly and accurately consider the merits and limitations of each proposed solution. Be sure to test *all* the alternatives, even if the first alternative seems to be a solution. The team may find a better solution in the third or fourth alternative.

If none of the alternative solutions clearly meets the criteria, combine two or more of the solutions until you create a solution that does. Or you may need to go back to Step 5 and generate additional alternatives.

The D&T team weighed each of the solutions generated in the meeting against the criteria they had established. Then they created the following chart to track each solution.

Solution Criteria	Allows us to live up to our agreement?	Allows for incentives if a flexible training solution is accepted?	Provides all the stakeholders a positive solution?	Can be implemented with minimal impact?
Move dates	No	Yes	Possibly, need more info.	?
Train the trainer	Yes and No	Yes	Possibly, need more info.	Yes
Joint training	Yes	Yes	Yes	Yes

Step 7: Formulating a Solution

Once you have found a solution that meets the criteria, clearly state the solution so that all the team members understand the direction the team will take. This statement will be used to create your report or presentation.

The D&T team developed the following proposal.

> *We propose that the sales team offer an incentive for both clients to participate in joint training at the corporate office and offer both clients a 20% discount for anyone attending the training. Alternatively, each client could designate a trainer who could attend the training for free and then train other members of his or her company.*
>
> *If this solution is unacceptable, we suggest that the sales team approach each client to determine if other training dates are a possibility and offer a 20% reduction in the cost of training as an incentive for changing the dates.*
>
> *Any reduction in course fees will be shifted back to the D&T budget from the Sales budget.*

Step 8: Presenting the Solution

The goal of the final step in the problem-solving process is to present a convincing argument to the charging authority or stakeholder in the organization. In many cases, presentation of the solution will be made in person, by written report, or via email. Rarely does anyone have the time or the patience to read a long report in business today. Frequently, solutions to a problem are offered in an email response. To be certain your audience is familiar with all of the components of the problem, you should include the following information:

- A recap of the background.
- Who is affected by the problem and the solution.
- The timeframes involved (deadlines, how long the problem has been going on, etc.).
- The relevant facts gathered during the fact-finding phase.
- A brief summary of the alternative solutions and the criteria used to weigh the alternatives.
- The recommended solution, including the cost, resources, and timeframes required to implement the solution.

Delivering as a Team

When the D&T team met with the Sales team to present their solution, Shannon provided a brief history of the problem, the stakeholders affected, and the facts that emerged during fact-finding. She then summarized the alternative solutions, after which she presented the team's recommended solution and the alternate, detailing the costs involved and the revenue losses that would result from the discounts on class fees. The head of Sales, Kurt, asked for a short break while he phoned each client and presented the team's proposal. In 15 minutes, Kurt was back and he was smiling.

"Thanks, guys, for a great effort. I spoke with both clients and both agreed that joint training on-site here is a great solution," Kurt said. "The fact that they are getting a nice discount for cooperating didn't hurt," he added. "We definitely owe you guys!"

"Well," said Shannon, "you could start repaying us by putting some procedures in place that ensure this doesn't happen again."

"We've already thought about that," said Kurt. "In fact, I have a couple of people working on a program that allows our sales teams to record all the aspects of a sale as they are negotiating. The program will kick out any discrepancies like overlapping delivery dates or training. We really did learn a lesson from this. It won't happen again."

"Glad to hear it," Shannon said as they were leaving. "Let us know if there is anything else we can do to help your team."

Most people think that teamwork is delivered primarily in formal meetings. However, more and more organizations are realizing that meetings are a drain on resources and time. Most informal team communication occurs in clusters of team members working around someone's computer or at a whiteboard. Formally, however, teamwork is delivered in five ways:

- Memos and reports
- Staff briefings and weekly sessions

- Planning and problem-solving meetings
- Virtual meetings
- Conferences, workshops, and seminars

Let's examine each of these delivery methods in more detail.

Memos and Reports

With the rise in popularity of email and its prevalence in organizations, most memos and reports are delivered online. In fact, we cannot remember the last time someone handed us a paper copy of a memo or report. One of the benefits of conveying reports and memos online is that it allows the reader to determine if the information needs to be printed, thus reducing the paper load anyone in business is faced with daily. Another advantage is that information gets to the recipient fast and responses generally are turned around quickly.

Memos

Memos are quick snippets of information. They should focus on one concept, and the information in them should be direct and easy to follow. The format for memos is fairly standard, but memos should allow for style variations that reflect the information you are relaying. An example of an email memo is shown below.

```
Internal Training

To: Kurt Lansing
Cc: Team Leader List members
Bcc: < click here to enter blind carbon copy recipients >
Subject: Internal Training

Internal Training for the 3.50 release of Bilin-BtoB is available and we are eager for your feedback! As you know, Internal Training provides us with a test of the training materials and environment before we deliver training to our first new client.  It is important that your team members participate.  To register your team members for training, please respond to this email no later than May 25.  Thanks in advance for your support!

Dates:   June 17 - 18

Location:  Training Room C

Schedule:      June 17 -  Trading Partner Access     8:30 - 12:00
                          Lunch                     12:00 -  1:00
                          Customer Support           1:00 -  5:00

               June 18 -  Application Setup          8:30 - 12:00
                          Lunch                     12:00 -  1:00
                          Application Maintenance    1:00 -  5:00

Snacks will be served at the 10:00 break.  Please do not bring cell phones or beepers to class.
```

Reports

Reports convey detailed information about a topic or a group of related topics. In today's busy organization, few people have the time or the desire to read a long, detailed report. Before you begin drafting a detailed report, ask yourself the following questions:

- Who is my audience?
- What do they need to know?
- How will they use the information I am providing?
- When will the action need to occur?
- Am I including information that is irrelevant to or unnecessary for my audience?

Depending on its length and intended audience, a business report may include the following elements:

- Cover page
- Executive Summary
- Table of Contents
- List of Illustrations (usually included in technical or scientific reports)
- Abstract (usually included in technical or scientific reports)
- Text (should be kept to 7–12 pages)
- References
- Appendices

Staff Briefings and Weekly Sessions

The most common type of meeting in a business or professional setting is the weekly staff briefing. Generally, these group meetings are organized for the purposes of *sharing information* and *making plans for organizing work*. They are typically held in a conference room, with each group member seated around a large table. Meeting leaders should:

- Provide an agenda for the meeting in advance
- Call the meeting to order
- Follow the agenda and not allow the meeting to get off course
- Acknowledge the efforts of team members
- Ask questions
- Recap the main points
- Recap points of consensus
- Make assignments

The briefing or staff meeting ends when the leader, manager, or facilitator terminates it. In most cases, these meetings occur on an established schedule (for example, Mondays at 9 a.m. or Wednesdays at noon).

Planning and Problem-Solving Meetings

Most organizations recognize that planning and problem-solving meetings are an important part of their everyday operations. *Planning sessions* are held to create a shared vision and mission, to establish core business values, and to organize the development, manufacturing, marketing, and delivery of new services or products. *Problem-solving meetings* are used when gaps appear between the organization's vision or core values and the actual daily operation of the business, or when a particular issue arises that may negatively influence the development, marketing, manufacturing, or delivery of the service or product. The elements of a problem-solving meeting were detailed in the section on Coordinating the Problem-Solving Process.

Virtual Meetings

Virtual meetings (e.g., video conferencing, networks, telephone conference calls, online chat) may occur across a wide geographical space. They use technology as the principal delivery system. They may include members of your team, members of cross-functional teams, vendors, suppliers, or customers. As the technology for virtual meetings has improved, the reasons and possibilities for conducting virtual meetings have increased.

Virtual meetings may not be defined by the standards applied to traditional face-to-face meetings. In virtual meetings you may find that:

- Members include people from inside and outside the organization.
- Teams using virtual meetings may form, break up, and reform as a need arises.
- Participants in virtual meetings have reporting responsibilities to different parts of the organization.
- Participants in virtual meetings may have goals and objectives that are different from or at odds with the goals and objectives of other participants.

In order to be successful, participants of virtual meetings and teams need to recognize that:

- It isn't the technology that should influence the team, but rather, the way the technology is used and for what purpose.
- Never substitute a virtual meeting for a face-to-face meeting if the face-to-face meeting is possible.
- If participants have multiple goals and objectives, the goals of a virtual meeting should be collaboration and communication rather than total agreement or consensus.

Conferences, Workshops, and Seminars

Conferences are large group meetings designed to facilitate talk about a specific topic or area of common interest. Workshops and seminars are smaller group meetings designed to improve knowledge and skills associated with task performance.

Conferences, workshops, and seminars often make use of *panel presentations* as a preferred format or agenda. Panels of three to six participants or experts are assembled, and each panel member presents a brief individual talk before opening the session up for general questions and remarks from others in attendance. Seminars and workshops also make use of specialized formats, such as problem-solving and brainstorming techniques. Many divide time between brief oral overviews (usually accompanied by computer-assisted slide shows) of a skill or idea delivered by the seminar or workshop leader, followed by actual practice in that skill or application of the idea by the participants.

Summary

In this chapter, we discussed many of the communication skills needed to be both an effective team member and leader. We placed these skills in the context of CCCD. We examined the need to choose strategies that provide team leaders and members with ways to help the team accomplish its goals. We discussed creating a vision and objectives that allow team members to feel vested in the team and the organization. We looked at coordinating as a means for problem solving in teams and across teams. We talked about the importance of coordinating with all the teams within an organization. Finally, we discussed ways that teams deliver their information both within the team and to outside team members.

COMMUNICATING IN PROFESSIONAL CONTEXTS ONLINE

Use your **Goodall Connection CD-ROM** for quick access to the electronic study resources that accompany this text. Included on your CD-ROM is access to:

InfoTrac College Edition

The World Wide Web

A demo of **WebTutor** for *Communicating in Professional Contexts*

The **Communicating in Professional Contexts Website** at the Wadsworth Communication Café. The Communicating in Professional Contexts Website offers chapter by chapter learning objectives, activities, quizzes, and a digital glossary.

You can review and complete the following sections online at
http://www.wadsworth.com/communication_d/

What You Should Have Learned

After reading this chapter, you should:

- Understand the differences between groups and teams.
- Apply the eight strategies for effective team leadership.
- Apply strategies for effective participation in teams.
- Develop criteria for selecting team members.
- Discuss adaptive skills and behavioral flexibility as an adaptive communication skill.
- Develop agendas for team meetings.
- Discuss the concepts of vision, goals, and objectives and how they affect a team.
- Discuss the concepts of creativity and constraint in problem solving.
- Use the scientific method for team problem solving.
- Use brainstorming as a team skill.
- Determine the best method for delivering team communication.

Activities

The following activities can be completed online and, if requested, submitted to your instructor, under Student Resources, Activities for Chapter 10 at the Communicating in Professional Contexts Website at the Wadsworth Communication Café http://www.wadsworth.com/communication_d/.

1. Break into teams. Your assignment is to create a criteria list for team participation on a group presentation. Think about your experience in other groups and teams. What are your needs and expectations? How do they mesh with other members of your team? Generate criteria for your team that will balance the needs of the individual with the needs of the team.

2. Think about a leadership experience you have had. Write a paper discussing how you did or did not apply the eight strategies for an effective leader. What would you have done differently, now that you have this information?

3. As a team, create a vision for your final presentations. Go through each of the stages of creating a vision. Share your vision with the class. How are they similar?

Communicating in Groups and Teams

Surfing the Net

Any sites referred to in the following activities are maintained under HyperContents for Chapter 10 at the Communicating in Professional Contexts Website.

1. Do a keyword search for *brainstorming* on the Internet. Download a demo of a brainstorming application. Think of a problem that would benefit from brainstorming. Use the application you downloaded to conduct a brainstorming session. Write a brief paper or journal entry about your experience. Did the application help the process? Would you use it again?

2. Search for information on business writing on the Internet. Develop a list of resources you can use to assist you with writing business reports, proposals, memos, etc. Print out your list and any useful samples you might find. Share your samples and list with your team members. Develop a file of business writing information for future reference.

3. As a team, conduct one of your team meetings on-line. Have the team leader send out a question for the group ahead of time and have everyone respond to the question. Write about your experience. What techniques did you use to facilitate the process? How did the process succeed or break down? What could your team have done differently?

Key Terms

adaptive skill *(250)*
agenda *(251)*
constraint *(256)*
creativity *(256)*
goal *(247)*
jamming *(250)*
memo *(264)*
objective *(247)*
report *(265)*
synergy *(245)*
team *(244)*
virtual meeting *(266)*
vision *(252)*

Breakthrough Skill:
Handling Team Interviews

Break into teams and solve the following problem using the scientific method provided in this chapter for problem solving.

Student parking has been slashed 25% as a result of new building on campus. While everyone agrees the new buildings are necessary, a solution to the limited student parking must be found.

Communicating in Professional Contexts In Action!

Communicating In Professional Contexts In Action! is available on your Goodall Connection CD-ROM and features model group presentations which utilize the CCCD approach. Improve your own group presentation skills by watching, listening to, critiquing and analyzing the Group Presentation featured on this program. After completing a presentation evaluation and answering the questions provided, you can compare your work to our suggested responses.

Chapter Eleven

Informative Presentations in the Workplace

After three years as an investment broker, Sam was finally asked to develop a presentation for his group. In the past, Sam had presented information about his company's investment programs using presentations that others had developed. Now, Sam was charged with developing a presentation for his company's newest investment vehicle—a modified 401K program. Sam had attended a number of seminars and training classes about the new program and was confident he could put together a good presentation. However, Sam wanted his presentation to go beyond good. This was a chance for him to really stand out.

That night at dinner, Sam confided his concerns about the presentation to his girlfriend, Beth. Beth laughed. "Don't you remember a few months ago when I had to do that major presentation on a new advertising campaign for a client? I used a process from a workshop I'd been to, and the presentation went great! I'll give you all my notes. You'll do fine."

"Now that you mention it, I remember how excited you were when the presentation was over. You were gloating about how you had all your bases covered and everything went like clockwork," Sam said. "Your presentation went that well because of a process you learned at a workshop?" he asked.

"Yes, and it will work for you. After dinner, I'll show you how it works."

Revisiting the CCCD Process for Organizing a Presentation

This chapter focuses on the components of an *informative* presentation in a business setting. We explain the difference between an informative and a persuasive presentation. In addition, we show you how to design effective presentations using PowerPoint or other presentation software.

As you may recall from Chapter 3, Beth used the CCCD process for organizing her *persuasive* presentation. The CCCD process along with a series of worksheets were used to organize her ideas, gather the information she needed, and manage the expectations of the audience. In this section, we will follow Sam as he uses the CCCD process and worksheets to organize an *informative* presentation. If you need additional information on any of the CCCD steps, please refer to Chapter 3.

For a brief review of how the CCCD process is used to organize a presentation, let's look at the outline that Sam wrote for himself after going over Beth's notes and getting familiar with the worksheets.

Choose: This is where I choose the goal for the presentation, but first I have to think about the people I will be speaking to, what their expectations are, and how they might interpret what I say.

Create: This is where I lay out a strategic and ethical plan for getting across my message. I also have to think about the

Coordinate: This is where I coordinate the presentation with the other members of the company who might have an influence on how successful I am.

Deliver: This is a biggee. This is where I practice until I know the presentation backwards and forwards, and then I deliver my presentation.

verbal, nonverbal, and visual appeals I will include in my message.

Choosing a Goal for Your Presentation

Sam realized that the first step in the CCCD process would be *to establish a goal for his message*. According to Beth's notes, he needed to determine the type of presentation he was going to give. Basically, there were two ways to go: *informative* or *persuasive*.

Informative vs. Persuasive Presentations

Informative presentations attempt to present facts and information in an objective, nonpersuasive manner. They can be short briefings, long reports, or detailed training presentations. Each type of informative presentation serves a specific purpose.

- *Briefings* allow a speaker to disseminate a concise number of facts in a short amount of time. Briefings are best used when it is important to get information out quickly so that it can be acted upon. For example, when a sales manager has received changes to a sales program, she would brief her sales staff on the facts of the changes.

- *Reports* allow a speaker to introduce and explain information over an expanded period. Reports are best used when information needs to be presented in greater detail. For example, when a sales manager is presenting a *new* sales program to her sales staff, she would do so using a report style presentation that could be supplemented with a hard copy report.

- *Training presentations* are most often used when examples, exercises, and practice are required for participants to grasp the ideas that are being presented. Training often occurs over a period of hours or days and can be accompanied by extensive online and hard copy materials. For example, when a sales manager wants the sales staff to feel confident with a new process for financing office equipment, she would walk them through the new process in a training class that would allow them to practice the process before meeting with clients.

Persuasive presentations are designed to bring the audience to a decision or to cause them to take some type of action. (Chapter 12 describes preparing a persuasive presentation.) This didn't seem right for Sam's presentation. While the ultimate goal might be for clients to invest in the new program, the short-term goal was to educate investors. He knew from experience that knowledge was important to investors, and that when they sensed a sales pitch, most of them quickly lost interest in the conversation. So Sam decided he was going to do an informative presentation. With that decision made, he began thinking about what his audience was like and what their needs and expectations would be.

Developing an Audience Profile

An early step in organizing a presentation is to determine the audience's characteristics, needs, and expectations. (Chapter 3 discusses how to assess your audience's needs and expectations; Chapter 12 describes how to prepare a needs assessment and explains an audience analysis.) As Sam thought about his audience, he made the following notes:

- savvy, experienced investors
- very busy people with little spare time for long presentations
- successful business leaders who would not respond well to being bored or talked down to

Given these points, Sam knew that the overall tone of his presentation would be very important. He would need to emphasize knowledge distribution rather than trying to sell his audience on the product or solve a problem.

Although Sam's main audience was this savvy group of investors, he knew that his colleagues and boss would also be an audience. After thinking about their needs and expectations, Sam wrote:

- Brokers need a well-designed presentation they can give to other clients.
- My boss needs to know that I can develop presentations that meet the needs of the firm's clients.

With his audience groups in mind, Sam worked through a couple of drafts before choosing the goals on the following page for each audience and himself.

Establishing Credibility

Persuasive presentations require the speaker to identify the reasons the listener might agree or disagree with the speaker. Informative presentations don't require this step. Informative presentations are based on the presentation of **facts**—what is known to exist or has been proven to be true. In an informative presentation, the audience members are free to interpret the facts however they like.

Since Sam would be doing an informative presentation, it was not his job to gain consensus or persuade. However, it was important for him to think about the types of facts, authorities, examples, and truths he would use to establish

Informative Presentations in the Workplace

Step 1: CHOOSING A GOAL—Audience Needs and Expectations	
Audience	**Needs and Expectations**
Existing clients	♦ Learn about a potential investment vehicle without a lot of pressure to make a decision right away.
	♦ Gather as much information as possible, in the shortest amount of time, from an informed source.
Brokerage firm	♦ Introduce a new product and provide the client with information without it sounding like a sales pitch.
	♦ Convince the audience that providing information is a key component of the relationship between the firm and the client.
Sam	♦ Make a professional-quality presentation that is well received by both the clients and the other brokers.
	♦ Make a favorable impression on his boss and stand out a bit from the other brokers at his level.

credibility—believability and trustworthiness—with the audience. The audience had to feel that they could believe the information he was presenting to them and that they could trust him to give them the facts.

Sam believed he had the credibility to speak about the new investment. He certainly had attended enough workshops and seminars on the topic. He had been with the firm for three years. He had a number of good clients with strong accounts who were trusting him more and more with their investments. But was that enough to establish his credibility with this audience? Beth's notes didn't provide him enough information, so he decided to browse the Internet. Within just a few clicks, he found a number of sites that had information on credibility. He learned that he could demonstrate credibility in several ways:

♦ *Education:* list the workshops, seminars, courses, or training you have attended. List the degrees, honors, and awards you have received for research in a particular area.

♦ *Expertise:* talk about your length of time in a particular field or with a company. List any panels you have participated in, articles or books you have written, and professional associations you belong to that are relevant to the topic.

♦ *Empathy:* demonstrate to the audience that you have their best interests in mind. The information you are presenting is useful and important to them. Talk about the goals you have in common.

♦ *Enthusiasm:* show that you are interested in the topic and in providing your audience with information on the topic. Your enthusiasm will catch

on and help to engage your audience, which will increase your credibility. If you don't care about your topic, why should your audience?
- *Appearance:* dress the part. If the majority of your audience consists of successful business leaders who are likely to show up at your talk in business attire, wear a suit. However, if you are hosting a seminar for a group of young, newly minted dotcom entrepreneurs, you might want to lean toward business casual. Wear what your audience wears.

Sam knew that his opening statement would need to establish his credibility. How well he demonstrated his credibility would have a direct link to the success or failure of his presentation.

Establishing Informative Outcomes

According to the CCCD process, Sam had to develop a set of outcomes for his presentation. What did he want his listeners to know, believe, or do as a result of his presentation? As Sam knew from perusing Beth's notes, there were four possible communication outcomes: informing, persuading, entertaining, and improving the relationship with the listeners.

Sam already knew that the primary purpose of his presentation was to inform, but what about the other three? He immediately shelved persuading as an outcome because it didn't fit with the goals he had established. He also ruled out entertaining as an outcome. As much as he would like to think that he could entertain his audience, he was realistic about how entertaining investments could be. However, improving relationships was definitely an outcome he would like to have as a result of his talk. Investments are all about relationships, and if he could improve his relationships and those of the firm as a result of his presentation, that would be a major benefit. Sam filled in the Personal Outcomes section of the worksheet, as shown on the following page.

Developing Criteria to Measure Success

According to Beth's CCCD notes, the criteria used to measure the success of a persuasive presentation were the audience's adoption of the position, product, or decision put forth in the presentation. But how do you measure success for an informative presentation? What type of feedback would signal that Sam had successfully communicated his message?

Sam fell back on what every broker uses as criteria: numbers. If the requests for information, phone calls, and movement from current investments to the new investment went up, Sam would know he had been successful. On the relationship side, if clients who attended his presentation sent more business to the firm or called for additional investment advice of any kind, he would know that the clients would feel more vested in their relationship with the firm.

Step 1: CHOOSING A GOAL—Personal Outcomes

Audience	Needs and Expectations	Personal Outcomes
Existing clients	• Learn about a potential investment vehicle without a lot of pressure to make a decision right away. • Gather as much information as possible, in the shortest amount of time, from an informed source.	• Confirm that the firm has the investor's best interest in mind. • Weigh the information gained to determine if changes need to be made in the investor's portfolio.
Brokerage firm	• Introduce a new product and provide the client with information without it sounding like a sales pitch. • Convince the audience that providing information is a key component of the relationship between the firm and the client.	• Have a presentation that can be used for qualified clients. • Feel they have met all of the clients' informational needs with the presentation.
Sam	• Make a professional-quality presentation that is well received by both the clients and the other brokers. • Make a favorable impression on his boss and stand out a bit from the other brokers at his level.	• Be told that he has created a presentation that other brokers can and will want to present. • Believe that he did the best job possible. • Have his boss tell him that he approved of the presentation and the results.

Within his firm, if his boss asked him to repeat the presentation or made it available to other brokers, Sam would know he had been successful. If the other brokers asked for his notes and additional information, Sam would have met their needs. He filled in the Criteria section of the worksheet as shown on page 278.

Creating an Informative Presentation

Sam was finished with Step 1 of the CCCD worksheet—Choosing a Goal. As he looked back over the ideas he had put on paper, he could actually feel his confidence growing. Looking at the CCCD worksheet for Step 2, Creating the Message, Sam saw that he needed to establish the purpose, main points, support, transitions, and introduction and conclusion for his talk. He didn't think he would have much trouble with purpose and main points; both seemed fairly straightforward. He reviewed the types of organizational patterns in Beth's notes and decided to follow a topical pattern, which would allow him to present the key pieces of information an investor would need to understand the new 401K product.

Step 1: CHOOSING A GOAL—Criteria

Audience	Needs and Expectations	Outcomes	Criteria
Existing clients	♦ Learn about a potential investment vehicle without a lot of pressure to make a decision right away. ♦ Gather as much information as possible, in the shortest amount of time, from an informed source.	♦ Confirm that the firm has the investor's best interest in mind. ♦ Weigh the information gained to determine if changes need to be made in the investor's portfolio.	♦ Increased requests for information about the new investment vehicle. ♦ Movement from established investments to the new investment. ♦ New business moved to the firm, signaling a stronger relationship.
Brokerage firm	♦ Introduce a new product and provide the client with information without it sounding like a sales pitch. ♦ Convince the audience that providing information is a key component of the relationship between the firm and the client.	♦ Have a presentation that can be used for qualified clients. ♦ Feel they have met all of the clients' informational needs with the presentation.	♦ The other brokers nod and smile throughout the presentation. ♦ They ask for additional information and are ready to launch the presentation and product for their clients. ♦ Sam's boss asks that the other brokers begin using the presentation.
Sam	♦ Make a professional-quality presentation that is well received by both the clients and the other brokers. ♦ Make a favorable impression on his boss and stand out a bit from the other brokers at his level.	♦ Be told that he has created a presentation that other brokers can and will want to present. ♦ Believe that he did the best job possible. ♦ Have his boss tell him that he approved of the presentation and the results.	♦ Feels good about the presentation and walks away knowing he has passed on useful information. ♦ He doesn't second-guess his information, presentation, or ability. ♦ His boss thanks him for his hard work.

Sam made notes about the main points he wanted to cover. He wrote a few drafts of his purpose and thesis statement, focusing on the informative intent of his presentation. When he was satisfied, he filled out the first two columns on the Step 2 worksheet.

Sam reviewed his thesis statement. He felt it did a good job of setting audience expectations while at the same time remaining neutral about the product. In his first draft he had said "an exciting new investment opportunity" but decided that "exciting" was a persuasive word he didn't want to use in his talk.

Informative Presentations in the Workplace

Step 2: CREATING THE MESSAGE — Purpose, Thesis, and Main Points

Introduction

Purpose and Thesis Statement	Main Points	Support	Transitions
♦ To provide accurate and factual information about a new investment product to our existing clients. ♦ Today, I will present information on a new investment opportunity. After my talk, you will be equipped to make an informed decision about whether or not this investment is right for you.	♦ First, I will discuss who should consider investing in the product. ♦ Second, I will go over the investment rules and laws associated with the product. ♦ Third, I will examine the tax considerations associated with the product. ♦ Finally, I will cover the performance expectations for the product.		

Conclusion

Hint

When developing informative presentations, do not use words that are designed to entice your audience or motivate action. Words and phrases like those listed below are not appropriate for an informative talk.

Apply Now!	Free	Advantages
Flexibility	Easy	Fun
Simple	Available for a	New and Improved
Limited Quantities	Short Time Only!	
Exciting		

Conducting Research

Sam realized that if he wanted to develop his main points and subpoints, he would need to do some research. Throughout high school and even into college, most students are taught to do research by finding articles in sources like *Time*, *Newsweek*, and the *New York Times*. By now, you may have been encouraged by some of your professors to turn to the Internet to conduct research on a particular topic. However, for business presentations, you need to become even more specific. You need to begin developing a list of resources for information in your chosen field.

Using the right resource can make the difference between instant credibility or laughter in the professional arena. For example, if you are giving a talk about investing to a group of investors, you might cite the *Wall Street Journal, The Economist, Barron's,* or *Forbes*. If you have conducted research online, you could site *CNNfn, CNET Investor,* or *The Wallstreet Journal Interactive*. If your audience consists of younger, hipper investors, you might even mention *The Motley Fool* site.

One of the best methods for finding good information is to follow the paper trail. In most industries, there are a handful of top people that the majority of people in that field consider the best sources for information. Print out five to 10 articles on your topic and flip to the references. Who has been referenced over and over in most of the articles you printed? Those are your most credible sources for information in your field. Now, go back to the Internet or the journal index and find articles by those sources. Use those articles as the main source of information for your presentation.

Tips for Conducting Research

- Determine the most credible sources within your field by following the paper trail. What experts are cited over and over again in articles published on your topic?
- Read widely. Read the trade publications (magazines and newspapers), journals, and Internet publications associated with your field. Don't simply read the most popular publication.
- Ask for help. If you aren't sure where to find the information you need, ask. You can ask a librarian, a co-worker, or your boss or mentor.
- Don't wait until the last minute. If you know your boss expects a presentation on Tuesday at 1:00, don't wait until Tuesday at 9:00 to do your research. Good, thorough research takes time. Give yourself plenty of time to gather information and to read and assimilate what you find.

Sam conducted research on the Internet and reviewed all the research materials he had gathered on the product. As he went through his notes and the other information, he made a list of potential subpoints for each of his main points. After completely reviewing his materials, Sam added several subpoints to his worksheet.

Informative Presentations in the Workplace

Step 2: CREATING THE MESSAGE—Subpoints			
Introduction			
Purpose and Thesis Statement	**Main Points**	**Support**	**Transitions**

• To provide accurate and factual information about a new investment product to our existing clients.
• Today, I will present information on a new investment opportunity. After my talk, you will be equipped to make an informed decision about whether or not this investment is right for you.
	• First, I will discuss who should consider investing in the product.
	   ◊ Type of investor
	   ◊ Type of portfolio
	   ◊ Amount of investment
	• Second, I will go over the investment rules and laws associated with the product.
	   ◊ Percentage of portfolio rule
	   ◊ Early withdrawals
	   ◊ Penalties and charges
	• Third, I will examine the tax considerations associated with the product.
	   ◊ Estate planning
	   ◊ Early retirement
	• Finally, I will cover the performance expectations for the product.
	   ◊ Conservative estimates
	   ◊ Aggressive estimates		

Conclusion			

Sam was beginning to see what Beth meant by support. After outlining the subpoints, he could clearly see where he needed charts, graphs, and figures to lend credibility to his information. In addition, there were places where showing the SEC rulings and the tax code would help clarify certain points. He also realized that examples would be extremely helpful when he was discussing who should invest. Sam completed the Support section of the worksheet.

After outlining the types of support he would use, Sam decided to do a slide show presentation using PowerPoint, a software program that he had used before.

Step 2: CREATING THE MESSAGE — Support			
Introduction			
Purpose and Thesis Statement	**Main Points**	**Support**	**Transitions**
✦ *To provide accurate and factual information about a new investment product to our existing clients.* ✦ *Today, I will present information on a new investment opportunity. After my talk, you will be equipped to make an informed decision about whether or not this investment is right for you.*	✦ First, I will discuss who should consider investing in the product. 　◇ Type of investor 　◇ Type of portfolio 　◇ Amount of investment ✦ Second, I will go over the investment rules and laws associated with the product. 　◇ Percentage of portfolio rule 　◇ Early withdrawals 　◇ Penalties and charges ✦ Third, I will examine the tax considerations associated with the product. 　◇ Estate planning 　◇ Early retirement ✦ Finally, I will cover the performance expectations for the product. 　◇ Conservative estimates 　◇ Aggressive estimates	✦ Examples by investor type ✦ Examples by portfolio type ✦ Examples by investment amount ✦ Slide with SEC ruling ✦ Graph of percentages ✦ Graph showing early withdrawal penalties ✦ Graph showing other penalties and charges ✦ Cite the tax code and examples ✦ Graph showing performance expectations for a conservative and aggressive investment approach.	
Conclusion			

Effective PowerPoint Presentations

Multimedia, computer-assisted presentations have outstripped any other type of visual aid in the business environment. While whiteboards abound in board and conference rooms across the country, flip charts and overhead projectors are virtually nonexistent. In fact, most companies don't even stock transparencies anymore. Walking into corporate America brandishing hand-lettered posterboard sales charts just might get you fired. It is simply not done.

Throughout this section, we will refer to the PowerPoint software program. However, the information presented here can be applied to any of the presentation software on the market, including Autograph, Corel Presentations, Media Pro, and Presentation Pro. The main benefit of presentation software is that it allows a speaker to organize a variety of visual elements into one easy-to-use slide show. The software lets you incorporate whatever type of information you need, including audio and video.

Using presentation software like PowerPoint, you can create slides that show:

Bulleted talking points	Maps	Diagrams
Graphs and charts	Photographs	Schematics
Flowcharts	Tables	Product images

Many corporate employees are expected to know how to use PowerPoint or other presentation software. Knowing how to design and deliver these types of presentations could be critical to your presentation and career success. Just because everyone uses presentation software, however, doesn't mean everyone is using it effectively. But there's no reason you can't.

Tips for Using PowerPoint

Use Slides as Support

The number one rule when designing any type of visual aid, but especially PowerPoint presentations, is to remember that the slides are a *supplement* to the talk, not the entire talk. The biggest mistake you can make is to cram the slides with every word you plan to say and then read from the slides. Not only will you bore your audience, but you will lose all credibility. This type of presentation is offensive to the audience and can cause your listeners to shut down before the presentation has gotten very far.

Start with a Blank Slate

Many people begin their PowerPoint presentations with a fancy title page that states the title or subject of the talk and the speaker's name. A typical reaction from the audience is a long groan accompanied by "Not another PowerPoint

(continued)

presentation!" Before you have even begun to talk, your audience is preparing to be bored.

You can change the audience's expectations by using the following strategy.

1. Begin your talk with a blank screen.
2. Introduce yourself and your topic, stating the main points and subpoints you outlined in the CCCD worksheets.
3. When you reach a point in the talk that requires a visual aid, bring up the first slide.
4. When you have completely explained the slide, bring up another blank screen.
5. Continue to talk, using the slides where necessary to enhance your talk, and using blank screens in between visuals.

Your audience will sit up and take notice of the screens you use and will marvel at your ability to integrate your talk with your visuals. That's how PowerPoint should be done!

Limit the Number of Slides

One of the biggest mistakes a speaker can make in a PowerPoint presentation is having *too many slides* that contain *too much information*. Follow these basic rules:

- No more than one slide per subpoint.
- No more than four to six lines of text, or one sentence and three bullets, or one example or graphic per slide.
- Remember: slides are used to *enhance* your talk, not replace it.

Use Transitions

In PowerPoint, transitions are the methods used to switch from one slide to another within a slide presentation. They range from simply replacing one slide with another, to over-the-top explosions that break one slide into a million pieces that come back together to form the next slide. Here are the basic rules for transitions:

- Pick one transition technique and stick to it all the way through the slide show. *Cover left,* for example, moves the new slide onto the screen from right to left, covering the previous slide.
- Keep whizzy-bang transitions to a minimum.
- Use blank slides while you are talking, so the audience is not distracted by the slide for the previous point.

Transitions should not be distracting or interfere with the verbal message and the message on the slide. Most business people have seen so many slide shows that whizzy-bang transitions don't stun and amaze us anymore; we simply find them an annoying waste of time.

Use a Readable Font Size

Font size refers to the size of the lettering you are using for the text elements of your presentation. Choosing the right font size can make the difference between an effective presentation and a waste of time. Make the wording readable for the audience. The examples on page 286 show some basic font sizes and the distance from which they can be read.

Use a Readable Font Type

Font type refers to the particular style of the text characters, such as Times Roman or Arial. Simply put, stick to the sanserif fonts Arial or Helvetica. Sanserif fonts (those without curly ends) are the most readable fonts from a distance. On paper, other fonts might be more attractive, but trying to read these on a screen 30 feet away is very difficult. As you get more proficient, you can try other fonts, but for now, sticking to Arial or Helvetica ensures a clean readable presentation.

Use Colors Wisely

Developing your first presentation is not the time to discover the artist within. It is amazing how often people create truly hideous "works of art" for business presentations that no one can read or bear to look at. As with many other areas within the world of business communication, apply the acronym "Kiss"—*Keep it simple, stupid.* Like transitions, color can be used incorrectly. It can be distracting and ruin your credibility. Perhaps the biggest thing to keep in mind when selecting color is that we all have our favorites; what I like best, you might hate. Neutral choices are best.

There is also a readability issue with color. While some colors work well together on paper, those relationships may not translate well to a light medium like a computer screen. Listed below are a few basics for using color.

- Never use more than three colors per slide.
- Stick to the same three colors for the entire slide show.
- White is a color.
- 10% of the population is colorblind and cannot distinguish reds and greens, so unless it is Christmas or these are the colors in your company logo, you might want to avoid this combination.
- The greater the contrast between colors, the greater the readability.
- Using light colors like white, light gray, yellow, or cream on a dark background is more readable in a room where the lights will be dimmed.
- Use color to signal a key point or to highlight significant information.
- Use blocks of color to set off important information.

(continued)

36 point	This size font can be read from 5 feet away. Unless you are using a LCD panel, which actually magnifies your presentation, this point size is almost useless.
72 point	This size font can be read from 10 feet away. You can get approximately 10 words of text on the slide using this size font.
144 point	This size font can be read from 20 feet away. You can get approximately 3 words of text on the slide using this size font.

Use Clip Art Wisely

Clip art consists of all the prepackaged, ready-to-use pictures, cartoons, and graphics that people add to their presentations. When it comes to clip art, the rule is *less is more,* or better yet, *none at all.* However, if you feel you must use clip art, here are some things to keep in mind:

- Use one style of clip art on all your slides. Don't switch from animation to pictures to graphics.
- Use clip art only if it enhances a given slide.
- Be *very* selective about the clip art you use. If you can't find exactly the right image, don't use anything.

The bottom line is that PowerPoint is a very visual presentation aid that should be used to add emphasis, support a point, and add interest to your talk. Before using a PowerPoint presentation in front of an audience, practice your talk, using the slides, preferably in front of a colleague or friend.

Verbal and Visual Support

Sam expected to have 20–25 people attend his presentation. He would be speaking in the firm's large conference room. The last row in the room was about 35 feet from the screen, but luckily the conference room was equipped with a "smart screen" projector that would magnify his presentation and allow him to simply touch the screen to move to the next slide. In addition to the technology available, Sam's firm already had in place a corporate standard that defined the graphics, colors, fonts, and other elements that he would be required to use.

Sam looked back over each type of support he had indicated on the worksheet. Let's follow Sam as he decides whether to use *verbal or visual support* for each of the points he will make in his presentation.

Examples

There is a difference between verbal and visual examples. *Verbal* examples are comparisons that help to make a point within your talk. Verbally, Sam might refer to other plans that have similar performance expectations or plans that allow a variety of investment options.

Visual examples walk an audience through a complex concept. Sam decided that he could clarify at least three of his points using visual examples. He created the slide shown in Figure 11.1 on page 288 for one of these points.

References

A **reference** is a citation of a noted authority. Including citations in your presentations lends authority and weight to your talk. They can also be used to

Figure 11.1

Aggressive Investors

year 1	$100,000	x 27%	$127,000
year 2	75,000	x 27%	256,540
year 3	50,000	x 27%	389,305
year 4	50,000	x 27%	557,918
year 5	50,000	x 27%	772,055
year 6	50,000	x 27%	1,044,010

back   next

clarify a point or to underscore the importance of a concept. However, unless there is a particular word or phrase in the reference that you can highlight using color, boldface type, or underlining, do not put a reference on a slide.

In Sam's case, he knew he needed to cite both the SEC and tax code rulings that applied to the new investment. It was important that his audience know about these rulings. He also needed to demonstrate that *he* was aware of the rulings. Referencing these agencies would lend credibility to his talk.

Here are some tips for using references effectively:

- Use only references that are meaningful and appropriate to the audience. For example, a quote from a respected medical professional would be appropriate for an audience of healthcare workers. Using a quote from a medical professional to an audience of auto workers wouldn't work, unless you were discussing healthcare.
- Keep references brief. If the passage you are quoting is long, paraphrase the passage. Don't try to read the entire passage. You can say, "Dr. Carver confirms these findings, adding that the percentages are growing every day."
- Begin by citing the source of the reference if your audience will easily recognize the source.
- Make sure your references and quotes *accurately* reflect the intentions of the original source.

Statistics

Statistics refers to information presented in the form of numbers, such as percentages and averages. Don't use statistics unless they are needed to clarify or strengthen your talk. When you do use statistics, be sure that they meet the following guidelines.

- Use statistics that are relevant for your point. For example, when Sam is talking about early withdrawal penalties, he might say: "Thirty-five percent of investors lose a portion of their initial investment when they withdraw their investment early." However, referring to the percentage of early withdrawals when talking about types of portfolios wouldn't make sense and would confuse the listener.
- Use statistics that can be easily absorbed. If you are working with large numbers, round off so that your listeners can easily assimilate the information. For example, instead of saying "over 78,918 people have invested in this vehicle to date," say "almost 80,000 people have invested to date." The second number is much easier to grasp.

Graphs and charts are a visual representation of numbers. To be effective, they must be clear and simple. They must also accurately reflect the type of information you need to present. Some numbers are more easily absorbed if presented as a pie chart rather than a bar graph. Choose the right format for your

Figure 11.2

statistics. For example, pie charts work well to present percentages, while bar graphs work well to compare data from year to year. Sam prepared the pie chart in Figure 11.2 for his presentation to show the different types of investors.

Visual Cues

Visual cues can be statements, quotes, or other information placed on a slide to emphasize or strengthen a point. Often, seeing the words displayed as well as hearing them will make the point more strongly than simply hearing the words. Shown below in Figure 11.3 is a slide that Sam created to emphasize one of his statements during the presentation.

Effective Transitions

As part of creating his message, Sam had to fill in the Transitions column on the CCCD worksheet. **Transitions** connect one topic or point to another. They help the audience listen more effectively. Some transitions signal a change in the point being made. Some transitions summarize what has been said and signal what is to come. (See Chapter 3 for more information on making transitions.)

Sam thought about the types of transitions he might use. Then he put his ideas in the Transitions column on the CCCD worksheet. He included a transition statement for each of his main points.

Figure 11.3

Investors are limited to an investment of 23% of their total portfolio in the modified structured investment vehicle.

SEC

back   next

Informative Presentations in the Workplace

Step 2: CREATING THE MESSAGE — Transitions

Introduction

Purpose and Thesis Statement	Main Points	Support	Transitions
◆ To provide accurate and factual information about a new investment product to our existing clients. ◆ Today, I will present information on a new investment opportunity. After my talk, you will be equipped to make an informed decision about whether or not this investment is right for you.	◆ First, I will discuss who should consider investing in the product. ⬥ Type of investor ⬥ Type of portfolio ⬥ Amount of investment ◆ Second, I will go over the investment rules and laws associated with the product. ⬥ Percentage of portfolio rule ⬥ Early withdrawals ⬥ Penalties and charges ◆ Third, I will examine the tax considerations associated with the product. ⬥ Estate planning ⬥ Early retirement ◆ Finally, I will cover the performance expectations for the product. ⬥ Conservative estimates ⬥ Aggressive estimates	◆ Examples by investor type ◆ Examples by portfolio type ◆ Examples by investment amount ◆ Slide with SEC ruling ◆ Graph of percentages ◆ Graph showing early withdrawal penalties ◆ Graph showing other penalties and charges ◆ Cite the tax code and examples ◆ Graph showing performance expectations for a conservative and aggressive investment approach.	◆ Introduction ⬥ Preview the flow of the talk ◆ Who should invest ⬥ Now that we have discussed who should invest and the amount of investment, I would like to review the rules and laws associated with the product. ◆ Tax considerations ⬥ Another important factor you need to consider are the tax implications of investing in the product. Let's spend a few minutes discussing the tax implications. ◆ Performance expectations ⬥ Examining the projected performance expectations of the product will provide you with additional information as you consider the product. Let's take a look at the performance expectations. ◆ Wrap up and call for questions ⬥ Review main points

Developing an Effective Introduction and Conclusion

In her notes about presentations, Beth had drawn a big circle around the words "Introductions and conclusions are circular. The conclusion should always tie back to the introduction so the audience feels that your presentation has come full circle." Sam thought about the introduction to his presentation. According to Beth's notes, he should begin with an attention-getter. As he read through each of type of attention-getter, he considered how each would work for an informative presentation. Sam made the following notes about each type.

Attention-Getter	Informative Use
Interesting question	This might work if I were talking about a subject that is less conservative than investing.
Startling statement	I don't think I want to startle my audience. My goal is to educate not scare or sway.
Quotation	Too pushy. All the quotes I can think of would sound like a sales pitch.
Personal experience	This is a possibility. Maybe I could tie in my learning experience with the product and use this as a way to highlight my credibility.
Story	Can't think of one that would work with the subject.
Captivating image	Nothing comes to mind for investing.

His best option clearly was his personal experience learning about the new investment vehicle. After writing a draft of his introduction, Sam made the following entries on his worksheet.

Step 2: CREATING THE MESSAGE—Introduction and Conclusion	
Introduction	◆ As a broker, one of the most important aspects of my job is to learn as much about the products we offer as I possibly can. This ongoing commitment to learning ensures that I can pass on to our customers the information they need when they request it. Today, I will share the information I have gathered from the modified 401K seminars and workshops I have attended over the past six months. Statement of Thesis.
◆ Preview of main points.
◆ After listening to my presentation, you will be able to determine if the modified 401K program should be incorporated in your portfolio.

Because he was giving an informative talk, he wanted to make sure that he didn't begin to sell in his conclusion. So he decided a simple review and closing sentence would be the most effective way to conclude.

Conclusion	Today, we discussed the benefits, penalties, and tax considerations of the modified 401K investment program. I hope you have found the information valuable and will take from my talk the information you need to make an informed decision about our new product. If you have any additional questions, I will be happy to stay and speak to you individually. Thank you for your time.

Sam now had his presentation organized. When Beth telephoned to see how he was doing, he told her, "All I have to do is write about what I want to say for each main point, then practice, practice, practice."

Coordinating an Informative Presentation

Sam went into the office with a full text of his presentation and his PowerPoint slides prepared. He sent a copy of the text and slides to the other brokers in his group and his boss. He asked that everyone review the presentation and the slides and give him any feedback they might have by Wednesday. He also asked that they provide him with a list of clients that should receive notice of the seminar.

By Wednesday afternoon, everyone in his group had responded to his request. Frank, the most senior member of the group, provided a number of good ideas that Sam decided to work into his presentation. Most of the remaining comments were "Good job!" or "You know way more about this than I do. I learned a lot."

The next Monday, Sam called the head of the marketing group, Ben, and asked for some of his time.

"Sure, Sam, what are you working on?" Ben asked.

"I have developed a seminar on the new modified 401K program. I need your help developing a brochure that reflects the information we are providing. Do you have the time?"

"How about tomorrow at 4:00? In the meantime, if you could send me some information on the seminar, that would help me to prepare."

"I'll go one better," Sam said. "I'll send you a copy of the text and my Power Point slides."

"Great! If you can do that, I can have some ideas ready and we'll go from there. Anything else I should know that isn't in your text or slides?" Ben asked.

"Yes," said Sam. "The approach we are taking to the talk is informative. We don't want the brochure to be a sales pitch. I'll send you the client list too. That should give you a solid idea about the target audience."

"You're making my job so easy," Ben said. "I'll see you tomorrow."

Informative Presentations in the Workplace

The next day, Sam went to Ben's office. Ben showed him a draft of the brochure that he had designed. He had done a great job of presenting the seminar as an information gathering opportunity. Ben had used one of Sam's PowerPoint slides on the front of the brochure and had inserted two sentences from his text on the inside as quotes.

"Thanks!" Sam told him. "I would like to run this by the rest of the group, but I think everyone will be as excited as I am." He couldn't help but be thrilled by how well Ben had interpreted his message. "How soon do you think we need to send the brochure out to our clients?"

"By the first of next week at the latest," Ben said. "Your audience books up pretty quickly. If you send me your changes by Thursday, I'll have it in Monday's mail."

Sam made copies of the brochure and circulated them to the members of his group along with a memo requesting any changes be submitted by the end of the business day on Wednesday. He then called Sarah, the office supervisor, to ask her to reserve the seminar room for his presentation and order the standard seminar refreshments.

Delivering an Informative Presentation

Sam was really pleased at how well his presentation had come together. He had followed CCCD, and so far, the feedback he had received from his co-workers and boss was beyond his expectations. Beth's notes emphasized how important practice was, so Sam took out his planner and scheduled two practices a week for the next three weeks. He then called Sarah and booked the seminar room for the afternoon before his presentation. He wanted to have one practice session in the room, using the equipment and his PowerPoint slides.

The morning of the presentation, Sam put on one of his most conservative suits. He made sure that his shoes were polished and his tie was straight. He felt confident and ready.

That afternoon, he went to the seminar room early to make sure everything was set up correctly. He distributed cards that clients could fill out and return to him if they wanted more information about the new investment. When the audience was in place, Sam delivered his presentation. Afterward, a number of people came up and asked him questions. Before leaving, 27 people filled out cards asking for additional information. When Sam returned to his office, he discovered that his boss had sent him an email telling him how pleased he was with Sam's presentation. Sam called Beth to tell her all about it.

"Things went well?" Beth asked.

"Unbelievable!" Sam said. "I felt so good about the whole thing. What I said was right on, my materials were really good, and the response was great. Thanks for your help, Beth."

"Hey, you did all the work. I just gave you the process to use," Beth told him.

Summary

In this chapter we discussed the basics of preparing an informative presentation. We contrasted some of the elements of an informative presentation against those for a persuasive presentation. We also explained how to use presentation software and provided tips for preparing an effective PowerPoint presentation, including choosing the number of slides, transitions, colors, and fonts. We provided examples of PowerPoint slides and discussed when each type of slide would be appropriate. We discussed verbal and visual supports, transitions, and introductions and conclusions for informative presentations. We also highlighted the importance of coordinating your efforts with others in your organization. Finally, we emphasized the importance of practicing for a smooth delivery of your presentation.

COMMUNICATING IN PROFESSIONAL CONTEXTS ONLINE

Use your **Goodall Connection CD-ROM** for quick access to the electronic study resources that accompany this text. Included on your CD-ROM is access to:

InfoTrac College Edition

The World Wide Web

A demo of **WebTutor** for *Communicating in Professional Contexts*

The **Communicating in Professional Contexts Website** at the Wadsworth Communication Café. The Communicating in Professional Contexts Website offers chapter by chapter learning objectives, activities, quizzes, and a digital glossary.

You can review and complete the following sections online at
http://www.wadsworth.com/communication_d/

What You Should Have Learned

Now that you have read Chapter 11, you should be able to:
- Distinguish between an informative and a persuasive presentation.
- Discuss the types of informative presentations.
- Discuss issues of credibility and develop ways to lend credibility to your presentations.
- Determine the best type of support to use for the points of an informative presentation.

Informative Presentations in the Workplace

- Use PowerPoint or other presentation software effectively.
- Understand the importance of coordinating your efforts with others in the organization to ensure a successful outcome.
- Recognize the connection between preparation and practice and the success of a presentation.

Activities

The following activities can be completed online and, if requested, submitted to your instructor, under Student Resources, Activities for Chapter 11 at the Communicating in Professional Contexts Website at the Wadsworth Communication Café http://www.wadsworth.com/communication_d/.

For each of the activities listed below, you need to pick a topic for an informative presentation. Be sure your topic is something you already know something about and have an interest in developing further.

1. What makes you a credible speaker for this topic? Go through each of the types of credibility discussed in this chapter and describe how you can demonstrate your credibility. Make a list of your sources of credibility.

2. Brainstorm in your group the goals for a presentation on a particular topic. Remember that your job is to inform, not persuade. After 20 minutes, stop and discuss your results. Is your goal an informative one?

3. Pick an informative presentation you have heard recently. You can select a speech, a news story, or a class lecture. Were there elements that were more persuasive than informative? What were they? How did this affect you as a listener? How did these elements affect the speaker's credibility? What could the speaker have done differently?

Surfing the Net

Any sites referred to in the following activities are maintained under HyperContents for Chapter 11 at the Communicating in Professional Contexts Website.

1. Use the Internet to research the topic for your informative presentation. Make a log of the sites you found and rate their helpfulness. Share your resources with your group members if you are developing a group presentation.

2. Go online and find examples of PowerPoint presentations. You can do this by typing "PowerPoint examples" in the search field on your browser and hitting Enter. Critique the example presentations you found. How effective were they? Did they meet the criteria for a good presentation established in this chapter? Explain why or why not.

Key Terms

clip art *(287)*
credibility *(275)*
fact *(274)*
font size *(285)*

font type *(285)*
informative presentation *(273)*
persuasive presentation *(273)*
reference *(287)*

statistics *(289)*
transition *(290)*

Breakthrough Skill Development:
Developing an Informative Presentation Using the CCCD Worksheets

This is your opportunity to apply much of what you have learned throughout this course. In addition, you have the opportunity to create a well-planned and practiced presentation in a classroom setting, before your job or career depends on your success. Take full advantage of this opportunity by treating it as if you are speaking to a group of your professional peers. Think of your instructor as your boss. The grade you receive might reflect how well you would do in this type of situation in the workplace.

Select a topic within your chosen major and prepare a 10-minute informative presentation using the CCCD worksheets provided. Keep the topic focused on either a business or professional aspect of the field you are pursuing. For example, if you are a nursing student, you could give a presentation on giving injections or a new drug. If you are an accounting major, you could give a presentation on a new tax law.

Whatever topic you choose, remember your goal is to inform, not persuade. You should also use PowerPoint or other presentation software. If this technology is not available in your classroom, mount enlargements of your slides on foam board and provide handouts to your instructor.

Make sure that you think about ways to demonstrate your credibility to your audience. Dress for your presentation exactly as you might in the workplace. And practice, practice, practice.

Communicating in Professional Contexts In Action!

Communicating In Professional Contexts In Action! is available on your Goodall Connection CD-ROM and features a model presentation which utilizes the CCCD approach. Improve your own presentation skills by watching, listening to, critiquing and analyzing the individual presentation featured on this program. After com-

Informative Presentations in the Workplace

pleting a presentation evaluation and answering the questions provided, you can compare your work to our suggested responses.

Chapter Twelve

Making the Persuasive Case at Work

George sat musing over his cup of coffee as he waited for his best friend, Alex, to meet him for dinner. He had been a vice president for six months and hadn't seen Alex since his promotion. When George called and invited him to dinner Alex said, "I want to hear all about your new job and how it feels to be out of sales."

"Out of sales," George thought. "I spend more time selling as a VP than I ever did when I was in sales."

A few minutes later, Alex sat down. They spent the first hour or so catching up on family and friends. Eventually, the conversation turned to work and George began to recount his week. "No really, Alex, all I do is sell," George said. "Every day, I have to convince someone of something. This month alone, I had to persuade an employee to either accept demotion or be let go, convince the executive board to adopt our new marketing strategy, sell our new marketing strategy to our distributors, and close a contract that made the difference for launching the strategy. Instead of selling the product, I am selling concepts, ideas, policy, and the organization. Almost everything I do requires some form of persuasion."

"Yeah, but you're good at it," Alex said. "I can tell by listening to you, you know exactly how to sell in any situation you encounter. It must be because you come from a sales background."

"My sales background helps, but that isn't why I've been so successful," George told him. "I did some research about effective communication, and I learned a process called CCCD that really helps me organize what I need to say and how to say it to a particular audience. I use the CCCD process almost every day. It has really helped me through some tough situations. I also did some research on the Internet and got some books about persuasion."

"Really," said Alex somewhat surprised. "You've never been a book guy."

"Well," George said, "maybe I'm evolving."

"That'll be the day!" Alex laughed. "Tell me about what you're reading."

"For one thing, there's the idea of concierge persuasion—persuading through personal connection."

Concierge Persuasion

To succeed in business, we need to adopt an attitude of **concierge persuasion.** Concierge persuasion has been described as a persuasion "of discrete problem-solving and assiduous service" (Bennet, 2000). For example, a concierge in a hotel might provide one hotel guest with theater tickets, another a table in a good restaurant, and another the assurance that his dog will get walked at 2:00 every day. The purpose of having the concierge provide all these services is to convince the hotel guests that they have selected the best hotel and that they should stay there again.

This concierge concept applies at work. In each situation that arises, you have to persuade your audience you have the best approach, contract, or product. We do this to keep our existing employees and customers and convince new employees and customers to come on board.

Just as the hotel concierge adapts to each hotel guest's needs, we must adapt our persuasion strategies to each situation in business. What is required is a *personal connection* between the participants and an understanding of the persuasive strategy that works best in each type of situation. While some situations may require a subtle strategy, others may require a more direct, blunt strategy. The persuasion continuum in Figure 12.1 illustrates when a particular persuasive strategy might be used.

As you can see in the continuum, the persuasive strategies range from brutal to mindful. As we move across the continuum, we also increase the range of choices available to the audience. In addition, the speaker becomes more focused on the needs of the audience and less focused on the simple goal of persuasion.

While the goal is to be more mindful in most business situations, there are times when one of the less mindful persuasive strategies is necessary. That is to say, *not every business situation is about choice*. Although situations offer choices, those choices may not always be good choices for the audience. When faced with a situation that requires you to provide your audience with little or no choice, you may find yourself using a brutal strategy.

In this chapter we will examine how each persuasive strategy in the continuum might be applied in a business context. We will also show how the CCCD process can be applied to each type of persuasive situation. We will use George's experiences to illustrate:

- Choosing a persuasive strategy
- Creating a persuasive message

Figure 12.1 Persuasion by Personal Connection

Brutal	Rational	Rational/Emotional	Mindful	CONSCIOUS COMMUNICATION CHOICES:
Characterized by one-sided persuasion. Uses the hammer method of persuasion. Provides the listener with no choice. Strong pathos	Characterized by two-sided exchanges. Uses the pro vs. con method of persuasion. Allows listener to test alternatives before coming to a conclusion. Logos	Characterized by mass appeal to a large audience. Uses Monroe's Motivated Sequence to persuade. Presents listener with attention-getter, need, solution, and call to action. Pathos	Characterized by the connection between audience and speaker. Uses understanding of a need and a personal commitment to satisfy the need as persuasion. Emphasizes personal choice in decision-making. Ethos	A mindful approach to persuasion; appropriate in any context, but it takes more work by all parties.

Mindless Persuasion - - - - - Mindful Persuasion

- Coordinating the strategy with the message
- Delivering the message using a persuasive style

Logos, Pathos, and Ethos

Logos: the ability of a speaker to sway an audience using logic.
Pathos: The ability of a speaker to sway an audience using emotion.
Ethos: The perceived credibility or expertise of a speaker.

Conscious Persuasion in the Workplace

One of the few things George didn't like about being a vice president was dealing directly with other people's conflicts. For the past three months, Ivan, the head of Implementation, and Mary, the head of Product Development, had been going at it like small children. Every meeting was the same. Ivan would accuse Mary of meddling in Implementation, and Mary would accuse Ivan of being stubborn. George had repeatedly asked the two of them to work through their problems, but Ivan and Mary couldn't have a meeting without a fight.

Over time, George had come to the conclusion that this was not a business process conflict, but a personal conflict, and at the root of it was Ivan's resistance to change. Ivan, a longtime employee of the company, had been head of Implementation for seven years and was stuck in a "this is how I have always done things" frame of mind. He was resistant to Mary's ideas and had resisted any efforts to compromise. Ivan was a valuable employee, but his resistance to change was hurting his department, his relationships with other department heads, and the organization.

After much thought, George decided to place Ivan in charge of the new Custom Development area. This department was just getting started and would require a good bit of product and implementation knowledge, something that Ivan certainly had. However, it was a much smaller department than Implementation and could be viewed as a demotion. How should he tell Ivan about the transfer? George needed to choose a persuasive strategy that was appropriate for the situation and for Ivan.

Choosing a Persuasive Strategy

George decided to use a selection criteria strategy worksheet to help him choose the best strategy. His chart looked like the one shown on the following page.

After completing the chart, George realized that a **brutal strategy** was needed. A brutal strategy (Covino and Jolliffe, 1995; Woods, 1997) is appropriate when:

- You are not offering the audience a choice, yet you want to convince your audience that clearly this is the best approach.

STRATEGY SELECTION CRITERIA WORKSHEET

Strategy	Brutal	Rational	Rational/ Emotional	Mindful
What type of presentation would work best?	☑ One-on-one	☐ Any audience	☐ Any audience	☐ Any audience
What are the needs of your audience?	☑ Not considered	☐ Clearly definable	☐ Somewhat definable/ somewhat fluid	☐ Clearly definable
What type of choices will your audience be presented with?	☑ None or either/or	☐ Multiple with best alternative presented	☐ Call to action	☐ Choice that reflects personal responsibility and organizational accountability
How open to your position, product, or idea has your audience been in the past?	☑ Closed or resistant	☐ Open	☐ Unaware or open	☐ Open
What method of persuasion would work best?	☑ Strategic control—the use of authority to warrant compliance	☐ Logos—an appeal that is based in evidence and logic	☐ Logos/Pathos—a logical appeal that induces the emotions of the audience	☐ Ethos—an appeal that is based on the credibility of the speaker and his or her ability to follow through on commitments
What personal trait does your argument rely on: organizational authority, personal credibility, knowledge or expertise?	☑ Authority	☐ Knowledge or expertise	☐ Credibility	☐ All
What is your goal?	☑ Compliance	☐ Consensus	☐ Action	☐ Commitment

- Your audience has a history of being resistant or closed to your ideas or product.
- The needs of your audience are less important than the outcome you are presenting.

- You need to make the presentation in a one-on-one setting to avoid publicly embarrassing or undermining your audience.
- Your ability to persuade your audience lies more with your position of organizational authority than your personal credibility.
- All other forms of negotiation and persuasion have failed.
- Your main goal is compliance in the form of agreement to your position or proposal.

George wasn't offering Ivan a choice. Ivan could either take the new position or resign. He had considered Ivan's needs when he tried to negotiate with him and when he tried to resolve the conflict between Ivan and Mary, but now George had to think about what was best for the company, not what was best for Ivan. He definitely wanted to present his proposal to Ivan one-on-one to avoid embarrassing him. George had the authority to move Ivan, and as much as he wished it hadn't come to this, George knew he had to use a brutal strategy.

Creating the Message

George knew that it would be difficult to script a conversation for his meeting with Ivan. There were just too many variables. He didn't know what Ivan would say, how emotional he might become, or how he might respond. However, George believed he could keep the conversation focused if he clearly stated the problem, the evidence, and his proposal. To clarify these goals, George created the following chart.

George decided to keep the chart on the desk in front of him during the meeting, to refer to as a visual cue.

Step	Your Message
+ Clearly state the problem.	+ Ivan's resistance and inability to change are hurting the company.
+ Cite any supporting evidence for your case.	+ Ivan refused to incorporate Mary's ideas, even when I asked him directly to do so.
+ Clearly state the proposal.	+ Ivan must take the position of department head for Custom Development or find a new job.

Coordinating the Message

George's next step was to call his boss, Alita, the president of the company. He explained his decision to Alita and his plan of action. She agreed with George that this was the best way to handle the situation and thanked him for updating her. She appreciated George's effort to keep her informed. As a result, Alita would not be caught off guard if Ivan decided to come to her after his conversation with George. Then, George called Ivan and asked him to meet with him in his office the next day at 4:00.

Delivering the Message

Before meeting with Ivan, George reviewed his strategy for delivering a brutal message. He had to be clear, straightforward, and nonemotional. He also knew he had to remain neutral and not allow Ivan to make him angry or defensive. He thought he could do that, given that he knew what he wanted to say. He had mentally rehearsed some of his statements. He felt prepared to present his case to Ivan.

"Thanks for coming, Ivan," George said when they began their meeting. *"Have a seat."*

Ivan sat down and looked around the room. "Looks totally different from when Bob was VP," he said. "This office hadn't changed in almost nine years before you became VP."

"Really," George said, *"that amazes me. I've made so many changes in the past six months, I am surprised anything can stay the same for very long in this business."*

"Well, change for change's sake isn't always a good thing," Ivan said defensively.

"I agree," George replied. *"While I don't think processes or people should be changed without careful consideration, I also don't think resisting change is good for business either. I have been giving a lot of thought to Mary's ideas and to your resistance of them."*

"It's not that I don't think there may be a few good points to what she has to say," Ivan told him. *"I just don't think anything is wrong with the way we are doing things. We have been implementing systems successfully for years, and I don't see stirring up a bunch of change if things are working fine the way they are. We've been over this already, George."*

"Yes we have, Ivan, and the last time we spoke I explained to you that I agreed with Mary's ideas and wanted you to come up with a plan to incorporate her ideas into your current processes. Have you done that?" George asked.

"No, I don't see the point. I told you then I didn't, and I still don't."

"Well," said George, *"given that you have resisted all efforts to implement the changes that I have asked for, I think it is time to take a different approach."*

"Like what?" Ivan asked a bit apprehensively.

"As you know, we are putting together a Custom Development department. This position requires someone with knowledge of both the product and the implementation process. Initially, it will be a small department, but we expect it to grow over the next five years. Ivan, I would like you to become the head of that department."

"You want me to leave a position I've held in this company for seven years and start some lame department that may never come to anything?" Ivan lamented. "This is insulting!"

"The Custom Development department has a lot of growth potential for the right person," George replied. "And it will provide you and the Implementation department with a change that is needed right now."

"What if I refuse?"

"The offer is not negotiable, Ivan," George said. "This company has to be open and willing to change. We change our products to keep them current in the marketplace, we change our clients as new lines of business open up, and we have to change the way we do business as new ideas are presented to us. We are offering you an opportunity to move to a new area and gain a fresh perspective. We value your contribution to the company. You're a valuable asset that we do not want to lose. However, you either accept the new position or we will begin putting together a severance package for you. I would like you to take some time to think about it and give me a call tomorrow."

The next day, Ivan called and accepted the new position. "You didn't give me much choice," he said.

"No, I didn't," George said. "But I'm glad you've decided to stay. I'll help you anyway I can to make your new position a successful move."

Tips for Using a Brutal Strategy

1. Be sure. Be absolutely certain *before* you walk into the room that a brutal strategy is *the only* choice you have to effect change or gain acceptance for your position. Only use the brutal strategy *when all else fails*. This should be the last method of persuasion you try.

2. Be kind. Just because you are using a brutal strategy doesn't give you license to embarrass, belittle, or humiliate. Use the brutal strategy only in one-on-one settings. If it is necessary to use this strategy with a team or a department, consider presenting your decision to the team leader or department head and allow that person to present it to the rest of the group. Or present your decision to everyone in a closed-door session with only those who are directly affected.

3. Be considerate. Give your audience some time to absorb your idea or proposal. They will need time to think about what you have said. They will also need time to develop a way to agree without losing face or looking bad in the process.

4. Be prepared. Lay out your case *before* your meeting. Have your reasons firmly in hand and present a clear and reasoned proposal to your audience.

5. Be firm. You will lose all credibility and authority with your audience if you cave in or back-peddle once you have stated your case in a brutal manner.

Persuading Through Reason

When George became vice president, one of the tasks he was assigned by the executive board was to come up with a new corporate marketing strategy. George formed a special Marketing Strategy Team composed of stellar employees from a number of departments. For the past few months, he had been meeting with this team, the Marketing department, advertising agencies, and the company's public relations firm, all in an effort to develop a new approach to marketing the company and its products. After much work, he and his team had developed a marketing plan around a new approach called "identity immersion." The idea was that they would market the company as something that their clients and vendors could identify with, and the products would then become identified with the company. It was similar to the approach Target, Coke, and Mercedes had been using, but it was a first for George's company.

Now George had to convince the executive board that all the time and money he had spent developing this concept was worth it. He needed their approval to begin developing the marketing campaigns that would take the concept to their customers. Because this was the first big initiative he would bring to the board, he wanted it to go well. If he succeeded, the board would have more confidence in him, which would pave the way for any changes he would present in the future. If he failed, the board would second-guess any future ideas he presented.

A lot was riding on this presentation: his credibility with the board, his ability to rally the board for future change efforts, and his ability to move ideas forward from concept to reality. He needed to plan this presentation to the board carefully if he was going to convince them.

George knew a brutal strategy was out. "No way would the board put up with me telling them what we are going to do," he thought. "I need a strategy that helps me to guide them to my point of view."

Choosing the Rational Persuasive Strategy

George decided to use a selection criteria strategy worksheet to determine the best strategy to use with the executive board. When it was finished, his chart looked like the one shown on the following page.

After completing the worksheet, George decided that a rational strategy would work well. Although he could see elements of the rational/emotional style in the situation, he didn't think appealing to the board's emotions was appropriate in this case. As for the mindful style, he was all for communicating mindfully, but his goal was really consensus rather than commitment. Also, the board's decision would have to be based on more than his credibility and past performance.

A **rational strategy** (Covino and Jolliffe, 1995) is appropriate when:

✦ You want to lead your audience to consensus after presenting alternatives and then the best alternative.

✦ Your audience is open and receptive to your ideas.

Making the Persuasive Case at Work

- The needs of your audience must be met within the presentation.
- Your ability to persuade your audience lies more with your knowledge of the subject or product than with your position of organizational authority or your personal credibility.
- Your main goal is consensus for your position or proposal.

STRATEGY SELECTION CRITERIA WORKSHEET

Strategy	Brutal	Rational	Rational/Emotional	Mindful
What type of presentation would work best?	☐ One-on-one	☑ Any audience	☑ Any audience	☑ Any audience
What are the needs of your audience?	☐ Not considered	☑ Clearly definable	☐ Somewhat definable/somewhat fluid	☑ Clearly definable
What type of choices will your audience be presented with?	☐ None or either/or	☑ Multiple with best alternative presented	☑ Call to action	☐ Choice that reflects personal responsibility and organizational accountability
How open to your position, product, or idea has your audience been in the past?	☐ Closed or resistant	☑ Open	☐ Unaware or open	☑ Open
What method of persuasion would work best?	☐ Strategic control—the use of authority to warrant compliance	☑ Logos—an appeal that is based in evidence and logic	☐ Logos/Pathos—a logical appeal that induces the emotions of the audience	☐ Ethos—an appeal that is based on the credibility of the speaker and his or her ability to follow through on commitments
What personal trait does your argument rely on: organizational authority, personal credibility, knowledge or expertise?	☐ Authority	☑ Knowledge or expertise	☐ Credibility	☑ All
What is your goal?	☐ Compliance	☑ Consensus	☐ Action	☐ Commitment

George wanted to build the presentation toward the idea of identity immersion by first presenting the other alternatives the team had considered. He knew his audience was open to new ideas, because they had asked him to come up with a new approach. He believed the board would be swayed by his knowledge of the product, the market, and the clients rather than by his authority or his credibility, especially given this was the first time he had presented an initiative to the board. But the most important factor was that he wanted to develop a consensus for his new approach. He wanted the board members to be in agreement with the approach and to feel they had a part in developing it. Given all of that, George decided he would use a rational strategy for his presentation to the board.

Creating the Rational Persuasive Message

Now that he had selected his persuasive strategy, George was ready to create his message. In his message, he wanted to present the charge from the board, the criteria they developed, the alternatives generated, and finally the best alternative. To help him create his message, George prepared a presentation organization chart. He worked for a couple of hours, carefully thinking about each heading. When he was finished, his chart looked like the example shown on the following page.

Coordinating the Rational Persuasive Message

One of the supports for George's meeting with the board was a PowerPoint presentation. George would have to coordinate this with Marketing, so he called Cynth. She was the best marketing designer the company had and she was also a member of his Marketing Strategy Team. He could develop the PowerPoint presentation himself, but he knew that Cynth would do a much better job.

"Sure, I'd be happy to whip up your slides," Cynth told him after George explained the project. "When do you need them?"

"I want to do a dry run for the team on Friday. Could you have everything to me by Thursday so I can practice it a couple of times before Friday?"

"No problem," Cynth said. "Do you have all the information for each slide?"

"Yes," George said. "I'll email it to you when we hang up."

"Good," said Cynth. "That will make things go very quickly."

George's next call was to Martin, another Marketing Strategy Team member. He asked Martin to send out an email asking the team to attend a dry run on Friday, to reserve the conference room, and make sure that the equipment he needed would be there and working. He also asked Martin to make arrangements for refreshments in the conference room.

After George's dry run on Friday, the team spent several hours fine tuning the presentation until it was as close to perfect as possible. The team members provided excellent

PRESENTATION ORGANIZATION CHART

Introduction	• Attention-Getter—Tell the story about the man and the elephant. • Statement of Thesis—Today I will show you that our new strategy meets the criteria we developed and gives us an edge over our competition. • Preview of main points. • Inducement		
Purpose and Thesis Statement	**Main Points**	**Support**	**Transitions**

• To inform the board about the progress George's team has made developing a new marketing strategy and to convince the board that identity immersion is the best strategy.
• I will show you that our new strategy meets the criteria we developed and gives us an edge over our competition.
	• First, I will introduce the members of the team and others who helped us with the process.
	  ◊ Team
	  ◊ Outside consultants
	• Second, I will walk you through the process we followed as we developed our strategy.
	  ◊ Establishing criteria
	  ◊ Generating alternatives
	  ◊ Selecting the best strategy.
	• Third, I present the strategy we selected.
	  ◊ Concept
	  ◊ Goals
	  ◊ What's next
	• Finally, I ask for your input and answer any questions you may have.
	  ◊ Questions
	  ◊ Vote for consensus
		• None required
		
		• PowerPoint
		  ◊ List of the criteria
		  ◊ List of alternatives
		
		  ◊ Slide showing the statistics of sales increase by company of organizations using an identity immersion marketing strategy
		  ◊ Slide with goals
			• Introduction
			  ◊ Preview the flow of the talk
			• Process
			  ◊ With the team in place, we began the process by generating the criteria our final strategy should include.
			  ◊ Once we had the criteria in place, it was time to develop possible strategies.
			  ◊ After reviewing all the possible strategies generated by the team and comparing each strategy to our criteria, it was clear that identity immersion was the best strategy.
			• Best Strategy
			  ◊ Now that we have discussed the general concept, I would like to explain the goals we have established for the strategy.
			  ◊ The logical next step in the process is to develop a marketing plan and a budget. I would like to spend a few minutes discussing a timeline for that process.
			  ◊ Return to introduction
			  ◊ Of course, to be effective, a corporate strategy requires corporate buy-in. However, before we take a board vote, I would like to give you all an opportunity to ask any questions you might have.

Conclusion	• Review of main points • We have to approach a new marketing strategy the way a blind man perceives an elephant. Identity immersion allows us the opportunity to be perceived by the market in a new way, which is the goal of a great marketing strategy.		

feedback that filled in the gaps in the presentation. George was ready for the board meeting the following week.

Delivering the Rational Persuasive Message

The morning of the board meeting, George selected a conservative suit and tie. He made certain that his shoes were shined and his hair and nails were groomed. There was no way he was going to allow his personal presentation to take away from his professional presentation.

An hour before the meeting, George went to the board room and checked the equipment. He made sure the refreshment table was set up. Then he went back to his office.

A few minutes before the meeting, George reviewed his preparations for delivering a rational message. He needed to follow his organizational chart and present his message in a straightforward and nonemotional manner. He also needed to be positive, upbeat, and ready for questions. He felt ready.

George was thinking about the presentation he had just delivered to the executive board when the phone rang. The call was from Alita, the company president.

"Congratulations, George," Alita said. "That was a great presentation. Very well organized and planned. Everyone was impressed."

"Thanks!" George said. "What was the outcome?"

"You got your consensus. Of course a couple of people had some reservations, but the decision was made to go with your strategy and move to the planning and budgeting phase," Alita said. "I'm pleased for you and I'm eager to start moving forward."

"I'm ready," said George. "I'll get the team together on Monday and we'll get started. Thanks for the support, Alita."

Tips for Using a Rational Strategy

1. Select an organizational pattern that allows you to present your case in a logical and organized manner. Many of the patterns discussed in Chapter 3 are effective, including cause/effect, problem/solution, and criteria/alternatives/best solution.
2. Prepare your organizational chart, laying out all the elements required for a complete and planned presentation.
3. Practice your presentation in front of your team or group. Ask for feedback to fill in any gaps you may have left in your preparation or planning.
4. Develop visual support that enhances your presentation. (See Chapter 11 for tips for developing visual support.)
5. Dress in a way that enhances your credibility and doesn't distract from your message.
6. Deliver your presentation with confidence and enthusiasm.

Persuading Through Emotion

Three months after George's successful presentation to the board, his team was ready to launch the first promotion based on the identity immersion marketing strategy. They had determined through research that their company had three advantages to promote: price points of its products, sound reputation for service, and a reputation for doing what they said they would do. The Marketing Strategy Team decided that they would launch a campaign that promoted value, service, and credibility.

They had buy-in from the board, but now they needed to sell the concept to their distributors. The team had determined that for identity immersion to be successful, they needed customers to identify with the company, their products, *and* their distributors. Their goal was to enter into as many co-advertising agreements as possible with their distributors. Thus far, the company had not been very successful with co-advertising, which split advertising costs between the company and the distributors. In the past, distributors had regarded advertising as the company's responsibility. George had a major sales job ahead of him to change their minds.

George wanted to present the identity immersion concept at the next quarterly distributors meeting. He needed to develop a presentation that would get the distributors excited about the concept. He wanted at least 25% of his audience to sign co-advertising agreements by the end of the three-day meeting.

Choosing the Rational/Emotional Persuasive Strategy

George knew from his sales experience that to get the distributors excited, he had to use a strong sales pitch. He prepared a strategy selection criteria worksheet to see if the rational/emotional strategy would work. When it was finished, his chart looked like the one shown on the following page.

After completing the chart, George decided that a rational/emotional strategy would work well. Although there were elements of the other strategies present in the situation, the rational/emotional strategy seemed the best choice. A **rational/emotional strategy** is appropriate when:

- Your goal is a call to action.
- Your audience is open and receptive to your ideas.
- You need to persuade your audience that you can meet their needs, especially when they might be unaware of what their needs are.
- Your ability to persuade your audience lies more with meeting the emotional needs of your audience and personal credibility.

George's goal was to persuade at least 25% of the distributors to sign a co-advertiser agreement by the end of the meeting. He knew that his audience was open and receptive to his products because they were already distributors. However, he needed to make them aware of the advantages of co-advertising within

STRATEGY SELECTION CRITERIA WORKSHEET

Strategy	Brutal	Rational	Rational/Emotional	Mindful
What type of presentation would work best?	☐ One-on-one	☑ Any audience	☑ Any audience	☑ Any audience
What are the needs of your audience?	☐ Not considered	☐ Clearly definable	☑ Somewhat definable/somewhat fluid	☐ Clearly definable
What type of choices will your audience be presented with?	☐ None or either/or	☐ Multiple with best alternative presented	☑ Call to action	☐ Choice that reflects personal responsibility and organizational accountability
How open to your position, product, or idea has your audience been in the past?	☐ Closed or resistant	☑ Open	☑ Unaware or open	☑ Open
What method of persuasion would work best?	☐ Strategic control—the use of authority to warrant compliance	☐ Logos—an appeal that is based in evidence and logic	☑ Logos/Pathos—a logical appeal that induces the emotions of the audience	☐ Ethos—an appeal that is based on the credibility of the speaker and his or her ability to follow through on commitments
What personal trait does your argument rely on: organizational authority, personal credibility, knowledge or expertise?	☐ Authority	☐ Knowledge or expertise	☑ Credibility	☐ All
What is your goal?	☐ Compliance	☐ Consensus	☑ Action	☐ Commitment

the identity immersion strategy. Most of all, he wanted to get them excited about the new marketing strategy. He knew if he could get them excited, he could persuade them to sign up.

Creating the Rational/Emotional Message

George realized that a rational/emotional persuader is a facilitator. The rational/emotional speaker brings the audience to a particular action by showing them their needs, explaining how those needs can be satisfied, and helping them visualize how a product or service can meet those needs. In order to accomplish this at the distributors meeting, George had to figure out what the needs of his audience were. He decided to conduct a needs assessment.

Needs Assessment vs. Audience Analysis

In most cases, when you develop a presentation for a business situation, you know in advance who your audience is. For example, when George spoke to the board, he knew who each of the board members was, how long each had served on the board, what positions they held on other boards or in other organizations, how old each board member was, and each member's race and gender. These are the demographic traits that are commonly referred to as an **audience analysis.** George's company had an online database that could provide George with several factors:

- Geographic location of each distributor, sorted by the distributors' region, state, city, or zip code.
- Products a distributor had purchased in the last 10 years, sorted by product number, name, or price.
- Top management at each distributor location and a profile that included name, title, age, birthday, education, length of service, and hobbies.
- Notes that sales had entered after each visit, phone call, or email to anyone at a particular distribution site.

All this information gave George a solid profile of the group of people he would be speaking to. What it didn't give him was any information on what his audience needed from him and his company. His goal was to use his presentation on identity immersion to tap into a need of the distributors. But to do that, he had to determine what their needs were. George decided to conduct a **needs assessment**—a survey to find out what the audience needed or wanted, or what problems they might have. He called a meeting of the Marketing Strategy Team for the next morning.

> *"To sell the identity immersion concept to the distributors, we have to tap into a need that the distributors have," George explained to the team. "To do that, we have to conduct a needs assessment. We have two weeks to develop the needs assessment and a cover letter, distribute it, and get it back. We have one week to assimilate the information and develop the presentation. Can we do it?" George asked.*

"I was going to send out the invitations to the distributors dinner today," Cynth said. "I could hold off for two days and we could send the needs assessment with the invitations. If we make the assessment fit the RSVP envelope, I think we could expect a higher return than if we sent them out separately." Cynth turned to Nate, the director of Marketing and Sales. "Nate, what is the average RSVP rate for the dinner?" she asked.

"Normally, it's 75 to 78%," Nate said. "That sounds like a good plan to me, George. I don't mind holding the mailing two days if you think you can get the needs assessment to us by then. A needs assessment of the distributors is long overdue. The information you get back will be helpful to us as well. What else do you need from us?"

"How about some examples of the assessments you've conducted in the past and some of Cynth's time to pull everything together," George replied.

"Sure," Nate said. "Most of Cynth's time right now is dedicated to the distributors meeting anyway. And she helped develop the assessment we used for the sales force, so she is familiar with the process."

An hour later, Cynth and George sat at his conference table with her laptop and the printouts of the distributors database. "Let's start with the sales notes," Cynth suggested. "They usually have suggestions or complaints. Then we can create a list of what we find and develop the assessment from that."

"Good idea," George said. "Let's see what we have."

For two hours, George and Cynth poured over the sales notes. When they were done, they had created the following list.

More equity in pricing from distributor to distributor.

Better communication about special discounts and sales.

Higher-profile product advertising.

Education for the customer on the service process.

Advertising that is connected, rather than spread out across too many sources.

Lower-end products that could induce customer to buy up.

"I see two areas here that fit right into the direction we want to take," George said. "Let's design some questions around these topics and see what kind of response we get."

Later that night, when they finished their draft of the needs assessment, George emailed copies to the Marketing Strategy Team. He asked them to review the assessment and return it to him no later than 11:00 the next morning with any changes or concerns.

The needs assessment that was sent to the distributors is shown on the following page.

When the needs assessments were back, George and Cynth compiled the results. They developed the table shown on page 319 to organize the statistics drawn from the distributors' responses.

Assessment review

File Edit View Insert Format Tools Compose Help

From: George
To: Nate
Cc:
Subject: Review, urgent

As many of you know, we have been working to improve the services we offer you, the distributor.

You are a valued and indispensable member of our team. As such, we believe it is important for us to stay on top of your needs and to develop ways we can help make you more successful. To help us in the endeavor, please take a few minutes to answer the following questions. The completed assessment can be placed in your RSVP envelope. Thank you!

1. How important to you is pricing equity from distributor to distributor?
☐ Very important — we have to match other distributors' prices.
☐ Important — we try to match prices, but we don't have a policy that we will.
☐ Somewhat important — we'd like to keep prices low, but we don't have any competition.
☐ Not at all important

2. Should there be a price break based on distributor size or number of locations?
☐ Yes — if we sell more product, we should have a lower price point.
☐ No — all the smaller distributors combined sell as much or more than a few large distributors and that should be taken into consideration.

3. What would you like us to do to improve communication about special discounts and sales? Check all that apply.
☐ Use email bulletins for any sales notices.
☐ Send out notices by mail.
☐ Have my salesperson call me personally and let me know of upcoming sales.
☐ Announce sales or special discounts during the quarterly distributors meeting.
☐ Other _____

4. What advertising venues would you like to see us use to advertise the product?
☐ Television commercials
☐ Monthly magazines aimed at a targeted audience
☐ Trade publications
☐ Local newspaper
☐ Internet
☐ Radio

5. How important do you think it is to participate in an advertising campaign?
☐ Very important. Our customers can know all about a product, but if they don't know we have it, it doesn't do us any good.
☐ Important. However, we are a national chain and when our customers think about the product, they know we have it.
☐ Somewhat important. We are pretty much the only game in town, so customers come to us first anyway.
☐ Not important. We only have a budget for local advertising.

(continued)

6. How open would you be to co-advertising if the pricing structure was equitably defined and the benefits were obvious?
☐ Very. We do already participate in co-advertising with other companies.
☐ Open. We don't do much co-advertising now, but if we could see a benefit, we would consider it.
☐ Not open. We've tried co-advertising in the past, but it wasn't worth the costs.
☐ Not sure. We've never used co-advertising so we aren't sure why we would want to.

7. One recommendation we have received is to develop a more cohesive approach to marketing. Which of the following do you think would be the most effective approach?
☐ A national campaign that includes the product, the company, and the distributor.
☐ A single message about either the product, the services, or the value that is used across advertising venues.
☐ A strategy that allows the customer to identify the product with the company, service process, and the distributor.
☐ I like the approach you are currently using.
☐ Other _____

8. Many of you would like to provide your customers with more information about our service process. What method of customer education do you believe would be most effective?
☐ Make it part of an advertising campaign.
☐ Provide more information along with the product.
☐ Develop a training video that can be shown to your sales team.
☐ Develop a brochure that can be sent to customers after they make a purchase or given to a customer considering a purchase.
☐ Other _____

They zeroed in on the marketing questions and identified the following needs.

1. To develop an approach to advertising that would allow the distributor to participate. This need was considered very important or important by 70% of the distributors who had returned the assessment.

2. To develop a new campaign strategy that was either national in scope or centered around identity immersion. This need was supported by over 60% of the respondents.

In addition to these findings, George concluded that only 8% of the respondents believed the current campaign was working. More importantly, he discovered that 60% of his audience would be very open or open to co-advertising. He began to think his goal of signing 25% of the distributors by the end of the meeting was achievable. George sent copies of the assessments, his table, and his findings to Nate for further analysis by Marketing.

Monroe's Motivated Sequence

George concentrated on developing the message he would deliver at the distributors meeting. He would use a process called Monroe's Motivated Sequence: get the audience's attention, present the need, show how he could satisfy it, help

Pricing equity	Very Important	Important	Somewhat Important	Not Important
	38%	42%	18%	2%
Price break by size or location	Yes	No		
	24%	76%		
Communication about special discounts	Email	Mail	Phone calls	Quarterly announcements
	63%	12%	10%	15%
Advertising venues	Television	Magazines	Trade publications	Local newspaper
	21%	14%	12%	12%
	Internet	Radio		
	27%	14%		
Participation in advertising	Very Important	Important	Somewhat Important	Not Important
	57%	23%	22%	8%
Co-advertising	Very Open	Open	Not Open	Not Sure
	27%	33%	31%	9%
Cohesive approach	National campaign	Single message	Identity immersion	Current approach
	32%	13%	37%	8%
	Other			
	10%			
Customer education about the service process	Advertising	Information provided with the product	Training video for sales	Brochure
	12%	35%	23%	20%
	Other			
	2%			

the audience visualize it, and then call the audience to action (McKerrow, Grombeck, Ehninger, and Monroe, 2000).

George worked for a couple of hours on a chart to organize his ideas. When he was finished, his chart looked like the example shown on page 321.

Steps in Monroe's Motivated Sequence

Attention-getter: The story, joke, or first line of a message, designed to pull the audience into your message.

Need: The part of a message that details the audience's need or problem.

Satisfaction: The part of a message that conveys the solution to the audience's need or problem.

Visualization: The part of a message that helps the audience imagine the satisfaction of their need.

Call to action: The direct or indirect statement of action you want the audience to take after listening to your message.

Coordinating the Rational/Emotional Message

George, Cynth, Nate, and the rest of the team worked for two days to flesh out the presentation and develop the visual support it required. George practiced before the team a number of times to ensure that he was hitting each point of the presentation with just enough emotion. By the end of the week, he was satisfied. However, before he presented his message to the distributors, he wanted to share the presentation with the sales representatives and Alita, the CEO.

George sent out an email asking that all the sales reps in town for the distributors meeting attend a preview of his talk before the first session. He wanted to be sure that all the sales reps were on the same page with the marketing and sales teams. Even though he and Alita had had numerous discussions about the new marketing strategy, he wanted to be sure that Alita knew exactly what was in the presentation. The last thing he needed was for Alita to be caught off guard after his session. If she previewed the presentation, she would be able to address any questions that might arise from the distributors.

Delivering the Rational/Emotional Message

George knew there would be a fine line in his presentation between too much emotion and not quite enough. He wanted his audience to be excited about co-advertising and the new marketing strategy. However, he also wanted to maintain his credibility. He had to convince the distributors that they needed a new marketing strategy, and that the strategy he proposed would strengthen the customers' identification with the product, the company, and the distributor, which

MOTIVATED SEQUENCE ORGANIZATION CHART

Introduction

- Attention-Getter—Most of us have heard the story of the blind men and the elephant. According to the story, each man describes the elephant differently. One describes the elephant as a strong tree, one as a mighty sword, and one as a strong rope. However, the real beauty of this story is that to learn about the elephant, the blind men must first learn that they need to learn. Second, the blind men need to listen to each other and set aside their previous notions of what an elephant is. Third, they need to understand that only together will they develop a true understanding of the whole elephant.

  In the past, our advertising efforts have been similar to the efforts of the blind men identifying the elephant. Our new approach identifies the bits and pieces that we have often overlooked. What we need is a new approach to marketing that gives our customers the whole picture.

Purpose and Thesis Statement	Main Points	Support
◆ To convince the distributors that we need a new approach to marketing and that they are critical to the success of the new approach.	◆ *Need*—new approach is needed ◇ Past efforts ◇ Sales figures ◇ Customer survey conducted on the current approach to advertising ◆ *Satisfaction*—identity immersion ◇ Create identity with customer for the product, company, and the distributor ◇ Provides a cohesive advertising strategy ◇ Discuss the impact of co-advertising ◆ *Visualization* ◇ Show an example of a successful identity immersion campaign ◇ Discuss the sales figures from before identity immersion campaign and after ◇ Show the distributor's logo on sample ads ◆ *Action* ◇ For this new approach to be successful, we need you the distributor to join us. ◇ Outline the points of the co-advertising agreement.	◆ Slides showing examples of past advertising from a variety of media and different campaigns ◆ Slide showing sales figures before and after each campaign ◆ Slide showing results of customer survey ◆ Slide showing a diagram that links all the elements of the campaign together ◆ Slides and video that show an example of the TV, magazine, and newspaper ads from an identity immersion campaign ◆ Slide showing before and after sales figures ◆ Slide showing a sample ad with a distributor's logo ◆ Slide that outlines the points of the agreement.

Conclusion

- *Call to Action*—When our customers see our products, we don't want them to see just a product. We want them to see our product, our excellent service policy, exceptional value, an established and innovative company, and a local distributor who is knowledgeable and dependable. We want them to see the whole elephant! Join us in this exciting new approach, sign up today as a co-advertiser, and together we will create a marketing strategy the customer can identify within a new way, which is the goal of a great marketing strategy.

would result in increased sales. He needed to hit a note of excitement mixed with credibility. That was the balance he was looking for. After all his practice sessions and the preview for Alita and the sales reps, he was confident he had it.

As he spoke, George kept an eye on his audience. He was looking for feedback: a nod, a smile, a bored look. As the speech progressed, the nods increased and the smiles widened. The distributors liked what they were hearing. George gauged their reaction and put a bit more excitement into his voice. He increased the strength of his voice and the audience went along, nodding and smiling more. A few times, George saw one distributor nudge another and nod as if to say, "See, I told you that's what we needed." By the end of his presentation, George was sure he had the 25% sign-up he had hoped for.

Tips for Using a Rational/Emotional Strategy

1. Determine your purpose and your audience.
2. Identify the needs of your audience and ways that their needs can be served by your purpose.
3. Use Monroe's Motivated Sequence to organize your ideas. Clearly lay out the need, satisfaction, visualization, and call to action for the audience.

4. Practice your presentation, modulating the emotion of your appeal to ensure you have the right balance for your audience.
5. Develop visual support for your presentation that enhances the visualization portion of the presentation and draws your audience toward the call to action.
6. Deliver your presentation with strength, and use words that help generate the emotions you want to elicit from the audience.

Persuading Through Mindful Communication

Charlotte Lansing represented one of the largest distributors on the East Coast. After George's presentation at the distributors meeting, she asked to meet with him the next morning to discuss the details of the co-advertising agreement. They set up a breakfast meeting for 8:00 in George's office. George realized that if he could convince Charlotte to sign the agreement, most of the other distributors would be easy to sign.

To help him decide the best approach to use with Charlotte, George prepared a strategy selection criteria worksheet. When he was done, his chart looked like the one shown on the following page.

After completing the chart, he decided that a **mindful strategy** would work. A mindful strategy (Covino and Jolliffe, 1995) is appropriate when:

- Your goal is for the audience to make a commitment to your position, product, contract, or candidate.

- Your audience has a history of being open to your concept, idea, or product.

- The needs of your audience are vital to the outcome you are presenting.

- Your ability to persuade your audience lies as much with your position of personal credibility as it does with your organizational authority and knowledge of the situation or product.

George's main goal was for Charlotte to *commit* to being a co-advertiser and sign the co-advertising agreement. To get her to sign, he knew it was important that she trust him and believe he would honor his commitments, something he had demonstrated in the past. He also knew he would have to show Charlotte that he understood her company's needs and concerns and that he would work hard to ensure that those needs were met. Although he could see elements of the other strategies, overall he thought that a mindful strategy would work best.

STRATEGY SELECTION CRITERIA WORKSHEET

Strategy	Brutal	Rational	Rational/Emotional	Mindful
What type of presentation would work best?	☐ One-on-one	☐ Any audience	☐ Any audience	☑ Any audience
What are the needs of your audience?	☐ Not considered	☑ Clearly definable	☐ Somewhat definable/somewhat fluid	☑ Clearly definable
What type of choices will your audience be presented with?	☐ None or either/or	☐ Multiple with best alternative presented	☑ Call to action	☑ Choice that reflects personal responsibility and organizational accountability
How open to your position, product, or idea has your audience been in the past?	☐ Closed or resistant	☐ Open	☑ Unaware or open	☑ Open
What method of persuasion would work best?	☐ Strategic control—the use of authority to warrant compliance	☐ Logos—an appeal that is based in evidence and logic	☐ Logos/Pathos—a logical appeal that induces the emotions of the audience	☑ Ethos—an appeal that is based on the credibility of the speaker and his or her ability to follow through on commitments
What personal trait does your argument rely on: organizational authority, personal credibility, knowledge or expertise?	☐ Authority	☐ Knowledge or expertise	☑ Credibility	☑ All
What is your goal?	☐ Compliance	☐ Consensus	☐ Action	☑ Commitment

Creating a Mindful Persuasive Message

To communicate mindfully, George would need to do the following.

- Analyze the situation.
- Adapt his message to the audience.

Making the Persuasive Case at Work

- Evaluate feedback as it occurred.
- Be willing to take risks that might lead to a better understanding.
- Listen consciously to what was said during the meeting.
- Provide feedback.

In the past, George had relied heavily on wit, charm, and a fast-paced conversational style to close deals. Thinking back, he marveled at how often he joked about "leaving so and so in the dust" and how "so and so didn't stand a chance once I walked into the office." While it was true that George did live up to his end of the contracts he signed and the promises he made, he was beginning to see that those promises were clearly tipped in his favor. He also began to see that his meeting with Charlotte was a very different situation. The message he gave Charlotte not only would pave the way for future interactions with his company's largest distributor, but it could set the tone for negotiations with a number of the other distributors. He wanted to let Charlotte know that he and the company valued her business and their working relationship. He thought a mindful approach would help him do just that.

To help him organize his ideas, George prepared a persuasive message worksheet, shown below.

PERSUASIVE MESSAGE WORKSHEET	
Step	**Your Message**

Analysis of the situation	- Convince Charlotte that signing the co-advertising agreement is:
	  - Vital to the success of the new marketing strategy.
	  - In her company's best interest.

Audience needs	- Charlotte needs to clearly see:
	  - How co-advertising will benefit her company.
	  - How co-advertising complements the new marketing strategy.

Necessary risks	- May need to make disclosures that will assure Charlotte I am being honest.

George realized that he could not script his conversation with Charlotte. He printed out the worksheet and made some notes on the page. His annotated worksheet is shown on the following page.

Persuasive Message Worksheet

Step	Your message
Analysis of the situation	Convince Charlotte that signing the co-advertising agreement is: 1. Vital to the success of the new marketing strategy. 2. In her company's best interest.
Audience needs	Charlotte needs to clearly see: 1. How co-advertising will benefit her company. 2. How co-advertising complements the new marketing strategy.
Necessary risks	May need to make disclosures that will assure Charlotte that I am being honest.

Stop Talking!

Listen! — for position, motivation, intention.

Recap.

Ask for confirmation.

Make Suggestions!

Listen to Feedback!

George would use this sheet as his guide through the conversation. If he looked at the notes, he would remember to stop talking and listen. Hopefully, the notes would remind him not to fall into his pattern of talking, charming, and schmoozing his way into a deal. His goal was not just a signed agreement, but a true partnership with Charlotte's company that set a tone for the distributor relationship in the future.

Coordinating the Mindful Persuasive Message

Before leaving the office, George put the notes he made in a folder on his desk. He added a copy of the presentation he had delivered at the distributors meeting. He wanted to have that on hand in case Charlotte had a specific question from the presentation. George stopped by his administrative assistant's office and asked her to make the arrangements to have breakfast set up in his office in the morning. There were no charts to prepare and no one else to coordinate with for his meeting tomorrow. The rest was up to George.

Delivering the Mindful Persuasive Message

George arrived in the office at 7:30. He reviewed the notes he had made the previous day. He had spent most of the previous night turning the conversation over in his mind, playing out possible questions and objections.

When Charlotte arrived, they spent a few minutes chatting about the distributors meeting and eating breakfast before Charlotte opened the topic of the agreement.

"As I said yesterday, George, I was very impressed by your presentation. I have thought you needed a new approach to marketing for a year or so."

"So have I," George agreed. "It was very frustrating for the sales reps to work as hard as they did to get the product to you and the other distributors and then have it languish on the shelves because of a lack of marketing focus."

"I am a bit surprised to hear you admit that," Charlotte said.

"It isn't a big secret that our past approach to marketing has been a problem. We've known it and the distributors have known it. However, I give the board credit for recognizing the problem and for giving me the resources to deal with it. We are confident our new strategy will address the problems we have had in the past." He started to continue but looked down at his sheet and realized that he needed to stop talking and listen.

"Which is why I wanted to meet with you today," Charlotte said. "It was clear to me that the company has made an investment in this new approach. I spoke with Tom, our CEO, last night and he thinks we should give you a shot at making this work. However, we do have a few reservations."

"I would be surprised if you didn't," George said. "This is a new direction for us. Why don't you tell me what your reservations are and we will walk through each one and see if we can come to terms on them."

"Okay," said Charlotte. "First, we don't want to commit a year to the co-advertising program. We think six months is plenty of time to see if the ads are working. After six months, if the numbers haven't improved significantly, we want to terminate the agreement. Second, we think that in the first year of the agreement, a 60–40 split is too high. We would like to amend the agreement so that you pay 70% of the advertising costs for the first year. If the numbers come in the way we hope, we will agree to a 60–40 future split. Finally, we need to have final approval over anything that our name is going on. The agreement states that we will have approval at the creative level, but we would like to have approval at the editing stage. If we can agree to those points, I can sign the agreement today."

While Charlotte was talking, George was making notes and scanning his worksheet. When Charlotte finished, he said, "Let's take each point one at a time, so that we are both clear. First, I believe I understand your concerns about the length of the agreement. If the new strategy doesn't pan out, you don't want to be forced to continue with an ineffective program. Is that right?"

"Yes," Charlotte said.

"Okay, then I propose that we amend the agreement to read that you can terminate the agreement six months after the first ad runs. It is important to the success of the program that we have at least six months to run the numbers and evaluate the saturation of the message."

"I can live with that," Charlotte said. She made a few notes on her copy of the agreement.

Point by point, George restated his understanding of what Charlotte had said and they discussed any accommodations that could be made.

"That was actually pretty easy," Charlotte said when they finished their discussions. "I was expecting you to try to sell me or talk me out of each point. Instead, I feel as if we just had a really good negotiation that worked out for both of us."

George smiled. "To be honest, six months ago that is exactly what I would have done. But since becoming VP, I have realized that a hard sales approach doesn't always work. Sometimes, you have to be willing to give a little to get a little. I'll call Frank in legal and ask him to amend the agreement with our changes. He should be able to run it up in about 15 minutes."

Tips for Using a Mindful Persuasive Strategy

1. Analyze the situation before you begin. Develop a deep understanding of the positions of each party before you enter the conversation.
2. Listen. You cannot be mindful if you aren't listening to the other parties involved. Listen for intention, position, objections, and emotion.
3. Recap. Make sure that you understand the positions of the other parties by recapping what they have said. Then, ask for confirmation before moving on.
4. Give feedback. Make sure that the other parties understand your position by giving them accurate and clear feedback.

Summary

In this chapter, we explored the notion of concierge persuasion—persuasion through personal connection that is intended not only to meet the immediate needs of a situation, but to develop long-term relationships. We discussed four strategies of persuasion: brutal, rational, rational/emotional, and mindful.

Activities

The following activities can be completed online and, if requested, submitted to your instructor, under Student Resources, Activities for Chapter 12 at the Communicating in Professional Contexts Website at the Wadsworth Communication Café http://www.wadsworth.com/communication_d/.

1. Jon is required to pass a certification test before he can use a specific piece of machinery. He has failed the test three times and refuses to take the test again. You want to keep Jon as an employee, and eventually you would like to promote him to a team leader's position, but you can't until he passes the test. What persuasive strategy would you use to persuade Jon to retake the test? Write a 3–5-page paper discussing your choice of strategy and the possible outcome.

2. In your group, share a persuasive situation you recently had. Analyze the persuasive strategy you used. How successful were you? What would you do differently, having read this chapter?

3. Select a television, Internet, or print ad. Analyze the ad using Monroe's Motivated Sequence. What were the attention-getter, need, satisfaction, visualization, and call to action used in the ad? Was the ad successful? Why or why not?

Surfing the Net

Any sites referred to in the following activities are maintained under HyperContents for Chapter 12 at the Communicating in Professional Contexts Website.

1. Enter the words *logos, pathos*, and *ethos* in a keyword search. Select two or three articles to read. How did what you find improve on your understanding of the strategies discussed in this chapter?

2. Enter the term *needs assessment* in a keyword search. Browse through the Websites and articles provided by the search. Print out a few examples of assessments that you can use to create your own needs assessment.

Key Terms

attention-getter *(320)*	**ethos** *(303)*	**pathos** *(303)*
audience analysis *(315)*	**logos** *(303)*	**rational strategy** *(308)*
brutal strategy *(303)*	**mindful strategy** *(323)*	**rational/emotional strategy** *(313)*
call to action *(320)*	**need** *(320)*	**satisfaction** *(320)*
concierge persuasion *(301)*	**needs assessment** *(315)*	**visualization** *(320)*

Making the Persuasive Case at Work

We laid out the reasons for using each type of strategy and provided worksheets to organize the messages for each strategy. We also showed how CCCD applies to a persuasive situation. We hope this discussion has helped you reframe your thinking of persuasion as a necessary part of communicating in a business and professional environment.

COMMUNICATING IN PROFESSIONAL CONTEXTS ONLINE

Use your **Goodall Connection CD-ROM** for quick access to the electronic study resources that accompany this text. Included on your CD-ROM is access to:

InfoTrac College Edition

The World Wide Web

A demo of **WebTutor** for *Communicating in Professional Contexts*

The **Communicating in Professional Contexts website** at the Wadsworth Communication Café. The Communicating in Professional Contexts Website offers chapter by chapter learning objectives, activities, quizzes, and a digital glossary.

You can review and complete the following sections online at
http://www.wadsworth.com/communication_d/

What You Should Have Learned

Now that you have read Chapter 12, you should be able to:

- Discuss the concept of concierge persuasion and how choosing the right persuasive strategy helps to build relationships.
- List the four persuasive strategies and the uses for each strategy.
- Discuss a situation for which a brutal strategy might be required.
- Discuss the criteria for choosing a brutal strategy.
- Give examples of situations for which a rational strategy might apply.
- Discuss the criteria for choosing a rational strategy.
- Discuss situations for which a rational/emotional strategy might be required.
- Discuss the criteria for choosing a rational/emotional strategy.
- Discuss situations for which mindful persuasion might be required.
- Discuss the criteria for choosing a mindful persuasive strategy.
- Use the worksheets provided in this chapter to create a persuasive message.

Breakthrough Skill Development:
Show What You've Learned

Throughout this book, we have emphasized CCCD (choose, create, coordinate, deliver) and conscious communication. In this exercise, you will be asked to use much of what you have learned in this book to create a successful presentation. Review the main topics in the book and the CCCD process. Before you begin, make a list of the topics you might find helpful to complete the project.

Situation: You have been asked to create a new handheld personal digital assistant specifically for a college market. The head of research and development would like to hear your ideas in two weeks. He has asked that you provide him with an overview of the market, a needs assessment, and a name for the product. To gather this information, you need to conduct interviews, surf the Net, and develop a needs assessment. You will then need to prepare a presentation that persuades the head of research to produce the product you propose. Good luck!

Communicating in Professional Contexts In Action!

Communicating In Professional Contexts In Action! is available on your Goodall Connection CD-ROM and features a group presentation which utilizes the CCCD approach. Improve your own group presentation skills by watching, listening to, critiquing and analyzing the CCCD worksheet used in the Group Presentation and featured on this program. After completing a worksheet evaluation and answering the questions provided, you can compare your work to our suggested responses.

Appendix

CCCD Worksheets for Persuasive or Informative Presentations

Step 1: CHOOSING A GOAL

Audience	Needs and Expectations	Outcomes	Criteria
Client	♦	♦ ♦	♦ ♦ ♦
Firm	♦	♦ ♦	♦ ♦ ♦
Self	♦ ♦	♦ ♦	♦ ♦

CCCD Worksheets for Persuasive or Informative Presentations

Step 2: CREATING THE MESSAGE

Introduction	<ul><li>Attention-Getter</li><li>Statement of Thesis</li><li>Preview of main points</li><li>Inducement</li></ul>		
Purpose and Thesis Statement	**Main Points**	**Support**	**Transitions**
<ul><li>*Purpose*</li><li>*Thesis Statement*</li></ul>	<ul><li>*Main Point 1*<ul><li>*Subpoint*</li><li>*Subpoint*</li></ul></li><li>*Main Point 2*<ul><li>*Subpoint*</li><li>*Subpoint*</li></ul></li><li>*Main Point 3*<ul><li>*Subpoint*</li><li>*Subpoint*</li></ul></li></ul>	<ul><li>*Support for Main Point 1*</li><li>*Support for Main Point 2*</li><li>*Support for Main Point 3*</li></ul>	<ul><li>*Transition 1 Transition between Main Point 1 and Main Point 2*</li><li>*Transition 2 Transition between Main Point 2 and Main Point 3*</li></ul>
Conclusion	<ul><li>Review of main points</li><li>Return to the Attention-Getter and wrap up</li></ul>		

Motivated Sequence Organization Chart		
Introduction	✦ *Attention-Getter*	
Purpose and Thesis Statement	**Main Points**	**Support**

✦ *Purpose*
✦ *Thesis Statement*
	✦ *Need*
	  ◇
	  ◇
	  ◇
	✦ *Satisfaction*
	  ◇
	  ◇
	  ◇
	✦ *Visualization*
	  ◇
	  ◇
	  ◇
	✦ *Action*
	  ◇
	  ◇
		◇
		◇
		◇
		
		◇
		◇
		◇
		
		◇
		◇
		◇
		
		◇
		◇

Conclusion	✦ *Call to Action*	

Types of Visual Support and Audiences

Type of Visual Support and Audiences	Should Be Used To:	Don't:	Things to Keep in Mind
Slide presentations (see Chapter 11 for tips on using presentation software)			
Appropriate for: ♦ Business and professional groups that are familiar with technology or operate in a technologically comfortable environment	♦ Stay on agenda ♦ Provide transitions between multiple speakers ♦ Present statistical support in the form of graphs, or graphic charts, or pictures	♦ Create elaborate complicated slide shows that distract from your message ♦ Get bogged down in moving the slides along and forget to speak to your audience ♦ Develop or use without practice, practice, practice	♦ Make sure that the technology to support your slide show is available at the talk site or plan to bring your own ♦ Develop a backup plan in case something goes wrong with the technology ♦ Be prepared to veer from your use of the slide show if your audience shows signs of boredom or visual fatigue
Internet-based presentations			
Appropriate for: ♦ Audiences doing business on the Internet ♦ Audiences that will access your Internet site ♦ Internal customers that will access the company Intranet site	♦ Demonstrate the capabilities of your site ♦ Demonstrate the type of information available on your site ♦ Highlight the advantages of your site vs. other sites	♦ Get bogged down in the features of a site and forget the important points of your presentation ♦ Get bogged down in the technical aspects of the site, especially if your audience is not technical ♦ Deliver a presentation based on Internet technology without practice, practice, practice	♦ Make sure that the technology to support your Internet-based presentation is available at the talk site ♦ Develop a backup plan in case something goes wrong with the technology ♦ Be prepared to veer from your use of the Internet if your audience shows signs of boredom or visual fatigue

Appendix

Types of Visual Support and Audiences

Type of Visual Support and Audiences	Should Be Used To:	Don't:	Things to Keep in Mind

Slide presentations (see Chapter 11 for tips on using presentation software)

Videotape

Appropriate for: ♦ Audiences that require visual demonstration of a sales technique, product, or competitor's product or service ♦ Audiences that are geographically dispersed ♦ Cases where the featured speaker (CEO, president, or motivational speaker) is unavailable for an appearance	♦ Demonstrate the capabilities of your product or service ♦ Demonstrate a technique or process ♦ Deliver personal message from a CEO, motivational speaker, or other source not available for a personal appearance	♦ Simply turn on the videotape and walk away. Videotape should be used to enhance a presentation, not substitute for one ♦ Use poor quality video. If you can't find or develop a video that has high audio and video quality, find another type of support ♦ Deliver a presentation based on video technology without practice, practice, practice	♦ Make sure that the technology to support the portion of your videotape presentation is available at the talk site ♦ Develop a backup plan in case something goes wrong with the technology

Models

Appropriate for: ♦ Presentations that require a 3D or visual demonstration of a product or idea ♦ Cases where a visual representation is important or will improve understanding. For example, architects often use models to present building concepts	♦ Illustrate or clarify points that are confusing. For example, crime scene models are often used in court cases to help with a witness's testimony ♦ Create excitement about a product or idea that is in the development stage	♦ Use models that have not been professionally prepared ♦ Rely on the model to make your case or sell your idea. The model is a support for the presentation, not the presentation	♦ Should be professionally prepared. ♦ If model is a large visual model, be sure that it is backed on foam board. Foam board is more stable than poster board and doesn't buckle when placed on an easel

Types of Visual Support and Audiences

Type of Visual Support and Audiences	Should Be Used To:	Don't:	Things to Keep in Mind
Flip charts Appropriate for: ♦ Audiences that will be brainstorming or generating ideas on the fly ♦ Audiences that are less formal in nature, like teams or groups, or for meetings ♦ Audiences meeting in places where technology is not available ♦ Training classes	♦ Brainstorm or draw ♦ Collate the ideas or views of a group or meeting	♦ Allow flip charts prepared in advance to become dated or soiled ♦ Use poor-quality flip charts in professional situations. With the availability of technology, few audiences have any tolerance for hand-drawn charts or hand-labeled graphics ♦ Use flip charts in a technological environment. Learn the technology that is appropriate for the audience you are speaking to	♦ Make sure you have an easel or other way to display the charts ♦ Use charts big enough for the space you are speaking in. If you are speaking to more than 20 people, chances are someone in your audience will not be able to see your flip chart
Whiteboards Appropriate for: ♦ Audiences that will be brainstorming or generating ideas on the fly ♦ Audiences that are less formal in nature, like teams or groups, or for meetings ♦ Audiences meeting in places where technology is not available ♦ Training classes	♦ Brainstorm or draw ♦ Collate the ideas or views of a group or meeting	♦ Use whiteboards as your primary visual aid for a formal presentation	♦ Write legibly and large enough for everyone to read what you put on the board ♦ Erase completely ♦ Bring markers and erasers with you if you aren't sure they will be available

Appendix

Types of Visual Support and Audiences

Type of Visual Support and Audiences	Should Be Used To:	Don't:	Things to Keep in Mind
Transparencies Appropriate for: ♦ Audiences meeting in places where higher levels of technology are not available ♦ Training classes	♦ Collate the ideas or views of a group or meeting ♦ Present training points ♦ Back up higher technology options when technology fails or is unavailable	♦ Keep using transparencies that have become dated or faded ♦ Use transparencies simply because you don't want to learn new technology	♦ Make sure an overhead projector is available at your site. These have become rare in most business environments ♦ Use overheads big enough for the space you are speaking in. If you are speaking to more than 30 people, chances are someone in your audience will not be able to see your transparancy
Handouts Appropriate for: ♦ Audiences meeting in places where higher levels of technology are not available ♦ Cases where supplemental materials are necessary ♦ Training classes or where hard-copy supporting materials are needed	♦ Provide hard-copy supporting materials ♦ Provide graphics to large groups where technology is not available or would not be clearly viewed by the entire audience ♦ Back up higher technology options when technology fails or is unavailable	♦ Distribute unless what is on the paper is highly valuable. We all have too much paper to deal with ♦ Dump your entire presentation to a handout that you then read from	

Chalkboards—Seen one lately?

Tips for Successful Interpersonal Communication

Type	Definition	Tips for Success
Downward Communication	Communication flows from the top of the organizational chart down. Some examples are: • Goals, values, and vision • Tasks • Schedules • Policies and procedures • Performance appraisals and raise information	1. When communicating tasks to subordinates, tell them how to do a task and why the task is important or fits into the overall scheme of the business. 2. When discussing a problem or conflict, stay on the topic and deal with the employee's behavior, rather than the person. 3. Use written messages only when appropriate and with follow-up and feedback.
Upward Communication	Communication flows from the bottom of the organizational chart up. Some examples are: • Task reports, monthly memos, and status reports • Suggestions for improvement • Complaints about working conditions or co-workers • Problems to be resolved • Feedback about messages from a supervisor	1. Don't conceal or sugarcoat bad news or problems. Eventually, your supervisor will discover the problem and you will lose credibility. 2. Do not distort the facts about a situation that occurs with a co-worker. State the facts and give your manager time to respond to the situation. 3. Keep you supervisor aware of your and your team members' significant achievements.
Peer Communication	Communication flows from side to side, between team members, work groups, or department members. Some examples are: • Task coordination • Job sharing scheduling • Invitations to lunch	1. Keep gossip out of the workplace. Gossip is not only detrimental, it is unethical professional behavior. 2. Be helpful, be kind, and be smart. Never say or write anything you don't want repeated.

Tips for Successful Written Communication

Type	Definition	Tips for Success
Email	Short, brief written conversations that call for a quick decision, impart specific or general knowledge, or provide opportunities for networking. Some examples are: ✦ Request for a decision ✦ Directions to a customer's site ✦ Appointment confirmations ✦ Invitation to a group lunch ✦ Follow-up on a memo or report	1. Don't send memos in email form. Studies show that people have limited time in the day to respond to email messages. Emails that contain detailed information or complex instruction sets may not be given the attention they deserve. Write a brief email describing the memo and requesting the reader print and read the attached memo. 2. Don't abuse email. You will lose credibility if you send out emails without purpose or substance. 3. Purge and archive emails regularly to avoid becoming overwhelmed by your inbox.
Memos	Official company messages that impart *specific* information or a *specific* request. Examples are: ✦ Changes in policies or procedures ✦ Changes to schedules ✦ Sales reports ✦ Status reports ✦ Requests for equipment or staff	1. Memos should be 1–5 pages. Beyond 5 pages, the memo becomes a report. 2. Memos should cover 1–3 specific *and* related topics. 3. Memos should contain a request for feedback where necessary. 4. Use subheads for memos that are longer than 2 pages to orient your audience.
Reports	Informational messages that contain large amounts of complex or detailed knowledge. Examples are: ✦ Corporate prospectus ✦ White papers ✦ Quarterly and annual sales reports ✦ Needs assessments ✦ Requests for equipment or staff	1. Begin by outlining the purpose, scope, and major headings for the report. 2. Analyze the audience for the report. 3. If you are preparing a report for the first time, request copies of previous reports to use as an example. 4. If you are stating a problem, end with recommendations for improvement. 5. Provide only the information that is necessary to inform, educate, and lead your audience to an appropriate decision or conclusion.

Tips for Successful Group and Team Communication

Type	Definition	Tips for Success
Groups	Work groups, departments, or units formed for specific projects. In groups the operation is more informal, jobs are less connected, and the charge of the group is less specific than in teams. Some examples are: ✦ Committee formed to plan the 25th anniversary celebration of a school ✦ Managers that meet once a month to discuss customer complaints ✦ Committee formed to review a faculty member for tenure	1. Help your group define the purpose of the group and stay on track. 2. Don't belittle other group members' ideas or contributions. 3. Complete group assignments on time and with a high level of quality. 4. Keep information about the group in the group unless all group members agree to make the information public.
Teams	Formally appointed groups of employees whose jobs cut across departments, function, or capability. Teams are given a specific charge to solve a problem, design a product, or change a procedure. Examples are: ✦ Reengineering group charged with redesigning the accounting department ✦ Y2K team charged with bringing your organization into compliance ✦ Product design team charged with creating a car for the 2010 auto show	1. Don't allow conflict or disagreements to interfere with the effectiveness of the team. 2. Ask team members for feedback to ideas you offer and be open to the feedback received. 3. Keep team meetings short and to a minimum. 4. Recognize when your team has accomplished its goal and is no longer needed.

Appendix

STRATEGY SELECTION CRITERIA WORKSHEET

Strategy	Brutal	Rational	Rational/ Emotional	Mindful
What type of presentation would work best?	☐ One-on-one	☐ Any audience	☐ Any audience	☐ Any audience
What are the needs of your audience?	☐ Not considered	☐ Clearly definable	☐ Somewhat definable/ somewhat fluid	☐ Clearly definable
What type of choices will your audience be presented with?	☐ None or either/or	☐ Multiple with best alternative presented	☐ Call to action	☐ Choice that reflects personal responsibility and organizational accountability
How open to your position, product, or idea has your audience been in the past?	☐ Closed or resistant	☐ Open	☐ Unaware or open	☐ Open
What method of persuasion would work best?	☐ Strategic control—the use of authority to warrant compliance	☐ Logos—an appeal that is based in evidence and logic	☐ Logos/Pathos—a logical appeal that induces the emotions of the audience	☐ Ethos—an appeal that is based on the credibility of the speaker and his or her ability to follow through on commitments
What personal trait does your argument rely on: organizational authority, personal credibility, knowledge or expertise?	☐ Authority	☐ Knowledge or expertise	☐ Credibility	☐ All
What is your goal?	☐ Compliance	☐ Consensus	☐ Action	☐ Commitment

	Example Interview Script
Establish rapport	These questions should put the interviewee at ease and break the ice. Examples are: ✦ How was your flight? ✦ Did you have trouble finding us?
Define the interviewee's experience	These questions arise from the cover letter, resume, and references. Examples are: ✦ I see that you majored in communication. How has your major prepared you for this job? ✦ Tell us a little about your current position. ✦ What are two things about your current job that you find challenging? ✦ What are two things about your current job that you dislike? ✦ What has been your biggest accomplishment at your current position? ✦ What will you miss most about the company you work for? ✦ Of all the jobs you have had, which has been the best fit and why?
Clarify the requirements for the position	These questions zero in on the requirements for the position. Examples are: ✦ This position requires hiring and developing a team of writers and trainers. How would you go about doing that? ✦ In this position, you will be required to manage a team. What qualities do you think are important in a team environment? ✦ As a manager, you will be required to report the progress of your team. How do you feel about providing regular status reports? ✦ An important function of this position is liaison to other teams. What skills do you have that will facilitate this function? ✦ How would this position further your career goals?
Present the organization	These questions open a discussion of the organization. Examples are: ✦ What do you know about Bilin.com? ✦ How do you feel about working for an Internet start-up, coming from such an established company? ✦ Bilin is a small, young company and we can't offer the benefits some organizations can. Is that a problem? ✦ We have just signed three major contracts, which has tripled our deliverables overnight. To meet our schedules, we know that we have to work extremely long hours. Is there anything to prevent you from working long weeks when necessary?
Provide closure	These questions signal the interview is ending and allow for a final opportunity to clarify information. Examples are: ✦ Do you have any additional questions? ✦ If offered the position, when could you start?

	Employer Performance or Grievance Review Checklist
Before the Review	✦ Ask for a written evaluation from the employee of his or her performance. ✦ Carefully read the employee evaluation *before* you complete your evaluation. ✦ Review (if a record exists) the employee's past two performance appraisals. ✦ Outline the areas of the employee's performance that exceeded expectations, met expectations, and fell short of expectations for the appraisal period. ✦ Indicate areas that over the past two review periods have fallen below expectations. ✦ Outline a course of action for the employee to follow that will meet expectations. ✦ Document the course of action in a memo for both you and the employee to sign.
During the Review	✦ Present the evaluation to the employee beginning with areas that exceeded expectations, followed by those that met expectations, and ending with those that were below expectations. ✦ Keep the focus on the employee's job performance and team and group interactions. ✦ Avoid making vague references to the employee's "attitude" or other subjective references. ✦ Present the course of action for improvement. ✦ Ask the employee if he or she has have questions. ✦ Offer the employee a brief period to think about the evaluation and respond either in writing or in person. ✦ Indicate that you expect the memo to be signed by the employee by a specific date and that a nonresponse on the part of the employee indicates agreement with the memo as is.
After the Review	✦ Follow up on the memo if the employee has not signed it by the date specified. ✦ Continue to document problems as they arise, but don't harp on problems that have been discussed and solved. ✦ Praise the employee for changes and progress made. ✦ Follow up with additional reviews as needed at 3-month periods.

Employee Performance and Grievance Review Checklist

Before the Review	✦ Prepare a written evaluation of your work prior to the manager's evaluation.
	✦ If you are not asked for a self-evaluation, check with your manager two weeks before your review date and request the opportunity to provide a self-evaluation.
	✦ In your evaluation, give an honest assessment of your performance. Include the areas where you believe you went above and beyond the requirements of the job and the areas where you need improvement.
	✦ Outline goals for the next review cycle. The goals you outline should reflect your individual and team goals.
	✦ Submit a well-thought-out, well-reasoned, organized appraisal of your work.
During the Review	✦ Listen, listen, listen. By now, your manager knows what you think. Now, it is his or her turn. Listen carefully to everything your manager has to say.
	✦ Take notes.
	✦ Be gracious when given praise or high marks for doing well.
	✦ Acknowledge areas you know need improvement.
	✦ Ask for a period to reflect on and respond to areas that may be in dispute.
	✦ Walk away from the appraisal without being defensive, negative, or closed to suggestions offered by your manager.
After the Review	✦ Spend some time honestly thinking about your appraisal.
	✦ Don't talk about it with co-workers or vent only your side to friends and family.
	✦ Submit a well-thought-out, well-reasoned, organized assessment of your appraisal, if you believe any areas were unfair.
	✦ Indicate areas of agreement and areas that you think were unfair or too harsh. Suggest ways to remedy the disagreement. Indicate that you are willing to work on your performance and toward an amicable conclusion.
	✦ Give your employer an opportunity to respond.

Glossary

adaptive skill *The ability to adapt behaviors to the needs and expectations of others.*

agenda *A functional document used to organize a meeting.*

ambiguity *Expressing oneself in terms that are unclear or open to multiple interpretations.*

attention-getter *The story, joke, or first line of a message, designed to pull the audience into your message.*

audience analysis *A demographic reading of an audience based on findings like age, race, gender, years of service, position.*

audience needs and expectations *What the listener should gain and expects to gain from a presentation.*

bookmark *A way of tagging information on the Internet so you can return to it quickly for future reference.*

brutal strategy *A one-sided strategy of persuasion that offers the listener little or no choice.*

bureaucracy *A system of organization marked by hierarchy, set rules, and fixed divisions of labor.*

call to action *The direct or indirect statement of action you want the audience to take after listening to your message.*

causal pattern *A cause and effect organizational structure for a presentation.*

CCCD *A four-step process of choosing, creating, coordinating, and delivering a conscious communication message.*

channel *The thoroughfare a message takes from sender to receiver, including electronically mediated methods of message delivery such as radio, television, computers, and satellites, as well as the full range of print media such as office memos and letters, newspapers, magazines, advertising flyers, brochures, and books.*

choosing *Analyzing the possible outcomes of a communication situation to select the best strategy for a given communication goal.*

chronological *An organizational structure for a presentation that relies on past, present, and future or a series of dates to frame a talk.*

clarity *The quality of being clear and unambiguous.*

clip art *Prepackaged, ready-to-use art and graphics that can be dropped into a document to add impact or interest.*

closed questions *Questions that require specific, concrete responses and provide little opportunity for elaboration.*

communication *All forms of speaking, listening, relating, writing, and responding, both human and electronically mediated.*

communication history *The cumulative record of communication events between participants.*

concierge persuasion *Persuasion that is adapted to fit a particular person and situation.*

conflict *Feelings or perceptions of imbalance that arise in a relational setting.*

conscious communication *Communication that has been carefully chosen, created, coordinated, and delivered.*

conscious listening *Listening openly to a speaker's point of view and reflecting on how talk affects the whole.*

constraint *A restriction or limit.*

context *The physical, historical, and cultural environment that informs a communication situation or episode.*

coordinating *The act of bringing together everyone required to successfully deliver the message.*

creating *The process of developing a presentation plan designed to carry out a chosen strategy.*

creativity *What results from giving people the freedom to explore alternatives beyond the traditional ways of doing things.*

credibility *A demonstration of believability and trustworthiness.*

criteria *The parameters against which you measure the success of a presentation.*

critical listening *The ability of a listener to deliberate on what is said by exploring the logic, reason, and point of view of the speaker.*

cultures *The evolved standards of communication practice, acquired through observation and experience, that may be unique to an organization.*

delivery *The process of practicing and articulating your message for an audience.*

dialectic *The interaction of two arguments that by nature are oppositional.*

dialogue *Communication that focuses on mutuality and relational growth, rather than self-interest.*

diversity The cultural, gender, racial, religious, and socioeconomic differences that inform communication in the workplace.

downward communication Communication that occurs between you and anyone lower than you within the organizational hierarchy.

electronically mediated communication Includes radio, television, computers, and satellites, as well as the full range of print media, such as office memos and letters, newspapers, magazines, advertising flyers, brochures, and books.

email Electronic mail transmitted to or from your computer almost instantaneously anywhere in the world.

employment interview An interview designed to bring together potential employees and employers to test the fit of someone for a position.

empowerment The process of enabling and motivating employees, mainly by removing roadblocks, which builds feelings of personal effectiveness and control.

environment The integral parts of an organization that overlap to create a space for communication and understanding.

equity The principle that we should be treated fairly by others and in turn should treat them fairly.

ethos The perceived credibility or expertise of a speaker.

exclusive message strategies Autocratic communication that reveals a me-oriented pattern of behavior.

fact Something that is known to exist or has been proven to be true; basic, empirically verifiable information that has credibility for a given audience.

feedback The responses provided to the communication, ideas, and identities received in a message; an evaluation of the effectiveness of the actions of others.

fluency Smooth or effortless articulation of a speech or presentation.

focus group A group assembled to help explore an idea or test a product or a concept.

font size The size of the lettering in a text.

font type A particular style of text characters, such as Times Roman or Arial.

formal interview A structured, tightly scripted interview that centers on questions designed to gather specific information.

gendered talk Conversation marked by the differences between the way men and women tend to communicate.

goal A concrete, achievable end.

goals The set and planned accomplishments of an organization.

haptics The study of touching as nonverbal communication.

hearing The passive and physical process of listening.

hierarchical noise The shadings in meaning attributed to rank or status within an organization.

hierarchy The system of authority, rank, and status within an organization.

hostile work environment An environment in which intimidating or offensive verbal or nonverbal communication interferes with someone's work.

human relations movement A theoretical movement that viewed employees as sources of group information and skill that could be developed through training and education.

identity The way people see and respond to you in the workplace, including your organizational persona, credibility, and savvy.

inclusive message strategies A democratic form of communication taking into account the group or culture, thoughts and feelings of others, and others' contributions and differences.

informal interview An unstructured interview that covers a wide variety of topics and uses open questions.

information interview An interview designed to gather specific information, further understanding, or test a concept.

information overload What occurs when too many forms of communication intersect at one time, making decision-making and response difficult.

information transfer model A model that posited information was passed directly from sender to receiver.

informational listening The stage in the listening process where meaning is assigned to the words we hear.

informative presentation A presentation that attempts to present facts and information in an objective, nonpersuasive manner.

interdependence The pattern of contingent decision-making that understands the need to revise decision-making based on new information and the effects of past decisions.

interpretation The meanings we assign to messages.

interrogation A one-sided form of interviewing that concentrates on the negative aspects of a problem.

interview script A plan of questions used for an interview.

jamming Engaging in a spontaneous, energetic group session in which the members are totally coordinated.

job description A description of an open position that usually includes experience, salary, and education requirements.

job goals The type of position you want and the outcomes you want from your employment.

kinesics The study of body movement, including facial expressions, eye contact, and gestures.

learning organization An organization marked by conscious systems-based thinking and an ability to continually adapt communication to organizational, cultural, and individual changes.

listening The process of hearing and interpreting messages.

Glossary

logos The ability of a speaker to sway an audience using logic.

Luddite A person who refuses to adapt to new forms of technology.

memo A short document containing information about a specific topic.

mental models The images, assumptions, and stories that permeate the minds of the people working in organizations.

message What is said and done during a communication interaction, both verbally and nonverbally.

mindful communication An approach to communication that is both purposeful and strategic and emphasizes the audience and expected outcomes.

mindful strategy A persuasive appeal that emphasizes a deep connection between the speaker and the audience.

mindless communication Episodes of small talk or automatic talk that occur in familiar situations.

monitoring Checking the accuracy of your perceptions and questioning the factors that lead to those perceptions.

motivation The force or reason that drives us to do something.

narrative The representation of experience in the form of a story.

naturalness An easy, genuine manner of speaking.

need The part of a message that details the audience's problem or need.

needs assessment A survey or questionnaire developed to find out what an audience needs or wants or what problems they might have.

netiquette The rules of etiquette that govern online interaction on the Internet.

network Two or more computers that are connected either locally (within a company or building) or widely (across different geographic locations) by cable, phone lines, or satellite.

noise The physical, semantic, and hierarchical influences that either disrupt or shape the interpretation of messages; any sound that disrupts or interferes with the delivery of a message.

nonsupportive messages Messages that communicate superiority, disrespect of others, and lack of cooperation in the workplace.

nonverbal competence The ability of a speaker to maintain eye contact, use gestures and body movement to enhance the speech, and incorporate visual aids in the presentation.

objective A task required to reach a goal.

oculesics The study of the eyes as a source of communication information.

open questions Questions that require more than yes or no responses and that allow you to discuss your experience or perspective.

organizational credibility The values associated with being a trustworthy, honest, responsible, fair, and ethical person in the organization.

organizational culture The histories, habits, values, and rules for conduct that make working in an organization feel unique.

organizational persona The position, status, rank, years of service, and role in a company that determine who we are perceived as within an organization.

organizational savvy The ability a person has to successfully negotiate political and social boundaries in an organization.

outcome What you achieve as a result of a presentation.

pathos The ability to sway an audience using emotion.

perception The way we process and interpret cues from a person's outward appearance, voice, and language usage.

performance review A review or critique of an employee's work and job performance.

person prototypes The stereotypes we assign to people when we first meet them.

personal constructs The specific evaluations we make of people based on our assessment of their habits and behaviors.

personal mastery A form of empowerment that emphasizes the need for continuous growth and renewal as vital to the individual and the organization.

personal space The spatial distance we keep between ourselves and others.

persuasive interview A sales-oriented form of interviewing intended to convince a client or customer to buy into an idea or make a purchase.

persuasive presentation A presentation designed to bring the audience to a decision or action.

phatic communion The patterned sequences of talk or scripts we use every day.

physical diversion Any physical element that disrupts or interferes with the delivery of a message.

policies The guidelines that oversee conduct in the workplace.

power The sources of influence derived by an individual within an organization; our ability to influence others and outcomes.

problem-solution pattern An organizational structure that begins with a problem and offers a solution or potential solutions.

proxemics The study of interpersonal space and distance.

quid pro quo "This for that"—an exchange of favors or actions.

rational strategy *A two-sided persuasive exchange that presents alternatives and a best solution.*

rational/emotional strategy *Persuasion that appeals to logic and emotion and makes use of need, satisfaction, visualization, and a call to action.*

receiver *The person to whom a message is directed.*

reference *A citation of a noted authority, which lends credibility to a presentation.*

report *A document containing detailed coverage of one or more related topics.*

resume *The formal statement of who you are; it combines autobiography, work history, and sales presentation.*

reward *The benefit received from an activity (e.g., money, identity, power, support, companionship, a skill set) in relation to what it costs (physical labor, mental and emotional stress, free time, time away from families, subordinating personal goals, dealing with difficult people, harassment).*

rules *The taken-for-granted assumptions and formal pronouncements for communication among employees.*

satisfaction *The part of a message that conveys the solution to the audience's need or problem.*

schemata *The mental pattern recognition plans that help us identify and organize incoming information.*

scientific management *The theory that posited organization should be operated as efficient machines governed by scientific principles, rules, and laws.*

scripts *The patterned sequences of talk we use every day.*

self-disclosure *Providing personal information within a conversation.*

self-reflexive listening *Listening for the way in which a message applies to the listener's life.*

semantic noise *The differences people have for the meanings of words, which include the gender, racial, and cultural biases of the receiver as well as jargon and misunderstandings.*

sender *The originator of a message.*

sense-making *Our attempt to construct the versions of reality we perceive and respond to based on our own experiences, knowledge, feeling, needs, and expectations.*

sensitivity *Taking into consideration the speaking differences of a communication partner.*

sexual harassment *In the workplace, any form of sexually explicit verbal or nonverbal communication that interferes with someone's work.*

shared vision *An organizational vision and mission that is built upon a foundation of trust, openness, empowerment, and honesty.*

statistics *Any basic, empirically verifiable numerical representation of information; information presented in the form of numbers, such as percentages or averages.*

strategic communication *Communication that is planned with specific audiences and intentions in mind.*

supportive messages *Messages that communicate concern and respect for others, and cooperation.*

synergy *The shared knowledge, diversity of experience, and collaborative energy that results from mindful team communication.*

systems thinking *A perception of an organization as a system of interconnected individuals and teams.*

team *A group that shares a unifying goal and recognizes the synergy of shared knowledge, diversity of experience, and collaborative energy.*

team learning *The conscious, coordinated action that translates shared vision, mental models, and personal mastery into thinking and acting as a team.*

technological diversion *Any technological element that disrupts or interferes with the delivery of a message.*

telecommuting *Working from your home or away from your company's primary location, but connected by telephone, fax, and computer.*

thesis statement *A simple, declarative sentence that introduces your message and announces your intentions.*

topical pattern *An organizational structure that allows development of a talk based on a theme and the logical topics associated with the theme.*

transactional process model *A model that posits all persons are continually sending and receiving messages and constantly affecting each other.*

transition *A connection of one point or topic to another; a movement from one item to another.*

upward communication *Communication that occurs between you and anyone higher than you within the organizational hierarchy.*

video conferencing *Conducting a conference between two or more participants at different sites by using computer networks or audio and video equipment.*

virtual communities *Communities that exist primarily on the Internet.*

virtual meeting *A meeting that may occur over wide geographical space and that uses technology as the principal delivery system.*

vision *The overall, far-reaching idea of what a team or organization should accomplish and the values that should inform those accomplishments.*

visualization *The part of a message that helps the audience imagine the satisfaction of their need.*

vivacity *Energy and enthusiasm used in a speech or presentation.*

voice mail *Messages left on a telephone answering system.*

References

Abernathy, D. J. (1999, May). A chat with Chris Argyris. *Training and Development 53*, 80–85.

Albrecht, K. (1992). *The only thing that matters: Bringing the power of the customer into the center of your business*. New York: HarperBusiness.

Allen, M., & Caillouet, R. (1994). Legitimation endeavors: Impression management strategies used by an organization in crisis. *Communication Monographs 61*, 44–62.

Alvesson, M. (1993). *Cultural perspectives on organizations*. New York: Cambridge University Press.

Andersen, P. A. (1993). Cognitive schemata in personal relationships. In S. Duck (Ed.), *Individuals and relationships*. Newbury Park, CA: Sage.

Andersen, P. A. (1999). *Nonverbal communication*. Mountain View, CA: Mayfield.

Andersen, P. A., Andersen, J. F., & Landgraf, J. (1985). *The development of nonverbal communication competence in childhood*. Paper presented at the annual convention of the International Communication Association, Honolulu.

Andersen, P. A., Todd-Mancillas, W. R., & DiClemente, L. (1980). The effects of pupil dilation in physical, social, and task attraction. *Australian Scan: A Journal of Communication 7 & 8*, 89–95.

Anderson, J. (1987). *Communication research: Issues and methods*. New York: McGraw-Hill.

Anderson, R., Cissna, K., & Arnett, R. (1994). *The reach of dialogue*. Cresskill, NJ: Hampton Press.

Anderson, W. T. (1995). *The truth about the truth*. New York: Tarcher/Putnam.

Argyris, C. (1994, July–August). Good communication that blocks learning. *Harvard Business Review*, 77–85.

Argyris, C., & Schon, D. (1978). *Organizational learning: A theory of action perspective*. Reading, MA: Addison-Wesley.

Arnett, R., & Cissna, K. (1996). *The reach of dialogue: Confirmation, voice, and community*. Cresskill, NJ: Hampton Press.

Ashford, S., & Cummings, L. (1983). Feedback as an individual resource: Personal strategies of creating information. *Organizational Behavior and Human Performance 32*, 370–398.

Atkouf, O. (1992). Management and theories of organizations in the 1990s: Toward a critical radical humanism? *Academy of Management Review 17*, 407–431.

Axley, S. (1984). Managerial and organizational communication in terms of the conduit metaphor. *Academy of Management Review 9*, 428–437.

Bales, R., & Strodtbeck, F. (1960). Phases in group problem solving. In D. Cartwright & A. Zander (Eds.), *Group dynamics: Research and theory* (pp. 624–638). New York: Harper & Row.

Banta, M. (1993). *Taylored lives: Narrative productions in the age of Taylor, Veblen, and Ford*. Chicago: University of Chicago Press.

Bantz, C. (1993). *Understanding organizations: Interpreting organizational communication cultures*. Columbia: University of South Carolina Press.

Barker, R. T., & Camarata, M. R. (1998). The role of communication in a learning organization. *Journal of Business Communication 35*(4), 443–467.

Barley, S. (1983). Semiotics and the study of occupational and organizational culture. *Administrative Science Quarterly 23*, 393–413.

Barnard, C. (1938/1968). *The functions of the executive*. Cambridge, MA: Harvard University Press.

Barnet, R., & Cavanagh, J. (1994). *Global dreams*. New York: Simon & Schuster.

Barnlund, D. (1994). *Communicative styles of Japanese and Americans*. Belmont, CA: Wadsworth.

Bateson, G. (1992). *Sacred unity: Further steps toward an ecology of mind*. San Francisco: HarperSanFrancisco.

Bavelas, A. (1951). Communication patterns in task oriented groups. In D. Lerner & H. Laswell (Eds.), *The policy sciences* (pp. 193–202). Stanford, CA: Stanford University Press.

Baxter, L. A. (1988). A dialectical perspective on communication strategies in relational development. In S. Duck (Ed.), *Handbook of personal relationships*. Chicester, UK: Wiley.

Baxter, L.A., & Montgomery, B. M. (1996). *Relating: Dialogues and Dialectics*. New York: Guilford Press.

Bellah, R., Madsen, R., Sullivan, W., Swidler, A., & Tipton, S. (1985). *Habits of the heart*. Berkeley: University of California Press.

Bellah, R., Madsen, R., Sullivan, W., Swidler, A., & Tipton, S. (1991). *The good society*. New York: Knopf.

Benne, K., & Sheats, P. (1948). Functional roles of group members. *Journal of Social Issues 4*, 41–49.

Bennis, W. (1999). *Managing people is like herding cats: Warren Bennis on leadership*. Provo, UT: Executive Excellence.

Berger, C. R., & Calabrese, R. J. (1975). Some explorations in initial interaction and beyond: Toward a theory of interpersonal communication. *Human Communication Research 1*, 99–112.

Berger, P., & Luckmann, T. (1967). *The social construction of reality*. Garden City, NY: Anchor.

Berlo, D. (1960). *The process of communication*. New York: Holt, Rinehart & Winston.

Beyer, J., & Trice, H. (1987). How an organization's rites reveal its culture. *Organizational Dynamics 15*, 4–35.

Bingham, S. (1991). Communication strategies for managing sexual harassment in organizations: Understanding message options and their effects. *Journal of Applied Communication Research 19*, 88–115.

Birdwistell, R. L. (1970). *Kinesics and context*. Philadelphia: University of Pennsylvania Press.

Blumer, H. (1969). *Symbolic interactionism: Perspective and method*. Englewood Cliffs, NJ: Prentice-Hall.

Bochner, A. (1982). The functions of human communication in interpersonal bonding. In C. Arnold & J. Waite-Bowers (Eds.), *Handbook of rhetorical and communication theory* (pp. 544–621). Boston: Allyn & Bacon.

Bochner, A. P. (1994). Perspectives on inquiry II: Theories and stories. In M. L. Knapp & G. R. Miller (Eds.), *Handbook of interpersonal communication* (pp. 21–41). Newbury Park, CA: Sage.

Bochner, A. P. (1997). It's about time: Narrative and the divided self. *Qualitative Inquiry 3*, 418–439.

Boje, D. (1991). The storytelling organization: A study of story performance in an office-supply firm. *Administrative Science Quarterly 36*, 106–126.

Boje, D. (1995). Stories of the storytelling organization: A postmodern analysis of Disney in "Tamara-Land." *Academy of Management Journal 38*, 997–1035.

Bracci, S. (1999, November). *Visions of community: Ethical issues in public relations and community building*. A highlighted panel, National Communication Association annual meeting, Chicago.

Brown, M., & McMillan, J. (1991). Culture as text: The development of an organizational narrative. *Southern Communication Journal 57*, 49–60.

Brownell, J. (2002). *Listening: Attitudes, principles, and skills*. Boston: Allyn & Bacon.

Browning, L. (1992). Lists and stories as organizational communication. *Communication Theory 2*, 281–302.

Browning, L., & Hawes, L. (1991). Style, process, surface, context: Consulting as postmodern art. *Journal of Applied Communication Research 19*, 32–54.

Buber, M. (1985). *Between man and man* (2nd ed.). New York: Macmillan.

Buck, R. (1979). Individual differences in nonverbal sending accuracy and electrodermal responding: The externalizing-internalizing dimension. In R. Rosenthal (Ed.), *Skill in nonverbal communication: Individual differences*. Cambridge, MA: Oelgeschlager, Gunn, & Hain.

Buckman, R. H. (1997). [Interview, vice chairman of Buckman Laboratories International].

Bullis, C., & Bach, B. (1989). Socialization turning points: An examination of change in organizational identification. *Western Journal of Speech Communication 53*, 273–293.

Bullis, C., & Glaser, H. (1992). Bureaucratic discourse and the goddess: Towards an ecofeminist critique and rearticulation. *Journal of Organizational Change Management 5*, 50–60.

Burke, K. (1989). *On symbols and society*. Chicago: University of Chicago Press.

Burke, W. (1986). Leadership as empowering others. In S. Srivasta (Ed.), *Executive power* (pp. 51–77). San Francisco: Jossey-Bass.

Buzzanell, P. (1994). Gaining a voice: Feminist organizational communication theorizing. *Management Communication Quarterly 7*, 339–383.

Calas, M., & Smircich, L. (1993). Dangerous liaisons: The "feminine in management" meets "globalization." *Business Horizons 36*, 71–81.

Canadian Manager Office Team. (1999). *Canadian Manager 24*(2), 20.

Cheney, G., & Mumby, D. (1997). Communication and organizational democracy: Introduction. *Communication Studies 48*, 277–279.

Chiles, A., & Zorn, T. (1995). Empowerment in organizations: Employees' perceptions of the influences on empowerment. *Journal of Applied Communication Research 23*, 1–25.

Clair, R. (1993). The use of framing devices to sequester organizational narratives: Hegemony and harassment. *Communication Monographs 60*, 113–136.

Clair, R. (1998). *Organizing silence*. Albany: State University of New York Press.

Clegg, S. (1989). *Frameworks of power*. Newbury Park, CA: Sage.

Coles, R. (1989). *The call of stories: Teaching and moral imagination.* Boston: Houghton Mifflin.

Conger, J., & Kanungo, R. (1988). The empowerment process: Integrating theory and practice. *Academy of Management Review 13,* 471–482.

Conquergood, D. (1991). Rethinking ethnography: Towards a critical cultural politics. *Communication Monographs 58,* 179–194.

Conrad, C. (1983). Organizational power: Faces and symbolic forms. In L. Putnam & M. Pacanowsky (Eds.), *Communication and organizations* (pp. 173–194). Beverly Hills, CA: Sage.

Conrad, C. (1991). Communication in conflict: Style-strategy relationships. *Communication Monographs 58,* 135–155.

Contractor, N. (1992). Self-organizing systems perspective in the study of organizational communication. In B. Kovacic (Ed.), *Organizational communication: New perspectives.* Albany: SUNY Press.

Covey, S. (1990). *Seven habits of highly effective people.* New York: Simon & Schuster.

Covino, W. A., & Jolliffe, D. A. (1995). *Rhetoric: Concepts, definitions, boundaries.* New York: Longman.

Csikszentmihalyi, M. (1990). *Flow: The psychology of optimal experience.* New York: Harper & Row.

Csikszentmihalyi, M. (1997). *Finding flow: The psychology of engagement with everyday life.* New York: Basic Books.

Cusella, L. (1987). Feedback, motivation, and performance. In F. Jablin et al. (Eds.), *Handbook of organizational communication* (pp. 624–678). Beverly Hills, CA: Sage.

Czarniawska-Joerges, B. (1988). Dynamics of organizational control: The case of Berol Kemi Ab. *Accounting, Organizations, and Society 11,* 471–482.

Damasio, A. R. (1999). *The feeling of what happens: Body and emotion in the making of consciousness.* New York: Harcourt Brace.

Dansereau, F., & Markham, S. (1987). Superior–subordinate communication: Multiple levels of analysis. In F. Jablin et al. (Eds.), *Handbook of organizational communication* (pp. 343–388), Beverly Hills, CA: Sage.

Davis, K. (1953). Management communication and the grapevine. *Harvard Business Review 31,* 43–49.

Deal, T., & Kennedy, A. (1982). *Corporate cultures.* Reading, MA: Addison-Wesley.

Deetz, S. (1991). *Democracy in an age of corporate colonization.* Albany: State University of New York Press.

Deetz, S. (1995). *Transforming communication, transforming business.* Albany: State University of New York Press.

Deetz, S., & Mumby, D. (1990). Power, discourse, and the workplace: Reclaiming the critical tradition. In J. Anderson (Ed.), *Communication Yearbook 13,* 18–47.

Dillard, J., & Miller, K. (1988). Intimate relationships in task environments. In S. Duck (Ed.), *Handbook of personal relationships* (pp. 449–465). New York: Wiley.

Dillard, J., & Segrin, C. (1987). *Intimate relationships in organizations: Relational types, illicitness, and power.* Paper presented at the Annual Conference of the International Communication Association, Montreal, Canada.

Donnellon, A. (1992). Team work: Linguistic models of negotiating difference. In B. Shepard et al. (Eds.), *Research and negotiations in organizations* (Vol. 4). Greenwich, CT: JAI Press.

Dove, L. (1998). CPA standards elevated for complex profession. *Wichita Business Journal 13*(22), 16.

Dutton, J., & Dukerich, J. (1991). Keeping an eye on the mirror: Image and identity in organizational adaptation. *Academy of Management Journal 34,* 517–554.

Eisenberg, E. (1984). Ambiguity as strategy in organizational communication. *Communication Monographs 51,* 227–242.

Eisenberg, E. (1986). Meaning and interpretation in organizations. *Quarterly Journal of Speech 72,* 88–98.

Eisenberg, E. (1990). Jamming: Transcendence through organizing. *Communication Research 17,* 139–164.

Eisenberg, E., & Goodall, H. L. (2001). *Organizational communication: Balancing creativity and constraint.* New York: St. Martin's.

Eisenberg, E., Monge, P., & Miller, K. (1983). Involvement in communication networks as a predictor of organizational commitment. *Human Communication Research 10,* 179–201.

Eisenberg, E., & Phillips, S. (1991). Miscommunication in organizations. In N. Coupland, H. Giles, & J. Weimann (Eds.), *"Miscommunication" and problematic talk* (pp. 244–258). Newbury Park, CA: Sage.

Eisenberg, E., & Witten, M. (1987). Reconsidering openness in organizational communication. *Academy of Management Review 12,* 418–426.

Ehninger, D. (1974). *Influence, belief, and argument: An introduction to responsible persuasion.* Glenview, IL: Scott, Foresman.

Ekman, P. (1978). Facial expression. In A. W. Siegman & S. Feldstein (Eds.), *Nonverbal behavior and communication.* Hillsdale, NJ: Erlbaum.

Etzioni, A. (1988). *The moral dimension: Toward a new economics*. New York: Free Press.

Evered, R., & Tannenbaum, R. (1992). A dialog on dialog. *Journal of Management Inquiry 1*, 43–55.

Fairhurst, G., & Chandler, T. (1989). Social structure in leader–member interaction. *Communication Monographs 56*, 215–239.

Fairhurst, G., Green, S., & Snavely, B. (1984). Face support in controlling poor performance. *Human Communication Research 11*, 272–295.

Fairhurst, G., Rogers, E., & Sarr, R. (1987). Manager–subordinate control patterns and judgments about the relationship. *Communication Yearbook 10*, 395–415.

Fairhurst, G., & Sarr, R. (1996). *The art of framing*. San Francisco, CA: Jossey-Bass.

Farace, R., Monge, P., & Russell, H. (1977). *Communicating and organizing*. Reading, MA: Addison-Wesley.

Farley, L. (1978). *Sexual shakedown: The sexual harassment of women on the job*. New York: McGraw-Hill.

Fayol, H. (1949). *General and industrial management*. London: Pitman.

Feldman, S. (1991). The meaning of ambiguity: Learning from stories and metaphors. In P. Frost et al. (Eds.), *Reframing organizational culture* (pp. 145–156). Newbury Park, CA: Sage.

Fisher, A. (1980). *Small group decision making* (2nd ed.). New York: McGraw-Hill.

Fisher, W. (1984). Narration as a human communication paradigm: The case of public moral argument. *Communication Monographs 51*, 1–22.

Fisher, W. (1987). *Human communication as narration: Toward a philosophy of reason, value, and action*. Columbia: University of South Carolina Press.

Ford, J. D., & Ford, L. W. (1995). The role of conversations in producing intentional change in organizations. *Academy of Management Review 20*, 541–570.

Ford, R., & Fottler, M. (1995). Empowerment: A matter of degree. *Academy of Management Executive 9*, 21–31.

Fox, M. (1994). *The reinvention of work*. San Francisco: HarperCollins.

Franz, C., & Jin, K. (1995). The structure of group conflict in a collaborative work group during information systems development. *Journal of Applied Communication Research 23*, 108–122.

French, R., & Raven, B. (1968). The bases of social power. In D. Cartwright & A. Zander (Eds.), *Group dynamics* (pp. 601–623). New York: Harper & Row.

Fritz, J. (1997). Men's and women's organizational peer relationships: A comparison. *Journal of Business Communication 34*(1), 27.

Fulk, J., & Mani, S. (1986). Distortion of communication in hierarchical relationships. *Communication Yearbook 9*, 483–510.

Fulk, J., Schmitz, J., & Steinfeld, C. (1990). A social influence model of technology use. In J. Fulk & C. Steinfeld (Eds.), *Organizations and communication technology* (pp. 143–172). Newbury Park, CA: Sage.

Furnham, A. (1999). Gesture politics. *People management 6*, 52.

Geertz, C. (1973). *The interpretation of cultures*. New York: Basic Books.

Geffen, D., & Straub, D. W. (1997). Gender differences in the perception and use of e-mail: An extension to the technology acceptance model. *MIS Quarterley 21*, 389–401.

Geist, P., & Dreyer, J. (1992). *A dialogical critique of the medical encounter: Understanding, marginalization, and the social context*. Paper presented at the Annual Meeting of the Speech Communication Association, Chicago.

Geist, P., & Dreyer, J. (1993). The demise of dialogue: A critique of medical encounter ideology. *Western Journal of Communication 57*, 233–246.

Gersick, C. (1988). Time and transition in work teams: Toward a new model of group development. *Academy of Management Journal 31*, 9–41.

Gersick, C. (1991). Revolutionary change theories: A multi-level explanation of the punctuated equilibrium paradigm. *Academy of Management Review 16*, 10–36.

Gilsdorf, J. (1998). Organizational rules on communicating: How employees are—and are not—learning the ropes. *Journal of Business Communication 35*(2), 173.

Goodall, H. L. (1983). *Human communication: Creating reality*. Dubuque, IA: Brown.

Goodall, H. L. (1989). *Casing a promised land*. Carbondale: Southern Illinois University Press.

Goodall, H. L. (1990a). Interpretive contexts for decision-making: Toward an understanding of the physical, economic, dramatic, and hierarchical interplays of language in groups. In G. M. Phillips (Ed.), *Teaching how to work in groups* (pp. 197–224). Norwood, N.J.: Ablex.

Goodall, H. L. (1990b). Theatre of motives. In J. Anderson (Ed.), *Communication Yearbook 13*, 69–97.

Goodall, H. L. (1993). Empowerment, culture, and postmodern organizing: Deconstructing the Nordstrom's Employee Handbook. *Journal of Organizational Change Management 5*, 25–30.

Goodall, H. L., Jr. (1995). Work-hate narratives. In R. Whillock & D. Slayden (Eds.), *Hate speech*. Thousand Oaks, CA: Sage.

Goodall, H. L., Jr. (1996). *Divine signs: Connecting spirit to community*. Carbondale: Southern Illinois University Press.

Goodall, H. L., Jr. (2000). *Writing the new ethnography*. Walnut Creek, CA: AltaMira.

Goodall, H. L., & Phillips, G. M. (1985). *Making it in any organization*. Englewood Cliffs, NJ: Prentice-Hall.

Goodall, H. L., Wilson, G., & Waagen, C. (1986). The performance appraisal interview: An interpretive reassessment. *Quarterly Journal of Speech 72*, 74–87.

Gouran, D. S. (1970). A response to the paradox and promise of small group communication research. *Speech Monographs 37*, 217–218.

Grantham, C. (1995, September–October). The virtual office. *At work: Stories of tomorrow's workplace, 4*(5), 1, 12–14.

Gray, B., Bougon, M., & Donnellon, A. (1985). Organizations as constructions and destructions of meaning. *Journal of Management 11*, 83–98.

Gray, J. (1992). *Men are from Mars, women are from Venus*. New York: HarperCollins.

Greene, J. O., & Sassi, M. S. (1997). Adult acquisition of message-production skill. *Communication Monographs 64*, 181–201.

Gronn, P. (1983). Talk as the work: The accomplishment of school administration. *Administrative Science Quarterly 28*, 1–21.

Hackman, R., & Associates. (1990). *Groups that work (and those that don't): Creating conditions for effective teamwork*. San Francisco: Jossey-Bass.

Hall, E. T. (1968). Proxemics. *Current Anthropology 9*, 83–109.

Hall, E. T. (1973). *The silent language*. New York: Anchor Books.

Hall, S. (1997). *Representation in media*. Amherst, MA: Media Education Foundation.

Hammer, M., & Champy, J. (1993). *Reengineering the corporation*. New York: HarperCollins.

Harshman, E., & Harshman, C. (1999). Communicating with employees: Building on an ethical foundation. *Journal of Business Ethics 19*(1), 3.

Hawes, L. (1974). Social collectivities as communication: Perspective on organizational behavior. *Quarterly Journal of Speech 60*, 497–502.

Hawken, P. (1992). *The ecology of commerce*. New York: HarperCollins.

Hellweg, S. (1987). Organizational grapevines: A state of the art review. In B. Dervin & M. Voight (Eds.), *Progress in the communication sciences 8*. Norwood, NJ: Ablex.

Heslin, R. (1974). *Steps toward a taxonomy of touching*. Paper presented at the annual convention of the Midwestern Psychological Association, Chicago.

Hirokawa, R., & Rost, K. (1992). Effective group decision making in organizations. *Management Communication Quarterly 5*, 267–388.

Hofstede, G. (1983). National cultures in four dimensions. *International Studies of Management and Organization 13*, 46–74.

Hofstede, G. (1991). *Culture and organizations: Software of the mind*. New York: McGraw-Hill.

Holt, G. (1989). Talk about acting and constraint in stories about organizations. *Western Journal of Speech Communication 53*, 374–397.

Homans, G. (1961). *Social behavior: Its elementary forms*. New York: Harcourt, Brace & World.

Huber, G. (1990). A theory of the effects of advanced information technologies on organizational design, intelligence, and decision-making. In J. Fulk & C. Steinfeld (Eds.), *Organizations and communication technology* (pp. 237–274). Newbury Park, CA: Sage.

Isaacs, W. (1993). *Dialogue*. New York: Currency Doubleday.

Jablin, F. (1979). Superior–subordinate communication: The state of the art. *Psychological Bulletin 86*, 1201–1222.

Jablin, F. (1985). Task/work relationships: A life-span perspective. In M. Knapp & G. Miller (Eds.), *Handbook of interpersonal communication* (pp. 615–654). Newbury Park, CA: Sage.

Jablin, F. (1987). Organizational entry, assimilation, and exit. In F. Jablin, L. Putnam, K. Roberts, & L. Porter (Eds.), *Handbook of organizational communication* (pp. 679–740). Newbury Park, CA: Sage.

Jackson, S. (1983). Participation in decision-making as a strategy for reducing job-related strain. *Journal of Applied Psychology 68*, 3–19.

James, J. (1996). *Thinking in the future tense: Leadership skills for a new age*. New York: Simon & Schuster.

Janis, I. (1971). *Victims of groupthink* (2nd rev. ed.). Boston: Houghton Mifflin.

Jhally, S. (1997). *Advertising and the end of the world* [Videotape]. Amherst, MA: Media Education Foundation.

Johnson, D., et al. (1993). *Circles of learning*. Edina, MN: Interaction Books.

Kellett, P. (1999). Dialogue and dialectics in managing organizational change: The Case of a mission-based transformation. *Southern Communication Journal 64*, 211–231.

Kellett, P., & Dalton, D. (2001). *Managing conflict in a negotiated world: A narrative approach to achieving dialogue and change*. Walnut Creek, CA: Sage.

Kellett, P., & Goodall, H. L. (1999). The death of discourse in our own (chat) room: "Sextext," skillful discussion, and virtual communities. In D. Slayden & R. K. Whillock (Eds.), *Soundbite culture: The death of discourse in a wired world*. Thousand Oaks, CA: Sage.

Kendon, A. (1967). Some functions of gaze direction in social interaction. *ACTA Psychologica 26*, 22–63.

King, P., & Sawyer, C. (1998). Mindfulness, mindlessness, and communication instruction. *Communication Education 47*, 326.

Kotter, J., & Heskett, J. (1992). *Corporate culture and performance*. New York: Free Press.

Kramer, M. (1993). Communication and uncertainty reduction during job transfers: Leaving and joining processes. *Communication Monographs 60*, 178–198.

Kramer, M. (1995). A longitudinal study of superior–subordinate communication during job transfers. *Human Communication Research 22*, 39–64.

Kraut, R. E., & Johnson, R. E. (1979). Social and emotional messages of smiling: An ethological approach. *Journal of Personality and Social Psychology 37*, 1539–1553.

Krippendorff, K. (1985). *On the ethics of constructing communication*. International Communication Association presidential address, Honolulu, Hawaii.

Krivonos, P. (1982). Distortion of subordinate to superior communication in organizational settings. *Central States Speech Journal 33*, 345–352.

Kunda, G. (1993). *Engineering culture: Control and commitment in a high-tech corporation*. Philadelphia: Temple University Press.

Lacy, D. (1995). *From grunts to gigabytes: Communication and society*. Urbana: University of Illinois Press.

Langer, E. (1989). *Mindfulness*. Reading, MA: Addison-Wesley.

Langer, E. (1992). Interpersonal mindlessness and language. *Communication Monographs 59*, 324.

Langer, E. (1997). *The power of mindful learning*. Reading, MA: Addison-Wesley.

Lodge, D. (1997). *The practice of writing*. New York: Penguin.

Louis, M. (1979). Surprise and sense-making: What newcomers experience in entering unfamiliar organizational settings. *Administrative Science Quarterly 23*, 225–251.

Lovitt, C. R., & Goswami, D. (1999). *Exploring the rhetoric of international professional communication: An agenda for teachers and researchers*. Amityville, NY: Baywood.

Luhmann, A. D., & Albrecht, T. L. (1990). *The impact of supportive communication and personal control on job stress and performance*. Paper presented at the International Communication Association, Chicago.

Marshall, A., & Stohl, C. (1993). Participating as participation: A network approach. *Communication Monographs 60*, 137–157.

Marshall, J. (1993). Viewing organizational communication from a feminist perspective: A critique and some offerings. In S. Deetz (Ed.), *Communication Yearbook 16*, 122–143.

Martin, J. (1992). *Cultures in organizations: Three perspectives*. New York: Oxford University Press.

Maslow, A. (1965). *Eupsychian management*. Homewood, IL: Irwin.

Maslow, A. (1970). *Motivation and personality* (2nd ed.). New York: Harper & Row.

May, S. (1993). *Employee assistance program and the troubled workers: A discursive study of knowledge, power, and subjectivity*. Unpublished doctoral dissertation, University of Utah.

Mayo, E. (1945). *The social problems of industrial civilization*. Cambridge, MA: Graduate School of Business Administration, Harvard University.

McGregor, D. (1960). *The human side of enterprise*. New York: McGraw-Hill.

McKerrow, R., Gronbeck, B. E., Ehninger, D., & Monroe, A. H. (2000). *Principles and types of speech communication*. New York: Longman.

McPhee, R., & Corman, S. (1995). An activity based theory of communication networks in organizations, applied to the case of a local church. *Communication Monographs 62*, 132–151.

Mead, G. (1934). *Mind, self, and society*. Chicago: University of Chicago Press.

Meyer, G. J. (1995). *Executive blues*. San Francisco: Franklin Square Press.

Miller, J. G. (1978). *Living systems*. New York: McGraw-Hill.

Miller, K. (1995). *Organizational communication: Approaches and processes*. Belmont, CA: Wadsworth.

Miller, K., Ellis, B., Zook, E., & Lyles, J. (1990). An integrated model of communication, stress, and burnout in the workplace. *Communication Research 17*, 300–326.

Miller, K., & Monge, P. (1985). Social information and employee anxiety about organizational change. *Human Communication Research 11*, 365–386.

Miller, K., & Monge, P. (1986). Participation, satisfaction, and productivity: A meta-analytic review. *Academy of Management Journal 29*, 727–753.

Miller, K., Stiff, J., & Ellis, B. (1988). Communication and empathy as precursors to burnout among human service workers. *Communication Monographs 55*, 250–265.

Miller, V., & Jablin, F. (1991). Information seeking during organizational entry: Influences, tactics, and a model of the process. *Academy of Management Review 16*, 92–120.

Mintzberg, H. (1973). *The nature of managerial work*. New York: Harper & Row.

Mitroff, I., & Kilmann, R. (1975). Stories managers tell: A new tool for organizational problem-solving. *Management Review 64*, 18–28.

Monge, P., Bachman, S., Dillard, J., & Eisenberg, E. (1982). Communicator competence in the workplace: Model testing and scale development. *Communication Yearbook 5*, 505–528.

Monge, P., Cozzens, M., & Contractor, N. (1992). Communication and motivational predictors of the dynamics of organizational innovation. *Organizational Science 3*, 250–274.

Monge, P., & Eisenberg, E. (1987). Emergent communication networks. In F. Jablin et al. (Eds.), *Handbook of organizational communication* (pp. 204–342). Beverly Hills, CA: Sage.

Monge, P., Farace, R., Eisenberg, E., Miller, K., & Rothman, L. (1984). The process of studying process in organizational communication. *Journal of Communication 34*, 22–43.

Morgan, G. (1986). *Images of organization*. Newbury Park, CA: Sage.

Morrison, E., & Bies, R. (1991). Impression management in the feedback-seeking process: A literature review and research agenda. *Academy of Management Review 16*, 522–541.

Motley, M. (1992). Mindfulness in solving communicators' dilemmas. *Communication Monographs 59*, 306.

Moxley, R. (1994). *Foundations of leadership*. Greensboro, NC: Center for Creative Leadership.

Mumby, D. (1987). The political function of narratives in organizations. *Communication Monographs 54*, 113–127.

Mumby, D. (1993). *Narrative and social control*. Newbury Park, CA: Sage.

Mumby, D., & Putnam, L. (1993). The politics of emotion: A feminist reading of bounded rationality. *Academy of Management Review 17*, 465–486.

Noer, D. (1993). *Healing the wounds: Overcoming the trauma of layoffs and revitalizing downsized organizations*. San Francisco: Jossey-Bass.

Ochs, E., Smith, R., & Taylor, C. (1989). Detective stories at dinnertime: Problem solving through co-narration. *Cultural Dynamics 2*, 238–257.

Okabe, R. (1983). Cultural assumptions of East and West: Japan and the United States. In B. Gudykunst (Ed.), *Intercultural communication theory* (pp. 212–244). Newbury Park, CA: Sage.

Oldham, G., & Rotchford, N. (1983). Relationships between office characteristics and employee reactions: A study of the physical environment. *Administrative Science Quarterly 28*, 542–556.

O'Reilly, B. (1994, June 13). The new deal: What companies and employees owe each other. *Fortune*, 44.

Osborn, J., Moran, L., Musselwhite, E., & Zenger, J. (1990). *Self-directed work teams*. Homewood, IL: Business One Irwin.

Ouchi, W., & Wilkins, A. (1985). Organizational culture. *Annual Review of Sociology 11*, 457–483.

Pacanowsky, M. (1988). Communication in the empowering organization. In J. Anderson (Ed.), *Communication Yearbook 11*, 356–379.

Pacanowsky, M., & O'Donnell-Trujillo, N. (1983). Organizational communication as cultural performance. *Communication Monographs 50*, 126–147.

Papa, M. (1989). Communicator competence and employee performance with new technology: A case study. *Southern Communication Journal 55*, 87–101.

Papa, M. (1990). Communication network patterns and employee performance with new technology. *Communication Research 17*, 344–368.

Perrow, C. (1986). *Complex organizations: A critical essay* (3rd ed.). New York: Random House.

Peters, T., & Waterman, R. (1982). *In search of excellence*. New York: Harper & Row.

Pettigrew, A. (1979). On studying organizational cultures. *Administrative Science Quarterly 24*, 570–581.

Phillips, G. (1991). *Communication incompetencies: A theory of training oral performance behavior*. Carbondale: Southern Illinois University Press.

Philpott, J. S. (1983). *The relative contribution to meaning of verbal and nonverbal channels of communication: A meta-analysis*. Unpublished master's thesis, University of Nebraska.

Pinchot, G., & Pinchot, E. (1993). *The end of bureaucracy and the rise of the intelligent organization*. San Francisco: Berrett-Koehler.

Poole, M. S. (1981). Decision development in small groups I: A comparison of two models. *Communication Monographs 48*, 1–24.

Poole, M. S. (1983). Decision development in small groups II: A study of multiple sequences in decision making. *Communication Monographs 50*, 321–341.

Poole, M. S. (1992). Structuration and the group communication process. In L. Samovar & R. Cathcart (Eds.), *Small group communication: A reader* (6th ed.). Dubuque, IA: Brown.

Poole, M. S. (1996, February). *A turn of the wheel: The case for a renewal of systems inquiry in organizational communication research*. Conference on Organizational Communication and Change, Austin, Texas.

Poole, M. S., & Desanctis, G. (1990). Understanding the use of group decision support systems: The theory of adaptive structuration. In J. Fulk & C. Steinfeld (Eds.), *Organizations and communication technology* (pp. 173–193). Newbury Park, CA: Sage.

Poole, M. S., & Holmes, M. (1995). Decision development in computer-assisted group decision making. *Human Communication Research 22*, 90–127.

Poole, M. S., & Roth, J. (1989). Decision development in small groups V: Test of a contingency model. *Human Communication Research 15*, 549–589.

Putnam, L., & Pacanowsky, M. (1983). *Communication and organizations: An interpretive approach*. Beverly Hills, CA: Sage.

Quinn, R. (1977). Coping with Cupid: The formation, impact, and management of romantic relationships in organizations. *Administrative Science Quarterly 22*, 30–45.

Rafaeli, A., & Sutton, R. (1987). The expression of emotion as part of the work role. *Academy of Management Review 12*, 23–37.

Rafaeli, A., & Sutton, R. (1991). Emotional contrast strategies as means of social influence: Lessons from criminal interrogators and bill collectors. *Academy of Management Journal 34*, 749–775.

Ralston, S., & Kirkwood, W. (1995). Overcoming managerial bias in employment interviewing. *Journal of Applied Communication Research 23*, 75–92.

Ray, E. (1987). Supportive relationships and occupational stress in the workplace. In T. Albrecht & M. Adelman (Eds.), *Communicating social support* (pp. 172–191). Newbury Park, CA: Sage.

Redding, W. C. (1991). *Unethical messages in the organizational context*. Paper presented at the annual convention of the International Communication Association, Chicago.

Redding, W. C. (1985a). Rocking boats, blowing whistles, teaching speech communication. *Communication Education 34*, 245–258.

Redding, W. C. (1985b). Stumbling toward identity: The emergence of organizational communication as a field of study. In R. McPhee & P. Tompkins (Eds.), *Organizational communication: Traditional themes and new directions* (pp. 15–54). Beverly Hills, CA: Sage.

Rehfield, J. (1994). Cited in D. C. Barnlund, *Communicative styles of Japanese and Americans*. Belmont, CA: Wadsworth.

Richmond, V., & McCroskey, J. (1995). *Nonverbal behavior in interpersonal relations*. Englewood Cliffs, NJ: Prentice-Hall.

Roberts, K., & O'Reilly, C. (1974). Failures in upward communication: Three possible culprits. *Academy of Management Journal 17*, 205–215.

Roy, D. (1960). Banana time: Job satisfaction and informal interaction. *Human Organization 18*, 156–180.

Sahlins, M. (1976). *Culture and practical reason*. Chicago: University of Chicago Press.

Salopek, J. (1999, September). Is anyone listening? *Training and Development 53*, 58.

Salopek, J. (1999, November). Liar, liar, pants on fire. *Training and Development 53*, 16.

Sailer, H., Schlachter, J., & Edwards, M. (1982, July–August). Stress: Causes, consequences, and coping strategies. *Personnel 59*, 35–48.

Samovar, L., Porter, R. E., & Jain, N. C. (1991). *Understanding intercultural communication*. Belmont, CA: Wadsworth.

Scheidel, T., & Crowell, L. (1964). Idea development in small discussion groups. *Quarterly Journal of Speech 50*, 140–145.

Schein, E. (1991). The role of the founder in the creation of organizational culture. In P. Frost et al. (Eds.), *Reframing organizational culture* (pp. 14–25). Newbury Park, CA: Sage.

Scollon, R., & Scollon, S., (1995). *Intercultural communication*. Cambridge, MA: Blackwell.

Scott, J. (1990). *Domination and the arts of resistance: Hidden transcripts*. New Haven, CT: Yale University Press.

Senge, P. (1991). *The fifth discipline: The art and practice of the learning organization*. New York: Doubleday/Currency.

Senge, P., Roberts, C., Ross, R., Smith, B., & Kleiner, A. (1994). *The fifth discipline fieldbook*. New York: Doubleday/Currency.

Shockley-Zalabak, P., & Morley, D. (1994). Creating a culture. *Human Communication Research 20*, 334–355.

Shorris, E. (1984). *Scenes from corporate life*. Hammondsworth, England: Penguin.

Sias, P., & Jablin, F. (1995). Differential superior–subordinate relations, perceptions of

fairness, and coworker communication. *Human Communication Research 22*, 5–38.
Simon, H. (1957/1976). *Administrative behavior* (3rd ed.). New York: Free Press.
Smith, D. (1972). Communication research and the idea of process. *Speech Monographs 39*, 174–182.
Smith, H. (1995, May 14). *The three faces of capitalism*. Public Broadcasting System.
Smith, R., & Eisenberg, E. (1987). Conflict at Disneyland: A root metaphor analysis. *Communication Monographs 54*, 367–380.
Sommer, R. (1969). *Personal space*. Englewood Cliffs, NJ: Prentice-Hall.
Sundstrom, E., DeMeuse, K., & Futrell, D. (1990). Work teams: Applications and effectiveness. *American Psychologist 45*, 120–133.

Tannen, D. (1990). *You just don't understand: Women and men in conversation*. New York: Morrow.
Tannen, D. (1994a). *Gender and discourse*. New York: Oxford University Press.
Tannen, D. (1994b). *Talking from 9 to 5: Women and men in the workplace, language, sex, and power*. New York: Simon & Schuster.
Taylor, F. (1913). *The principles of scientific management*. New York: Harper.
Taylor, F. (1947). *Scientific management*. New York: Harper.
Tjosvold, D., & Tjosvold, M. (1991). *Leading the team organization*. New York: Lexington Books.
Trenholm, S. (2000). *Thinking through communication: An introduction to the study of human communication*. Boston: Allyn & Bacon.
Trenholm, S., & Jensen, A. (1992). *Interpersonal communication*. Belmont, CA: Wadsworth.
Triandis, H., et al. (1988). *Handbook of industrial and organizational psychology*. Palo Alto, CA: Consulting Psychology Press.
Trujillo, N. (1985). Organizational communication as cultural performance: Some managerial considerations. *Southern Speech Communication Journal 50*, 201–224.

Van Maanen, J. (1991). The smile factory: Work at Disneyland. In P. Frost et al. (Eds.), *Reframing organizational culture* (pp. 58–76). Newbury Park, CA: Sage.
Van Maanen, J., & Barley, S. (1984). Occupational communities: Cultural control in organizations. In B. Staw & L. Cummings (Eds.), *Research in organizational behavior* (Vol. 6, pp. 265–287). Greenwich, CT: JAI Press.

Varner, I., & Beamer, L. (1995). *Intercultural communication in the global workplace*. Chicago: Irwin.
Victor, D. A. (1994). *International business communication*. New York: HarperCollins.
Von Bertalanffy, L. (1968). *General systems theory*. New York: George Braziller.
Vroom, V. (1964). *Work and motivation*. New York: Wiley.

Waldron, V. (1991). Achieving communication goals in superior–subordinate relationships: The multi-functionality of upward maintenance tactics. *Communication Monographs 58*, 289–306.
Walster, E., Walster, G. W., & Bersheid, E. (1978). *Equity theory*. Boston: Allyn & Bacon.
Watzlawick, P., Beavin, J., & Jackson, D. (1967). *The pragmatics of human communication: A study of interactional patterns, pathologies, and paradoxes*. New York: Norton.
Weber, M. (1946). *From Max Weber: Essays in sociology*. H. Gerth & C. Wright Mills (Eds.), New York: Oxford University Press.
Weick, K. (1979). *The social psychology of organizing* (2nd ed.). Reading, MA: Addison-Wesley.
Weick, K. (1980). The management of eloquence. *Executive 6*, 18–21.
Weick, K. (1995). *Sensemaking in organizations*. Newbury Park, CA: Sage.
Wellins, R., Byham, W., & Wilson, J. (1991). *Empowered teams*. San Francisco: Jossey-Bass.
Wenberg, J., & Wilmot, W. (1973). *The personal communication process*. New York: Wiley.
Wheatley, M. (1992). *Leadership and the new science*. San Francisco, CA: Berrett-Koehler.
Wilkins, A. (1984). The creation of company cultures: The role of stories and human resource systems. *Human Resource Management 23*, 41–60.
Wilson, G., & Goodall, H. L. (1991). *Interviewing in context*. New York: McGraw-Hill.
Witmer, D., & Katzman, S. L. (1997). On-line smiles: Does gender make a difference in the use of graphic accents? *Journal of Computer-Mediated Communication 2*(4). http://www.ascusc.org/jcmc/vol2/issue4/.
Wood, J. (1977). Leading in purposive discussions: A study of adaptive behavior. *Communication Monographs 44*, 152–165.
Wood, J. (1996). *Gendered relationships*. Mountain View, CA: Mayfield.
Wood, J. (1997). *Communication as a field of study*. Belmont, CA: Wadsworth.

Index

Page numbers followed by *f* or *t* indicate figures or tables, respectively.

A
Abstraction, 121
Accommodating, in conflict situations, 183
Adaptive skills, in group/team communication, 250
Agendas, in group/team communication, 251–252, 252*f*
Ambiguity, of verbal communication, 120–121
Andersen, Peter, 131
Apology, 125
Appearance. *See* Personal appearance
Aristotle, 126
Articulation, of voice, 132
Artistic format, of resume, 223–224
Assignments, in group/team communication, 247
Assumptions, and identity of communication, 118–119
Attention-getter, in Monroe's Motivated Sequence, 320
Audience
   analysis of, in rational/emotional persuasion, 315–318
   of communication event, 64–65
   of informative presentations, 274
   needs and expectations of, 64–65
Authoritative sources, 76
Authority, and credibility, 126
Automatic talk. *See* Mindless communication
Autonomy-togetherness dialectic, 181
Avoiding, in conflict situations, 183
Awareness, of communication of self, 117–118, 117*t*

B
Barker, Randolph, 53
Bias, in language, 122, 127–128
Body language, 133–136
Bohm, David, 257
Bookmarks, in Web-based research, 160
Bottom-up communication, 47
Boundaries
   in interpersonal communication, 170–172
   of personal space, 137
Brainstorming, in problem-solving, 260–261
Breakthrough skills, 2
Briefings, 273

Brutal persuasion, 303–307, 343
Buckman, Robert H., 152
Bulletin boards, 159
Bureaucracy, in management, 35
Business and professional communication, 2–3
   and communication history, 10–11
   components of, 3–11
      channels, 7
      context, 7–11
      feedback, 6–7
      message, 5
      noise, 5–6
      receiver, 5
      sender, 4–5
   cultural context of, 9–10, 10*f*
   functions of, 11–15
      interpretation, 13–15
      organizing tasks and people, 12–13
      sense-making, 13–15
   listening in, 106–110
   models of
      current, 6*f*
      top-down, 3, 4*f*
      updated, 5*f*
   physical situation of, 7–9
   and systems theory, 41–42
   timing of, 9

C
Call to action, in Monroe's Motivated Sequence, 320
Camarata, Martin, 53
Campus recruitment office, 217–219
Career placement centers, job announcements in, 204
Casual pattern, of communication event, 72
Casual zone of interaction, 137
CCCD. *See* Choose, Create, Coordinate, and Deliver
Channels, in business and professional communication, 7
Charts, in informative presentations, 289–290
Chatrooms, shorthand in, 157
Choose, Create, Coordinate, and Deliver (CCCD)

Choose, Create, Coordinate, and Deliver (CCCD) (*continued*)
   in communication event, 63
   in conscious communication, 15–18, 15f
   in group/team communication, 244–267
   in informative presentations, 272–295
   in interpersonal communication, 167–188
   in interviews, 200–205
   in job search, 214–238
   in persuasion, 303–328
Choosing, 63
   in communication event, 64–69
   in conscious communication, 15, 15f, 16
   in group/team communication, 245–251
   in informative presentations, 273–277
   in interpersonal communication, 167–175
   in interviews, 200–205
   in job search, 215–219
   in persuasion, 303–305
Chronic complaints, 109
Chronological pattern, of communication event, 72
CIOS. *See* Communication Institute for Online Research
Clarity, of verbal communication, 120–121
Clip art, in PowerPoint presentations, 287
Closed questions, in interviews, 232
Clothing, 130–132
Coercive power, 44
Collectivist cultures, 185, 186t
Collegial peers, 171
Colors, in PowerPoint presentations, 285
Commodity value, 177–178
Communication
   bottom-up, 47
   business and professional (*See* Business and professional communication)
   conscious (*See* Conscious communication)
   downward, 122–123, 340
   dramatistic, 187
   dysfunctional, 101–102
   electronically mediated, 3
   group/team (*See* Group/team communication)
   importance of studying, 55
   as information transfer, 36
   interpersonal (*See* Interpersonal communication)
   mindful, 50–52
   mindless, 49–50
   nonverbal (*See* Nonverbal communication)
   ordinary, 48, 49f
   and organizational culture, 43–52
   phatic, 48, 49–50, 49f, 169
   and power, 43–52
   pragmatic, 187
   strategic, 15–18
   top-down, 3, 4f
   as transactional process, 39
   upward, 122, 340
   verbal (*See* Verbal communication)
Communication continuum, 48, 49f
Communication culture researcher, 14
Communication event
   audience needs and expectations in, 64–65
   and Choose, Create, Coordinate, and Deliver process, 63
      choosing, 64–69
      coordinating, 85–86
      creating, 69–85
      delivery, 86–89
   conclusion of, 80–85
   criteria for success, 68–69
   fluency of, 88
   goal of, 64–69
   introduction of, 80–85
   naturalness of, 88
   nonverbal competence in, 89
   organization of, 63–89, 72
   outcomes of, 66–68
   practicing for, 87–89
   timing of, 87
   transitions in, 80, 81t, 82
   vivacity of, 88
Communication history
   in business and professional communication, 10–11
   and listening, 101–102
Communication Institute for Online Research (CIOS), 159
Communication networks, 40
   effective use of, 42–43
   feedback in, 42
   flow in, 41
   formal, 41, 42–43
   informal, 41, 42–43
Communication profile, 22–30
Communication skills, 2
Community. *See* Organizational culture
Company employees, in job search, 216–217
Company tours, in job search, 217
Complaints
   chronic, 109
   legitimate, 108–109
   listening to, 108–109
Compromising, in conflict situations, 183
Computer-assisted communication technology, 153–154
Computer-assisted decision-aiding technology, 153–154
Computer networks, 156
Concierge persuasion, 301–303
Conclusion
   of communication event, 80–85

Index

in informative presentations, 292–293
Conferences, 267
Confirming messages, 124–125
Conflict situations
    in interpersonal communication, 183–184
    listening in, 107–108
Conscious communication, 15–19
    and Choose, Create, Coordinate, and Deliver process
        choosing, 15, 15f, 16
        coordinating, 15, 15f, 17–18
        creating, 15, 15f, 16–17
        delivery, 15, 15f, 18
    diversity in, 19
    and information technology, 151–152, 152f
    preparation for, 60–92
    principles of, 18–19
Conscious listening, 95t, 105–106
Consensus, in group/team communication, 247
Constraints, on problem-solving, 256–257
Contemporary format, of resume, 222–223
Context, of business and professional communication, 7–11
    communication history, 10–11
    cultural, 9–10, 10f
    physical situation, 7–9
Contingency, in systems thinking, 40
Continuous improvement, 38, 42
Coordinating, 63
    in brutal persuasion, 305–306
    in communication event, 85–86
    in conscious communication, 15, 15f, 17–18
    in group/team communication, 255–263
    in informative presentations, 293–295
    in interpersonal communication, 184–187
    in interviews, 205–209
    in job search, 226–230
    in mindful persuasion, 326–327
    in rational/emotional persuasion, 320
    in rational persuasion, 310–312
Cover letter, 225–226
Covey, Stephen, 50
Creating, 63
    in brutal persuasion, 305–306
    in communication event, 69–85
    in conscious communication, 15, 15f, 16–17
    in group/team communication, 251–255
    in informative presentations, 277–293
    in interpersonal communication, 175–184
    in interviews, 205
    in job search, 219–226
    in mindful persuasion, 323–326
    in rational/emotional persuasion, 315
    in rational persuasion, 310–312
Creativity, in problem-solving, 256–257

Credibility
    in informative presentations, 274–276
    personal, 126
    professional, 126
    of speaker, 102–103
Criteria
    of communication event success, 68–69
    of informative presentation success, 276–277
    for problem-solving solutions, 259–260
Critical listening, 95t, 102–104
    and message, 103
    and motivation, 103–104
    and speaker credibility, 102–103
Crowding, of personal space, 137
Cultural approach, to power, 45–46
Cultural bias, in language, 122
Cultural context, of business and professional communication, 9–10, 10f
Cultural differences
    and eye contact, 136
    in interpersonal communication, 171, 184–185, 186t
    and listening, 97–99
    and sexual harassment, 140
    in voice, 133
Cultures
    collectivist, 185, 186t
    individualist, 185, 186t
    transaction, 185
Cziksentmihalyi, Mihalyi, 38

D

Decision-making
    contingent nature of, 40, 41
    and ethics, 172–175
Deetz, Stan, 46
Deintensification, in nonverbal communication, 134
Delivery, 64
    in brutal persuasion, 306–307
    in communication event, 86–89
    in conscious communication, 15, 15f, 18
    in group/team communication, 263–267
    in informative presentations, 295
    in interpersonal communication, 187–188
    in interviews, 208–209
    in job search, 230–238
    in mindful persuasion, 327–328
    in rational/emotional persuasion, 320–322
    in rational persuasion, 312
Democracy, and power, 46–47
Density, of personal space, 137
Dialectics
    autonomy-togetherness, 181
    expressive-protective, 181
    in interpersonal communication, 181–182
    novelty-predictability, 181

Dialogue, 47–48, 49f
  in interpersonal communication, 181–182
  in learning organizations, 53–54
Disclaimers, 187
Disclosure, in interpersonal communication, 177–179
Disconfirming messages, 124–125
Discussion groups, online, 159
Discussions, in group/team communication, 246
Display rules, in nonverbal communication, 133–134
Diversity
  in conscious communication, 19
  and power, 45–46
Downward communication, 122–123, 340
Dramatistic communication, 187
Dysfluency, of voice, 132

E
Education, and credibility, 275
EEOC. *See* Equal Employment Opportunity Commission
Electronic mail. *See* Email
Electronically mediated communication, 3
Email, 154–156
  and gender differences, 151
  shorthand in, 157
  tips for, 341
Emotion, and persuasion. *See* Rational/emotional persuasion
Empathy, and credibility, 275
Employment interviews, 199
Empowerment, 119
Ends justify the means, 173
Entertainment, as communication goal, 66
Enthusiasm, and credibility, 275–276
Environment, in systems thinking, 40
Equal Employment Opportunity Commission (EEOC), 139, 140, 142
Equity, 119–120
  in interpersonal communication, 176–177
  mental, 120
  narrative, 120
Ethics
  and interpersonal communication, 172–175
  and interviews, 205
  and mindful communication, 51
Ethos, 303
Evaluating, in group/team communication, 247–248
Examples, 76–77
  in informative presentations, 287, 288f
  listening to, 103
Exclusive messages, 123–124
Expert power, 44
Expertise, and credibility, 275
Expressive-protective dialectic, 181

Eye contact, 133–136
Eye movement, 135

F
Facial expressions, 133–136
Fact-finding, in problem-solving, 258–259
Facts, 75–76
  in informative presentations, 274
  listening to, 103
Fax machines, 153
Fayol, Henri, 34
Feedback, 85–86
  in business and professional communication, 6–7
  in communication networks, 42
  giving, rules for, 180
  in interpersonal communication, 179–181
  negative, 40
  positive, 40
  in systems thinking, 40
The Fifth Discipline (Senge), 253
First impressions, 167–169
  and person prototypes, 167–168
  and personal appearance, 130–132
  and personal constructs, 168–169
  and scripts, 169
Flexibility, in interpersonal communication, 187
Flip charts, in presentations, 338
Flow, in communication networks, 41
Flow theory, 38
Fluency, of communication event, 88
Focus groups, 197–199
Font size, in PowerPoint presentations, 285
Font type, in PowerPoint presentations, 285
Ford, Henry, 34
Formal communication networks, 41, 42–43
Formal interview, 232
Friends, as job search source, 217
Friendship-warmth touching, 139
Functional-professional touching, 138

G
Geertz, Clifford, 43
Gender bias, in language, 122
Gender differences
  in information technology use, 150–151
  in interpersonal communication, 185–187
  in listening, 99–100
  in voice, 133
Gendered talk, 127–128
Goals
  of communication event, 64–69
  definition of, 247
  in group/team communication, 247
  of informative presentations, 273–277
  of interviews, 200–202

Index

of job search, 215–219
and self-reflexive listening, 104
in systems thinking, 40
Goodall, H.L., 48
Graphs, in informative presentations, 289–290
Great Depression, 36
Grievance review, 345–346
Group/team communication, 243–270, 245f
adaptive skills in, 250
agendas in, 251–252, 252f
and Choose, Create, Coordinate, and Deliver process
choosing, 245–251
coordinating, 255–263
creating, 251–255
delivery, 263–267
effects on worker morale, 37
jamming in, 250
leadership in, 246–248
meetings in
conferences, 267
planning meetings, 266
problem-solving meetings, 266
seminars, 267
staff briefings, 265–266
virtual meetings, 266
weekly sessions, 265–266
workshops, 267
memos in, 264
organization of, 245–251
participation in, 248–249
problem-solving in, 255–263
process of, 257–263
reports in, 265
selection of team members in, 249–250
shared vision in, 252–255
successful, 342
and working with other groups, 256–257

H

Handouts, in presentations, 339
Harassment, 139–142. *See also* Sexual harassment
Hawthorne Effect, 37
Hawthorne Studies, in human relations movement, 37
Head hunters, 204–205
Hearing, 94–96. *See also* Listening
blocks to
noise, 95
overcoming, 96
physical diversions, 95
technological diversions, 96
Hierarchical noise, 6
Hierarchy
legitimate power in, 122
in management, 33

Hierarchy of needs, in human relations movement, 37–38, 38f
Homans, George Caspar, 177
Hostile work environment, 140
Human relations movement, 36–38
and Hawthorne Studies, 37
and hierarchy of needs, 37–38, 38f
and power, 44–45

I

Identity. *See also* Nonverbal communication; Verbal communication
communication of, 117–126
and assumptions, 118–119
and awareness, 117–118, 117t
and workplace equity, 119–120
creation of, 13
definition of, 117
monitoring of, 118
and self-reflexive listening, 104
Image, and personal appearance, 130–132
Imperato, Gina, 1
In-person interview, 228–229
Inclusive messages, 123–124
Individualist cultures, 185, 186t
Inequity, 176–177
Inflammatory language, 121
Informal communication networks, 41, 42–43
Informal interview, 232
Information interviews, 198–199
Information overload, 150
Information peers, 171
Information technology, 146–165
approach to, 149–150
appropriate levels of, 161–162
computer-assisted, 153–154
computer networks, 156
and conscious communication, 151–152, 152f
development of, 148–149
downside to, 149
electronic mail, 154–157
and gender differences, 150–151
in job search, 216
in memos/reports, 264
PowerPoint presentation, 283–287
and resume, 220
and team-based communication, 12
types of, 153–158
video conferencing, 157–158
and virtual meetings, 266
voice mail, 154–156
web-based research, 159–160
Information transfer model of communication, 36
and clarity of verbal communication, 120
goal of, 66

Informational listening, 95t, 96–102
    and communication history, 101–102
    and cultural differences, 97–99
    and gender differences, 99–100
    and language differences, 97–98, 100–101
Informative presentations, 271–299
    audience of, 274
    and Choose, Create, Coordinate, and Deliver process
        choosing, 273–277
        coordinating, 293–295
        creating, 277–293
        delivery, 295
        worksheet for, 333, 334
    conclusion of, 292–293
    credibility in, 274–276
    criteria for success of, 276–277
    examples in, 287, 288f
    goal of, 273–277
    introduction of, 292–293
    outcomes of, 276, 277
    PowerPoint, 283–287
    references in, 287–288
    research for, 279–282
    statistics in, 289–290, 289f
    support in, 287–290
    transitions in, 290–291
    visual cues in, 290, 290f
Intensification, in nonverbal communication, 133
Intensity, of voice, 132
Interdependence
    in decision-making, 41
    in systems thinking, 40
Internet. *See also* Information technology
    in job search, 216
    Web-based research, 159–160
Internet-based presentations, 336
Interpersonal communication, 166–191, 170f
    boundaries of, 170–172
    and Choose, Create, Coordinate, and Deliver process, 167–188
        choosing, 167–175
        coordinating, 184–187
        creating, 175–184
        delivery, 187–188
    and cultural differences, 184–185, 186t
    and dialectics, 181–182
    dialogue in, 181–182
    equity in, 176–177
    and ethics, 172–175
    expectations of, 170–172
    feedback in, 179–181
    first impressions in, 167–169
    and gender differences, 185–187
    limitations on, 171
    peer relationships in, 171
    relational conflict in, 183–184
    risk-taking in, 177–179
    self-disclosure in, 177–179
    successful, 340
Interpretation, 13–15
Interrogation interviews, 194
Interviews, 192–212, 194f
    appearance during, 131
    and Choose, Create, Coordinate, and Deliver, 200–210
        choosing, 199–205
        coordinating, 205–209
        creating, 204–206
        delivery, 208–209
    employment, 199
    and ethics, 205
    example of, 235–238
    goals of, 200–202
    in-person, 228–229
    information, 198–199
    interrogation, 194
    parameters of, 200–205
    performance reviews, 195–197
    personal appearance during, 230
    persuasive, 194–195
    phone, 208–210, 227–228
    practicing for, 232–234
    preparation for, 226–230
    questions in, 206–207
    sales, 194–195
    screening, 208-210
    scripts of, 204–206, 344
    setting up, 205–209
    styles of, 231–232
        formal, 232
        informal, 232
Intimate zone of interaction, 137
Introduction
    of communication event, 80–85
    in informative presentations, 292–293

J

Jamming, in group/team communication, 250
Jargon, 121
Job announcements
    and head hunters, 204–205
    in local newspapers, 202–204
    in online job databanks, 204
    in professional association databanks, 204
    in trade publications, 204
    in university career placement centers, 204
Job description, 201–204
Job interview. *See* Interviews

Index

Job search, 213–242, 214f. *See also* Interviews
  and Choose, Create, Coordinate, and Deliver process
    choosing, 215–219
    coordinating, 226–230
    creating, 219–226
    delivery, 230–238
  and cover letter, 225–226
  goals of, 215–219
  research in, 215–219
    campus recruitment office, 217–219
    company employees, 216–217
    company tours, 216–217
    friends and relatives, 217
    Internet, 216
  and resume, 219–226
Johnson, Patrice, 94

K
Kellett, Peter, 182
Kinesics, 133
Kvale, Steiner, 31

L
Labor laws, and scientific management, 35
Labor unions, 36
Lacy, Dan, 148
Language, bias in, 122
Language differences, and listening, 97–98, 100–101
LANS. *See* Local Area Networks
Leadership, in group/team communication, 246–248
Learning organizations, 52–55, 54f
  and dialogue, 53–54
  disciplines of, 52–53
    mental models, 53
    personal mastery, 52–53
    shared vision, 53
    systems thinking, 52
    team learning, 53
Legitimate complaints, 108–109
Legitimate power, 44, 122
Library, and web-based research, 159
Lies, detection of, 128, 136
Listening, 14, 93–113, 95t, 97f
  in business and professional contexts, 106–110
  to complaints, 108–109
  in conflict situations, 107–108
  conscious, 95t, 105–106
  critical, 95t, 102–104
  and hearing, 94–96, 95t
  informational, 95t, 96–102
  in meetings, 107
  roadblocks to, 80
  self-reflexive, 95t, 104–105
  when asked for help, 109–110
Local Area Networks (LANS), 156
Logos, 303
Lone Ranger model, of business communication, 17
Love-intimacy touching, 139
Luddite, 151

M
Management
  and bureaucracy, 35
  classical period of, 32–35
  hierarchy in, 33
  and human relations movement, 36–38
  scientific, 33–35
  theories of, 32, 33f
  top-down, 33
Manager, job of, in scientific management, 34
Masking, in nonverbal communication, 134
Maslow, Abraham, 37–38
Meetings
  conferences, 267
  listening in, 107
  planning, 266
  problem-solving, 266
  seminars, 267
  staff briefings, 265–266
  virtual, 266
  weekly sessions, 265–266
  workshops, 267
Memos
  in group/team communication, 264
  tips for writing, 341
Mental equity, 120
Mental models, in learning organizations, 53
Messages
  in business and professional communication, 5
  clarity of, 121
  confirming, 124–125
  in conscious communication, 16–17, 18
  and critical listening, 103
  disconfirming, 124–125
  exclusive, 123–124
  goals of, conflict and, 51
  inclusive, 123–124
  in interpersonal communication, 175–184
  interpretation of, 52
  main points of, 72–75
  nonsupportive, 125–126
  practicing, 87–89
  subpoints of, 74–75
  supporting materials for, 75–80
    verbal, 75–77
    visual, 77–80
  supportive, 125–126

Messages (*continued*)
   undesirable consequences of, 51
Mindful communication, 50–52
Mindful persuasion, 304, 323–328, 343
   coordinating, 326–327
   creating, 324–326
   delivery, 327–328
Mindless communication, 49–50
Models, in presentations, 337
Monitoring, of identity, 118
Monroe's Motivated Sequence, 318–320, 335
Motivation
   in hierarchy of needs theory, 37–38
   and listening, 103–104

N
Narrative equity, 120
Narrative recovery technique, 47
Narratives, 76–77
   organizational, 47–48
National Communication Association (NCA), credo for ethical communication of, 174–175
Naturalness, of communication event, 88
NCA. *See* National Communication Association
Needs, in Monroe's Motivated Sequence, 320
Needs assessment
   for communication event, 64–65
   for rational/emotional persuasion, 315–318
Negative feedback, 40
Netiquette, 156
Networks
   communication (*See* Communication networks)
   computer, 156
Neutralization, in nonverbal communication, 134
Newspapers, job announcements in, 202–204
Noise
   in business and professional communication, 5–6
   hierarchical, 6
   and listening, 95
   semantic, 6
Non-native speakers, 97–98
Nonsupportive messages, 125–126
Nonverbal communication, 114–145, 128–139. *See also* Identity
   awareness of, 117–118, 117*t*
   and body movement, 133–136
   and clothing, 130–132
   in communication event, 89
   and eye contact, 133–136
   and facial expressions, 133–136
   and feedback, 180
   and lies, 136
   paralanguage, 132–133
   and personal appearance, 130–132
   and personal space, 136–138
   and touching, 138–139
   and voice, 132–133
   and workspace, 128–130
Nonverbal competence, in communication event, 89
Novelty-predictability dialectic, 181

O
Objectives, definition of, 247
Oculesics, 133
Off-stage power, 46
On-stage power, 46
Online discussion groups, 159
Online job databanks, 204
Openness, in systems thinking, 40
Order, in system, 40
Ordinary communication, 48, 49*f*
Organization, of communication event, 63–89, 72
Organization theories, 32
Organizational change, 48
Organizational credibility, 13
Organizational culture, 14, 42, 43–52
Organizational learning, 38, 41
Organizational narratives, 47–48
Organizational persona, 13
Organizational relationships, limitations on, 171
Organizational savvy, 13
Organizational stories, 47
Organizational system, definition of, 40
Organized communication theories, 32
Outcomes
   of communication event, 66–68
   of informative presentations, 276, 277

P
Paralanguage, 132–133
Participation, in group/team communication, 248–249
Pathos, 303
Pause, in voice, 132
Peer relationships, 171, 340
Peers
   collegial, 171
   information, 171
   special, 171
Perception, and first impressions, 167
Performance reviews, 195–197, 345–346
Person prototypes, 167–168
Personal appeals, listening to, 103
Personal appearance, 130–132
   and credibility, 276
   during interview, 230
Personal connection, and persuasion, 302, 302*f*
Personal constructs, and first impressions, 168–169
Personal credibility, 126
Personal mastery, in learning organizations, 52–53
Personal narratives, 48, 49*f*

Personal space, 136–138
  and crowding, 137
  and density, 137
  and territoriality, 137
  and zones of interaction, 137
Personal zone of interaction, 137
Persuasion, 300–331, 302f
  and Choose, Create, Coordinate, and Deliver process
    choosing, 303–305
    coordinating, 305–306
    creating, 305
    delivery, 306–307
  as communication goal, 66
  concierge, 301–303
  and emotion, 313–323
  and personal connection, 302
  strategies of
    brutal, 303–307, 340
    choice of, 303–305, 340
    mindful, 304, 323–328, 340
    rational, 304, 308–312, 340
    rational/emotional, 304, 313–323, 340
Persuasive interviews, 194–195
Persuasive presentations, 273–274, 333, 334
Phatic communication, 48, 49–50, 49f, 169
Phone interviews, 208–210, 227–228
Physical diversions, to listening, 95
Physical situation, in business and professional communication, 7–9
Pitch, of voice, 132
Placement centers, job announcements in, 204
Planning meetings, 266
Policies, and interpersonal communication, 171
Pollack, Judith, 94
Positive feedback, 40
Postponing, in conflict situations, 183
Power, 43–52
  classical approach to, 44
  coercive, 44
  cultural approach to, 45–46
  and democracy, 46–47
  and difference, 45–46
  expert, 44
  human relations approach to, 44–45
  legitimate, 44, 122
  off-stage, 46
  on-stage, 46
  and organizational culture, 44–47
  referent, 44
  reward, 44
  systems theory approach to, 45
  and verbal communication, 127–128
PowerPoint presentations, 283–287
  clip art in, 287
  colors in, 285
  font size in, 285
  font type in, 285
  slides in, 283, 284
  transitions in, 284
Practicing
  for communication event, 87–89
  for interviews, 232–234
Pragmatic communication, 187
Presentations. *See also* Communication event
  informative (*See* Informative presentations)
  Internet-based, 336
  persuasive *vs.* informative, 273–274
  PowerPoint (*See* PowerPoint presentations)
  slide, 283, 284, 336
  training, 273
  visual support in, 336–339
Preview statement, 73
Problem-solution pattern, of communication event, 72
Problem-solving
  brainstorming in, 260–261
  constraints on, 256–257
  and creativity, 256–257
  in group/team communication, 255–263
    and working with other groups, 256–257
  process of, 257–263
    fact-finding, 258–259
    phrasing the question, 258
    solution alternatives, 260–261
    solution criteria, 259–260
    solution formulation, 262
    solution presentation, 262–263
    solution testing, 261–262
    understanding the charge, 257–258
Problem-solving meetings, 266
Professional association, and job announcements, 204
Professional credibility, 126
Proxemics, 136–138
Public zone of interaction, 137
Pupil dilation, 135
Purpose, and thesis statement, 70

Q
Qualifiers, 187
Quality improvement, in scientific management, 35
Questions
  closed, 232
  in interviews, 206–207, 232
Quid pro quo sexual harassment, 140

R
Range, of voice, 132
Rational/emotional persuasion, 304, 313–323, 340
  audience analysis in, 315–318
  coordinating, 320
  creating, 315

Rational/emotional persuasion *(continued)*
   delivery, 320–322
   needs assessment in, 315–318
Rational persuasion, 304, 308–312, 340
   coordinating, 310–312
   creating, 310
   delivery, 312
Receiver, in business and professional communication, 5
Reciprocity, 176
References, in informative presentations, 287–288
Referent power, 44
Relational conflict, in interpersonal communication, 183–184
Relationship building, as communication goal, 66
Relatives, in job search, 217
Reports, 265, 273, 341
Research
   for informative presentations, 279–282
   in job search, 215–219
   Web-based, 159–160
Resonance, of voice, 132
Restitution, 120
Resume, 219–226
   format of, 220–224
      artistic, 223–224
      contemporary, 222–223
      traditional, 221
   words to avoid on, 224
Reward power, 44
Rewards, 119, 176
The Rhetoric (Aristotle), 126
Rhythm, of voice, 132
Risk-taking, in interpersonal communication, 177–179
Rules, and interpersonal communication, 171

S
Sales interviews, 194–195
Satisfaction, in Monroe's Motivated Sequence, 320
Schemata, and first impressions, 167
Scientific management, 33–35
Screening interviews, 208–210
Scripted responses, 49
Scripts
   and first impressions, 169
   of interviews, 205, 344
Search engines, in Web-based research, 160
Self. *See* Identity
Self-disclosure, in interpersonal communication, 177–179
Self-reflexive listening, 95t, 104–105
   and identity, 104
   and personal goals, 104
   and sensitivity, 105
   and understanding, 105

Semantic noise, 6
Seminars, 267
Sender, in business and professional communication, 4–5
Senge, Peter, 31, 42, 52, 53–54, 105, 253
Sense-making, 13–15
Sensitivity, and self-reflexive listening, 105
The Seven Habits of Highly Effective People (Covey), 50
Sexual harassment
   avoidance of, 140–141
   defining, 140
   and hostile work environment, 140
   quid pro quo, 140
   victims of, recourse of, 141–142
Sexually arousing touch, 139
Shared vision
   in group/team communication, 252–255
   in learning organizations, 53
Shorthand, in chatrooms/email, 157
Silence, as opportunity to listen, 14
Simulation, in nonverbal communication, 133
Skilled conversation, 48, 49f
Slide presentations, 336
   PowerPoint, 283, 284
Small talk. *See* Mindless communication
Social-consulting zone of interaction, 137
Social-polite touching, 138–139
Speaker, credibility of, 102–103
Special peers, 171
Staff briefings, 265–266
Stakeholder organization, 46–47
Statistics, 75–76
   in informative presentations, 289–290, 289f
   listening to, 103
Stereotyping, and personal appearance, 130–132
Strategic communication, 15–18
Stress, and inequity, 119–120, 176
Success
   of communication event, 68–69
   of group/team communication, 248
   of informative presentation, 276–277
Summarizing, in group/team communication, 247–248
Supervisor/employee relationships, 122
Supporting materials, of message, 75–80
   verbal, 75–77
   visual, 77–80
Supportive messages, 125–126
Synergy, 245
System
   components of, 40
   definition of, 40
Systems thinking, 40
   and business and professional communication, 41–42
   in learning organizations, 52
   and power, 45

Index

T

Tag questions, 187
Talk, types of, 48, 49f
Tannen, Deborah, 99, 186–187
Taylor, Frederick, 33
Team. *See also* Coordinating; Group/team communication
   definition of, 244
Team-based model, of business and professional communication, 12–13
Team communication. *See* Group/team communication
Team learning, in learning organizations, 53
Technological diversions, to hearing, 96
Technology. *See* Information technology
Telecommuting, 156
Tempo, of voice, 132
Territoriality, of personal space, 137
Testimonies, 76
Theory of flow, 38
Thesis statement
   creation of, 70–71
   preview of, 73
Three Musketeers model, of business communication, 17
Time, of communication event, 87
Timing, of business and professional communication, 9
Top-down communication, 3, 4f
Top-down management, 33
Topical pattern, of communication event, 72
Touching, 138–139
Trade publications, job announcements in, 204
Traditional format, of resume, 221
Training presentations, 273
Transaction culture, 185
Transactional process, communication as, 39
Transitions
   in communication event, 80, 81t, 82
   in informative presentations, 290–291
   in PowerPoint presentations, 284
Transparencies, in presentations, 339
Trenholm, Sarah, 167
Trust, and credibility, 126

U

Uncertainty-reduction theory, 130
Understanding, and self-reflexive listening, 105
University career placement centers, job announcements in, 204
Upward communication, 122, 340

V

Values clarification, 173–175
Verbal communication, 114–145. *See also* Identity
   awareness of, 117–118, 117t
   clarity *vs.* ambiguity of, 120–121
   confirming *vs.* disconfirming messages, 124–125
   and credibility, 126
   downward, 122–123
   exclusive *vs.* inclusive messages, 123–124
   and lies, 128
   and power, 127–128
   problems with, 120–128
   supportive *vs.* nonsupportive messages, 125–126
   upward, 122
Verbal support, for message, 75–77
Video conferencing, 153, 157–158
Videotape presentations, 337
Virtual communities, 156
Virtual meetings, 266
Vision, shared
   in group/team communication, 252–255
   in learning organizations, 53
Visual cues, in informative presentations, 290, 290f
Visual support, 77–80, 336–339
Visualization, in Monroe's Motivated Sequence, 320
Vivacity, of communication event, 88
Voice, 132–133
Voice mail, 154–156
Volume, of voice, 132

W

WANS. *See* Wide Area Networks
Web-based research, 159–160
Web sites, 159, 173, 216
Weber, Max, 35
Weekly sessions, 265–266
Whistleblowers, 172–173
Whiteboards, in presentations, 338
Wide Area Networks (WANS), 156
Withdrawing, in conflict situations, 183
Work-hate narratives, 47
Worker morale, 37
Working conditions, in scientific management, 35
Workplace equity. *See* Equity
Workshops, 267
Workspace, 8–9, 128–130
Written communication, successful, 341

Z

Zones of interaction, 137